ARCHAISM
AND
ACTUALITY

THEORY IN FORMS

SERIES EDITORS

Nancy Rose Hunt, Achille Mbembe, and Todd Meyers

ARCHAISM AND ACTUALITY

JAPAN AND THE GLOBAL FASCIST IMAGINARY

HARRY HAROOTUNIAN

DUKE UNIVERSITY PRESS   DURHAM AND LONDON   2023

© 2023 DUKE UNIVERSITY PRESS
Designed by Matthew Tauch
Typeset in Alegreya by Westchester Publishing Services,
Danbury, CT

Library of Congress Cataloging-in-Publication Data
Names: Harootunian, Harry D., [date] author.
Title: Archaism and actuality : Japan and the global fascist
imaginary / Harry D. Harootunian.
Other titles: Theory in forms.
Description: Durham : Duke University Press, 2023. |
Series: Theory in forms | Includes bibliographical references
and index.
Identifiers: LCCN 2022061832 (print)
LCCN 2022061833 (ebook)
ISBN 9781478025221 (paperback)
ISBN 9781478020363 (hardcover)
ISBN 9781478027355 (ebook)
Subjects: LCSH: Capitalism—Japan—History. | Fascism—Japan—
History. | Marxian historiography. | Philosophy, Marxist. | Japan
—History—1868—Historiography. | BISAC: PHILOSOPHY /
History & Surveys / Modern | HISTORY / Asia / Japan
Classification: LCC DS881.95 .H37 2023 (print) LCC DS881.95 (ebook)
| DDC 320.50952—dc23/eng/20230419
LC record available at https://lccn.loc.gov/2022061832
LC ebook record available at https://lccn.loc.gov/2022061833

Cover art: Kazou Shiraga, *Black Fan in front of Red (J-108)*,
1966. 27 cm × 24 cm. Courtesy of the artist's estate and
Fergus McCaffrey Gallery.

For the memory of Tetsuo Najita

Despite diverse arguments, Japanism is a version of a Japanese type of fascism. To the extent that this is not seen it will be impossible to coherently grasp it as a link in an international phenomenon and explain the unique circumstances of how Japanism employed a good deal of European fascist philosophy.

—**Tosaka Jun,** *Nihon ideorogiron*

CONTENTS

ix   PREFACE

xix   ACKNOWLEDGMENTS

1   1   In the Zone of Occult Instability

36   2   Restoration

99   3   Capitalism & Fascism

145   4   Actuality & the Archaic
              Mode of Cognition

223   Epilogue: Déjà Vu

245   NOTES

261   BIBLIOGRAPHY

269   INDEX

PREFACE

Any account of Japan's momentary embrace of fascism in the 1930s, like accounts of similar events in many other societies, may appear somewhat out of joint with the concerns of contemporary life. Yet despite technological advances that distract, displace, mediate, and even control lives more thoroughly than ever before, the present remains plagued by familiar problems of the past that apparently have never gone away. There are still foreign wars, whether fought by proxies or directly; acute and increasing inequality; global economic uncertainty that behaves cyclically and repetitiously; and political failures of systems that have long outlived their shelf lives—all of which lead to new violent divisions that are beginning to tear apart the fabric of already frayed so-called democratic orders, with the reappearance of the vague silhouette of fascism falsely promising to restore wholeness.

The principal question of levels of historical life comes into focus here because it invariably points to the necessity of accounting for and explaining the relationship between forms of ideological production and how they penetrate diverse social constituencies in everyday life to become articles of mass belief. The phenomenon of the so-called big lie in contemporary American political life is only the most recent example of the persistence of this question, whose history undoubtedly stretches back to earlier fascist successes in mobilizing large numbers of people to subject themselves to unquestioned obedience and followership, violence, and ruin. This is not to say that what is occurring today in a number of societies like the United States is simply a replay of what happened in the 1930s, since the two moments are too different and belong to vastly different temporal registers. The principal difference between these two moments of fascism was marked by the inversion of the earlier experience into what prevails today. What this means is that if the historic fascism seized the opportunity to exploit the economic, political, and social chaos produced by a world historical crisis in the 1930s, the more recent forms initiated by Donald Trump, Jair Bolsonaro, Reçep Tayyip Erdoğan, and other like-minded aspirants have no crisis to resolve, as such, or one that is fixable; they project no other plan but vague promises of bringing back some made-up golden age when things were better to relieve the present of the crises they have generated. They believe in nothing more than their own self-interest and identify its realization with their conception of a new order. But the fact that we seem to be compelled to recall the earlier episodes of fascism at this moment suggests the fear of the return of a shapeless historical revenant, of a corpse long dead.

One way to respond to the unknown is to appeal to allegory, which allows the historian to focus on some other's past or another present to draw attention away from what is closer at hand without directly engaging with it, especially if that historian is driven by the Gramscian conviction that politics is primary. A distant account substitutes for a nearby one, even if the former is not immediate and contains risks leading to censorship, imprisonment, and worse that are always imminent but indefinite. in fascist regimes and other authoritarian regimes. In the dark days of the late 1930s, Japanese historians like Hani Gorō turned to their more remote past to speak critically about the impending dangers of their immediate present. This has led me to imagine the possibility of both looking at the formation of Japan's earlier fascist experience from the perspectives supplied by the contemporary era and recognizing in that experience a vague parallelism to what seems to be the shape of our current situation. Part of the impulse to do so stems from the practice of history and its preoccupation with the past—either distant or near, but rarely the immediate past in which that practice is carried out. To allegorize what is close by substituting another time or place for one's own is a rhetorical device with political ambitions: a form of action, not a determination of historical knowledge. At the same time that such allegorization interrupts the normal procedure of historical practice, it discontinues the movement of history from past into present and suspends its dedication to demonstrating historical continuity with an unmoving present. The allegorization of history thus transmutes the discipline's diachronic vocation into the standstill of synchronic displacement and removes history's reliance on narrative linearity and its fixed subject in a closed chain that demands meaning (that is, interpretation). And the initial premise of a direct causal relationship serves only to maintain the idea of historical continuity necessitated by the linear trajectory, while we have learned that historical continuity itself is a reification. But allegorical perception, at most, provides only an imprecise road map of where we might have been and the possibilities that history may bring us. Walter Benjamin acknowledged the limitations of allegorization when he remarked that "even the story of the life of Christ lent itself to that turning of history into nature" and "what remains is a living image amenable to all corrective interventions."[1]

It is worth recalling that, the Japanese literary critic Kobayashi Hideo (of whom I say more below) was more right than wrong when he explained his reason for rejecting history and considering it useless in a reasonable manner that is more persuasive today than when he first articulated it before World War II. Kobayashi early observed that history was framed by chronology that both limited it and hindered it from achieving full disclosure because its patterning "imitates the movement of things" instead of giving us self-knowledge. His solution was to recommend the exercise of a hermeneutic "entry" into or access to the world expressed in archaic words to suggest how the ancient Japanese lived and looked upon their world. While Kobayashi believed that this method of reading could be carried on in every present and proposed this strategy as an alternative to historical practice, its horizon was limited to those who were members of a specific "language community," such as the Japanese in Japan. His historicist solution was no improvement. Yet his critique inadvertently implied that history was characterized by progressive linearity, if not punctuated by stages, a procedure shared by both Marxian and bourgeois historians. In this connection, it has been said that Michel Foucault once confessed, somewhere, that he could not tell the difference between bourgeois and Marxist historiography and pointed out the evident similarity of the two practices in their uncritical fidelity to linear narrative form, distinguished by a unidirectional progressive movement of time and interspersed by epochal stages as regular as train stops, marking a before and after. Marx went further, critically discerning in the form of history a concealed theory that privileged the nation-form as the primary unit of organizing the historical field, with history adopting capitalism's accountancy of time from its successive production processes. History was thus turned into a one-way street moving toward the bourgeois concept of progress (capitalist modernization), following the itinerary demanded by a society constructed on the principle of commodity exchange.

It was, I believe, this observation that preoccupied prewar thinkers like Benjamin and Ernst Bloch, especially, as well as their successors like Jean-Paul Sartre, Frantz Fanon, Henri Lefebvre, Peter Osborne, Daniel Ben-Said, and Massimiliano Tomba. The question for such thinkers was what form should history itself take. In this instance, the concealed theory in the form that Marx uncovered was eventually rethought and referred to as "real abstraction" or the "commodity exchange system" that generates an abstracted "social synthesis" rather than labor and value rather than use-value.[2] Thus, the system was capable of producing accumulated abstractions that prevailed in 1930s Japan like idealist philosophy and epistemology, as well as a culture that, according to the philosopher Tosaka Jun, performed the work of ideology, which he called the "Japanist ideology."

The issue for thinkers who turned to interrogating history's form and its conception of time was the inadequacy of the figure of linearity that structured and disposed historical narratives (as it did the form of biography, a condensation of history). In this discourse, the principal proponents were philosophers and historians were usually absent, which confirmed Jacques Rancière's view that discussions of time, even historical time, belonged to the domain of philosophy rather than history. Historians, excepting Reinhart Kosellek, rarely saw the importance of the form of historical time as such, often confusing it with chronology. Historical narratives accepted as unproblematic the figure of unilinearity without rethinking the question of causal progression from a past to the present by bracketing the present in which the practice was carried out on the assumption that they were starting from the past. By the same measure, it is difficult to know what provoked Marxian philosophers to undertake the labor of thinking about the necessary rejection of conventional linearity and to begin imagining the relationship between time and history as a suitable detour that would allow them to envision an adequate form of history. Those philosophers may have been prompted by the lingering residues of the interwar period's controversy over historicism and history's failure to explain how pasts led to presents, as well as residues of the critique of excessive historical production that threw into doubt the discipline's capacity to avoid the relativizing of values. In this connection, the Western Marxism that emerged in the interwar years turned away from the concreteness of the historical and toward the abstraction of a critical appraisal of prewar Marxian orthodoxy and bourgeois science, which never led back to the concrete (which Marx had projected it would).[3] The turn stemmed less from the Russian Revolution's priority of addressing the practical problem of constructing a new everydayness than it did from the advent of the more urgent question of determining the consequences of revolutionary consciousness and agency under a maturing capitalism, in which the commodity form seemed to be approaching its completion and value was finessing history as its result. Considerations of the conception of everydayness in the West turned from Lenin's emphasis on matters of politics and history to issues of philosophy and value.[4] In time, this hegemony of value over history (use-value) obscured the Marxian historical vocation, and it is hard not to conclude that the embrace of value by some of its more enthusiastic proponents was encouraged by that embrace's offer of a convenient alibi for forgetting history altogether. In such cases, value theory thus strove to empty history of its capacity for independence and difference and sought to make it essentially indistinguishable from capital. Under certain conditions of rupture, history's countertemporality was able to provide a release or exist from an outside[5] represented by the received social order through intervening in the present.[6] But in areas like Latin America, Asia, and Africa, the practical and historically concrete problem of constructing new societies after World War II, aided by new readings of Marx, led to a shift to history furnished with a new conception of form that no longer depended on linearity and unidirectionality.

In this book I have tried to envision historical practice as a mode of intervening in the past from the present as a telescoping, which is the only experiential perspective available. It is the time in which historical practice is carried on and when the past is animated and brought to life. This practice requires confronting the problem of historical time and responding to the need to think about it alongside capital's dominant structuring of everyday life and to consider the exits to the outside that the practice might offer. In this regard, I have relied on Benjamin's pertinent reflections on historical time and Bloch's protean notion of the multiversum, along with Antonio Gramsci's conception of passive revolution in the context of uneven development, which characterized not only Japan's capitalist development since the Meiji Restoration of 1868 but also most societies in their modernizing political transformations, leaving them laden with coexisting different temporalities (levels of time) in the present that mixed with, collided with, and rubbed against each other to produce the figure of constant friction and tensions that Tomba has usefully named "chronotone."[7] Gramsci's conception of passive revolution provided what is still a timely warning of how a fascist outcome was invariably able to develop from the political ground of liberal democracy: it was initiated by passive revolution through inverting the conditions that had enabled an earlier active revolution. This process has the historical authority to back up more recently identifiable signs of the spectacles that have already begun to appear in certain European states like Hungary and Poland, as well as in Turkey and India, and is now confronting American society. In this regard, the arrival of signs of fascisms must be seen as signifying the possibility of a dialectical reversal, whereby all the putative circumstances and resulting institutional safeguards said to have ensured the safety of liberal democratic polities can be easily reversed to enable the turn to oligarchic authoritarianism and demagogic fascism.

Concern with the agency of historical time has steered me to primarily focus this study on what might be called the contemporizing of the past that produced the figure of contemporary noncontemporaneity or synchronic nonsynchronisms, as well as the reverse of that production, the domination of the noncontemporary over the contemporary with the rise of fascism and its relentless campaign to banish history altogether and replace it with archaic myth or ideological fictions of an imagined past, what Benita Parry named fascist "symptoms of morbidity." Benjamin's rethinking of historical practice led him to designate the act of contemporizing the past, unmaking and refiguring it to serve the capitalist present, to express the historical materialistic principle of "actuality," "in order for part of the past to be touched by the present instant"—that is, *Aktualität (jissai in Japanese)* praxis, or political intervention into the present. At the same time, "if part of the past is to be touched by the present instant," there must be no continuity between them.[8] What this requires is an approach to the past that relieves it from its fixed point of history, turning " political categories into theoretical categories" to intervene and politically interrupt the present, by making history yield a political meaning it had repressed or forgot.[9] But the idea of contemporizing pasts was prefigured by Marx (in *Capital*), where he proposed that capital was positioned to appropriate what was at hand from prior economic modes like labor and to reconfigure them if necessary to put them to work for capitalism's new production agenda. Hence, contemporizing signified a momentary coming together "in a flash" of part of the past with the "now" of the present to form a "constellation." The result was an intense production of congested heterogeneous temporalities that Benjamin named "dialectics at a standstill."[10] By the same token, "the history that shows things" as they really were is a delusion and "was the strongest narcotic of the century."[11] The true method of "making things present" compels us to "[represent] them in our space."

"We don't displace our being," Benjamin warned, "into theirs; they step into our life."[12]

The thematic thread of Japan's modern history shows the experience of uneven and combined development inaugurated by the Meiji Restoration and its program dedicated to transforming the country into a modern society, instantiating capital's initial use of practices from the past to enable or enhance its own production system. While unevenness was not limited to latecomers to capitalism and implicated all societies committed to its production program, we are obliged to respond to capital's demand of a global perspective, as Marx proposed in the 1860s with his acknowledgment of the formation of the world market.

It should be stated here that while earlier Marxian interpretations saw the appearance of unevenness as a stage to be reached in the linear trajectory that ultimately would be overcome by a more progressive one, my reading, explained in detail later, proposes that all societies experience the status of unevenness the moment they embrace the capitalist agenda and remain permanently bound to it, even as the capitalist endowment may mature and advance. The reason for this comes from the uneven distribution of resources, which is capitalism's founding presupposition that is continually reproduced. In other words, capitalism, from its inception, has appropriated practices presupposed by prior modes of production to function with procedures derived from capitalism itself, thus assimilating what is outside of it to its inside and implanting an irresolvable contradiction at its origin. In this respect, unevenness refers to both the mixed methods capitalism appropriates and uses from the past with those it innovates and devises in the present to augment its production process, which widens the material disparity between those who must work for their subsistence and the owners of the means of production for whom they work. This approach results in putting an end to the necessity of following a tradition of linear history comprised of progressively moving from one stage to another imposed by an earlier Marxism for a temporal configuration consisting of capitalism's mixed unevenness and the possibility of its future overcoming, which is not linear but an inversion leading to its replacement.

Since given the appearance of multiple different routes to capitalist development, there could be no pure development of capitalism or the certainty that one size would fit all. Unevenness thus pointed to a plurality of societies, relationality, and different pathways toward the development of capitalism that made each experience manifestly worldly. Each also brought in its train survivals from the past to the present, observable in contemporaneous noncontemporary temporalities that coexisted and indexed their different historical formations. It is precisely this dialectical encounter between history and capital's logic for producing combinations out of what appear to be incommensurables that brings us back to the importance of memory's vocation to restore the true meaning of the incommensurate and the critical restraints it puts on history's ambitions.

I have organized Japan's modern historical past into three separate montage-like moments, not causally connected to each other as if in a chain. Yet they are still readable not as stories but as temporalized political images in the manner of a palimpsest, from the Meiji Restoration to the world crises in the 1930s that drove Japan, along with other societies, to fascism and to its postwar life filled with dormant traces of the past ready to be reawakened. The appearance of such lingering residues of a dangerous past in the postwar present provides us with what Kristin Ross once called the "figurability of the present."[13] This refers to the recognition of presents as "landscape[s]" capable of offering occasions of figurability at moments when capitalist time is interrupted by the unanticipated arrival and forcible entry of untimeliness brought about by the reanimated coexisting traces of what Marx described as the "inherited evils arising from the passive survival of archaic modes of production, with their accompanying train of anachronistic social and political relations"—that is, unwanted remains of the past bursting into the present.[14] With the mobilization of figurability we have moved to a different perspective on what earlier might have seemed like a familiar scene, from vistas of "unchanging abstraction" to the possibility of catching sight of "the colour of the concrete."[15] The moment of figurability thus signals the appearance of heterogeneous temporal congestion, whose presence requires overcoming the addiction of "abstraction" inflicted by the historicist hermeneutic of empathetic entry. Among historians, this approach had been an unquestioned matter of common sense and had been employed for a long time, substituting the act of feeling oneself into subjects in the past (or standing in their footprints) for the politics of "actuality" in historical understanding. It had made history interpretative rather than an interventionist interruption of the present, precisely the critique that Tosaka directed against the Japanist ideology. The scandals that have lain dormant in every present can be energized to surface in moments of contemporary crisis to show their presentness: they appear as significant and function as forms to stimulate the presence of mind, which puts forth the possibility of completion. But Benjamin's conception of "mindfulness" also sparks the reappearance of remembrance, of what had been forgotten, and it encourages the need for completion, for finishing business.[16] In the Japan (as well as a good part of the rest of the world) of the 1930s, conjunctural forces led to an economic crisis that fused with efforts to find political solutions. This provided the ground for the rise of fascism in a number of nation-states that ultimately led to worldwide conflict. In Japan, it was a configuration that summoned the archaic form of primal mythic and fictive histories—which, as Benjamin observed, made "semblance in history still more delusive by mandating nature as its homeland."[17] The Japanese response to the situation resulted in the construction of a Japanist program based on archaism, which recruited its followers from diverse social classes and promised to replace the troubled present by installing a nonexistent but supposed historical experience of the originary past of deities and the first emperor, which elicited a powerful critique dedicated to articulating a strategy founded on actuality (praxis) and the primacy of politics. Like the Meiji Restoration, remembrance ignited the claims of historical apocatastasis in the demand for a second restoration in the 1930s, completing what Japanists believed had remained unfinished, which was an even more magical fable than its predecessor. Postwar Japan experienced déjà vu in the steady reappearance of archaism in the activities of revived Shinto associations and in cultural expressions that sought to continue the rhythms of a Japanese historical consciousness in the archaic stratum and the desire for the archaic by showing the solidarity of a "linguistic community" rooted in the ancient "spirit of words." The archaic was thus seen as pointing to an "origin" (not as a "genesis" or another beginning) and as calling for "restoration" or "restitution" (referring to something that remained unfinished and required completion).[18]

ACKNOWLEDGMENTS

I owe a great and probably unpayable debt to Carol Gluck for taking the time to thoroughly read an earlier version of the manuscript for this book, systematically going through the writing and arguments and vastly improving both. My thanks go to Hyun Ok Park and Gavin Walker for their valuable comments and observations, which I have tried to incorporate. Thanks also go to two anonymous readers who raised important questions about the manuscript (which I have sought to satisfy) and to Kristin Ross for her continuing and perceptive reflections on the difficult problem of the changing relationship between politics and culture, which is at the heart of this book. I also want to remember and thank the members of the reading group in which I have been a participant for the intellectual companionship they have provided: Laura Neitzel, Carol Gluck, Kim Brandt, Alan Tansman, Ramona Bajema, Yukiko Hanawa, Marilyn Ivy, Yukiko Koga, Brian Hurley, Jack Wilson, Tom Looser, Andrea Arai, Janet Poole, Louise Young, Hyun Ok Park, Tom LaMarre, and Chris Nelson.

I want to thank Ken Wissoker, Senior Executive Editor at Duke University Press, for years of constant support for innumerable projects dealing with the Asia-Pacific region and my own work. I also want to thank Jessica Ryan, Editorial Production Manager, for her crucial help during the process of reading over an unreasonable example of copyediting of the manuscript. I also to want to thank Nancy Rose Hunt, a coeditor of the series Theory in Forms, particularly for her encouragement of the project realized in this book.

IN THE ZONE OF OCCULT INSTABILITY

The Problem: History and Time's Multiple Arrows

This book principally concerns Japanese society in its modernizing moment, with brief comparative asides about other societies that have experienced the political form Antonio Gramsci named passive revolution or restoration/revolution, the subject of the next chapter, distinguished by capitalism's law of uneven and combined development. Gramsci was the first to classify Japan's transformation associated with the Meiji Restoration of 1868 as an example of his conception of passive revolution, and as far as I know, James Allinson and Alexander Anievas (in a prescient essay) were the first to connect the Meiji Restoration to the form of passive revolution in Leon Trotsky's formula of uneven and combined development.[1] The book focuses particularly on exploring the relation of a political form—passive revolution—and its production of a form of historical time consisting of coexisting plural historical times that signify unevenness in development, different levels of social life, and various combinations resulting from the bringing of practices from prior modes of production together with the demands of a new mode in the domain of political economy. I call this form of historical time contemporizing the past. Empowered with agency, it seeks to incorporate selected elements of the past into the present and at the same time accommodate unused survivals and remnants. Identities of the originating pasts are rarely, if ever, entirely eliminated: what often has been appropriated to function in a different time can retain a signature of the moment when it first appeared. My aim is to work through the consequences and effects of this form in the case of Japan while remaining committed to the prospect of comparability, suggesting that similar resonances will occur in other societies that have either followed the route of passive revolution or approximated some of the principal characteristics of its strategy that lead to political transformation and economic and social modernization. It is my conviction that forms of historical temporalities act to totalize cultural experiences and organize meaning in specific moments. Hence, the objective of this book is to consider the relationship of fascism to regimes of historical time in Japan's modernizing experience. I am particularly concerned with accounts of Japan's epochal capitalist modernization and how concepts of modernization (bourgeois and Marxian) were invariably employed to narrate the progressive movement from a precapitalist past to a modern capitalist present. It has so far gone unrecognized that these accounts were culturally mediated historically totalized forms and representing moments produced by orders of time seeking to appear natural—what Marxian philosopher Tosaka Jun would describe as phenomenological time.[2]

Japan, like other societies coming to capitalism, encountered a process of temporalization that obliged it to navigate through fractious multiple times in a present filled with residues and remnants of pasts that had not yet been mastered. Too often, the category of lateness, which clearly is about time, ranks societies like those of Japan, India, China, and other countries as uneven by claiming a higher status for the chronologically earlier capitalism that developed in Western Europe and the United States. But this hierarchical grading originated in a West that could claim no immunity to the unevenness it imposed on others, since using the status of unevenness or being under development to classify societies principally outside of Euro-America was actually a displacement of the unevenness found in advanced capitalist societies and served to temporally and spatially distance Euro-Americans from the newcomers.

In fact, it should be said at the outset that the idea of uneven development was perhaps no more beneficial to capitalism than to those societies waiting in the wings of historical progress to catch up with advanced societies, which earlier had successfully embraced the new quest for capital accumulation and surplus value. In the capitalist lexicon of terms, unevenness implied the possibility of eventually realizing an achieved evenness that capitalism had promised everywhere it had installed its production process. Whatever the meaning of its original derivation, the reverse of uneven development was nothing more than a necessary illusion serving capital. The promise of providing a trajectory of linear progress leading the underdeveloped to parity with advanced capitalist societies was not simply an ideological misrecognition, a masquerade, since maintaining unevenness constituted the natural state of capital's mode of operation, its unspoken law and program, which if abandoned to raise all societies to parity would lead to capitalism's self-destruction.

Given capital's capacity to produce unevenness everywhere, the real task is not to typologize societies according to a system that ranks them as advanced, late, or underdeveloped but rather to identify the combinations of capitalism and whatever national experience will offer for appropriation from the different pasts at hand. What I am proposing is that all societies that have entered the orbit of capitalism experienced uneven and combined development. In this regard, I will concentrate on how the figure of the archaic embodied in the Japanese emperor and its anachronic associations were employed at the moment when Japan embarked on a capitalist transformation to a modern nation-state form. As a remnant seemingly enwrapped in the archaic (whose beginnings were said to have derived from a distant origin), the putatively divine emperor was employed first as the flash point by samurai activists, who later would become known as a movement of imperial loyalists that struggled to overturn the Tokugawa shogunate and subsequently to secure the loyalty of the populace to the new capitalist state, making sure that Japanese would work for that state and die for it in its successive imperial wars. I will also examine how combining this archaic form with capitalism inverted capitalism into an obligation dedicated to serving a godly emperor and fulfilling the divine mandate of origin and how the appeal to the timelessness of the mythical origin became the principal political fuel for dismantling the structure of contemporary noncontemporaneity in the 1930s, as that appeal became the dominant way to temporalize and authorize Japan's fascism. While the national gods had created the archipelago, the moment of origin was seen as a timeless presence identified with the emperor, who claimed divine descent and had inaugurated an imperial genealogy said to have persisted in unbroken succession down to the present. In this way the archaic aura, represented by the emperor, was converted into a temporal register to constitute what looked like a lasting anachronism in the heart of a modern social formation. Thus, the sociopolitical order was constructed on a deeply implanted contradiction with divisive forces that only an emperor endowed with divine aptitude could bring together. That order was either a great anachronism or not one at all, since returning the emperor to rule was the entry of the timeless into historical time.

Societies like Japan that were said to have come late to capitalist modernization found passive revolution to be the most appropriate political form to use in transforming older political practices to promote the new political economy of the nation-state. While premodern experiences are mediated by local circumstances, the form (which appears less fixed and more elastic than its contents) can produce and account for the differences necessary to distinguish one society from another while allowing societies to share a collective kinship if they adopt the same political configuration and form of historical time. It was not lateness among societies determined to become nation-states but capitalism itself that produced unevenness—which means that no society, despite its claims of early entry into modern nation-statehood and supposed realization of advanced status, was exempt from the consequences of uneven development. Capitalism followed a path to development that sought to bring together what it considered useful from past modes of production that were still available and combine them with the new economic mode driven by a different production agenda, pursuing a reorganized working day and the goal of accumulating capital. The political character of passive revolution corresponded closely to this model of combined development by emphasizing the relationship between the hegemonic leadership of an emerging social class, usually an active minority bourgeoisie aligned with political practices, institutions, and constituencies from the past, either as found or in some reconfigured form or invented to serve a new sociopolitical environment. For example, Gramsci saw the alliance between urban industrial workers in the north and semifeudal peasants in the south as bringing together Italy's past and present, two incommensurate temporalities representing different forms of the country's social life.[3]

Karl Marx has reminded us that at the exact moment when insurgents carried out the French Revolution, aiming to wipe the historical slate clean of inherited oppressions and social inequalities to establish a new time and calendar, the upheaval yoked their revolution to an example "transmitted from the past." In that precise moment of revolutionizing—"in creating something that has never yet existed"—the conjured "spirits of the past" are summoned and "its names, battle cries and costumes" borrowed to mask the "new scene of world history." For Marx, this sudden appeal to the past in a time of rapid and unprecedented change was no historical accident but a "time-honored disguise":

> Thus Luther donned the mask of St. Paul, the Revolution of 1789 to 1814 draped itself alternately as the Roman republic and the Roman empire, and

the Revolution of 1848 knew nothing better to do than to parody, now 1789, now the revolutionary tradition of 1793 to 1795. . . . Thus the awakening of the dead in those revolutions served the purpose of glorifying the new struggles, not of parodying the old, of magnifying the given task in imagination, not of fleeing from its solution in reality; of finding once more the spirit of revolution, not of making its ghost walk about again.[4]

Yet Marx was not simply recommending the combining of past and present, which would distinguish the more moderate Gramscian conception of the "revolution without revolution." Rather, he was identifying the importance of how insurgents in every present see the necessity of contemporizing the past to make accessible what had been repressed, blocked, and forgotten or left unfulfilled, or of grasping the familiar from another perspective that separates it from its established or fixed context. This reemplotment of the past was not an affirmation of the continuity from past to present (as if the past were obliged to lead to the present) but rather the reverse, exemplifying how an event or episode from a past should be invoked and reactivated to overcome the immediate present or compel it to confront the dangers it faced. In this regard, the past is always unpredictable. With this observation Marx was not proposing that history moved along a linear track. Instead, he was perceiving the historical as a repetition of moments when presents are agitated to recall an experience from the past to resolve the crises or dissatisfactions at hand. In this regard, he was pointing to the repetition of recall to use the past to assist the present in changing its course and renewing itself. What was thus being repeated was not the content of a specific event, as such, but the form that directed the present to return to the past for renewal and thus to the work of how the present reconfigured the past. In Japan such a moment was named restoration, and not only did each moment of and movement toward restoration differ in time, circumstance, and goal, but also the desire that appeared in different presents to complete restoration was, in one respect, always new and unconnected with what came before. Yet in another sense, the figure of restoration constituted a constraint since it invariably referred to the monarchy and initially was announced to resolve a clash between imperial claimants. Furthermore, the restorations did not fall in a causal linear continuum. Elsewhere, where the historical figure of restoration may not have been available or invoked, the occasion that usually prompted the summoning of the past differed in terms of time and place, as would the specific recalled past. But all societies recognized that the past and its recall were always available in the present and ready for reactivation. The act of rebooting had less to do with memory, even though that was an important consideration, than it did with renewing the present through reawakening and reconfiguring a specific historical experience. This was the path of Gramsci's conception of passive revolution, which worked to "transmute historically given experiences and categories into the present."[5] But the reversal of this past and often its fictionalizing have led to the projection of forms of archaism to displace and even eliminate the actuality of the present. In its most extreme manifestation, this reversal of the temporal dominant (whereby the past or some fictional version of it is summoned to replace or guide what is considered to be a failed present or to address dissatisfaction with the present) disclosed the purpose of fascism or fascist-like political imaginaries. Implicit but unintended in Marx's "time-honored disguise" provided by the appeal to the past was the widening of the horizon to include its reversal as well, in which the "ghost" was unleashed to "walk about again," narrowing the imagination and allowing people to avoid providing a solution by parodying the actuality of the present in re-creating something old.

Gramsci saw in the early expression of the Italian Risorgimento an instantiation of passive revolution. He eventually broadened the scope of passive revolution to identify the route to modernity, which often resembled the adoption of a similar figure by a number of societies embarked on the path toward nation-statehood, especially those "lacking in the radical-popular 'Jacobin moment,' which had distinguished the experience of the French Revolution."[6] This was the case not only in fascist regimes like those in Italy, Japan, and Germany, but also in other states like Hungary, Romania, and nationalist China, which clearly appealed to forms of archaism.[7] While this claim might be restricted to fascist regimes, like Japan, Germany, Italy, and others claiming exceptionalist cultural and historical endowments, this may have also been the context of temporal characteristics found in other societies in less politically intense forms recently named by a number of writers "post fascisms" (though I would call them not quite or even not yet fascisms, like those in Turkey, Hungary, and Japan, not to forget the United States).[8] I think that this privileging of the archaic might be better expressed in the form of a challenging possibility rather than that of an established fact everywhere we see the implementation of capitalist modernity. If there will be a demand for the construction of a new temporal terrain based on the "poetry of the future," as Gramsci predicted, to avoid the baneful effects of the past, the future that is imagined will still include usable traces of the past and will not always call for a complete rupture with it. Above all, the archaic, in Japan's historical trajectory, must not be simply mistaken for another way of centering the emperor, whose status must be seen as only one of its effects or attributes—like the folk, familism, primitivism, communalism, land, and spirit of language—that cannot be separated from it.

In any case, the kinship Gramsci discerned between the passive revolution and modernity appeared at the moment when the politically leading class, which had secured the consent of the masses, began to forfeit its revolutionary initiative and focus on the acquisition and consolidation of dominance with the goal of foreclosing other classes' opportunity for political advancement—thus renouncing the project of political progress it had once embraced.[9] For our purposes, the historical importance of passive revolution appears in its imperative to synchronize asymmetrical temporal unevenness in some way to prevent the friction resulting from efforts to link contemporary capitalism with a received past in a workable unity. The relationship was achieved by subsuming the old in the new of contemporary capitalism—though this was always incomplete, as the consent of leaders and followers invariably fell short of realizing the pursued promise of capitalist modernization to spark a reversion to more conservative and even coercively reactionary positions like fascism. In Japan, Marxists saw the development of capitalism freezing into an unfinished state of semifeudalism and fascism that was centered on the apparatus of an imperial bureaucratic absolutism (tennōsei zettaishugi)—which in turn resulted from what they described as a counterrevolution or refeudalization, which reenlivened ghostly remnants of the feudal past to direct the present and future.

If Gramsci's *Prison Notebooks* appear to disclose a shift of hegemonic interests representing different groups and temporalities in which he considers the effects of noncontemporaneous contemporaneity, prompted by an opaquely fractured present filled with contending claims that prevent it from certifying an identity with itself, it can be said that fascism arose from the spectacle of an increasingly degraded, failing passive revolution that had been removed from the field of its revolutionary initiative.[10] Gramsci was convinced that the liberalism of the nineteenth century was the principal form of passive revolution and was succeeded by fascism in the following century in 1930s Japan and elsewhere.[11] In this connection, he wrote that "a new liberalism under modern conditions—wouldn't that be, precisely, 'fascism?'" As we shall see, this is a sentiment that was recognized and critiqued by Tosaka and by Herbert Marcuse of the Frankfurt school in the mid-1930s. Fascism was thus the active politicization of nonsynchronous synchronicity that opened the path to accepting what might be referred to as Massamiliano Tomba's "returning of the archaic"—not simply as a primal history but as an invented founding myth conjoined with capitalism and the ideological premise of fascism. In Japan, this was precisely the understanding of archaism that its principal proponents promoted, as when Tsukui Tatsuo announced that Japanism (*Nipponshugi*) was the premise of national socialism. This understanding seeks to syncretize all times under a primal founding principle within the national form of capitalism. While this constituted a response experienced elsewhere to the global economic and political crisis of the 1930s, the appeal to the archaic and putting it at the head of the signifying chain (the nonsynchronous synchronicity) of historical time exaggerated the nature of contemporary conditions. This was often done in societies like those of Germany, Japan, and Italy, which smuggled in archaic mythologies masquerading as original histories— thus heightening the dangers nations would encounter by emphasizing an entirely different temporal register. In other words, these societies turned time inside out and called for a return to an archaic beginning, an *Urzeit* to which the present could be connected and subordinated for guidance and direction. This was precisely the function supplied by enacting a restoration of imperial authority in Japan in 1868 and, I believe, virtually everywhere else where similar transformations occurred in the wake of restoring something from the past in the present. The key component was a temporal dominant that subordinated the contemporary to the noncontemporaneous. To avoid this temporal dominant, it would be necessary to rewind the conception of passive evolution to determine the point at which the reversal of the contemporaneous noncontemporaneity took place and prevent the fateful slippage into fascist time. Special attention would have to be paid to the relationship between politics and the capitalist economy, the entanglements of capitalism in the liberal polity, and the curbing of the excesses of the former and the need to find a more communitarian model to replace the latter.

At the heart of the initially progressive program of passive revolution was the hegemonic bourgeois capacity of integrating dissimilar social groups and classes and subordinating some of them to others, which shared a family resemblance with capitalism's aptitude for appropriating what it needed from existing practices—which Marx called formal subsumption. He saw in this capital's early ability to take what it wanted from past labor practices and to integrate them and use them to serve the capitalist production process—in other words, appropriating older practices and putting them to work for capital accumulation. Hence, the principle of appropriation posited a relationship of subordination to what it took, instantiating the moment when the present retrieved a practice or experience from the past and resituated and enclosed it in a new economic program. The appropriated practice would either remain in its original state or be reconfigured for its new function in a different mode of production. This operation embedded the relationship in the activity of bringing together with contemporary capitalism temporally incommensurable practices, functions, and institutions and creating new combinations of elements from the past. Moreover, when Marx declared that different forms of subsumption could exist together with mature, advanced industrial production, he was initiating the practice of subsumption like hybrid and formal, which referred to mixing components of past modes of practices, and contemporary capitalism. My argument is that subsumption—incorporation, enclosure, subordination, and resynchronization—opened the way to active appropriation that was not limited to the economic sphere to explain the use of past labor practices and modes of exploitation. Instead, subsumption also implied the possibility of expanding appropriation into a broad theater of operation including politics, culture, religion, and law.

The subsequent appropriations and synchronizations of the 1930s thus sought to supplant what were considered to be unsatisfactory presents with new measures of time and their respective regimes, which paradoxically were rooted in the return of archetypal archaic moments. These moments not only claimed unquestioned authority for a timeless spatial sanctuary but also supplied a historically uncontaminated model to guide societies out of their crisis-ridden present and into a future that, metaphorically or allegorically, would repeat the exemplars of a remote past. Such a drastic measure was a response to a widely held belief that the world had fallen and that neither language nor cognitive faculties could any longer penetrate the reality of everyday existence, necessitating in Japan the reinstatement of the true essence of the country's national spirit set free from competing with alternative alien values.[12] The crisis of the present was thus brought on by history and could be gotten out of only by returning to the zone of archaic myth and atemporality (that is, no time) and the habitat of spirit, which offered the prospect of renewal through restoration. But everywhere this call to return to a prior golden moment to guide and ultimately replace a corrupted present represented accumulated abstractions like "spirit" that had no material existence, veiling the real abstraction, which was the work of social synthesis authorized by the commodity exchange system, whose transactions leave no trace of a remainder. In Japan, the appeal was to the beginning, which meant a return to the archaic age of the gods, the creation, and the first emperor. In Italy, ancient Rome was summoned and mythologized into Romanness (*Romanita*), and in Germany, the Third Reich was portrayed as the continuation of its two predecessors. Even in our time, we can observe the traces of this older ideological form in what might be called late democracies. Examples include Turkey's Reçep Tayyip Erdoğan's call for Neo-Ottomanism, the repeated mentions by Japanese Shintoists and politicians of the so-called glories of imperial Japan of the 1930s, Victor Orbán's new Hungary, Donald Trump's staged delusions about making America great again, and Vladimir Putin's Neo-Slavism and aggressive Russian cultural nationalism. All these ideologies were employed by the state to relieve society of conflict or the threat of it and prevent the spread of antagonisms generated by contradictions difficult to contain, with the goal of saving a variety of Neo-liberal capitalisms indistinguishable from the interest of oligarchs who preside over these regimes and thus order through both coercion and the constraining of subjective autonomy. The remaking of the present into an image of a mythic past was intended to serve as a fire wall against the erosions inflicted by history's contingent changes. Yet especially in Japan, it provoked a vigorous discussion among philosophers concerning the status of what constituted the real (*genjitsu*)—which, as it turned out, was not the same as actuality (*jissai*)—and grasped for support a desperate philosophical idealism that sanctioned using the aura of the archaic to bolster what was considered as the stable status quo of the present, that is, the way things have been.

Behind the rejection of history was the growing preoccupation with the so-called crisis of historicism, which preceded the political and economic collapse in the 1930s. Originating in Germany, this concern spread rapidly to Japan, where it generated energetic discussions in the interwar period focused on the view that the present suffered from the production of an excess of historical knowledge, with its untested claims of certainty and the runaway relativism of values it unleashed. It was observed that this proliferation of historical knowledge derived from accelerated specialization and fragmentation among the disciplines of knowledge, which resulted in a collapse of the stability of values—in turn making impossible the permanence of or confidence in evaluative judgments and putting into question whatever coherence historical practice might have once commanded. Since the ending of World War I it had been increasingly noticed that historical specialization and the surplus of historical knowledge were both undermining claims of standardized values (by seeking to understand pasts in and on their own terms, as if such a Rankean fantasy were ever attainable) and acknowledging that the historical discipline had constantly failed to explain how the present was produced by its pasts. In Japan, this worry ultimately led fascism to discount history altogether and resulted in the rallying of the interwar generation of intellectuals around the call to overcome modernity, which was another tactic devoted to fostering both the return to Japan (*Nihon kaiki*) and the prominence of the Japanese modernizing experience as a world historical mission. But this detection of the failure of one of history's central claims signaled an uneasiness over the discipline's exclusive concern with the past while ignoring analyses of the current situation, which would have required a conception of practice that concentrated on the historical present. It also incited widespread interest in exploring new possibilities for securing greater precision. Eventually, this observation led thinkers like Walter Benjamin, Ernst Bloch, Gramsci, Tosaka, and Jean-Paul Sartre to question the utility of historical linearity and turn away from the claims of consecutive stages and especially "all that which did not fit properly into laws of historical movement," which had dominated both bourgeois and Marxian historical practices to the extent of overlooking the problem of history's form.[13] Such a move required recognizing the way that coexisting past temporalities worked to undermine the present's capacity to identify with itself. The extensive presence of these lingering pasts in the present would become the basis of thinking through new perspectives of narrative exposition that were decisively political.

Behind these temporal rearrangements lay what Peter Osborne has called the "politics of time." He persuasively argued that modernity must be seen as a form of "historical totalization expressed in the medium of cultural experience." Specifically, the process of totalizing constitutes a distinct form of historical temporalization, consisting of the temporalization of history to bundle together the past, present, and future into the supposed unity of a single historical view.[14] Osborne also asserted that modernity includes the quality of a social experience, which—like capitalism—is an incomplete project.[15] Yet what is striking about this social experience, which the historian Reinhart Kosellek called "new time" (*neue Zeit*), is its claim of qualitative distinctiveness, whereby the "newness of time" is made to appear superior to all that has gone before. In this way, the mark of "newness" establishes a "differential to its own claim to qualitative superiority, which would thus see in the past what had come before" and shows an irremediable lack in its nonsynchronicity and noncontemporaneity. This was how historians would justify the superiority of a single linear time. Osborne seems to limit noncontemporaneity to colonial regions, whose alleged backwardness stands in dramatic contrast to the development reflected in modern, contemporaneous societies—whose capacity for colonizing themselves demonstrates the meaning of the concept of progress. What this differential of times between colonizer and colonized shows is a difference represented by economic and technological development, even though both types of development coexist in the same present—which Osborne, quoting Immanuel Kant, proposes "is the foundation for 'universal histories with a cosmopolitan intent.'"[16] But we know now that this qualitative differential is not so easily acceptable as a classification based on the differentiation between colonizer and colonized, since it is simply a distinction between advanced and contemporary, on the one hand, and backward (or underdeveloped) and noncontemporary, on the other hand, and that distinction derives from capitalism's ideological propensity for endless economic expansion, accumulation, and acquisition. The differential also overlooks the unevenness embedded in the capitalist history of the advanced society, which classifies late developers as backward. The relationship between claims to contemporaneity and noncontemporaneity are far more complex and their political and cultural consequences are more diverse than hitherto imagined. Moreover, their histories seek to establish a regime of homogenization that ironically is undercut by the very premise of temporal differentializing that informs its claim.[17]

The Problem of Form, or Contemporizing the Past

In Frantz Fanon's perceptive discussions of national culture in *The Wretched of the Earth* (1961), a momentary word of caution to his readers appears when he observes that entry into "the zone of occult instability" risked making a perilous move—what Benjamin might have described as an encounter with the moment of danger—into a domain that crouched behind a historicist mask concealing a world of unscheduled events, the vast asymmetries of uneven development and their peculiar combinations of the precolonial old and the capitalist new, and the swirl of plural temporalities colliding with one another in the present that they all occupied.[18] Colonial oppression of the colonized managed to reproduce the splitting of consciousness so presciently articulated by W. E. B. Du Bois at the beginning of the twentieth century, whereby the colonized see themselves through "the revelation of the other world" of the colonizer that "yields no true self-consciousness."[19] Fanon was certain that this dense, heterogeneous, and heterogeneously timed zone was one of "fluctuations," whereby the "development is uneven" and "the violent collision of two worlds has . . . shaken the old traditions and thrown . . . perceptions out of focus."[20] With this observation, drawn from experience, Fanon unveiled the mystery of the identity of a theory in the form of historical time, which appeared in the figure of contemporary noncontemporaneity. The process resembled a kind of refraction whereby the materiality of unevenness passed through a form of time. While undoubtedly describing the colonized world in its last days, he might as well have been judging capitalist modernity in the nineteenth and twentieth centuries. If Fanon was not the first to recognize the danger posed by using a form of time conspicuously distinguished by discordant and competing temporalities and the entailing difficulties they presented to negotiating the entanglements of everyday life, his naming of this environment as "the zone of occult instability" provides one of the best descriptions we have of modern life: it is a sphere of concealment that is hidden, opaque, unclear, and lacking constancy and certainty, renamed as "hell" by Benjamin. Benjamin explained "modernity, the time hell," as "The punishments of hell are always the newest thing going in this domain . . . that this newness remains, in every respect, the same. To determine the totality of traits which define this 'modernity' is to represent hell."[21] But Fanon, like others in the colonial world, early understood that Marxism spoke not only to the parochial islands of modern cultures of the West but to the wider epochal world at large. In *The Wretched of the Earth*, Fanon was addressing the conditions he found in colonial life and focusing on the specific experience of living in its layered temporalities in the present and pointing to the barriers in the path leading to a transformation into a national culture that might be something more than folklore. Years later in *The Arrow of God*, the novelist Chinua Achebe charted the collision between the time accountancy of village life by the priest–medicine man and the bureaucratic time enforced by colonial administrators. It is conceivable that Fanon—like Amilcar Cabral, Jose Carlos Mariategui, and others who lived in regions on the margins of so-called advanced capitalist societies—saw the consequential unevenness of colonized spheres more directly than their colonial masters and other foreigners did, which enabled them to perceive the wider pageantry of capitalist development everywhere it had migrated and implanted its mixed modes of life and social relationships. The Japanese philosopher Watsuji Tetsurō, returning to Japan from Europe in the late 1920s, noticed this difference between the mix constituting modern life in the colonial ports at which the ship stopped and concluded that this picture of similar difference had become the fate of modern Tokyo. Unevenness was viewed as signifying only the circumstances of colonized life (that is, the lateness of the colonized in acquiring capitalism's metabolizing mechanism), but like the form of dominating nations that circulated this myth, the presence of uneven development already proclaimed the forceful occurrence of capital's principal law everywhere. Hence, an unevenness designating only the conditions of colonized life appeared everywhere capitalism reconstituted its world through the repetitive accumulation of surplus value. Fredric Jameson has proposed that the "expression of marginally uneven and the unevenly developed issuing from a recent experience of capitalism are more often more intense and powerful, more . . . deeply . . . meaningful than anything the enfeebled center still finds itself to say." The importance of this observation is underscored in the recognition that unevenness still appeared in all the regions where capital has established its production process and signaled the precise "moment in which co-existing" different modes of production visibly combined to compose a "condensation of contradictions," capable of opening up the pathway of time to "revolutionary transformation."[22] While the colonial realm and late-developing nations like Japan would be seen as distorted reflections of Euro-America—what Benedict Anderson once described as a shrunken similarity diminished by looking at such societies through the wrong end of a telescope—it was more like a hall of mirrors reflecting one another, which was made possible by removing a mediating history of unevenness that existed throughout the capitalist world.

Not long before Fanon proposed the importance of knowing how to navigate both the dangerous terrain of coeval but spatially distanced temporalities that constitutes colonial capitalism and the received traditions from a precolonial period, Sartre noticed that Marxism was on its way to developing a conception of "real temporality" to avoid the hijacking and distortions inflicted by followers of Marx who had reduced the movement of time to linear "progress" (what Sartre called "Cartesian time"). Observations similar to those were made by Benjamin and Bloch before World War II. Sartre was clearly referring to the way Marx's theoretical intention had been appropriated by Marxism's Second and Third Internationals, which borrowed their idea of time from the process of capitalism's economy and thus sought to reflect history as a "signification of production, of monetary articulation of redistribution" and so forth. In Sartre's view, the chronological "distribution of the universal character as a phase of social development" differed widely from what might be generated by the dialectical determination of real temporality that constitutes the true relation of humans to their past and future.[23] What seems significant in Sartre's perceptive critique is that he saw that history had been contaminated by the movement of the capitalist mode of production and correctly accused international Marxism (and, by implication, bourgeois historians) of unknowingly using the process of production as the universal temporal template for determining human interactions and the history they made. Although he was ready to accept the content of capitalism's movement as a universally applicable chronological measure, he saw how a view based on emphasizing capital's template of production and distribution had been obliged to eliminate as a condition of its possibility the dialectical relationship between humans driven by different interactive rhythms. It is interesting to note in this connection that in the 1930s Tosaka had comparably noticed that phenomenological time had been borrowed to explain historical time and attributed the location of real time in the materiality of the working everyday everywhere instead to consciousness and its projection onto a perspective of history. Similarly, Miki Kiyoshi, a philosopher who was Tosaka's contemporary, was stalled in his effort to connect the everyday to world history, which represented different registers of historical time that could not be put together (I say more about these conceptions of time in Japan below). Implicit in these efforts to envision a temporality for history unburdened by "ideologically constructed instruments" of state power and relations between developed and undeveloped states was the denial by advanced capitalist societies of coevalness and the imposition of both spatial and temporal distancing on the latecomers to capitalism.

It should be noted that the initial signs of capitalism's process of uneven and combined development were detected by Lenin and Trotsky and were principally manifested in the developing societies and the colonial world. Unevenness was increasingly seen as a strategy of catching up, and it was possible to leap over the distance of time between advanced and underdeveloped societies—a point that was clearly emphasized by Lenin, who saw that the Russian agricultural countryside was progressively using new techniques introduced by capitalism alongside received practices from the past. Trotsky was persuaded that the "law of combined and uneven development reveals itself . . . in the character of Russian industry."[24] He invited countries whose growth had lagged behind or had been captured by some variant form of colonial domination to skip over epochs to find their own route, as Marx had already advised in his unsent letters to the Russian progressive

Vera Zasulich.[25] But it must be said that both Lenin and Trotsky contributed powerfully to the strategy of contemporizing the past in their recognition of the importance of combining new practices with the received old ones and capitalism's reproduction of uneven development. However, this particular search for real historical time moved in another direction and was continued and energized by thinkers like Bloch and Benjamin as they confronted the destructive threat of a fascism that promised to reverse the temporal register and eliminate history altogether and fill the vacated space with myth. The paradox is that even though Marx called for a return to the archaic, it was a strategy that subsequently was distorted by being emptied of history. Marx also reminded Zasulich that Russia would eventually have to undergo a social revolution. With fascism revolution meant a return to myth and desertion of history.

In the eye of the gathering conjunctural storm in the 1930s that led to global fascisms and World War II, Bloch and Benjamin began to think of time as both a totalizing dimension capable of producing effects no less material than other manifestations of uneven development and as an agent of unification shaping "non-linear time" and without "historical direction that is not fixed and monadic."[26] What Bloch was able to envision here was the figure of what he named contemporary noncontemporaneity— more literally, synchronous nonsynchronicity (*Ungleichzeitigkeit*)—which referred to temporal scenes in which residues and remnants from pasts now interacted dangerously with contemporary capitalism. Where Bloch and Benjamin departed from the discourse on combined and uneven development was in seeing the instance of capitalism's developmental consequences in the discordance of different times' colliding and clashing with each other, as remnants from other temporalities demanded differential responses and modes of negotiating ways through their regimes. By naming this temporal phenomenon synchronic nonsynchronicity (more popularly known as contemporary noncontemporaneity), Bloch proposed a way to grasp the wider psychological effects on people who occupied the same present but were living in a different time (Benjamin's conception of now-time), which clung closely to the archaic. The importance of Bloch's timely intervention in Germany in the early 1930s was to see contemporaneous noncontemporaneity and the uneven development it inflected as the principal temporal condition of capitalist modernity, presenting its acquisition of uneven times as its identity and noting its expansion of the objective conditions of the capitalist mode of production and inclusion of the breadth of more subjective intellectual, emotional, and cultural experiences. When Bloch argued that history does not advance along a single line, he was proposing that capital never realizes the final stage of completion, in which it would resolve and incorporate all previous ones. Rather, capital is *"polyrhythmic and multi-spatial . . . with enough unmastered and as yet by no means revealed . . . corners."*[27] The temporal crisis is announced by the explosion of discordant times. Convinced that the "economic substructures" still persisted in these remote and unattended corners of the social formation, "obsolete forms of production and exchange" had not yet passed away—"let alone the ideological superstructures," which could supply the content for romantic reveries and recoveries that could be used to prop up a failing capitalism in times of severe economic crisis.[28] Such crises would magnify and exaggerate contemporary noncontemporaneity by resorting to appeals to the timeless archaic and the installation of the content of archaism as the template capable of guiding an errant present. This response was clearly manifested in the fascist regimes of Germany, Japan, Italy, Romania, and other states in the period before World War II and remains the principal connection between more recent forms of fascism and these earlier historical episodes. But it seems evident that the form of the uneven temporal figure that fascism embraced was created by seeking to synthesize and smooth the present's discordant times and ridding it of conflict that produced historical anomalies, which in turn stood in the way of establishing mythic exemplars from the past. The intended purpose of the invocation of the archaic, which was invariably more myth and fantasy than historical reality was to resolve the immediate crisis of capitalism. What Bloch perceived is the extent to which capitalism had not yet integrated the whole of society within a contemporary order, which was still in process of completion.[29] Yet this suggests that Bloch believed that capitalism would achieve completion and somehow liberate itself from the rule of uneven development that repetitiously reproduced unevenness. A more likely scenario was that, first, capitalism would never completely realize itself to the degree that it would transparently identify with itself and that, second, the unevenness it continued to produce in all societies would end only with the end of capitalism itself. Hence, the appearance of lingering residues of a dangerous past in the postwar present, which announced the explosion of heterogeneous times, provides us with what Kristin Ross once described as the "figurability of the present."[30] This refers to seeing presents as a "landscape" (Ross's term) capable of offering occasions of figurability at moments when capitalist time is interrupted by the unanticipated arrival and forcible entry of untimeliness, which in turn is caused by reanimated coexisting traces of what Marx described as the "inherited evils arising from the passive survival of archaic modes of production, with their accompanying train of anachronistic social and political relations"[31]—that is, unwanted remains of the past bursting into the now of the present.

Both Bloch and Benjamin rejected vulgate versions of Marxism in the interwar period, especially claims of historical linearity that was punctuated by stages of epochal progressive advance leading to capitalism's completion as the necessary condition for a socialist revolution. With Benjamin, his break from the orthodoxies of the Second and Third Internationals prompted him to call into question the astonishingly astigmatic defects of an interpretive view based on imitating the progressive linearity and stagism of bourgeois narratives. Here, Benjamin was persuaded that this progressivism "dissolves history into stories that provide the bourgeoisie with an incognito in time."[32] This blindness prevented the bourgeoisie class from recognizing the importance of the present for a past referred to as once upon a time but in which time was absent. Like Bloch, Benjamin concentrated on the present and the platform it provided for historical analyses. He described this turn to the present as a mode of "awakening," a "turn to remembrance" that denoted a "Copernican Revolution in historical perception."[33] With this move, Benjamin was actually returning to Marx's own preoccupation in *The 18th Brumaire of Louis Bonaparte* and "The Class Struggles in France" and rejecting what formerly had been considered the "fixed point" of "what has been." Now, Benjamin proposed, it is necessary to confront its dialectical opposite—"the flash of awakened consciousness." But the "flash," like the famous "tiger's leap" in Benjamin's "Concept of History," has no temporal life beyond the instance of occurrence in his conception of "dialectics at a standstill." This constitutes a problem for his reversal of dialectical theory, to which I return below.[34]

Henceforth, "politics attains primacy over history," a sentiment also expressed by Gramsci at about the same time, although Benjamin's texts were probably unknown to him. Gramsci wrote that it was necessary "to treat the past (better: what has been) in accordance with a method that is no longer historical but political." In other words, political categories must be made into theoretical ones, insofar as political categories can be applied only in the sense of praxis, because only in the present. According to Benjamin, "the dialectical penetration and actualization of former contexts puts the truth of all present action to the test."[35] In this reversal, Benjamin reasoned that the facts become something that has just occurred to us when they awaken to stir memory. To instantly awaken in such a manner makes available the "affair of memory," or what remains closest to us—which Bloch recognized as the "darkness of the lived moment." He went on to say that the present ("this pernicious chasm") signaled the moment "to seize the day."[36] Lukács added that "as soon as history is forced into the present—and this is inevitable as our interest is determined in the last analysis by our aim to understand the present."[37] "Awakening," Benjamin proposed, "is namely the dialectical, Copernican turn of remembrance."[38]

In these fragmentary reflections on awakening and the capacity to secure a hold on remembrance, Benjamin is clearly repeating the interpretive trajectory of Freudian psychoanalysis and its investigation of the dreamworld, but he is using it as a model for a logic and strategy of historical knowledge. It is important to recognize that he chose not to start with results, as most historians did, but rather to begin with the dream.[39] However, his use of the act of awakening provides him with the way to penetrate that "hell of modernity," suddenly revealing its concealment of history—a lost "primal history" (*Urgeschicte*).[40] It is as if the observer finally wakes from what has been a dream and recognizes that what is before him or her is a world that has been lost, that he or she has been led back to a world that time had forgotten, and that which had been dreamt was a representation and ideology that called for progress. The object is thus to make the presence of the forgotten appear present: "It's not that what is past casts its light on the present, or what is present its light on what is past; rather, image is that wherein what has been comes together in a flash with the now to form a constellation. In other words, image is dialectics at a standstill. . . . Only dialectic images are genuine (that is not archaic)."[41] In calling for a fusing of opposites, Benjamin disclosed the primacy of form that embodies at certain moments the heterogeneity of different times, the encounter of the past and present, and the moment they are brought together to produce the contemporaneous noncontemporaneity that Bloch had described. But the joining of the past and the present occurred with a profound difference: "In order for a part of the past to be touched by the present instant (*Aktualität*) there must be no continuity between them."[42] In this connection, it is interesting to notice that Tosaka was using the same term in 1930s Japan to emphasize the importance of the real, rejecting contemporaries who were using reality (*genjitsu*) because it connoted the abstract and immaterial that was prior and superior to the lived reality of the everyday. Constrained by a hermeneutic metaphysics, Tosaka observed that it had lost its sense of time and movement, which he replaced with "actuality" (*akuchuaritei* [Japanese kana version of the English word] or *jissai* [the Japanese word]), spelling it out in the Japanese phonetic transcription of the German, followed by the word in Chinese characters. He identified its usage with material everyday life, instantaneity, movement, fact, and action.[43]

For Benjamin, the coexisting constellation of oppositions, made up of the most "heterogenous temporalities was best exemplified by the labyrinth it embodied in the cities. These temporal oppositions often seemed to overlap with his conception of "constellations of dangers"—and to imperil both tradition and continuity as well as those who believed in these categories of separate and distinct experiences.[44] The scene of these multiple dangers is played out in the city. "Whoever sets foot in the city," he warned, "feels caught up in a web of dreams, where the most remote past is linked to events of today."[45] According to Benjamin, the past prevails over any conception of continuous time, just as politics (praxis) takes precedence over history. It is the actualizing agent that brings the past to fulfillment in an act of correspondence, resembling the contemporization of the past in Bloch's formulation. The coming together occurs in an instant, which I have described as a monadic enactment that refigures historical time as a vertical stacking or constellation of congested and swirling times, a fusion of the now and then and the here and there. This refiguration announces the realization of "dialectics at a standstill," which was ultimately Benjamin's utopia. In one respect, his stacking of a combination of images and plural moments recalls Bloch's reflections on the figure of the multiversum arising out of different times from "heterogeneous contexts," which are the residues of prior pasts and temporal remnants occupying the same present that persuade people to live according to their different rhythms.[46] The two perspectives both privilege what Benjamin named the form of "mindfulness," which through "awakening" brings on a commitment to the work of remembrance (*eingedenken*) as a compressed and recalled historical experience and a task that remained unfinished.[47] In both perspectives, society remained in a state of incompletion that still demanded integration and recognized that it could never be transparent to itself. For Benjamin the idea of progress is embedded in the notion of catastrophe: "That things are 'status quo' is the catastrophe,"[48] and history provides a continuum from which historical materialism must "blast out." Opposed both to progress and to continuity, Bloch and Benjamin were fixated on establishing historical facts as an "affair of memory," which means that the facts "become something that just now happened to us" and appear as "nothing other than what here is secured on the level of the historical, and collectively." Collecting here becomes a "form of practical memory, and of all the profane manifestations of penetration of 'what has been' the most binding."[49]

According to Benjamin, "the new, dialectical method of doing history teaches us to pass through in spirit . . . through what has been, in order to experience the present as waking world, a world to which every dream at last refers."[50] Crucial to the critical perspectives of both Benjamin and Bloch was the search for a historical materialist view that could confront and overpower the insidious and dangerous spread of the "archaic form of primal history," which has been roused once more as it had been in every past, making "semblance in history still more delusive by mandating nature as its homeland" in the form of fascist morbidities.[51] It is in their respective dialectical methods that the two men's perspectives part company: Benjamin's "dialectic at a standstill" brought the dialectical process to its end and to history's end, recalling what Marx had referred to as the prehistory to revolutionary transformation. According to Rolf Tiedemann, the meaning of central concepts like "dialectic at a standstill" and "dialectical image" "remained iridescent" and slightly opaque and lacked "terminological consistency."[52] Benjamin's conception of dialectics arrested the dialectical process and appealed to a knowledge derived from a "nucleus of time hidden with the knower."[53] More importantly, that conception inverted Marx's understanding of a dialectic's movement, which "regards every historically developed form as being in a fluid state, in motion, and therefore grasps its transient aspect as well."[54] Tiedemann rightly proposes that the "freezing of the dialectical image was obviously not a method the historians could employ at any time. For him, as for Marx, historiography was inseparable from political practice: the rescuing of the past through the writer of history remained bound to the political liberation of humanity. Contrasted with the Marxian conception, however, according to which 'capitalist production begats, with the exorability of a law of nature, its own negation.' . . . 'In reality, there is not one moment that does not carry its *own* revolutionary opportunity in itself. [T]he particular revolutionary opportunity of each historical moment is confirmed for the revolutionary thinker by the political situation. But it is no less conformed for him by the power this moment has to open a very particular closed chamber of the past. Entry into this chamber coincides exactly with political action.' Benjamin's historical materialism can hardly be severed from political messianism."[55] While Tiedemann is undoubtedly correct to quote Marx's early declaration that capital would negate itself, there are others in his writings to provide the interpretative opening Benjamin took. Still, Tiedemann himself acknowledges that capitalism, by the 1930s, had not yet naturally passed away; there was no more time to wait, as Marx's pronouncement implied. As for Bloch, he kept faith in a dialectic that continually produced social forms combining elements and experiences of the past with contemporary capitalist life and culture in an uncompleted process. Moreover, Bloch (unlike Benjamin) seems to have embraced the strategy of combined and uneven development, inasmuch as it was committed to the stagism of unevenness and the prospect of overcoming it through a strategy of development designed for capitalism's latecomers rather than remaining in permanent standstill. At the same time unevenness disclosed the identity of developing combinations that brought together temporalities composed of incommensurables in every present as the sure sign of history's trajectory and its continuing lack of completion. It should be noticed that both Bloch's impulse to retrieve and contemporize the past and Benjamin's constructive historiography that "actualized" and "telescoped" the past by using the present (acknowledging that contemporary society was littered with residues of and survivors from a precapitalist past) represented an act of conservation.[56] Gramsci also shared these political formulations, which illustrated his sense of preserving what was believed to still possess utility and value for the present. Despite the differences between the programs of Benjamin and Bloch, it is important to remember that their critical interventions in a dangerous political time alerts us to the frequently attributed diminished explanatory role accorded to forms of historical temporality in signifying (instead of presuming to represent) life-forms, the complex relationships between a living present and a passed but still present past, and the relentless pathway undertaken by capitalist modernization everywhere it migrated to implant its regime of "occult instability."

It would be wrong to suppose that the fixation on history and time was limited to German intellectual life. While it was probable that Germans came to the subject sooner than others did and formulated a broad methodological platform capable of speaking to the experiences of societies in the wider world after World War I, the urgency with which German thinkers of different political persuasions pursued the questions raised by examining history's practical relationship to time was undoubtedly accelerated by the circumstances of their country's disastrous defeat in the war; the infliction on it of a punitive treaty by the victors; and the chaos of social, economic, and political dislocations in the newly established Weimar Republic. Nevertheless, it is possible to see similar preoccupations in countries throughout the world of industrial capitalism, such as Italy and Japan, inflected by conditions of their own historical experiences and the circulating atmospheric mood of the *après guerre*. In Italy there were bourgeois philosophers like Benedetto Croce, Marxists like Gramsci, and protofascist theorists like Giovanni Gentile, who each set their own agenda focused on Italian national regeneration as a completion of the Risorgimento, looking to Germany and Japan as models of modernization. It was with the sanction of an unfinished Risorgimento that some Italian theorists saw in fascism, fueled by the ideology of futurism, a political form committed to a modernization that was capable of overcoming an unsatisfactory present. In Japan bourgeois thinkers like Miki Kiyoshi and Watsuji Tetsurō, the native ethnologist Yanagita Kunio, and Marxists like Tosaka saw the everyday as the privileged site and turned the determination of history's time and entry into the essence of real existence and the alternatives it offered to Western-imposed historical narratives of progress. While Miki sought to consider historical time in connection with the fascist moment, Tosaka issued a searing critique in a book that he named the *Japanese Ideology* ideological claims of archaism and the philosophic hermeneutics that authorized them.

Critical and methodological interventions into the role played by forms of historical time invites us to revisit Marx's meditations on the logic of historical practice and time as a way of understanding Sartre's call for a "real temporality"—before Marx's thought was hijacked by linear progressivism and before the creation of the kind of theorizations behind Bloch's and Benjamin's critical formulations. It must be said that in Marx there is a crucial bonding between a conception of uneven development and the combining of received practices from prior modes of production with contemporary capitalism. According to him, appropriative subsumption and its ceaseless application constitute the foundation for history's logic of unevenness and combining. The procedure of subsuming economic practices like labor in a present involved in capitalist forms of production from a prior but still useful past was an early instance of what I am calling the contemporizing of the past, which would eventually lead to the inclusion in the range of choices of other spheres of past activities that configured contemporary noncontemporaneity. But it should be added that in this process of subsuming, residues of pasts were invariably suborned to contemporary capitalism. The act of what Marx called formal subsumption represented the basic rule governing all capitalist development and could coexist alongside the forms of advanced capitalist industrial production, a phenomenon that can still be observed throughout the capitalist world of production. In this operation, subsumption was the principal means by which economic practices were carried over from a prior mode of production (either converted, reconfigured, or left as they alone) and then served an entirely different mode of production—one committed to the accumulation of surplus value. But this act of bringing together what had been outside of capital and subordinating it into capital's production process required resynchronizing and contemporizing the heterogeneity of the selected components to make them conform to contemporary capitalism, forming an asymmetrical relation of unevenness between incommensurables capable of sharing the same temporality. In this way, the subsumption of older modes of production repetitively performed the work of contemporizing the past in the present by harnessing practices from older modes of production to capitalism. Accordingly, the idea of contemporaneity as an enclosure anchored noncontemporaneity and the plurality of historical time layers within it by providing "a single frame of reference."[57] In this regard, Étienne Balibar has proposed that in the history of capitalism there has been a pervasive "history of the *reactions* of the complex 'non-economic' social relations, which are the binding agent of a historical collectivity of individuals, to the de-structuring with which the value-form threatens them."[58] This observation suggests that the various forms of belonging are continuously being dissolved by the value-form at the same time that history, through use-value and living labor, is constantly being reinforced with new shielding that results from the constant application of formal and hybrid subsumption—which, by appropriating from the past, invariably rescues what otherwise might have been selected for historical disappearance. I believe that this is especially the case once the subsumptive process moves into other domains of human activity (like politics, culture, the social, and religion) to defend historical difference against the value-form's destructive fetishization of sameness. It is important to remember that Marx proposed coextending various forms of subsumption with advanced industrial capital—in other words, that earlier forms could continue to exist with later, more mature forms. This suggests that the desire to see the completion of real subsumption and capitalism represents both a commitment to a linear stagism and a romantically impatient desire to move on to the next stage of socialism, implying that the imperative is more political than economic.

Marx's conceptualization of subsumption appeared in volume 1 of *Capital* where he discussed absolute and relative surplus value in the larger context of the world market. His perspective changed in the 1860s, and he no longer limited what he described in *Capital* to England and Germany, applying it instead to the world at large. It became evident that the lived experience of uneven and combined development implicated all societies that were touched by capitalism and committed to its production of accumulation. For this reason, countries like England and France that came to capitalism earlier than others did were not immune to or exempt from the rule of unevenness, even though they would subsequently claim advanced status in a world increasingly organized along a divide between the developed and underdeveloped societies (referred to as backward to suggest that they remained in the disarray of infantile precapitalism). This hierarchical classification was a way of concealing the relationship between colonizing societies from their colonies, but it nonetheless disclosed an important truth: that there was neither a pure development of capitalism nor a unitary linear trajectory of growth modeled after the classic English experience, as had once been believed. Marx had observed in *Capital* that while England and the countries of Western Europe had followed a similar route to capitalist development, elsewhere capitalism could develop by pursuing different routes. By the 1870s, he had already rejected a conception of growth divided into successive stages and excoriated those who associated his writings with a philosophy of history that implanted similar experience of capitalism's beginnings everywhere its productive system was established, whatever their historical circumstances. Instead, he endorsed Russia's different developmental route. Here was Marx's conception of historicity, which he differentiated from the rest of Western Europe and was convinced that comparison of events and developments in diverse contexts might reveal similarities and repetitions with results that merited further study for the difference they might yield. The figure of unevenness and the combination of old and new pointed to the plurality of and relations among societies, as well as the multiplicity of paths of historical development of capitalism that made each manifestation intrinsically worldly and a subject of comparability. In these late formulations of Marx, we can see how he began to think about the shape of world history that resulted from the expanding world market. Yet it also retained a trace of his earlier formulation in *The German Ideology*, where he and Friedrich Engels noted the interaction between the "being" of particularity and the "universal being." It also showed the importance of the noncontemporaneous or nonsimultaneous moments within the developing capitalist world that each manifestation of subsuming passed through. What this course signified is that the relationship between forms of subsumption from prior received practices and capitalism produces different manifestations of unevenness and combinations. A superficial look at contemporary capitalisms in India, China, and Japan will disclose both the process of combining and the differences among them caused by their appropriations from their separate experiences.

There were also hybrid forms (*Zwitterformen*) of subsumption in places where the older mode of economic production still prevailed. As capitalism matured and evolved into advanced industrial forms of production (what Marx designated as real subsumption), he acknowledged that these differing forms could exist alongside of and would undoubtedly interact with each other. What distinguished formal from real subsumption was that the latter generated its own presuppositions, while the former did not. It should also be said that subsumptive procedures were forms, not stages that successively occurred according to a prescribed narrative trajectory or history. Above all else, it was capitalism that directed the course of appropriation and the mode of assimilating older economic practices into its production process and goals. In this way subsumption became the instrument of temporal contemporization, naming what it found useful from the past as noncontemporaneous or nonsimultaneous to it. As Bloch perceived, the content of "the non-contemporaneous contradiction . . . has released itself . . . in the *vicinity* of capitalist antagonisms," yet the contradictions are "traditional to the capitalist Now, in which they have been . . . destroyed and not replaced, . . . elements of ancient society") or, I would add, "a precapitalist society) which have not . . . died."[59] This is particularly the case of forms derived from the past and, indeed, of origin itself— whose attempted replication, certainly for the Japanese, was never fulfilled and would lead to an endless repetition of uncompleted restorations.

Not only did capitalism take what it needed from the past, but it was also empowered to produce combined and uneven configurations as a way of giving these elements rescued from the past a new lease on life by refurbishing them so they could realize their unfulfilled intentions in the present or by supplying them with a new intention. Politically, the effect of contemporization was employed to bolster a failing capitalist order by imposing greater ideological control over the populace, as shown in the cases of Germany, Italy, and Japan in the 1930s and their echoes today in the United States, Turkey, Hungary, Poland, and so on. But it should not be forgotten that the interaction between modes of subsumption constituting a capitalism streaked with components from another time was a reminder that capitalism itself was mixed with prior modes of production. The ideological tightening resulted in replacing a history, which was increasingly seen as the cause of the present's fallen condition and elevated a noncontemporaneous mythic fiction that would pose as the true history. In this operation, the political right wing has traditionally benefited most from embracing mythic ideologemes (the cell-like units of a larger ideology) in contrast to the historical, which it sees as the problem to overcome. Thus, the right wing pits the completion of archaic myth over the fear that history remained unfinished. Hence it is the nonpast, inspired by the unwanted zone of the remnant, which Marx blamed capital for compromising with feudalism. But, in reality, this view reflected an inability to see that he had already recognized capital's capacious appetite to take what it needed from the past—or at least the refusal to accept the idea that the nonpasts' linear scheme could not accommodate or assimilate the effects of the continuing contingent encounter between past and present modes of production. In contrast, fascism sought to master the contradictions produced by the inventory of noncontemporaneous heterogeneity to pursue its mission of saving capitalism presumably from itself.

Subsumption was a striking instance of enclosure, including elements from pasts and renewing them in different economic, political, cultural, and religious contexts. Through incorporation, this process of enclosure signified the appearance of the noncontemporaneous or nonsimultaneous moments that each manifestation of subsuming passed through. Just as capital constantly expanded its horizon of production to organize national economies through the process of subsumption, so its enclosing propensity was increased by a colonizing impulse that led to the spatial mix that Fanon called "the zone of occult instability," which exemplified the operation of bringing the outside partially into the inside yet paradoxically making the noncontemporaneous a way to elude the extremes of commodification. The contemporizing effect is also an example, as noted above, of Sartre's appeal to a "dialectical determination of real temporality" of the interaction of humans with their past and their anticipation of the future, illustrating the ability to generate combinations of the encounter of the incommensurate and the commensurate with the possibility that such an encounter offers for imagining a different materialist conception of history and its practice. What Marx implied from capital's logic of subsumption was its expansive appetite for incorporating and subordinating the past by appropriating practices from prior modes of production, which thus appeared outside of capital. In other words, capitalism subsumed its nonidentity, which was temporally and spatially different from the present's immediate production agenda. In inserting practices from the past into a different present to serve capitalism, metabolizing them with capital's processes, the status of the anachronistic remnant was avoided because what capital had taken from the past was designated to serve its contemporary interest. At the beginning of capitalism, economics as such was not considered separate from the larger matrix of social life: the modern differentiation of economics into semiautonomous spheres of action like politics, religion, culture, law, and so on had not yet been achieved. Patrick Murray reminds us, inadvertently recalling Balibar's previous observation, that Marx's theory "encompasses matters of fundamental social and moral significance. By bringing attention to the topic of specific social forms of needs, wealth, and labour, Marxian subsumption concepts disclose the socially, morally and politically qualitative dimensions of Marx's thought."[60] As capitalist political economy matured, its practice widened to include the spheres of politics and so forth. From its historical beginnings, capital did not recognize the independence of distinct spheres of activity, which more often than not overlapped with each other in strange combinations. The classic example of these combinations appears in Max Weber's observation that Protestant Christianity is related to capitalism and the latter could subordinate the former to its advantage and interest. Fascism (standing in for capitalism) was a curious combination of advanced technology and mythic or backward-looking time. We can see the unfolding of similar combinations in late developing societies like Japan and India, where religion was employed to enhance capital. The differentiation between the two occurred later, when they were made into modern forms of knowledge. But it is precisely this failure to recognize that differentiation and the barriers erected by independent knowledge areas that has blocked our capacity to see the operation of subsumption as something more than a narrow economistic category advanced by a later vulgate Marxism and to recognize it as capital's initial pursuit of the valorization of its own value and its expansive bringing together of different practices and institutions. Finally, the act of subsuming the past into the present also reinvests the historical with a sense of unanticipated contingency bonded to the moment when the appropriation takes place to meet capital's new demands.

While the archetypal model of uneven and combined development surfaced in Marx's description of conceptualization and description of "so-called primitive accumulation" in *Capital*, volume 1, as a cauldron of mixed and different temporalities that would continuously reappear, it also was an event that secured the social reproduction of a present hereafter filled with the multiversum of contemporary noncontemporaneity—or, according to Gramsci, it secured the opposite: the structure of historical time. If this panoply of swerving heterogeneous temporalities was driven by uneven developments (what else could be the case?), it is possible to envision a turn to its opposite, in which the temporal structure would become dominated by a noncontemporaneous contemporaneity. This reversed trajectory that privileges the noncontemporaneous over the contemporary encouraged the embracing of illusory temporalities from remote mythic times of origins or reconfiguring them to use the new ground of historicity to reconstitute the present. In the latter case, the past brought in its train symptoms of morbidity, the zombies of the awakened dead who, like dead labor, echo Marx's famous warning against the "dead seizing the living" to allow the living dead of labor to conquer the living.[61]

As noted above, Marx changed his perspective on history in the 1870s. This shift was prompted by his correspondence with Zasulich, then exiled in Geneva. Zasulich asked Marx to explain how Russia would be able to overcome the debilitating residues of the past in the present and to realize a modernizing transformation to capitalism that could set the stage for the subsequent transition to socialism. By this time, Marx had begun to study Russian and had been reading ethnographies that led him to the world beyond Western Europe. The letters disclosed that his geographic vision had not only broadened to include other routes to capitalism besides those imitating the Western European model sketched in *Capital* but had also started his conceptualization of a program of historiographic practice that dramatically departed from both the philosophy of history he had embraced earlier and the linear stagism attributed to his *A Contribution to the Critique of Political Economy* (1859). The principal model informing this practice came from his effort to respond to this request by Zasulich. Marx advised adopting the figure of geological stratifications of temporalized strata, which he likened to differing levels or periods of historical time.

In these letters Marx explicitly acknowledged the compatibility of combining the archaic Russian commune (*obschina*), still functioning in the present, with contemporary capitalism. Notable about this linkage is the emphasis he placed on capital's contemporaneity. Convinced that capitalism could benefit by using the enduring structure of the archaic commune, he reasoned that the combination of the two could enhance a revitalization of both the principle of communalism and national economic development.

It would return to the archaic with a new historical respect. At the same time, it would work to avoid the baneful vicissitudes inflicted by capitalism. With this example, Marx disinterred his earlier conceptualization of incommensurables, involving the immense time differential represented by each component of the combination, and recommended the combining of what was still at hand, derived from a remote past mode of production, with contemporary capitalism. Here was an extension and expansion of the subsumptive process he first proposed in *Capital*, which offered a rich strategic model for societies embarking on comparable economic development to draw upon their own pasts for useful institutions and practices to combine with capital. It seems instructive to compare this strategic appropriation to Trotsky's later refiguration that aimed to shorten the path forward of late-developing societies by yoking backwardness (that is, the old) with the new innovations of capitalism and technology, which he named "combined and uneven development."

Owing to the new strategy that Marx outlined in his letters to Zasulich, he had no trouble suggesting to her how the archaic could be harnessed to capital and that she no longer needed to fear its baleful associations. But he reminded her that Russia, like all capitalist societies, would eventually have to undergo a social revolution. Hence, the glimpse Sartre had perceived of a new approach to history's time was provided by Marx in a model that invites us to imagine a historical form combining a representative of the past and the contemporaneity of the capitalist present to produce a working synchronic nonsynchronicity. It will be recalled that Marx's *The 18th Brumaire of Louis Bonaparte* prefigured this conception of history when he observed how the the revolutionaries recalled the examples of the past. The perspective proposed in his letters to Zasulich, including the example of geological stratifications vertically imposed on top of each other, insisted clearly that capitalism followed not just one but many routes and histories, loosely joined in a unified world market. We must see the multiple and discordant temporalities crowding every present—and manifesting uneven and combined developments, collisions, breaks, and interruptions—not as subjective expressions of consciousness but rather as objective indices of the different levels of a social formation emitting "effects of its materiality."[62]

Japan's modernity was initiated by the Meiji Restoration, the imperial activists who had staged it announced an intention to install an archaic mythic figure embodied in a persisting monarchy to start a new history. The implication of this announcement was that history since antiquity down to the moment of the restoration had been a failure. But the act of restoring an emperor long absent from direct rule led to contemporizing the past in an unknown present dedicated to world historical change. Restoring the emperor meant introducing into time both anachrony and the universal temporality of the clock time of state and capitalism. While Meiji leaders continued the practice from antiquity of using the reign name of emperors as a standard measure of time, this measure was now made to coexist with the new clock time and the Gregorian calendar of the state's and capital's business.[63] It should be noted that the imperial reign name and calendar were used as much in everyday life as clock time and the Gregorian calendar were and should be seen as a way the state and capital sought to regulate time and prevent the proliferation of diverse claims that differing pasts could offer to the present.

Years later the binary of imperial state and business times was glossed by Watsuji Tetsurō, who conceptualized a theory of Japanese culture that he called its "stadial character" (jūōsei). In Zoku Nippon seishinshi kenkyū (Studies in the cultural history of Japan) (1935), Watsuji envisioned the totality of Japan's culture as a form of stadialized layers imposed on top of each other, a vertical index of the piling up of different cultures and times. At the beginning of Japan's modern era, he perceived that the enthusiastic Meiji enlighteners' abstract conception of enlightenment taken from Europe "lacked historical consideration." What he meant was that the intellectuals who embraced an abstract conception of enlightenment and civilization in the 1870s and 1880s tended to see in it a replacement for the entirety of Japanese life. According to Watsuji, in their quest for a new concrete modernity, these enlighteners produced a "crisis of abstraction," which resulted in a problem for Japanese culture. This was because one of the special characteristics of Japan's culture piled stratified layers from diverse occasions: "A German who did not sufficiently understand the special characteristic of Japanese culture called Japan a 'Nebeneinander country,' a country of co-existence (heizon)." Watsuji agreed and proposed that existing differences in daily life are neither "abandoned" nor "blended" but instead are "completely unified in the totality of everyday life as a so-called double life (nijū seikatsu)."[64] In other words, two levels of the everyday occupy different registers of time and space in their present coexistence. But Watsuji's model failed to account for the importance of change in the static arrangement of the two levels. At about the same time, Yanagita examined the coexistence of two levels of folk time with the binary of hare and ke, with the former denoting an extraordinary time such as a festival day and the latter referring to the ordinary time of everyday life.

The imperial loyalists who orchestrated the overthrow of the Tokugawa shogunate and return of an ancient figure of monarchical authority believed that the Meiji Restoration would rescue the long abandoned but limited imperial world of origin and start a new time. However, it should be pointed out here that these reformers, commonly referred to as men of high purpose (shishi), appropriated what in the received political tradition was available to them to seize authority by overthrowing the shogunate and establishing a centralized state with themselves at the helm. While they were able to exploit a tradition that from its origin had centered on an emperor who was said to embody divine descent, in calling for its restoration, they were also successful in manipulating and expanding the power vested in the imperial figure. In other words, they were determined to "seize the jewel" for themselves. They were driven by the force of their own ambitions, not lofty principles, and they restored a usurped political authority while claiming to act on behalf of a righteous moral cause. It was this trajectory that led from restorationism to fascism through the instrumentality of archaism in the 1930s. But the transformation let loose after the restoration did far more than restoring the emperor to his rightful role. In fact, the actual restoring of ancient polity (ōsei fukko) was soon turned into what became known as a renovation (ishin), leading to a vast transformation of the social, economic, and political structure to a configuration resembling a modern capitalist state and society. Yet when the renovation was made to appear as a natural outgrowth of the restoration and a natural part of a linear narrative history of Japan, it was an effect of the spectacle of temporal unevenness inscribed in the new political form, conforming to what Gramsci called "passive revolution" or "restoration/revolution." The subsequent renovation undoubtedly emerged from the new economic forces and cultural impulses developed in the prior Tokugawa period—which remained momentarily recessive in the awareness of the imperial loyalists—as well as Japan's more recent confrontations with a world from which it had been shut off until the early decades of the nineteenth century.[65] The rapid transformation of Japanese society exceeded the imaginings of the restorers of imperial legitimacy, creating a society founded on the fusing of the imperial past and the capitalist present. However, Japan's revolution could be only partial because of the role played by an active past in making the present. It may most resemble the image portrayed by Marxist thinkers in the so-called lecture faction (kōzha) like Yamada Moritarō, who complained that the retention of feudal remnants had blocked the revolution's completion. What Marxists of this faction saw as a failure resulting in a descent into political absolutism, Gramsci cast in the form of passive revolution in his comments on many comparable transformations in the nineteenth and twentieth centuries, a form consisting of a composite of received practices from the past, new elements provided by contemporary capitalism, and an everyday life regulated by the rhythms of uneven and combined moments. We can see the parallels between the political form of passive revolution, whereby an archaic imperial institution was restored, and the temporal form of contemporary noncontemporaneity, represented by capitalism, as something more than coincidence.

With the shift to archaism and the formulation of Japanist ideology (*Nipponshugi*) in the 1930s, the presence of anachrony proved—as Jacques Rancière has observed—to be a useful way to synchronize the past as a solution to a present perceived to be the cause of the crisis at hand. Rancière proposes that since anachrony is an object, idea, or practice that seems to have come from the past and lodged itself in the present, it is considered an anachronism (something out of its time) because it defies belief as defined by the particular time of the present. Accordingly, one must be contemporary in one's time, present with it, and belong to it, if one's time is to resemble eternity—that is, a "pure present."[66] But this perspective reduces the relationship between past and present to the historians' conviction that there exists only a single historical time that is subsumed in a larger chronology that moves progressively to some completed state, when before and after are converted into cause and effect. Rancière calls this identity of a specific time and belief the "knotting of time," which assures time's redemption.[67]

For historians committed to historical time as chronological linearity, every moment or period has its proper time. It is important to note that Rancière considers anachrony neither bound nor related to the horizontal order of things that characterizes chronological linearity. Rather, he sees it as a vertical division of this order. The movement of time runs from below to above. Implied in this temporal reconfiguration are two possibilities: the first appears in Marx's letters to Zasulich, when he proposed the shift in the view of historical practice to a vertical axis composed of layers or levels of time stacked on top of one another and resembling the strata of geological formations. Here, items on the vertical axis constitute a palimpsest, whose earlier layers can still be traced to those imposed on top of them. In the palimpsest, lower layers are never entirely blotted out by what has been deposited above them, and it was precisely this relationship that Marx recognized in the contemporary Russian commune whose predecessors came from a remote time. The advantage of a historical practice based on the vertical axis of the palimpsest over one based on linear horizontality is that the form of layers of the past, like the strata of rock formations, are never effaced. In contrast, in a practice based on horizontality the past is assumed to have passed away because of the inexorably progressive trajectory moving history forward toward a goal: the past is gone, irretrievable, and forgotten. The power of the palimpsest appears in its capacity to allow retrievability and reversibility because it is not driven by a fixed narrative ambition. Another possibility appeared in Marx's suggestion that the communal form, whose traces remained visible in the Russian countryside of the 1870s, could be retrieved and revitalized by combining with capitalism to enhance national economic development without incurring the disadvantages of capital. Clearly, this move of combining an institution fashioned in a precapitalist past with contemporary capitalism (which sanctioned the appropriation) mixed elements from two different modes of production. In this way, Rancière's conceptualization of a vertical axis of times strongly echoes the example in Marx's letters to Zasulich, in which the commune would have been considered as an anachronism in the environment of the late nineteenth century. Yet the example actually manages to break the spell of anachrony by contemporizing a residue, like the archaic, from the long-forgotten past in which it had originated. To dispose of the claims of anachronism, Rancière called forth the presence of a "multiplicity of lines of temporality present in any one 'time,'" or the plural times that inhabit his great work *La nuit des prolétaires*—times that are invariably produced by capitalism's law of uneven development and its dedication to contemporizing all pasts that are found useful, not only the archaic.

For Rancière, anachrony disappears with the recognition of the "new line of history, linked to the idea as a process in the making, and born of the rupture accomplished by the revolutions in England, America and France. . . . The multiplicity of temporalities, even senses of 'time,' included in the 'same time' is a condition of historical activity."[68] This production of a sense of time continued the process with the proliferation of passive revolutions from the nineteenth century on. While Japan's break with its immediate past was not a product of a capitalist past but rather a response to the threat of capitalism's present and future from the outside (threats also faced in France, England, and the United States), it was an anachronistic archaic imperative that opened the way for a transition to capitalism. At the same time, the break was a force that rolled back the entirety of Japan's long history to focus on an original moment that offered the "capacity to define completely original points of orientation to carry leaps from one temporality to another." In these jumps, Rancière reminds us, lies the "power" of anachrony to "make history."[69] If anachrony has "left its time," it has no identity with time as such, which allows it to perform similarly to the French Revolution, whose effect Marx noted in *The 18th Brumaire of Louis Bonaparte*. At the precise moment of a new revolutionary upheaval, the history that is being made is still yoked to and "transmitted from the past." In that time of revolutionizing, "in creating something that has never yet existed . . . , the 'spirits of the past'" are conjured up and its "names, battle cries and costumes" borrowed to masquerade as the "new scene of world history."[70] As an anachronism, the archaic would find its times: it made possible the Meiji Restoration that opened Japan's path to becoming a modern society, and it provided the central ideologemes that authorized the construction of fascism's virulent ideology in the wake of the Shōwa Restoration of the 1930s. Paradoxically, Marx's recommendation to return to the archaic was reversed like the negative of a photographic print when the promise of passive revolution and its modernity turned into fascism, abandoning history to embrace mythic morbidities. Yet these mythic associations, derived from the origin (believed by restorationists to have historical existence), came in the train of the restoration of imperial authority in 1868, which were and have remained inseparable from the figure of the Japanese emperor who embodied divinity. Unlike European kings, who ruled by divine right (the grace of God), the Japanese emperor ruled because he was a living deity. Predictably, this transformation to the primacy of a mythic archetype rather than a historical figure was accompanied by replacing the usual temporal order of contemporary noncontemporaneity identified with passive revolutions with noncontemporaneous contemporaneity, which led to fascism.

The journey of the archaic (which traveled through Japan's modern history in three moments) is recognized as the principal trajectory. The third moment began in the postwar period, resulting from wartime destruction and failure and the attempt of the U.S. Army of Occupation to reconstruct a new social order. This last moment remains incomplete in the view of the political theorist Maruyama Masao, who conceptualized a figure that might succeed where its predecessors failed. While it was his intention to link the moments in a narrative of succession, I see each as separate and unconnected to what preceded or came after it. They are not modes in a rectilinear history of stages but simply three epochal moments that share only the valorization of the archaic, and they valorized it for vastly different reasons.

2 RESTORATION

The Question of Passive Revolutions

What Karl Marx showed in his histories of the present was the importance of insurgent actors in every present and the way they relied on the necessity of contemporizing examples from the past to secure access to what had been repressed, blocked, or unfulfilled. This effort to reemplot the past by making it present appeared to involve affirming how the past led to the present, but instead it was the reverse: it showed how the past might be seen from a different perspective and summoned to overcome the dissatisfactions of the present. This was precisely the path and purpose that Étienne Balibar attributed to what seemed close to Marx's conceptualization of the forms of subsumption (based on history and difference) in the struggle to maintain the primacy and presence of living labor. According to Balibar, subsumption served to counteract the extreme effects resulting from the circulation of the value-form and its propensities to eliminate anything outside of it and to make production appear to be derived from it rather than from living labor. In this respect, pasts were always contingently unpredictable because they embodied diverse possibilities that presents had overlooked, forgotten, or even repressed. This was the direction envisioned by Antonio Gramsci when he conceptualized the strategy of passive revolution, which constituted a transmutation of "historically given experiences and categories" (resembling the act of formal subsumption) into the present.[1] Early exemplified in the Italian Risorgimento, Gramsci saw its broader appearance in the journey toward modernity taken by a number of societies on the course of nationhood but was "lacking in the radical-popular of the 'Jacobin moment,' which had distinguished the experience of the French Revolution."[2] The description pointed to the moment when a politically leading class of reformers, which previously had won the approval of the masses, begins to lose its revolutionary initiative and turn to autocratic dominance and the denial of political advancement to other classes—renouncing the progress it had previously embraced. The reformers had failed to take into account that in its functioning, passive revolution would tend to revert to more conservative and reactionary positions, which eventually lead to fascism. The importance of the political form of "passive revolution" or "restoration/revolution" is disclosed in the attempt to synchronize the unevenness resulting from the recent fusion of elements of a received historical past with the new contemporary capitalism. Here it is interesting to notice both in Japan during the years preceding the Meiji Restoration and in nineteenth-century China (nearly a century before the 1911 Republican Revolution), the appearance of thinkers who presciently envisioned the silhouette of the combination of elements from a precapitalist and modern capitalism. In the actual working out of the form of passive revolution, it is possible that these earlier observations were used later. However, it is more likely that the form's adoption was stimulated by the availability of more recent models that could be emulated.

Tōyama Shigeki, the great historian of the Meiji Restoration, asked rhetorically who occupied significant positions in the making of the Meiji Restoration, what guided them, and what role they played in bringing it about. In answering his own questions, he suggested that the principal actors in the restoration were not directly conscripted from the "contemporary relations of interest of their descendants," implying the absence of a commercial class of bourgeoisie that had prepared the way for the restoration.[3] Whatever their identity, the position of these figures was connected to a desire to rescue the diminished imperial system and the emperor, who with his predecessors had remained a virtual prisoner of Tokugawa feudal power for three hundred years. Undoubtedly an overstatement, it nonetheless represented the principal theorization of the activists who advocated what was commonly referred to as revering the emperor and expelling the foreigner (sonnō jōi) and who had no plan apart from restoring imperial authority. But these activists were often portrayed by historians like Tōyama as a movement when in fact they were little more than a congeries of self-anointed imperial loyalists representing different domainal interests. This kind of coherence attributed to a group of loosely linked activists is usually a totalizing abstraction based on the final result, not extracted from the lived experience of those who were involved.

Tōyama was clearly referring to the idea that the Meiji Restoration was brought about not by the existence of a historic bourgeoisie, whose interests demanded an immediate political change in both the structure of authority and social order, but rather by samurai activist loyalists driven by "pure, unhistorical ethical values."[4] Nor did he even hint at the existence of any sign attesting to the momentous shifting of economic plates that resulted in a new mode of production, even though he and the whole tradition of Marxian historical practice in Japan would have been sensitive to recognizing it as a strategy accounting for the restoration. This is not to deny the vast amount of historical writing dedicated to disclosing the inroads of a new mode of production in the late Tokugawa period—the veritable "sprouts of capitalism" that presumably would mature later. Yet the origin of modern Japanese society bypassed the "route of a modern urban revolution," reflecting the strong authority of tradition that impelled a restoring of ancient polity. But Tōyama acknowledged that the activists, who were "ruptured from history," were not driven to "create a new revolutionary social order" but were motivated only by a respect for a "surface history."[5] Hence, from the beginning only the historical form of "esteeming respect," when made into an instrument, vindicated the interests of the leaders of the restoration. Tōyama concluded that such a history evades the investigation of reality and instead despises and desecrates reality. Immediately after the Meiji Restoration, the gathering of materials related to its origins was put into the hands of a new governmental agency (the *Dajokan*). The agency's compilation of the materials suffered from an "impoverished historical consciousness" and produced only a chronological collection of materials. This early Meiji collection had no coherent point to it but subsequently provided a weapon to use in political disputes among the ruling class, which "pained the heart of those who perused a researched history of the Meiji Restoration."[6] What Tōyama objected to was the absence of scholarly expertise in assembling this compilation of historical materials yet it was projected in a way that such an allegedly official history suspended further inquiry because of the "opportunistic arbitrariness" of the leadership. He contrasted the domain-centered interests in the restoration to the critical and scientific research of the modern historical practice (like his own) to show that the latter was the only way to overcome the "absolutism" established by the Meiji Restoration.

But tradition here is simply another totalizing and unifying abstract category used to replace more modern historical categories, and it is just as problematic as they are. It is never clear what traditions might have meant for the diverse participants. Even if they could agree, as some did, on the centrality of the Mito domain and its relationship to the Tokugawa house, acceptance probably stemmed less from its position in the feudal arrangement of power than the development of a powerful discourse from the late eighteenth century that articulated a theory of vertical hierarchy capped by the emperor, not the shogun. While its influential arguments were widely disseminated throughout the early nineteenth century among diverse samurai groups, it was never clear what that discourse meant to each of the activists or how they might have understood it. Depending on the temporal circumstances, their comprehension of the discourse would have been mediated by their experience, and vice versa. Thus, these circumstances must be considered in any effort to imagine what they were thinking as they formulated their opposition to the shogunal regime.

Severed from history, the move to restoration did not generate the immediate creation of a new social order or the construction of an entirely new society through the agency of revolution. In fact, the decision to restore a young and inexperienced emperor and end Tokugawa rule came at the last possible moment and represented the action of individual bodies, carrying out a momentary decision—not an existing historical trajectory toward seizing political space and time without any other idea and with no appeal to authority other than an absent emperor by claiming to return to the imperial precedent of a mythic origin that possessed no empirical existence. The initial narrative of the restoration appeared to be a surface history made to show that the samurai activists who sacrificed themselves to restore the emperor were prompted not by historical determinants, such as their own socioeconomic situation and political aspirations in the feudal hierarchy, but by a purely ahistorical and ethical respect for the monarchy and the hierarchy it authorized. Tōyama reasoned that if the historical was the means through which to explain the advantages or disadvantages of the leading group of restorationist activists, it is evident that with the "shirking of the reality of the true facts," history itself was severely "slighted" and left to "lay in waste."[7] In fact, this kind of "shirking" of history would continue to inform the subsequent Marxist and non-Marxist historiography of the restoration, including that of Tōyama himself.

While Tōyama's judgment remains ambiguous, it pointed to a missing historical configuration that would explain the reason samurai activists in the late Tokugawa period were prompted to commit extreme acts of violence. The activists were not motivated by loyalty to a remote and abstracted emperor, who was anxious about being dragged into a national struggle and had no experience whatsoever in exercising authority over national policy. Rather, they were motivated by a variety of different reasons that could be sanctioned under the umbrella of the singular figure of the emperor—which had already been symbolized as a principle, though not a principal, of a hierarchical arrangement of authority in the early political discourse of Mito domain.

Tōyama argued that a proper history of the restoration could be produced only after its success, and such a history would portray a much more complex picture of a society that had failed to pass through the stages of a modern bourgeois revolution to create a new social order. And why should it have gone through these stages? What appears important about the complexities of this picture is that it consisted of components that would reveal a configuration of forces that had much less to do with a tradition of imperial loyalism than hitherto supposed. By relying on the authority of tradition, historians had managed to convey only its opposite. The outcome of this historiographical reversal was the realization of a historically rooted counterrevolution (sometimes called refeudalization) that included the installing of political absolutism and the reassertion of a principle of historical repetition, if in a different temporal register.

This conception was later expanded by Gramsci in the political sphere in his formulation of the category of passive revolution. It should be pointed out that initially the idea of passive revolution was a response to a conjunctural challenge demanding political change and was thus conceived of as a tactic.[8] But the use of combined political incommensurables closely resembled Marx's earlier formulations on formal subsumption and the bringing of past economic practices together with the new capitalist production process, which suggests the possibility in Marx of converting the forms of functional economic operations into modes of political action that lead to new political organizations. It was this model of time— combining temporal incommensurables and often bringing components of prior modes of production together with capitalism—that subsequently transformed Japan (and a number of other societies throughout the nineteenth and twentieth centuries) into a modern country with uneven and combined developments. But Tōyama, like many other historians, seems to have overlooked the relationship between event and historical time. He chose to rely on the unquestioned traditional convention of linearity and its predictable imaging of history's unfolding as an inevitable outcome of the trajectory through the stages required to reach its final destination. Tōyama elected to start with the end result, as if it represented the completion of the story. In fact, this mode of historical emplotment conveyed the inevitable triumph of imperial loyalism in overthrowing the Tokugawa shogunate and restoring absolute authority to the emperor. Yet what this model of historical practice produced was an effect that excluded the coexistence of other competing events, movements, and discursive claims operating in different spatiotemporal registers that, all of which seen from a different perspective, could have manifested their copresence and availability for activation in the same present. What these alternatives collectively managed to disclose was an incomplete story. Linear trajectories retrospectively see the result of what has happened in a past that actually has passed, is done with, has been overcome, and has been left behind by the newly installed present. If we start from the final result or presumed conclusion and moving backward in time to reveal how only it could have happened, the chain of causation of temporal reversion is made to appear as if the history had started from the beginning and followed the succession chronologically forward. The apparent law of linear movement seeks to securely anchor history's time in a one-way street, thus guaranteeing an inevitable outcome and insisting that the past has finished whatever task it had set out to accomplish and had given way to a new present. The coexisting alternative discursive reminders remained everywhere and in open sight in the present but were nonetheless invisible, a little like Edgar Allan Poe's purloined letter. The logic governing this movement requires that historical time be irreversible and move only forward, and that in any given present there can be only one temporality rather than a copresent crowd of different times. Historians, sounding the alarm, were alerted to the sign of the past implanting itself into the present because it was seen as an act (according to the French historian Lucien Febvre, who called it a "sin of sins"), an act that commits the violence of interrupting the alleged natural flow of linear time. Anachronism was seen as the way to identify and banish what appears to be out of time and its claims of belonging and presence.[9] But the use of anachronism is usually an overt denial that the work of history has not been completed and brought to a successful end, that the past is not yet over, and that a new beginning has been installed. It is interesting to note that this one-way movement was precisely the modality of historical time and narrative that both state and capital have been strenuously committed to defending as natural against the unleashing of forgotten or suppressed memories of both unexpected and unwelcome political alternatives and challenges, as well as repeated economic failures of the established order of things.

Tōyama's vision of the Meiji Restoration, like countless other accounts of epochal transformations around the world, makes the restoration appear as to be inevitable and a completed conclusion or a linear teleological outcome, sometimes accompanied by a transition pointing to a capitalist society that supported a linear movement, and that the restoration's nonoccurrence would have been inconceivable. Had he been acquainted with Gramsci's conceptualization of passive revolution, he might have given more thought to the structuring role played by the collisions of coexisting plural temporalities representing the work of different groups and to the way that new forces inevitably attempt to win over their adversaries by retaining components and experiences of an older order under a reordered hegemonic arrangement. In other words, what the template of passive revolution shows is never the creation of an entirely new society (what the French Revolution tried to achieve and what Paul Ricoeur called the "mother of all ruptures") but rather a more modest, limited rupture producing a restoration of prior practices and institutions and their subsequent refiguration to meet new political and economic demands. In many ways these limited ruptures often resemble permanent transitions. We have seen that Marx indicated how capital was able to take over past practices that remained close at hand and make them work for capital accumulation, although they had previously served other kinds of economic functions like subsistence and reproduction. To see Meiji Japan as the result of an aborted revolution, an incipient bourgeois revolution, or a counterrevolution is to misrecognize the nature of capitalist modernization. In all instances, the capitalist modernization was propelled by the idea of catch-up with advanced Western capitalisms and by the mistaken understanding that it would be completed. Yet we know that the quest for modernization that drove passive revolutions possesses a capacity for producing uneven and combined developments, as initially manifest in its program to limit what in the past would have been abandoned and to fuse older political and economic practices to newer. Although its desire for new possibilities is a common source of the overthrowing of an older regime, it is never complete and can lead to even more conservative political settlements that generate what Benita Parry has called "symptoms of morbidity," which often signal the turn toward fascism. It was precisely the manifestation of these symptoms in Japan that produced the attempts to insert a mythic archaic moment into the present and make it look like a lived past. This model of repetition appeared as the fatal legacy of the restoration, in which later people promised to complete what they believed had remained unfinished and to call for the Shōwa Restoration in the 1930s, and the recourse to the dangerous ideology of Japanism and its mission to replace the present with an origin from the fictional and nativist past.

Gramsci's concept of the passive revolution grew out of his reading of Italy's modern history and the way the nation's stalled transformation and barriers of persisting regional divisions provided the occasion for identifying the political form that produced an inventory of incomplete revolutions. His passive revolution was free of the burden of replicating the French Revolution, and his form was a model used by most subsequent revolutionary moments. In this regard, the call to unify urban industrial workers in the north of Italy and semifeudal peasants in the south into a new bloc—which brought together contemporary capital, the feudal past, and the specific historical form of the Risorgimento—prefigured his formulation of the larger explanatory category of passive revolution and its capacity to account for the occurrence of politically transformative events in diverse places and times. In other words, Gramsci conceived of the category of passive revolution as a historical form applicable to certain historical transformations. It was, he wrote, "precisely the brilliant solution of . . . (diverse) problems which made the Risorgimento possible, in the form in which it was achieved . . . as a 'revolution without a revolution,' or as a 'passive revolution.'"[10] In Gramsci's explanation of Edgar Quinet's use of "revolution-restoration" and Vincenzo Cuoco's earlier idea of passive revolution, what appears to be missing from Italian history is the historical fact of popular initiative. Hence, "progress occurs as the reaction of the dominant class to the sporadic incoherent rebelliousness of the popular masses—a reaction consisting of 'restorations' that agree to some part of the popular demands and are therefore 'progressive restorations,' or 'revolutions-restorations,' or even 'passive revolutions.'" This ambiguous arrangement would set the course of the transformation that would progressively move from restoration to revolutionary change. But the progressive trajectory could be stalled, leaving the nation between restoration and the achievement of a permanent revolution and suspended in an empty temporal duration, neither fully restorationist nor revolutionary. This in turn would lead to a "crisis of authority," which fascisms in Italy, Germany, and Japan would (more or less) seek to resolve, according to Peter Thomas, by "exaggerating" and "intensifying" the "logic" of the current situation.[11]

Gramsci could not have provided a better description of the Meiji Restoration, in which the lower echelon of the ruling elite overthrew a centralized feudal authority (the Tokugawa shogunate) partially in response to the countrywide disorder sparked by the "sporadic rebelliousness of the popular masses," which was reflected in a number of discursive movements calling for new conceptions of social and political space, social relations, and leadership in the late Tokugawa era. Added to this inventory of the components of a contemporary crisis was the forced opening of the country to foreigners after several centuries of near seclusion. Imperial loyalist activists carried out their response to the current situation in the name of and out of respect for the emperor, which masked their own ambitions and effectively refracted the historicity of the present in such a way that it would account for and explain their precipitate revolutionary move.[12]

While a number of Japanese historians have regarded the growing occurrence of peasant disturbances in the late Tokugawa period as mere background noise related to the main events being enacted in Kyoto by imperial loyalists, others have recently applauded the Meiji Restoration for having cost fewer lives than the terror of revolutionary violence in the French Revolution, even though Japan's population was larger than the French at the times of the two events. This line of argument proposes that the Meiji Restoration and the French Revolution had the same revolutionary ground, as if they were variations of the same model. But this view resembles an inversion of the failed model thesis articulated by lecture faction historians following the template of *Nihon shihonshugi bunseki* (Essay on Japanese capitalism) by Yamada Moritarō (the faction's principal theorist). This book saw the Meiji Restoration as a failed imitation of the French model, having produced state absolutism (*zettaishugi*) instead of a desired bourgeois liberal democracy. But it was never the intention of the activists and large feudal domains that brought down the Tokugawa shogunate to replicate a foreign model like the French Revolution, of which they could only have had the sketchiest information. Yet in any comparison between Japan's restoration and France's revolution, it must be asked whether we are to believe that the former was more controlled and self-disciplined than the latter and thus more successful, or that the former proceeded with the same purpose and ambitious goal and thus was less successful? How do we account for the differences in the two events' time (they were separated by nearly a century) and historical circumstances? Unless we begin with such questions, achieving a comparative perspective on them must remain a fantasy, since in fact the Meiji Restoration was vastly different from the French Revolution in almost every way. It should be remembered that the revolution sought to eliminate all vestiges of the feudal past to create a new society from scratch and start history anew in the present. It did not appeal to a return to a mystifying mythic origin in an indeterminate past that never actually existed anywhere except in the nation's political unconscious. In the Meiji Restoration, the archaic was little more than a default position used to buy time to choose a more permanent form of a political settlement once the institution of the shogunate was out of the way. The actual ambition of those involved in the Meiji Restoration was far less as expansive and incomparably more ambiguous than the determination of French revolutionaries to erase all preceding history and start anew, reflected in the adoption of a new calendar to chart the revolution's progress and measure the rhythms of everyday time and declarations of individual freedoms and equality. More importantly, the Meiji rebels wanted to bring back an emperor, while the French revolutionaries executed their monarch. It was precisely these kinds of differences that prompted Gramsci to classify the French Revolution as an unprecedented and unique form that put it beyond comparison with later nineteenth-century revolutionary transformations. One of the ironies of the recent attempts of historians in Japan to put the Meiji Restoration on a par with the French Revolution was to strive to make it—the Restoration—even more exemplary as a model of transformation that presumably did not result in mass violence. But in doing so they unwittingly reproduced the figure of Gramsci's passive revolution. In retrospect, the real difference between the two political events was that the revolution was characterized by enlightenment and an intellectual and ideological vision of an unlimited future to the French, while enlightenment for the Japanese came only after the resolution of the restoration.

The importance of the form of the passive revolution thus refers to the conservation of elements from the past that will be useful to the creation of newer components produced by capitalist political economy and whose retention is seen as necessary in bringing on board the enemies of the politically dominant group. In arranging the meaning of restoration, the act of restoring and thus preserving selected institutions or sets of practices from the past will address both newer demands and more progressive and even revolutionary claims in a new environment driven by capitalism. The figure of the passive revolution suggests that the past remains deeply rooted in the new present and its continuity constitutes a brake (recalling Walter Benjamin's "emergency brake" that halts the excessively fast-moving train of modernizing changes) on the unconstrained claims of the newly dominant capitalism. But the principal function of passive revolution seems to have been to show that the appearance of the new forces of capital had not yet become sufficiently hegemonic and would have to coexist with older political and economic practices of prior political forms and modes of production.

While it is tempting to see (as many Marxian and bourgeois historians have done) in this function a sign of transition, to do so is to misperceive

the fundamental persistence of unevenness of capitalism—which it always socially and repetitively reproduces by capitalism as if it constituted an imperative law. Unevenness remains a common characteristic
in those societies that realized a transformation to capitalism. Moreover,
the transformation would always remain incomplete in cases like Japan,
where the conspicuous presence of the past's active traces in the present
became bourgeois. Gramsci regarded such processes as gradualist rather
than anything akin to the explosive convulsions classically dramatized
by the French Revolution. According to him, transition would have
meant the working out of a specific narrative strategy leading to a desired
social order in the future, whereas gradualism remained a work in progress, moving away from an unsatisfactory past.

In his historical scenario, Gramsci thus skirted the modularity of the
French Revolution—which he saw as a classic example among bourgeois
revolutions but never as an accessible model for imitation—to propose the
passive revolution as the general form for or "framework" of the kind of
transformation Italy experienced, in which bourgeois leadership was not
dominant nor was the bourgeoisie large. Gramsci's creation of the form
of passive revolution was also an effort to provide a political explanation
to supplement, if not replace, the economistic arguments advanced by the
Comintern in its understanding of the origins of fascism.

Just as the Risorgimento presumed the existence of a leadership and
sought to subsume the subaltern remainder, with capital personified by
northern workers assuming leadership over the mass of semifeudal peasants, Gramsci was convinced that these coalitions constituted political acts
that employed what was at hand to further the interests of a hegemonic
group or class by unifying the national political order. In both cases, the
leading class was able to formally subsume the subaltern groups by responding or giving formal expression to some of their aspirations. In this
respect, it has been proposed that Gramsci saw the French example as an
exception, an event that helped explain why later revolutions assumed
the form of ambiguity embodied in "revolution-restorations."[13] This approach conforms to the work of a line of interpreters who have not only
seen parallel historical trajectories leading to revolutionary transformation in Italy and Japan but have also sought to expand the utility of the category of passive revolution to account for a broad range of revolutionary
events. While many of these interpreters fail to recognize the category primarily as a form, rather than a thematic content of a specific case of, or
even a stage in, a political process, this trap has been avoided by arguing

that the domination of the bourgeois in many so-called bourgeois revolutions closely conforms to a political strategy that, more often than not, depended on recruiting and mobilizing what was near at hand. This explains the passivity of form marking the ambiguous mix of different classes and political ambitions that comprised revolutions. Gramsci had already entertained the possibility of extending the category of passive revolution to include the Meiji Restoration, which for him resembled events in both England and Germany. "Japan," he noted, "comes to the English and German types of development—that is, an industrial civilization that develops within a semi-feudal framework—but as far as I can tell, more like the English than the German type."[14] India and China were not yet comparable cases. Gramsci was interested in showing the commonalities in, rather than the differences between, such national experiences as passive revolutions, especially local differences between various places and times. Moreover, he was convinced that the concept of passive revolution would apply to "those countries that modernize the state through a series of national wars without undergoing a political revolution of a radical-Jacobin type."[15] This observation pointed to the further possibility of broadening the form's scope to include other transformations in the world beyond Europe, such as the Kemalist Revolution in Turkey, the Iranian Islamic Revolution, and the Republican Revolution in China. I would further suggest that if we accept Marx's definition of formal subsumption as the general form for all capitalist development, it is possible to propose the category of passive revolution as a political form equivalent to an economic production process that privileged suborning what was near at hand (received from prior past practices) to serve capital's pursuit of accumulation. According to Gramsci, older political practices and institutions could be similarly appropriated and used to address newer political demands and create structures serving capital and its emerging classes. Moreover, the procedure of subsumption worked to pair cultural and religious incommensurables to serve the new requirements of the political economy, as in the reconfiguring of the emperor and Shinto in Meiji Japan. Recruiting an older religiosity to enhance and serve the new capitalist political economy, as Max Weber did in his famous thesis, appears to have been necessitated by the demands of capital's general rule of subsumption, despite Weber's desire to suggest that the coupling was a contingent combination. This is not to say that Weber was wrong or misinterpreted Marx, but rather to recognize that Weber's explanation of contingency was compatible and consistent with Marx's understanding of subsumption inasmuch as the latter operation was always mediated by time and place and what in the specific past was available to serve capital. None of these examples necessarily reflected the economic structure as such, but rather indexed and deflected its presence. Passive revolutions, according to Gramsci, were capable of embodying similar combinations of political practices and institutions—composed of dominant classes linked to capital accumulation that in turn was aligned with temporal associations belonging to received social configurations—with newer, contemporary political forms. In fact, he saw no difference between the political program of passive revolution and its economic goals.[16] In this connection, it is important to repeat what I suggested above: that Gramsci was dedicated to seeing how passive revolution worked historically to conserve useful parts of the past in new political environments. Precisely because subsumption was a form instead of an empirical example or a specific stage, it contained the possibility of a future tradition.[17]

We know that revolutionary transformations dominated by a single class enlisted both past political practices and personnel from prior regimes now yoked to serving a new political order, environment, and purpose, resembling the coming together of Benjamin's "then and now" in a flash or "tiger's leap." In fact, the Meiji Restoration might have exceeded Gramsci's expectation of its suitability as an instance of passive revolution. From the beginning its primary purpose was to merge past and present—according to the Imperial Charter Oath of 1868, old customs and new knowledge—using an archaic presence constructed out of a mythic no-time (*in illo tempore*, the moment of a realized origin and state foundation) capable of adjusting its narrative structure to provide a map for new presents. It is important to recognize that this archaic past was even more remote and different from the premodern scene that the ethnographer Torii Ryūzō and the poet Satō Haruo reported as the vast "temporal remove" of Formosan aboriginal life.[18] Early Japanese ethnographers who began fieldwork on Formosa (present-day Taiwan) in the late nineteenth and early twentieth centuries were convinced that they had discovered a "new continent" inhabited by an archaic people whose primitivity represented the original human community.[19] In contrast, Japan's passive revolution was carried out under the authority of both a restored emperor who was reclaiming an archaic authority and the status of a deity and the state's pursuit of capitalist development at the expense of realizing social development or widening the base of political participation. The preceding Tokugawa regime represented a form of centralized feudalism, and it began to fall apart in the early nineteenth century as what might be called

a centrifugal or secessionary impulse led to the withdrawal of certain regional and religious groups from the central authority, combined with the
threats both of foreigners' colonization (reinforced by the existence of colonized societies in South Asia and China) and of peasants' unscheduled protests becoming increasingly violent. One of the paradoxes of this historical
scene is that even though the Tokugawa order denoted a form of feudalism,
it yielded no discernible transition comparable to the classic Marxian formula leading to capitalism, since imperial loyalists brought it down before
such a process could begin. This is not to say that no incipient manufacturing or industrialism appeared in the last decades of the Tokugawa regime.
While the years before the restoration witnessed what Japanese historians
have frequently called the "sprouts of capitalism" or "proto-capitalist social
relations," the transition typically associated with the appearance of new
socioeconomic forces never happened. This task was left to Meiji restorers,
who opted to follow the example of an advanced industrial capitalism offered by contemporary England.

In many ways the restorers were compelled to address the regional splin-
tering and withdrawals, which seemed to resemble a centrifugal process—
meaning that the momentum leading to it represented a threat to undermine
both economic and political stability. During the 1870s and early 1880s, the
new regime was still facing a good deal of popular disorder related to the
effort to reduce class struggle among the peasantry, whose members continued disturbances inaugurated in the Tokugawa system but in a wider
geographical area. They proceeded as if no political change had occurred,
angered by the implementation of a new system of taxation that required
payments in money rather than in kind. Peasant outbursts were joined by
revolts instigated by members of the military class (the samurai) who saw
in the new political order the dissolution of their class privileges together
with the prospect of economic impoverishment and social disappearance.
Where the Meiji transformation differed from the Italian experience was in
its capacity to loosely combine fragmented constituencies that had seceded
from the center into the political unity of a nation-state, even though much
of Japan's modern history contains echoes of sporadic regional resentment
and the desire for a more complete social revolution.

It is important to note that a Marxian accounting of this revolutionary
makeover did not appear until the late 1920s and early 1930s, with the great
Marxian historiographical debate over the historical development of Japanese capitalism and the creation of an orthodox narrative of transition.
Marxian historical practice and its consideration of the problems and

aporetic status of capitalism highlighted the importance of modernity in late-developing societies like Japan and China, where there were major debates in the 1930s about how the historical was to be grasped. India had its own experience with the Comintern and the efforts of Marxian historians to identify the economic consequences of British imperial policies for the stunting of native industries. The beginning of the Japanese debate (*ronsō*) was initiated at about the same time as Gramsci was formulating his views of the nature of passive revolution. Even though his random thoughts would have been immensely useful to the Japanese debaters, it is doubtful that his ideas would have been adopted had they been available, given the control exerted by the Comintern. In any case, his views were not available to the Japanese until after World War II, by which time the lines of controversy had solidified. The Japanese debate concentrated on understanding the structure of Japan's capitalism and how it had developed since the late Tokugawa period. Even though the debate stimulated the opening up of the study of Japan's modern history and its rapid progress, differences of interpretation proliferated among the many participating historians. The debate focused on the issue of determining the effects of the feudal remnants persisting in contemporary Japan (the past in the new present, so to speak), producing two principal groups, one (lecture faction, *Kozaha*) associated with the Japan Communist Party, following the changing theses handed down by the Comintern, the other (Labor-Farmer faction, *Rōnōha*) opposed to it: the labor-farmer historians, who considered the restoration to be a genuine revolutionary event engineered from above, emphasizing the importance of agricultural developments in new patterns of land ownership among rural classes. The Labor-Farmer faction thus perceived the feudal remains in the present as an inheritance from a past that eventually would disappear; and the lecture faction historians held that the restoration had failed and that the feudal remnants were an insurmountable barrier to realizing a full and completed capitalism, leading to refeudalization (a permanent state of semifeudalism) and political absolutism (*zettaishugi*).[20] The principal feudal remnant, which could not be named, was the emperor.[21]

The two groups could agree on the conjunctural forces confronting Japan and the capitalist world of the 1930s and the fact that the restoration had brought about immense unevenness and the possibilities both of new combinations capable of serving capitalism (sparked by the persistence of unwanted residues from the past, or what Marx described in *Grundrisse* as "stunted" and "travestied" forms) and of the completion of the revolution. The difference between the groups in their views of the restoration was prompted by disagreements in the Communist Party about what strategy was most likely to bring about a contemporary revolutionary transformation. What the lecture faction especially failed to recognize was the trajectory that led all revolutionary transformations, even the most classic examples, to incompletion—although not necessarily destined to experience Japan's fate. Yamada expected that fate to be remaining in the frozen social state of semifeudalism or semirevolution. He considered the very feudal remnants that the lecture faction identified as preventing the further development of Japanese capitalism to be the deformation of the development of capitalism in Japan, a caricature he called "Japanese style capitalism." He condemned Japan to a permanent state of semifeudalism, even though he rarely referred to its surviving remnants that were said to have held back the development of Japanese capitalism. Japan, he proposed, had departed from some unexplained pure form that the absolutist state had pursued with a "Japanese style rationality." The problem with this analysis were that it presumed the existence of a pure form of what he conjured as Japanese rationality, which he was convinced offered no hope, since he saw no difference between the Farmer-Labor faction's advocacy of agricultural developments and the persistence of feudal remnants in his present.

The divide between the two Japanese Marxian factions resembled a narcissism of small differences more than an irreparable split. A close look at the groups' respective claims suggests that their commonalities outweighed their differences. Both groups believed that the Meiji Restoration was a revolutionary transformation directed from the top and that Karl Kautsky's view that absolutism characterized the new Meiji state was premised on the prior belief that some form of modern manufacturing capital was a necessary condition of Japan's claim to have expressed the sprouts of capitalism before the Restoration and the accompanying claim that the country was already poised for full development. According to some historians, this assessment appeared to have occurred after the opening of Japan's ports to the West in 1853.[22] Gramsci would not have known of this division among Japanese historians—which, ironically, was contemporary with his imprisonment in Italy. But he would have recognized in the Meiji era the persistence of uneven residues from a feudal past as the raw material for development and thus requiring a strategy to accommodate them in the construction of a political and economic edifice capable of merging with newer forms of capitalist innovation. This would signify a kinship with other political transformations that he had already recorded and classified as examples of passive revolution. Such combinations of the older forms of labor practices and exploitation from prior modes of production and the new capitalist working day based on time would serve capitalism's pursuit of accumulation and surplus value. But this combination would also range widely to include bringing together older and new technological innovations to traditional habits of production in textiles and dishware. In Japan, the obvious example was the refiguration of a divine emperor now made contemporary with modern capitalism and positioned to force the population to work and die for monarch and nation, as implied in the Meiji slogan of enriching the nation, strengthening the military (*fukoku kyōhei*).

In fact, Gramsci was persuaded that all "bourgeois revolutions involve a 'passive' element"—which required leadership from the top, with only a little role assigned to the lower classes. The transition was thus led to completion by the upper echelons whose members controlled the "exercise of state power" and were positioned to accommodate capital rather than mass insurgency.[23] This was precisely the course taken by the Meiji reforms after the 1870s, which principally were led by samurai from southwestern domains like Satsuma and Chōshū. Gramsci further observed that passive revolution had come in the wake of the French Revolution and the search for a new form, involving a struggle to find "superior forms," as he put it, to contain capitalism since that historical content had been already established. But he suggested that unlike the French Revolution, new forms would not immediately resort to "dramatic upheavals" by eliminating all feudal fetters but instead would use unevenness in new combinations. The form Gramsci projected in *The Southern Question* that would bring urban industrial workers in the north of Italy together with semifeudal peasants in the south resembled the results of a formally subsumptive appropriation that served the goal of progressive political reorganization rather than merely that of improving economic practices. What passive revolution thus entailed was a gradualist program of reforms within a sufficiently elastic framework, which would make it possible to avoid the apparatus of terror associated with the French Revolution.[24]

Gramsci employed his understanding of Italian history as the lens through which to read other historical experiences that might conform to the category of passive revolution. In one observation, he proposed that success in organizing a state in Italy had stemmed from its "victory over the feudal and semi-feudal classes" and favorable international circumstances. Gramsci is quoted by Neil Davidson as suggesting that "the bourgeois State thus developed more slowly, and followed a process which had not been seen in many other countries."[25] But this political trajectory could certainly be observed in Japan, where the bourgeoisie as a class began to develop only in the 1890s, decades after the initial restoration, when a constitutional order was issued. But this bourgeois state, according to Friedrich Engels, was empowered to execute vast changes by "new classes or dominant fractions . . . with the old oligarchy." Because these changes, in societies like Meiji Japan, occurred in the absence of "popular mobilization," "they remain partial, unfinished, and incomplete."[26] (Although the Meiji state early announced its decision to "wash away old abuses" and customs, it was actually slow in doing so.) In this regard, both Farmer-Labor and lecture faction Marxist historians found common ground in their views on the semirevolutionary state that had appeared in the late nineteenth century. This state was not as catastrophically extreme as Yamada Moritarō had expected. Rather, as the Farmer-Labor economist Uno Kōzō observed, the Meiji regime preserved the medieval village structure until there was sufficient industrial development to begin absorbing workers from the countryside in the early twentieth century, instead of releasing them (as in England three hundred years earlier) with no place to go or way to support themselves. As Michael Lowy wrote, "these 'semi-revolutions' or 'passive revolutions' (as Gramsci termed them)—together with certain limited 'bourgeois' reforms . . . laid the basis for the European revolutions of the 20th century. Precisely because these reforms from above were incomplete—leaving considerable feudal detritus and or vestiges of the absolute state the bourgeois would or could not destroy—they created the explosive contradictions that would allow the proletariat to raise the banner of democracy in its own name."[27] In this way, passive revolution also allowed (as Gramsci observed and Hasegawa Nyozekan and Tosaka Jun predicted) the extreme conservative move of the bourgeoisie and the turn of the state it dominated toward aligning with other groups to bring about fascism as a barrier to the proletarian formation of a democracy. After World War II, Maruyama Masao turned in one of his last works to examining what he called the "archaic stratum" (kosō) that directed the course of Japan's long history, dominated the country's archetypal history, and made demands on the present—which has yet to liberate itself from the thrall of that substratum.

In the end, it seems that one of the real but unnoticed consequences of passive revolution in Italy, Japan, or elsewhere is that such a revolution defers indefinitely the difficult task of resolving the relationship of present pasts and contemporary demands to find ways to overcome the barrier to the future—which leaves a country stalled in what might be called the historical present, or the permanent coexistence of pasts with the present. Clearly, what emerged from Gramsci's formulation of the passive revolution was the privilege accorded to the untimeliness of contemporary noncontemporaneity (hinted at by Rosa Luxemburg and expanded on by José Carlos Mariátegui in Peru), in which different temporalities were fused into a heterogeneous combination of past and present to produce an uneven configuration comprised of Incas and contemporary Spaniards. This historical representation was, I believe, made explicit in Gramsci's *The Southern Question*, with its ambiguous silhouette first appearing in his discussion of the juxtaposition of Italy's northern industrialism and its southern feudalism and the necessity of their unification. Similarly, in Japan an archaic emperor directed the unification of a modernizing society.

Figuring the Archaic

Late Tokugawa society witnessed a countrywide explosion of feudal domainal reforms from the 1840s to the 1860s, attempts to offset a Tokugawa-first policy that sought to weaken the domains or to spread new discourses calling for ways to overcome the constraints imposed by the traditional division between mental and manual labor. In the mid-1860s there appeared worrisome incidents of what some historians have described as mass hysteria in cities like Kyoto, where people claimed that heaven was sending sacred cards (*fuda*) with mystical messages indicating that the times were out of joint—messages that led to mass dancing in the streets and chanting of the question "why not?" (*ee ja nai ka*). What best describes this moment is Marx's observation of a process that he named "so-called primitive accumulation" but condensed into a historical trope that allows us to interpret the political and economic upheavals that jump-started capitalist development.[28] Using this condensed historical trope allows us to bypass the detailed description Marx gave of primitive accumulation, its long duration, enclosures, intense forms of expropriation and dispossession, widespread economic impoverishment, and proliferating global colonization (which had begun to manifest itself by the seventeenth century). It also enables us to see the trope's temporal superstructure as a sprawling archaeological space of dialectical interactions and plural levels of uneven time, incapsulating the "initial stockpiling" of the mass of raw material that constituted primitive accumulation in its production of plural temporalities. It, primitive accumulation, was a landscape torn by the complex appearance and collision of unequal political, economic, social, and religious forces in a world thrown into temporal flux, with people compelled to live in multiple and different registers of time existing in the same present. This perspective allows us to grasp what the linear model of successive stages has concealed or overlooked in the interest of anchoring time securely in an irreversible temporal linear trajectory that makes the outcome appear as a culmination of now-passed forces that belonged to a past but have been completed.

Hence, the late Tokugawa years marked an indefinitely permanent transformation of society—a permanent chasm between past and future—and the way people hereafter would look upon the world. If the period lacked the intensity of economic accumulation that Europe had experienced three centuries earlier, it nonetheless included energetic signs of capitalist practices that had taken hold in certain regions of Japan, often spurred by the domainal reforms of the 1840s; sporadic forms of manufacturing; the growing spread of a money economy; and new ideas about reorganizing the social and political environment on the basis of the acquisition of new perspectives, knowledge (often inspired by foreign sources), and conceptions of the body directed to close the division between mental and manual labor.[29] There was a sense of contemporaneity capable of encompassing and unifying the unfolding process of uneven and combined developments, while the insertion of mixed plural temporalities associated with various forms of communitarian withdrawal, growing peasant disturbances (hyakushō ikki), urban trashings (uchikowashi), and millenarian demands (yo naoshi) contributed to the uncertainties already raised by a failing central authority. In fact, the imperial loyalists credited with bringing about the restoration were confronted by the pressure of these demands and their accompanying claims for the implementation of an order based on a new understanding of everyday life. In some cases, these claims appeared to be less concerned with the exercise of power (which constituted the real challenge the imperial loyalists had to meet) than with the immediate necessity of restoring imperial respect and resolving the threat of foreigners by repelling them. Historians like Tōyama were mindful of the problem these new and unprecedented popular claims posed but finessed the danger, whereas other historians treated the popular challenge as a sideshow to the loyalists' restoration. Here is Tōyama's explanation:

> Because the rebellious dances of the "ee ja nai ka" caused a commotion in the public spirit (jinshin), according to anti-Tokugawa activists, it was only a rumor that [the movement] was intentionally generated. Historical material

we have not seen until recently accurately proves this. Whatever its origins the anti-Tokugawa activists used the *"ee ja nai ka"* disorder propagated in the environs of Kyoto, at the same time they were fostering it and agitating for social order; it is possible to guess that they [anti-Tokugawa loyalists] consciously concealed their planning from the shogunate's searches and in the view of the people were probably stimulated by unconscious class instincts. In preceding years why was the people's revolutionary energy that had matured to the stage of peasant-like warfare that easily could have become a rebellion end by being put to depraved use? The imminent collapse of shogunal authority is clearly reflected in popular opinion, seen in (observing) the weaving of [the ins and outs] comings and goings of loyalist activists in the streets and hearing the exaggeration of things the shogun was doing. . . . At that time the people rejoiced in the [prospect] of decline of the old oppressive system and threw themselves into hoping for a new polity that would come. Nevertheless, those who were lacking did not themselves have the capacity to construct a political movement and had not yet acquired the personal will power to pursue skills represented by the actions of *shishi* activists. . . . The weakness of revolution from below could not overtake the tempo of reform from above and the passion of the people was forestalled from going beyond the hardship of the rebellions, *uchikowashi*, *ikki*; responding to this (weakness), the people broke out in a loud voice without reason, dancing on hands and feet and shaking off the controls of officials, their feet trampling the homes of the rich against whom they had turned and, in the words of *ee ja nai ka*, (they) threw down an entire reality, drunk in the freedom of a worldly dream of the *"yo naoshi odori."* . . . These folks did not possess the consciousness and means to configure the conflict of the *ikki*, *uchikowashi* into (wider) political combat; in other words, the peasant disturbances, clearly seized by petit bourgeois leadership . . . could not bear the burden of concentrating on a political crisis that exposed their weakness in (carrying out) a singular action.[30]

The interesting disclosure in this passage is Tōyama's ambiguous willingness to attribute limited political agency to mass political action—an attribution that was a Marxian conceit of an earlier time, dating from the prewar discussions of the development of Japanese capitalism that carried over into the early years of the postwar era. Yet he was also convinced that they could go no further than their initial outbursts, which ultimately took the course of large-scale spontaneous demonstrations of singing and dancing in anticipation of the coming of some sort of millenarian transformation to a new time, recalling the distant rumor of the "chialistic dream visions" Engels attributed to German "plebians" in *The Peasant War in Germany*.[31] Japanese masses in the late Tokugawa period, like German Christian chiliasts, were dreaming of a miracle that would deliver them from unending oppression and bring them joy and happiness.

Tōyama and other historians of the lecture faction overlooked Engels's observation that such acts were temporally oriented, sought to exceed the present and reach out to the future, and were driven by violent desires that could not help but be dangerous. Instead, Japanese historians believed that the masses had exhausted their limited capacity of collective movements and had no will for further action. Engels and Karl Mannheim saw in the peasant wars of sixteenth-century Germany the beginnings of mass politics. Although it is difficult to see why Japan's most talented Marxian historians so easily wrote off the staying power of mass collective movements by gesturing toward their revolutionary energy yet simultaneously discounting their capacity to do more than stage "singular" outbursts and dance and sing in the streets of Kyoto. If prewar Marxists bypassed revolutionary peasant and millenarian mass movements, it was because of their faithfulness to the Comintern line and, at the time, a Marxian conceit that saw peasant masses yoked to private interest in land. But given the wartime disappearance of the Comintern, what this fidelity to repeating the older interpretation suggests is an adherence to a historiographic plotline shared by their bourgeois contemporaries, who were no more committed to peasant agency to generate change. It also entailed the unquestioned conviction that Japan's social transformation of 1868 could have come only from the loyalist political activists recruited from the feudal ruling classes. More important, what Marxist and bourgeois historians overlooked was the extent to which these large-scale gatherings were able to conceptualize and reveal a vision of a new kind of communitarianism (a new form of life and time rather than a different will to power) that appeared in some of the new religions and nativism and in later mass social outbursts. Putting into question a lived reality, Marxists were now rejecting the common chants and dances of the masses as expressions of hysteria that nonetheless prefigured the politics of a new communal will. Despite the failure of the collective revolutionary energy demonstrated by the masses in the late Tokugawa period, those masses provided the initial groundwork for subsequent mass movements in Japan's modern history. But Tōyama and others opted to juxtapose the possibility of revolutionary weakness from below to the tempo of reform at the top, inadvertently or intentionally contributing to a historical practice dedicated to conveying success stories of winners and ignoring Benjamin's forgotten nameless losers, whose memory we are obliged to exhume, honor, and resituate in the present from history's graveyard of silence.[32]

In an earlier passage, Tōyama had concluded that in three hundred years of history driven by Tokugawa feudalists, the people never abandoned their desire to be released from the constraints of despotic feudal rule, though they never attained a decent life. He argued that while the shogunate would inevitably have collapsed at some point, it was the advancing of a strategy for restoration by several lords and anti-Tokugawa samurai that apparently set the agenda for the Meiji Restoration.[33] The importance of the logic of this long and often contradictory account, which both valorized the people's power and doubted it, was that it was the prelude to writing off their political agency. Tōyama explained that the people had failed to carry out a revolution, an interpretation that apparently originated from his preference for a narrative demonstrating that loyalist activists, assisted by a few powerful lords, had accomplished the restoration. Implied in his acceptance of a long-standing thesis attributing the accomplishment of the restoration to imperial respect is the implied argument that the desire to return authority to the emperor was a condition of dealing with the foreign threat. If the view that internal disorder leads to external catastrophe (*naiyū gaikan*) was the commonly accepted way to interpret the situation in the late Tokugawa period, the obvious solution was to restore domestic order by returning the emperor to his rightful position, which would remove the foreign threat. But this was an immense simplification of the situation, and it was repudiated by the course of later events, which demonstrated that restoring imperial authority was the best way to rid Japan of the Tokugawa regime, which in turn opened the door for the seizure of power by the restoration plotters. This interpretation still necessitated downplaying the role of the people by undervaluing both their political function and their oppressed social condition to show that they could not have brought about the restoration. Of course, what determined the Marxists' adoption of this strategy was the conviction that modern Japan's failed revolution had led to absolutism and fascism. It is interesting to note that Tōyama focused on the movements (usually described as symptoms of mass hysteria) that inundated the last years of the Tokugawa regime, as if the popular masses already knew the restoration was just around the corner. The *ee ja nai ka* demonstrations—along with the emergence of groups whose members threw themselves into the frenzy of so-called world renewal dances—are finally discounted, according to historiographical opinion, because they were not able to translate their mass energy into a disciplined political organization dedicated to struggle. The urban trashings and peasant disturbances are similarly written off, since they appeared to have been captured by petit bourgeois leaders and, like a summer storm, were capable of only a short downpour (that is, of a single action).

Yet behind these symptomatic expressions of popular discontent were more permanent forms of social organizations that already had established themselves as secessionary, purposely pulling their particular constituencies away from the central authority and into the periphery because of the Tokugawa shogunate's failure to deliver on its principal moral obligations to provide relief to the people and maintain order.

What historians like Tōyama failed to consider was the play of new cultural forms that—expressed in the growth of contingent discourses on culture which began in the late eighteenth century—started to imagine new conceptions of perspective, the body, and political configurations commensurate with these cultural changes.[34] In the world of restoration historiography, there has been a strangely unanimous agreement that the principal ideological agent propelling the anti-Tokugawa movement was the loyalist activists, as they used the Mito discourse of the 1820s to envision a morally rehierarchicized sociopolitical order that situated the emperor at the head of the social pyramid, with the goal of reminding the shogunate of its proper place in a system presided over by the emperor. The theory, as originally envisaged by Mito thinkers, pointed not only to the program of transmuting the emperor from a principle of authority into the primary source of all authority but also to the goal of reinforcing the semi-autonomy of the several domains at the expense of diminishing Tokugawa claims to being first among equal lords. But this discursive formation was part of a much larger political and cultural transformation in the troubled years from the 1830s on that spawned a number of new religious and social formations. These formations constituted a virtual secessionary movement that unofficially withdrew from the central authority to a metaphoric periphery to put into practice newer conceptions of social and communal organizations. In other words, the spatial terrain was not (as supposed by the dominant historiography) the sole product of loyalist activists but was crisscrossed by discrepant discourses representing different social audiences that were willing, in some instances, to withdraw to set up new forms of communities based on differences with other forms. These discourses, which included those of nativism and the new religions, authorized the establishment of semi-autonomous communities whose different ways of life were rooted in place and fused new modes of existence with specific spatial environments—whereby both place and its environment became an integral part of people's lives. The greatest threat the discourses posed to a flagging political order like the shogunate was their promise to transfer the nature of daily existence to the form of everyday life, in which certain groups, like new religions, especially, would withdraw to take charge of their own communities, a beginning of a process of seceding from the center to the periphery that would constitute the replacement of the political by the social. In the case of nativist groups and new religions, the activity took the form of assistance and relief in daily existence as part of the management of everyday matters. All these discourses were anchored in a pervasive decentralized regionalism that was frequently rooted in affective communities, which prefigured the coming breakdown of centralized political control. In some instances (like the new religions), a new subjectivization appeared that included women and made unprecedented calls for equality, and nativism placed a new value on land and the work of its peasant cultivators. The echoes of this moment (similar to those of the peasant disturbances in the late Tokugawa that continued into the early Meiji period), were still audible in modern Japan.[35] We must, therefore, view the appearance of these various discourses and the populist-like movements they initiated in terms of the trope of primitive accumulation and as part of the dialectical temporal interactions and the world of flux they instigated and sought to manage.

Each of these discourses propounded a conception of restoration: Mito thinkers had early called for a restoration (*chūkō*), employing the sinified version of the word, which involved a moral revision of the hierarchical system whereby duties corresponding to names (*meibunron*, discourse on the discrimination of names) were modified by loyalists into the ideology of an anti-Tokugawa movement. In the late Tokugawa there appeared a number of calls to restoration that were directed against the shogunal system and differed from the loyalist version that referred to restoring the archaic polity of origins exemplified by the first emperor, the mythic Jinmu. Meanwhile nativists, especially the rural inflection articulated by Hirata Atsutane and his followers, called for a return to an adherence to the foundation or beginnings (*moto ni tsuku*)—that is, the divine origins of the land. Yet, it should be pointed out that Hirata's version of return applied to the creation itself by the deities of heaven and earth, which preceded the installation of the first emperor. Simultaneously, the appearance of several new syncretic religions, which argued for world renewal (*yonaoshi*) to remove the corrosions of contemporary history, as Tōyama noted, ulti-mately inspired mass rebellious groups and others to spontaneously per-form frenzied dances. And even proponents of wealth and power in some of the large domains connected to the shogunate (*fudai*) envisioned a fed-eration or conciliar arrangement that evoked China's archaic past (espe-cially the Three Dynasties) or leaders from Europe's early modernizing monarchs (despots like Peter the Great) rather than the shadowy Japanese priest-king master of ritual and ceremony who had not ruled for centuries. Armed with such notions of some sort of political restoration that sanc-tioned action in various spheres and political renewal often in different spatial environs that pointed to different times, each of these discourses tried in its own way to pull away from what had long symbolized the cen-ter and move toward an imagined periphery and margin. This surely ex-plains even the decision of activists to abandon Edo (later renamed Tokyo) for Kyoto as the locus of planning and the execution of terror: they ulti-mately turned to the domains for protection and access to useful military resources in the forthcoming struggle with the shogunate. Yet the move was transforming. Everyday life—which Marx had described at the time of the Paris Commune of 1871 as occupying the space of an everyday "work-ing existence"[36] on the margins of official culture and politics—moved to a terrain with many centers, not just one. These discursive formations en-visioned a plurality of centers or peripheries that seceded from the fixed center of Tokugawa power. But the move to a peripheral imaginary, signi-fying the formation of a new social configuration, also created the prospect of the publicity of political life and new ways of enfranchising the groups and classes that for too long had been kept out of the arena of political participation. The emergence of conciliar arrangements conceived by late Tokugawa domainal intellectuals like Yokoi Shōnan and Hashimoto Sanai exemplified this new political impulse, severely narrowed to include only feudal lords and exclude a number of other groups. Yokoi even proposed an arrangement based on the U.S. federal system. The expression of mass movements in the last years of the Tokugawa period may also be seen as a prefiguration of a broader political participation, as demonstrated by the subsequent appearance of new constitutions in the early Meiji period that clearly show the effort of rural commoners (petit bourgeois landowners) to widen enfranchisement to include people like themselves and to include their interests in new political forms (like the nation form).[37]

More than most discourses, the Mito/loyalist intervention used the pub-lic realm as a forum for discussing and even acting on issues that affected society as a whole, rather than merely the domain. What with discussions of the importance of the public realm as part of the "living existence" of everyday life and calls for immediate action to prevent countrywide disaster, it was often difficult to distinguish between the self-promoting declarations of Yoshida Shoin that few people besides himself cared for the fate of the realm and the seemingly more measured anxieties of Sakuma Shōzan that the welfare or public safety of the realm was in jeopardy. Mito-inspired loyalists envisioned the creation of a public space for "discussion" (*kōron*; also called public opinion or consultation) that was indistinguishable from other forms of expression—such as work, prayer, writing, and action. The existence of this new space would signal the presumably permanent dissolution of both an administrative politics in which the rigid division between ruler and ruled (and by extension between mental and manual labor) prevailed as well as the creation of a new political environment characterized by uncertain practices, in which even the identity of the contending forces was constantly shifting and requiring redefinition. The discursive field conspicuously included political practices that presupposed incompletion and an open character. Challenging the claims of closure with openness and even equality among the new religions, and pitting determinacy against indeterminacy, the new discourses and their adherents had to find a mode of mediation between the recognized need to stabilize society and promote production and local demands to preserve various social identities that had surfaced in the new space of restoration. New social and occupational identities had already begun to appear in populous cities like Edo in the late Tokugawa period, as reported by the pseudonymous Buyō Inshi in his *Seji kemmonroku* (1816). Urban life, he complained, was overflowing with new occupations to serve the demands of popular culture, and this attested to the diversity of identities and occupations that had not existed in an earlier time and were now challenging the coherence of the social order. These new identities were responsible for the polyphonic voices of the new discourses that began to address the importance of society's business as if it was their own—which led to the later Meiji effort to limit the vocal diversity and reconstitute the whole to accord with a single authoritative voice of the state.

Only the presence of a vast arena of semi-autonomous, heterogeneous, and unevenly developed discourses and the dangers they posed for imminent conflict made it possible to organize a hegemonic practice that could address the demands for order, political centralization, productivity, and difference. It is possible to imagine this terrain, occupied by different groups projecting a conception of restoration that reflected their everyday experience of a "living existence," almost as if they were competing to see which part would next stand in for the not yet envisioned whole. In this contest, loyalist activists possessed clear material advantages that enhanced their chances of leadership. Yet nothing in the loyalist discourse explicitly suggests the inevitability of the later establishment of the Meiji state and the elimination of competing social identities (regionally and religiously based) under the regime of a centralizing political apparatus. For many people, including loyalist activists, the restoration offered the vague promise that they could retain a space for their own restoration in the realization of some sort of hegemonic formation committed to stabilizing society and preserving the interests of production derived from daily life. While loyalist activists had led a number of failed restorationist coups in the early 1860s (which were seen in retrospect as rehearsals that focused on the unifying symbol of the emperor and the expulsion of foreigners with the goal of destroying domainal sectionalism), they had to acknowledge that the most powerful force in society was the traditional authority and military capability of the feudal domain. The expulsionist strategy of the loyalist activists concentrated on the foreign threat (specifically, the presence of foreigners in Japan) after the ending of the seclusion policy. It was driven by the belief that the country should never have been opened to foreigners and that the shogunal administrators responsible for that opening had acted out of weakness. Following this strategy, activists called for the return of the emperor to his rightful position of authority and the formulation of a policy aimed at expelling foreigners. After a series of setbacks, the activists retraced their steps and turned to a new strategy aimed at resolving the problem of domestic political crisis, which meant eventually abolishing the shogunate and unifying a country that was in the process of being torn apart and facing what many believed to be an imminent foreign intervention. It was at this juncture that the question of the shogun's status and the governance of the country had to be settled and the growing incidence of domestic disunity overcome—especially the threat of groups' withdrawal from the shogunal center and the continuing peasant disturbances. Samurai like Takasugi Shinsaku of Chōshū, Ōkubo Toshimichi of Satsuma, and Yokoi of Echizen were willing to promote a renewed version of sectionalism as an alternative to what they considered was a mistaken policy advocating expulsion that illustrated administrative mismanagement. They were referring to the ways in which the expulsion of foreigners led to the dangers of increased foreign naval attacks against the large domains in the southwest. After the failure of expulsionism, thinkers in some of the larger domains (*han*) began to support a policy of strengthening local territories. Sectionalism of this sort was first hinted at by Yokoi but developed by Takasugi and Ōkubo because it balanced the unitary structure symbolized by the emperor with the tenacious domainal interests. Nothing became more real than the domain for these activists in this new political environment. Thus, the strength of the realm as a whole depended on the collective power of the domains (especially the large ones), which Takasugi called a greater sectionalism (*dai kakkyo*). The new sectionalism was premised on the belief that the foreign problem could be solved by domainal military preparedness through adoption of Western military technology and organization, while the internal situation required the reinforcing of local authority so that domains could more effectively formulate countrywide policy. The conception of greater sectionalism reformulated to meet the demands of political order was linked to Ōkubo's desire for "public discussions within the realm" and his call for broader representation of other groups in society (namely, lords and samurai in the upper ranks) in councils of power. By the same token, the new discourses representing other kinds of social units like the villages that were the seat of the new religions and the home of rural nativists could easily support a restoration symbolized by an emperor, though he had not ruled directly for more than a thousand years. The contemporary representative of the imperial figure was a fifteen-year-old boy guided by an imperial court whose members promised nothing more binding than a return to archaic institutions of the seventh century. In this light, the proponents of differing opinions could agree with loyalist activists as long as the emperor provided order and the semblance of unity that allowed the "working existence" of the Restoration unhindered continuity. The initial restoration seemed to promise this kind of arrangement, with its announcement of a return to the foundation of Emperor Jinmu, a figure of mythic origin and the fictional founder of Japanese political unity (even though it is difficult to determine whether at the time that unity was seen as mythic and fictional or as historically real). What is important about the timing of the decree that restored imperial rule in 1868 is that it was sufficiently vague in its affirmation of the momentary status quo and its alliances. Yet it was precisely its appeal to a remote and indeterminate archaic moment that would later set the conditions for a widespread renovation (*ishin*), which in turn promised to lead to the establishment of a centralized nation-state with its own version of a "working existence" for all and a capitalist political economy for which everyone would work and die. This should not be taken to mean that the plural discourses were merely background noise to the restoration. Rather, they should be viewed as a challenge to the aspirations of those who brought off the coup d'état and captured the imperial institution. They would undoubtedly be classified in the same register as mass demonstrations (such as *ee ja nai ka, why not?* and *yonaoshi odori* [dances of world renewal]), peasant disturbances, and urban trashings: as components not of some sort of hegemonic arrangement of the political but as forces capable of contesting the work of the restoration plotters.

In this mix of plural temporalities, many people identified with new social imaginaries that were devised by withdrawing to the periphery and that offered a glimpse of the vast complexity of Japan in the late Tokugawa period. The restoration sought to resolve both the unceasing domestic disorder that held the country in its grip and the threat of foreign colonization, which a weakened political system would not be able to prevent unless the shogunate was brought down with military force. Yet the very privileging of the idea of restoration made the outcome appear to be a historical inevitability in which groups had played no discernible part and whose claims received no recognition. The restoration thus seemed to validate the thesis articulated by Tōyama that the loyalists were motivated solely by respect for the emperor and the desire to restore the imperial institution to its rightful place. But the narrowness of this interpretative account permits us to question a historiographical tradition, brilliantly followed by Tōyama and others before him, that made the restoration appear to be the inevitable result of a singularly temporal linear trajectory running from the Tenpō reforms of the 1840s and ending in 1877 with the defeat of the samurai leader Saigō Takamori's abortive rebellion against the emerging Meiji state he had helped to establish.[38] Tōyama saw the restoration as a formation of absolutism in the span of thirty-one years. Perhaps this shift to absolutism might be rewritten as the process of a totality or whole world falling into pieces that would be reconstituted with the aid of a new world. It began with domain reforms in 1841, which basically were an instance of "feudal reaction incited to restore a depleted and oscillating shogunal power."[39] The principal and undoubtedly unintended consequence was to bring forth new political representations of feudal leadership, which could not help conforming to the new movement of society. It was also nourished by the formation of a new feudal ethic formulated by intellectuals of Mito domain who sought to reinforce the basic relationship of the exercise of duties according to one's status in the rigidly hierarchical arrangement of authority (*meibunron*).

This became the foundation of the *sonnō-jōi* movement of loyalist samurai, which subsequent historiography has privileged as the principal agent that brought about the restoration. It should be noted that the Mito ethic also worked both to correct the relationship between the domains and the shogunate, implying that the latter had willfully pursued a shogun-first policy at the expense of the domains, and to provide a necessary reminder that the shogun was formally only the deputy of the emperor.

The Mito discourse was only one among several circulating in the late Tokugawa period that were generated by the masses. But it should be noted that Mito was a domain collaterally related to the Tokugawa house and that its discourse was explicitly devoted to addressing the lack of discipline and the disorder of the masses. It is also important to recognize that the masses were easily involved in the public convulsions of the *ee ja nai ka* demonstrations and that the state of affairs was strongly affected by the tradition of the *okage mairi*, traditional mass mobilizations of pilgrims who streamed toward the Grand Shrine of Ise every sixty years. These pilgrimages were countrywide movements composed of the aged and the young, men and women. More often than not lacking subjective or class consciousness and critical spirit, people were not prompted to participate because of authority, distress, or superstition but by following their desire do so, forming crowds prone to be dominated by suggestion, rumor, imitation, and rapture. Although the pilgrims did not possess a class consciousness capable of producing an emotional impulse of rebellion against the feudal order, the movement of large numbers of displaced people constituted one-time separations from the social system. Accordingly, the pilgrimage of 1830 reflected the agitation of class war and peasant disturbances.[40] A tradition of connections between mass disturbances like the pilgrimages and peasant uprisings was deeply ingrained in the social psychology of the masses. The political crisis of 1867 was situated in an unusual social framework that brought this tradition to the surface, radiating surges of revolutionary energy borrowed from this tradition that momentarily recalled the experience of religious rage and ecstasy.

It seems that blurred perceptions of the current situation and the narrowing of self-interest squandered this potentially revolutionary spirit. This was possible because loyalist activism was animated by what Tōyama and others accepted as selfless loyalty to the emperor, unmediated by historical considerations. It must be asked what kind of explanation accounts for the pure loyalty among a generation of samurai who, when declaring their undying devotion to the emperor, meant sacrificing their lives to carry out an imperial imperative or protect the monarch. Is it even possible to say that they were thinking about the contemporary occupant of the throne, Emperor Kōmei? Or is it more reasonable to assume that by that time the imperial figure had been held captive in the imperial palaces, unseen by the masses, for so long that he had been abstracted into a principle of political authority that capped an imagined hierarchical arrangement, as envisaged by Mito theorists in the late eighteenth and early nineteenth centuries? Kōmei may have provided the occasion for a restoration (though he died before it), inasmuch as his successor was a youth in his early teens who had even less experience in the business of imperial governance than his father. But it is still difficult to reconcile the avowed pure loyalism expressed by activists ultimately willing to die for the removed and abstracted figure of an emperor who entered the public scene in the 1850s for the first time in his life and who, like all his predecessors in the Tokugawa period, had been virtually held prisoner in the imperial palace in Kyoto. Yet, it was precisely the loyalism to the throne, which Mito discourse had popularized in emphasizing that the shogun was only the deputy of the emperor, subtly implying usurpation of authority. It was only with the opening of the country by Americans in 1853, regarded by Japanese as a forced entry, and the subsequent signing of unequal treaties with Western countries that Kōmei was dragged into the center of countrywide discussions about the weakness of this shogunal decision and the growing reverberations of the demand to revere the emperor (sonnō) and expel the foreigner (jōi). It should be pointed out that the second character in the term sonnō is sounded as oo, like the Japanese reading of the Chinese wang (king; kimi in Japanese). Nonetheless the ideograph means king or ruler, not emperor (tennō, in which the first character, ten, denotes heaven in Chinese and Japanese, and the second, ō, refers to the Japanese sumera [a prefix referring to a deity] or sumeragi [an archaic term used to designate local chieftains, later identified with the term for emperor]). What is important here is that the term basically conveyed the meaning of the imperial principle, not the principal or figure of authority or sovereignty. The Chinese association of king or monarch, which, after all, referred to the entire realm of heaven and earth (tenka) was used by Mito theorists when they discussed the issue of hierarchical authority, and it is difficult to imagine that activists at a later time did not have this sense of authority in mind—that is, that they did not revere the authority of the chief or king, without specification. Eventually the principle of rulership merged with the principal ruler (the emperor), but it never merged with a specific personality. What this suggests is that until the late Tokugawa period political thinking was preoccupied with only the principle of rulership and legitimation. By the end of the period political thinking turned toward considering the specific principal, that is, the occupant of the throne, the personality who, in time, became the larger-than-life figure of the Emperor Meiji. That transformation was the work of courtiers like Iwakura Tomomi in the last years of the Tokugawa period.

Although Tōyama clung to a traditional plotline (that loyalist activists dominated restorationist discourse), he also seemed to lament the loss of this energetic mass revolutionary spirit, which apparently lacked the necessary consciousness and resources to focus and build on the experiences of urban trashings and peasant rebellions by taking the next step.[41] Yet we know that peasant outbursts continued throughout the first decade of the Meiji era—ultimately morphing into politically oriented movements that protested the new government's oligarchic control—as did new religious constituencies that still pursued a separate utopian space. It is evident that mass movements had the necessary consciousness, which could be drawn from the deep recesses of popular memory of examples of prior countrywide religious mobilizations. The specific instances of urban trashings and peasant disturbances were too limited by time and place to serve as models for wider mobilization. Urban trashings were usually spontaneous events and constricted by local circumstances. So were peasant disturbances, which appeared and disappeared like momentary interruptions. These spatiotemporal constraints could have been the reason that kept troubled peasants from perceiving their distress and dissatisfactions as signs of a countrywide crisis, since they had no leadership capable of making such assessments and planning for a broader and sustained action. It was probably this limited vision that prevented peasants from linking their concerns to a wider program that could have produced a coherent position on the countrywide crisis and turned their outbursts into something more than unique local events.

In addition to these limitations, the masses were excluded from involvement by the feudal classes, which looked upon them as a problem rather than an aid to a solution. In fact, the consciousness of feudal leaders (lords and their samurai retainers in the upper ranks) was reduced by the setbacks to the domestic revolutionary force and its political energy during the last years of the Tokugawa period. The feudal classes misinterpreted the nature of the danger confronting the realm in 1867 by turning toward the problem of the foreign threat, which resulted in limiting the content of their reform consciousness to the Mito conception of a hierarchical imaginary based on "a division of duties and designations" (*meibunron*) that increasingly focused on a restoration. The result was an extreme reduction in the Meiji Restoration's identity as a social reform: it became a political change completely cut off from the movement of the people and principally directed at replacing the moral leadership of the shogunate.[42] It is here that we can see that the restoration was chiefly concerned with redefining power and bypassing the people, not transforming their quality of life. But it should not be forgotten that loyalist activists were already singularly preoccupied with the treasonable decision to open the country to foreigners that had presumably caused the foreign problem. For the feudal classes, the problem was the shogunate and its unethical arrogation of authority that they believed belonged to the emperor. Of course, it was possible for loyalists to see in the opening of Japan an opportunity to elevate the emperor by holding the shogunate responsible for acting recklessly in its negotiations with the Western powers. Its failed leadership was reflected not only in the decision to open the country after centuries of isolation but also in the growing incidence of peasant rebellions and disturbances that feudal authorities always considered as a sign (like pestilence, earthquakes, volcanic eruptions, and so on) of heaven's displeasure with the moral failure of the current leadership and the possibility of eventual withdrawal of the mandate to rule. Many lords of domains saw that the present situation appeared to provide a new opportunity to overturn a long-standing Tokugawa policy of expanding the power of the shogunate at the expense of the domains. This observation of a shogun-first policy had been at the heart of the Mito discourse earlier in the century, which now acquired renewed significance in the crisis-charged environment of the 1850s. In this regard, the feudal classes favored a strategy of reform rather than revolution. Instead of simply replacing the shogunate's administration with an imperial one, they hastily contrived a program change, advocating a return to ancient imperial authority within the limited framework of the Mito conception of the "division of designation and duties," classically expressed as early as the late eighteenth century by Fujita Yūkoku (one of Mito domain's principal theorists): "In the country, there are lords and retainers, and there are upper and lower orders. If the designation between the aristocratic and non-aristocratic classes blurs, the distinction between upper and lower orders will vanish. The strong will despise the weak, and the masses will be thrown into confusion and disorder."[43]

Accordingly, the Meiji Restoration could not help but be reduced as a transformational event, losing whatever revolutionary depth it might have attained under different historical circumstances. It certainly was not the advent of the bourgeois revolution imagined by Farmer-Labor historians or even of the lecture faction's legendary counterrevolution. Rather, it was at most a passive revolution or "restoration/revolution." Marxist historians have recognized that the restoration achieved a political transfer, led by large domains. These domains were able to exclude from discussions on reform the appearance of widespread mass disturbances and guarantee their subsequent role in any future structure of political power, as well as to make a social revolution impossible. Ultimately, the discussions that decided the abolition of the shogunate were reduced to a complex amalgam of mere self-promoting strategies.

The discounted power of the masses appeared in more permanent but unrecognized forms than merely unscheduled peasant uprisings, urban trashings, and large-scale demonstrations bordering on mass hysteria that historians never tire of recalling and banalizing. There seemed to be a deeper, unexpressed psychology, as Tōyama describes it, that was capable of supporting the discourses that ultimately were concretized into movements that offered a mode of producing communalism (articulated in alternative conceptions of community, social order, and social relationships), which required abandoning rebellion for their decision to withdraw and separate from the center to organize themselves differently—not in confronting the feudal powers. Despite attributing immense power to the masses, historians like Tōyama were persuaded to disregard the masses' political utility, apart from linking it to the atmosphere that produced political events led by samurai activists. In other words, the masses contributed only background noise. Collectively, the several discourses, Mito, nativism, new religious, and even sects and even some domains aligned with the Tokugawa represented a vast social imaginary and political space on a newly defined periphery that promised security, order, tranquility, and relief from the hardships inflicted by contemporary history—all moral obligations the Tokugawa were pledged to fulfill. In 1868, the failing moral realm of Tokugawa feudalism was replaced by an archaic nonplace that would periodically reveal its affinity for fascism and a willingness to serve as its ideological placeholder.

Restoration as Farce

The proclamation announcing the decision to "return to the imperial polity of antiquity" was released at the last possible moment.[44] This suggests that even though domainal activists planned to carry out a coup d'état to wrest imperial authority from the Tokugawa and "seize the jewel" (the emperor) for themselves, the idea of returning to the beginnings (Japan's archaic origins) was considerably different from restoring imperial authority and emerged at the last possible minute. Recognizing the immense distance between the restoration of political authority and improving the image of a fainéant imperial figure who had not exercised power for centuries and relying on a program hurriedly cobbled together to return to the beginning of Jinmu *tennō*'s foundation—that is, to return to the no-time of divine origins or the timeless *illud tempus* (time now and always), a mythic origin, and an emperor who had never existed—most historians tried to close the considerable gap between a remote mythic origin and the world of the 1860s by arguing that the appeal to a distant antiquity (*ko*) freed the proposed new polity from any association with a historical feudal past and made a great transformation possible. Yet this kind of interpretive fantasy made sense only if the subsequent survival of feudal remnants (material and psychological) was ignored. The fascist atmosphere of the 1930s, which relied on what Tosaka called the archaic phenomenon (to be discussed in chapter 4) was a throwback to feudalism, even though it was cloaked in the costume of a remote past that never existed. According to Mitani Hiroshi, the "return to antiquity" (*fukko*) was the name given to reform.[45] But what kind of reform, and for whom? Declarations of this order are a little like calling an oligarchical dictatorship a democracy. Little changes, according to Takayoshi Kido from Chōshū domain, led to greater changes, echoing the optimistic opinion during the meeting at the imperial palace that planned the coup d'état (he was one of the principal plotters who attended the meeting). He initially saw the coup as a comedy (*kyōgen*) that would inevitably lead to the accomplishment of a great performance, an expectation that sounds as if it might have been made after the restoration.[46] The historian Inoue Isao claimed that the restoration of imperial rule was combined with reform and that far from denying the present, the restoration "gave birth to a conception that planned the reconstruction of order, a hope that clearly came from the future."[47] Basically, the restoration's promotion of political change was progressive. This optimism ultimately invited comparisons with other revolutions, notably the French Revolution that had also appealed to a remote antiquity (in that instance, Rome) as a guide to the present. But the Meiji Restoration was unique in that it relied on a mythic origin, not a historical past. Tōyama was perhaps more hesitant than those who enlarged the comparative compass to rank it with the French Revolution, given his conviction that the restoration resulted in a counterrevolution and absolutist government. He could see how the restoration opened a pathway to reform. "Within the boundaries of an essential conservatism embedded in archaism [*fukko-shugi*]," he suggested (quoting from the Charter Oath [*Gokajō goseimon*] of April 6, 1868), the restoration "worked up an intellectual base and produced a reform consciousness to 'wash away old abuses' and 'renovate all things.'"[48] But the Charter Oath was a brief statement announcing the beginning of the reign of the Meiji Emperor and its high intentions (aimed at reassuring other nations), whereas the call to return to an archaic origin promised to provide a legitimating ground (indeed, a political ontology) for modern Japan.

Furthermore, this historiographical optimism seems to have overlooked a number of possible consequences of the restoration. To begin with, it is important to note that appealing to the archaic was a last-minute decision that clearly sought to head off other possible claimants to power. Loyalist activists had long upheld the ideal of imperial authority as a reminder of the shogun's formal position in service to the emperor, and they based their argument for rejecting the shogunate's decision to open the country on this principle. In addition, this view of the emperor supplied them and others with an unassailable principle of legitimation, which explains their desire to "seize the jewel" and grasp absolute power themselves.[49] In this effort they were assisted by court noblemen like Iwakura and others who saw in the moment the opportunity to rid the country of shogunal usurpation of power and a return of the courtier class to a position of authority that its members had not occupied since medieval times. The courtiers could offer the samurai activists from Chōshū, Satsuma, Tosa, and other domains access to the court and audiences before the emperor—who, regardless of his political impotence, still granted titles and authenticated the holding of official positions. The decision to exceed the mere restoration of the reins of authority to the emperor (*taisei hokan*) by returning to the beginning of Emperor Jinmu's foundation of imperial governance was more than a great leap backward into the unknown. The last months of 1867 were filled with failed plans to resolve the political crisis facing the Tokugawa shogunate. Retainers from Satsuma (Ōkubo, Komatsu, and Saigō) united in Kyoto with others from Chōshū (Shinagawa and Yamagata) to form an anti-Tokugawa strategy, while Iwakura (who had been under house arrest as a result of the emperor's censure) bonded with Ōkubo and Komatsu and explained to other courtiers the necessity of using military force to carry out the imperial restoration. Iwakura had been censured because of his earlier involvement in the antishogunal expulsionist program of the loyalist faction. He had perceived that because the throne relied on the shogunate, whose authority had now collapsed, it was incapable of "preventing countrywide 'internal disaster,'" which would lead to an "external catastrophe."[50] As a result. he turned to planning a program of action by large and powerfully armed domains like Satsuma and Chōshū. But before his "great undertaking" (*taiji*) could be accomplished, there was an attempt to get a number of domains to agree upon a pact sponsored by Satsuma and Tosa domains to "return the imperial administration to the emperor."[51] The main goals were to return the shogun's political power to the emperor, lower the shogun's status to the rank of feudal lord, and raise the prospect of a new deliberative assembly that would represent the several domains. At the heart of the plan was the effort to check the shogunate's military power by installing the shogun as the chair of the new assembly. But both Satsuma and Chōshū saw through the plan, recognizing that it would leave the shogun in power so that nothing would really change. The complications and attempted revisions that the plan generated provided the opportunity for the most radical members of the anti-Tokugawa forces to band together and carry out the militarily backed coup d'état announced by the proclamation of the restoration of imperial rule of 1867. The issue of the shogun's status remained unresolved, leading to the civil war called the Boshin War that removed the shogun from the politics of the Meiji epoch.

But the most fateful legacy of the restoration proclamation for modern Japan was its imposition of the figure of the archaic imperial authority on top of the heavy feudal inheritance from the preceding Tokugawa period, whose material and psychological presence would remain in evidence throughout the Meiji years and beyond. This was especially true of what was called the status system (*mibunsei*) of feudal society, which referred to the vertical hierachicization of social relations that would outlive the formal institutional system as an adhesive element in everyday life, keeping people fixed in their place. The emperor served as a daily reminder to the population of the archaic, which, like a serpent, was wrapped around the strength of these more durable feudal characteristics, in effect archaicizing the materiality of feudal social relationships by spiritualizing them with imperial authority.[52] These feudal remnants would continue to be seen as a sign of backwardness that occupied the modern social space and inhibited the nation's full development into a capitalist society, while the presence of the archaic (*ko*) elicited no comparable criticism.

The remnants also played a new and important role in the capitalization of the Japanese economy, reminding us of the Marxian observation of the way capitalism is able to appropriate from the past what is at hand to use for its own processes. In a sense, some remnants (like the imperial institution and shrines) were ready-made to be employed to get people to work and die for the nation. The emphasis on the emperor's status as a living deity and on new shrines like Yasukuni, the emperor's shrine dedicated to the war dead, went a long way toward securing loyalty and obedience from the masses while they were serving capitalism and fighting imperial wars. If the retention of feudal remnants in the Meiji era attests to its precapitalist historical existence and capitalism's recognizable work in fusing components on hand from the past with the new time to serve its production agenda, the archaic (together with all its associations) was nothing more than an invented historical fiction used to perform similar functions and provide in the imperial figure a guarantee of the maintenance of the sociopolitical order. The undeniable flaw in this equation was the premise that linked feudalism to the archaic without accounting for the historicity of the former and the mythic character of the latter.[53] The appeal to the archaic was thus hurriedly devised to serve as an anchor for the immediate event of restoring the emperor to authority: it reinforced his powers of legitimation by recalling the divine origins of Japan and its people as well as supplying cover for those involved in seizing the jewel for themselves. During this time the figure of the emperor was usually not familiar to ordinary folk and played no direct or indirect role in their daily lives, even though he may have appeared in legends and folk stories.

According to Yasumaru Yoshio, from the medieval period to Tokugawa times, the emperor had various designations (including *mikado, dairi,* and *tenshi*), but he was not identified as *tennō* until the Meiji Restoration. Nativist scholars like Yano Gendō added religious associations to *tennō* when they claimed that the emperor's first duties were to perform "ceremonies to the deities of heaven and earth." It is also in this historical context that the emperor acquired an association with divine providence (*ten-i*), and because he has the same body as heaven, he is called "heavenly emperor [*tennō*]."[54] In short, the emperor was transmuted from a mere principle of legitimation into a principal of divine will who possessed the aura of charisma "realized according to the 'blessings entrusted by the invisible assistance of the imperial ancestors and heavenly deities from the unseen world.'" We must recognize that the sole purpose of this bold fictionalizing act was to completely legitimize the plotters, who became the leading figures in the Meiji Restoration.[55] This transmutation was a giant leap that initially resulted in a reinvented and refigured image of the emperor and reached completion in the final fabrication of him as a man-god (*arahitogami*) in the Meiji constitution of 1889. The final constitutional form of the emperor exemplified the way in which capitalism successfully appropriates what is at hand and revises it as necessary to serve its process of capital accumulation.[56] Even though the plotters had no idea of the kind of polity associated with Jinmu's mythic inaugural reign, they could use a conception of imperial authority derived from this archaic moment (close to the age of the gods and the creation) to implement wide-scale reform and reorganization and to ensure that people would work and die for the nation. In fact, this hurried appeal to origins, Jinmu, and the divine foundations of the state became a primary narrative that would be allegorized into an ideology called Japanism in the attempt to solidify the permanence of the new political ontology.

The feudal heritage reflected the experience of the immediate historical past that the Meiji era had succeeded and whose remainders would enter its temporal precinct as remnants. In fact, the move to restore the timeless nonplace of origins and make it part of the new society emphasized the beginnings of Japan's unevenness that was to characterize most societies as they entered capitalist modernity. The use of the archaic dramatized the moment of precapitalism in a society dedicated to capitalist modernization, a nonplace and nontime at the center of a national place and historical present as well as an enduring absence securing the coherence of a filled space—a contradictory position still extant in Japan today.

The proclamation announcing the return of archaic imperial authority sought to mask the coup d'état directed at bringing down the Tokugawa house and the political and feudal social edifice over which it had presided for three hundred years. Takayoshi Kido best described the proceedings in a letter to Sakamoto Ryōma of Tosa domain, and he showed no reluctance in portraying the hastily organized plot as a farce and comparing the anticipated political changes to a play (*shibai*). As noted above, according to Takayoshi Kido the plot "began as a *kyōgen* and [we] progressed to a great drama [war]." Even though some who participated in the farce were dragged into complicity, Takayoshi Kido explained that the episode illustrated the means employed in skillfully staging the comic interlude—a skill that "gently made possible and (was) prepared by (proper) stage management which required eventually moving in a manner to concentrate on expanding the size [of the group]."[57] Takayoshi Kido was proposing a strategy of progressive movement that would lead to broader group participation or consensus with the goal of transposing the farce into a "great play" enacted on a "large stage" (that is, moving to the wider stage of a takeover and even a war).

What worried those who expressed reluctance to go along with the coup d'état without the participation of the current shogun (Hitotsubashi Keiki) was their suspicion that the principal plotters were interested in embracing the young and inexperienced emperor only so that they could seize authority. This view was shared by members of the court who feared that access to imperial authority would be taken out of their hands, which Saigō addressed with the threat that "if there is one short sword in the room, it puts things into order."[58] Even by that time, Saigō was known for his military prowess, and as a person who was quick to act. He apparently believed himself to possess the requisite sword and was sure of his willingness to use it. Nonetheless, the outcome of the conference was foretold since when it opened, a military force commanded by Saigō had fortified the gates of the imperial palace. Domainal lords like Yamauchi of Tosa recognized that a scheme that increased the power of the emperor would lead to the political domination of the Satsuma-Chōshū-court alliance and undermine any possibility for a broader conciliar arrangement. Yamauchi confronted Iwakura about the Satsuma-Chōshū conspiracy and denounced the conspirators for what they attempted to assert and mask at the same time by asking, "Embrace the infant emperor or steal the jewel?" Iwakura replied that the unprecedented work of the restoration was an accomplishment "that does not extend to [involving] imperial judgment," while the "great work" of the restoration "does not spread out to the imperial palace." Apparently he meant that the monarch was not directly implicated, but he added that the emperor possessed "unparalleled brilliance"—which was simply another fiction. In fact, Iwakura went even further: he suggested that the determination to move toward a restoration had been made by the young emperor, who in fact had no decision-making capacity or any known political vision.[59] More important, the authoritative character of the emperor that was being invented in no way characterized the cosseted fifteen-year-old youth, who lacked an individual aura that might be invested with the psychic energy of a traditional form of charisma. Because of this, it was opportune to divinize the emperor's authority by linking it to the passage of succession from the sun goddess (Amaterasu Ōmikami) and her mythic descendant, Emperor Jinmu, and to assert the unification of ceremony and governance (*saisei itchi*). It was ironic that when officials of the U.S. occupation began to worry about the status of the emperor after World War II, their learned advisers made a case for validating the retention of the emperor by silently passing over this lineage of succession, which implied accepting both its mythic derivation and the deliberate manufacturing of the emperor's putative charisma by the leaders of the restoration.[60] In 1869 the restoration government established a Department of Divinities (*Jingikan*) that would embody the unity of religious and political authority that had been articulated in 1866 by Iwakura, who had used the emperor's divine authority to legitimate it. Even though the ministry was short-lived and replaced by more modern institutions, the evocation of divine authority was widely used in Japan's subsequent history. In later life, the Meiji emperor had developed an aptitude for posing in photos and providing a spectacle of public imperial progress in military regalia, although he indulged more in unlimited sexual satisfaction and the consumption of *ayu* fish than in performing imperial governance. This was precisely what the restoration plotters had in mind when they spoke of seizing the jewel. The fact that the emperor played any role at all in this dramatic episode sprang from the deliberate intentions of activists bent on seizing political authority, which Tōyama later described as being driven by "strangely individualistic machinations" whose "reasons were probably coarse and vulgar,"[61] and which Yamauchi recognized and denounced at the time. This assessment runs counter to Tōyama's earlier conviction that loyalists were impelled to act solely by their loyalty to the emperor. But the acknowledged intention to "seize the jewel" betrayed a more complicated mix of reasons (both historical and personal) that had less to do with referring to the reformers as men of high purpose (*shishi*). When Meiji died, people mourned the end of the era that had taken his reign name. But Iwakura had been right when he told Yamauchi that "establishing the basis of imperial authority in Japan opened the gateway through which to enter the next period."[62] But it was not the emperor who actually opened the "gateway."

Apparently, the young emperor began his education as a ruler during his journey from Kyoto to Tokyo in 1868, as reported by the shrewdly ironic Takayoshi Kido, who accompanied him and recorded a poem in his diary the first time the emperor saw the Pacific Ocean:

> *The Throne, upon arriving, inspected the great sea*
> *Thereafter began the mutual shining of the open sea and imperial prestige*
> *In ceaseless affection.*

Takayoshi Kido was not inspired, we are told, by seeing the sea, to which he had grown accustomed on domainal trips to Edo. However, the emperor, who at this point had turned sixteen but had barely left Kyoto, had never seen the open sea. What animated Takayoshi Kido was the idea that the emperor had seen in the Pacific a prefiguration of the advent of a new period and a new position for Japan in the wider world. The open sea had special meaning: it symbolized Japan's path to joining the great nations of the West.[63] The open sea represented the promise of a new age and all it would offer for the future, including new technologies that already were reducing the time needed to cover the distance between Japan and the countries that lay beyond the sea and new contacts with the world at large from which it had been isolated for nearly three hundred years. It had little to do with the actual young emperor, his face hidden behind white powder, who played no part in making this transformation happen.

Yet the proclamation of the restoration emphasized that it had been founded on the intention of the emperor. Without knowing whether Jinmu's political beginnings were factual or fictional, no one chose to debate its authenticity because it went "hand in hand with emphasizing the emperor's authority."[64] The claim of factuality was supported by attributing to Jinmu the founding of a politics in the service of "renovation of all occasions," since Jinmu's "great work" was unprecedented. Widening this magnanimous archaic endeavor would seem to entail the necessity of acknowledging the changeability of suitable standards according to different times. Yet there was nothing in this origin narrative that remotely hinted at future times or changes to meet suitable standards.

What seems important in this account of the restorationist plot is the narrative used to explain the necessity of a return to the foundations of imperial governance in remote antiquity. The purpose of the proclamation was to establish the need to abolish the shogunate for its failure to perform its duties as imperial deputy and because it had demonstrated indecision and incompetence when confronted by crisis. After it had acquiesced to Commodore Matthew Perry's demands to open the country, bringing an unanticipated end to a seclusion policy dating from the seventeenth century, a countrywide crisis had ensued. The restorationists claimed that since the early 1850s the late emperor (Kōmei) had commented that the foreign problem and the shogun's inability to resolve it "yearly pained his heart" and that he saw the treaties Japan was forced to sign with several nations as an act of misgoverning on the part of the shogun.

Yet it is worth noting that at the same time as the proclamation sought to focus on the foreign problem, some shogunal officials and samurai intellectuals not associated with principal domains thought that the shogun's decision to open the country was more rational than the allegations of the anti-Tokugawa activists calling for expulsion of foreigners. Given the international environment and the maturation of Japan's economy, ending seclusion was a realistic option that would set Japan on a course toward capitalist modernization, while the strategy of expulsion was at least a transparent tactic to discredit the shogunate and possibly a destructive and even dangerous policy. In the proclamation, the critique of the shogun's decision was accompanied by a demand for a foreign policy suitable to the sacred "land of the gods" (*shinkoku*), whose divinity sanctioned the unparalleled emperor's unbroken lineage and the concept that Japan was a country possessed of greatness principally because it had successfully achieved the unity of a family. The emphasis here is on the archaic, rather than the historical, which, because it was full of changes, was deliberately bypassed to allow the emperor to be identified with a long lineage stretching back to the foundation of the state by the gods. In fact, the archaic stood as an unchanging emanation and apart from the historical, anchoring Japan's modern political ontology. The imperial family's genealogy exceeds history to become a sign of the archaic, and the emperor its living embodiment in every present. Since the 1850s advocates of restoration had linked it to its archaic precedents, and the proclamation's main point was its call for a return to ancient imperial authority. This move was in fact a masquerade designed to conceal the plotters' attempt to seize power in the name of the emperor. What the masquerade achieved was bringing the name of the emperor (previously an unseen, even ghostly, figure imprisoned in the imperial palace) into ongoing public discussions. Hence, the proclamation announced in formal language the return to the beginning and referred to the foundational work of Jinmu *tennō*, the first emperor, confidently proposing the archaic as a model free from the contamination of failed historical experiments and available for emulation in the present because it had accompanied the act of creation. On this basis the proclamation both recommended returning to the "great polity of august trust" from preshogunal times and called for the resignation of the Tokugawa government. The cause of Kōmei's pained heart since Perry arrived in 1853 and presented his demands to open the country had become an item of common knowledge among ordinary Japanese. The proclamation explained that "even though [it is] difficult to discern the emperor's pleasure and the rousing up of an Imperial Restoration on the (basis of) the august foundation to turn around the (loss of) of countrywide prestige (*kokui*), we must today carry out the abolition of the shogunate and temporarily set up three administrative offices to conduct state affairs. All matters shall seek the work of the foundation in the work in Jinmu tennō."[65] It is not clear who composed this text, but it is seems safe to say it did not come from the hand of Kōmei.

The drafters of the document had to determine when antiquity was. Eventually they decided that the whole panoply of institutions, organization, systems, and practices of governance during the alleged 2,500 years or so before 1868 had to be scrapped, thus setting aside the accumulated historical record of the country down to 1867 and inferring that it had all been a mistake. The subsequent restoration appeared not only as a historical blank sheet, emptied of all prior historical associations apart from the archaic work of Jinmu (a mythic story outside of history), but also as an ambiguous nontime that sanctioned the coupling of an indefinitely remote past with the newness of the present. This thinking undoubtedly derived from courtiers like Iwakura, who had already written a number of treatises on the possibility of realizing a restoration.[66] The concept of the restoration in nativist discourse identified the emperor with the land created by the gods and worked by the people, placing both land and people before the emperor. In contrast, loyalist activists emphasized an alternative tradition based on the primacy of the sun goddess and the imperial house said to derive from her authority, viewing the emperor only as an empowered legitimating principle of absolute authority over land and people. Courtiers like Iwakura saw in a restoration of the monarch the return to power of their class and an end to their serving merely as custodians of ceremony. Assigned the task of creating the restoration proclamation and a corresponding institutional framework that reflected the archaic exemplars, Yano was forced to abandon the ideals of communitarianism (the relationship of land and people, which had informed the reconstruction of nativist discourse by Hirata and his followers) for the sake of the primacy of politics (imperial rule).

The summons to return to Jinmu's establishment of the state's foundation meant that the present was subsumed in an archaic time, a mythic moment existing before and outside of history in the historical present of a modernizing society. In this regard, the archaic or antiquity (*furui*) was probably more important than the emperor, who was its messenger and whose presence was a reminder of its occurrence in each reign. But the temporal distance separating the present from an indeterminate origin was too great to make retrieving the beginning moment possible. Or perhaps it was not available for imitation or appropriation because of its timelessness and therefore offered too great a range of possible reenactments. After all, it is important to remember that the orchestrating of the plot was seen by one of its participants as a farce capable of developing into a play on a wider stage. Yet the proclamation implied that what was being rescued for the present was the auratic apparition of the archaic. The very impossibility of bringing it back was a sign of its authority carried by the emperor down through the ages. This impossibility stemmed from the fact that the archaic represented the moment of creation by the gods of heaven and earth.

The hopelessness of literally returning to the archaic and emulating it lay in the obvious fact that it was identified with the time of creation, which could never be re-created but only recalled as an unattainable exemplar that an invocation of restoration would imperfectly reproduce. Here it seems, the restoration became a metaphor that had no need to fear perfect reproduction; it had the capacity merely to call attention to this possibility of implementation, not to actualize it. In this sense, the restoration of the archaic meant that any subsequent call for a restoration could only aspire to point to an intention to realign with the archaic past. But the real problem it faced is that it could not actually accomplish such a realignment. As I show below, Maruyama referred to the archaic as an archetype that flowed continuously, like a subterranean stream determining Japan's history. What he failed to add is that Japan's subsequent history was jump-started by the concept of origin that remained outside of historical time, a bit like capital being set on its way by noncapital primitive accumulation, which capital would subsequently seek to conceal. But unlike primitive accumulation, the creation could only be a one-time event. What appeared important to the planners calling for a restoration was not the obvious impossibility of reproducing the archaic but the fact that it predated the feudal system and could therefore sanction the overthrow of the shogunal order. Yet this attempt to realize an impossibility marked as contradictions both the idea of restoration and the emperor who embraced it. In this regard, the Japanese seemed to be replicating Marx's advice to Vera Zasulich, when he suggested that she need not fear the term *archaic* or its return. After all, Marx had recommended that the existing Russian commune, which had originated in a precapitalist time and place, be used with contemporary capitalism to enhance national economic development and avoid the worst excesses of capital. The mixture of components of earlier modes of production with capitalism was what Japanese Marxists saw as feudal remnants stalling the development of capitalism in Japan, even though the remnants had played important roles in the development of capitalism virtually everywhere capital had established its regime of production. These remnants were historical practices from earlier times that had been given a new lease on life in capitalism. Moreover, the Japanese restoration of the archaic exemplar and its imperial figure inverted, rather than followed, Marx's advice that a precapitalist commune could be used to enhance national development. When Marx advised Zasulich that she need not fear the term *archaic*, he had changed his perspective on history. He had come to envision historical formations in which periods functioned analogously to vertically layered geological strata stacked on top of each other. Even though early layers had been exceeded by later ones in a long history originating in the precapitalist epoch, they remained, and any contemporary manifestation was related to its predecessors. In contrast the Japan archaic was a mythic representation that had no subsequent historical development. Since it could claim no historical existence, it could not develop further, and any attempt to improve upon it would risk forfeiting its paradigmatic role. In fact, the imperial figure carefully reimagined in the Meiji period was immensely different from his putative historical prototype.

The archaic—which the plotters of the restoration may well have believed had existed in a remote past—in fact had no historical existence, but only a fabricated mythic attribution. This fact produced an absolute contradiction that the Meiji constitution of 1889 would enshrine and the U.S.–sponsored postwar constitution of 1946 would continue: the figuration of the emperor as a symbol of national unity. An emperor who was in and of history yet also outside it remained a contradiction and an illusion conjured up by magical thinking, whether claims of divinity were asserted or, as was the case after the war, denied. Someone once said that the appeal to symbol making appears when it is difficult to figure out solution.

In liberating Japan from the Tokugawa shogunate, the restoration leaders were obliged to reinstate the emperor and court to their allegedly proper place as the administrative apparatus of imperial authority. Iwakura called such an arrangement a "restoration of the court" (*kōshitsu chūkō*), not of the emperor, which meant that Tokugawa "private intentions" would be replaced by a foundation of "public principle" or "opinion." But it is obvious that his principal purpose was to return to the class of courtiers the power they had once enjoyed. It is also important to note that the term he used for "restoration" (*chūkō*) was the Japanized version of the Chinese political concept, not *fukko*, a word mired in a mythic origin. Iwakura had written before 1867 that restoring countrywide prestige and crushing the "foreign barbarians" hinged on unifying the realm by a single ordinance like a restorationist decree, which only the court could issue. Changing the basis of the new government would constitute the "great task" that would initially entail carrying out a general survey of contemporary conditions and discussions before the emperor. Once this was accomplished, the final edict, drafted by the nativist scholar Tamamatsu Hisao (a student of the last major nativist thinker of the Hirata persuasion Ōkuni Takamasa) would explain how the new government would "endeavor" to make all things "adhere to the beginnings of Jinmu *tennō*'s establishment." This standard demanded a return to the origin of creation, which already provided a determined "plan to unify all (things) in the universe . . . in order to correspond to a renovation (*ishin*) of all things."[67]

Michel Foucault has argued that the origin of creation "is by no means the beginning—a sort of historical dawn of history from which (man's) ulterior acquisitions have accumulated." It is rather the way in which humans "articulate" themselves "upon the already begun of labor, life, and language." We see in the Japanese summons of the archaic that it appears at the juncture where humans apply their labor to a world that has already been made and "worked for thousands of years," encountering a life that has been lived long before and has derived from the "first organic formations" and is expressed in words and sentences that are never before uttered but repeated time and again, that are "older than memory" itself.[68] For this reason the archaic must be seen as an allegory of any present and the promise of the new. We know that allegories usually function to disguise communications, displacing them to different registers of meaning, in order to address something that appears immediately disturbing and even dangerous that direct criticism would risk censorship or worse. By the same measure this act of displacement implies a political purpose which denies what had been said. This was particularly true in the 1930s, when the archaic was used to bolster fascism—a role that has recently been reprised in contemporary Japan. With the proclamation's call for political changes in the immediate present (in effect, a call for the sweeping away of all historical institutions and practices), the plotters revealed the radicality in their desire to reach back to the putative moment of state foundation (the legendary time when the gods appeared) and place the emperor in a temporal neighborhood of first-generation rulers who descended from the mythic heavenly palace, Kashiwara no miya. In this connection, it is interesting to notice that in Maruyama's later meditation on the "archaic substratum" running through Japan's history and directing its rhythm, the archaic was seen less as an allegory than as a powerful and unchanging principle that committed Japan to the permanence of an unchanging presence and implied that every present was simultaneously shadowed by the figure of an archetypal past. Moreover, this view sought to displace the idea of a divine emperor by turning to the engine driving the historical process in Japan, which appeared to follow the principle of repetition claimed by restorationists and an emperor whose divine self (housing both a human and political body) guaranteed the unity of governance and religious ceremony. That principle may have been the intended result of the Meiji Restoration in its early days.

The Archaic Imaginary

Because the archaic referred to a mythic moment removed from history, it was free from the materiality that usually is associated with the historical. But this role of the archaic demanded that all history must derive from the archetypal paradigm, as layers of historical time successively imposed on top of each other, like a deck of cards, constituted a vertical axis that would still afford every present access to the authorizing moment at its foundation. Once history departed from the archaic paradigm's divine mandate, it would signal the time for restoration to start anew. Hence, a misty invention in which the historiography of Japan's national narrative tried to overlook and even finesse political failure, which merely illustrated that historical representation for Japan, like all modern societies, became the fixed category of national history and vocation of historical practice, glorifying the achievements of the nation-state and making sure that the omissions remained omitted. On the contrary, the archaic was an immaterial force, both spiritual and spiritualizing, that invited the development of a contradiction that combined a native communal and spiritual structure and patterns of behavior into the foundation of a rapid and institutionalized modernization from the top to the bottom of Japanese society. The use and preservation of the antique communal figure facilitated the authoritative acceptance of the concept of *kokutai*, the mystical national body—a mystical body politic that was eventually centered on the modern state and its sacred meaning. But the communal figure deepened the contradictions and complications of modernization, and claims of communitarianism undermined the possibility of developing a space of subjective conduct and coping.[69] It should be said that the appeal to a communitarian ideal could easily be identified with and grafted onto the religiosity of origin and archaism. Through its spiritualizing power, the archaic became a modern form of unconsciousness that was bonded to the new nation-state's material pursuit of capital accumulation and played an important part in turning the reality of passive revolution into the formation of a fascist community—which was dedicated to turning the present into an indefinite past. The archaic unconscious (another important form) made the repetition inscribed in restoration regularly accessible as a way to leave the endless linearity of history's progressive movement—that is, its routinization and unrealized promise of completing unfinished business. Yet the entry of the archaic into the present in the form of a restoration that would once more realign the human order with an unattainable origin staged the encounter of the here and now with the then and there that brought to the synchronic surface the anachrony of the past. How could a timeless figure signify anachrony? In this scenario the emperor appeared as the manifestation of the archaic fixed in a modern present but not necessarily of it (given his role as a man-god), both in and outside of history, and mediating between the ancestors and gods on the one hand and the contemporary folk on the other. The emperor thus embodied the contradictions between past and present as well as between anachrony and synchrony, with the former privileged over the latter in both cases, and he represented the impossible unity of the unevenness that divides times and which the call to restoration was periodically delegated to realign in the world of humans—where, it was believed, its moral failure had resulted in friction and conflict. The emperor was the living embodiment of the temporal figure of contemporary noncontemporaneity, always positioned to turn into its reverse: the politically more retrograde noncontemporaneous contemporaneity of fascism. In this sense, the archaic was enlisted to support capitalism's cyclical production of mixed temporalities with uneven development and unexpected combinations. Similarly, the emperor was made to represent not so much the possibility of "eternal return" as that of "eternal recovery," or the bestowal of a prototypical past in the present, "giving the present" the form of "back then."[70] But as I have already suggested, he is instead the repository of an originating past that has never been present and has never historically existed.

This identification of the emperor with the origin and his primal divine ancestors created an eternal image of the archaic and the timelessness of the inimitable moment of *illo tempore* in contrast to a given experience with a historical past. In this way, Japan since the Meiji era has been constructed on the basis of a genuine anachronism of a mythic past: the historical present is unified in the figure of the emperor and the availability of a new beginning promised by restoration. In time Japan, like all modernizing capitalist societies, would be composed of temporalized spaces signifying capital's ability to continually produce forms of uneven and combined development. These mixed spaces of coexisting but different temporalities constituted modernity's true space-time coordinates that pointed to the presence of contemporaneous noncontemporaneities, rather than to frozen feudal remnants stranded in the new time of modern society and indefinitely forestalling the complete realization of capitalism. The archaic must be considered an anachrony (even though the claim of timelessness grants it an exemption), principally because its temporal referent is nonexistent and truly out of time because it has no time. In contrast, contemporary noncontemporaneous combinations can claim historical existence in the residues from the past that were combined in their survival in a new present, where they are made to function in one way or another. In this instance, Jacques Rancière is correct to see anachrony as inseparable from the historians' devotion to chronology, the regulator of correct time in spite of the imposture of the untimely. The unevenness produced by capitalism in modern Japan and its capacity to produce fissures, social discord, and class conflict meant that an emperor who already served to unify opposites could also be seen as a figure capable of resolving the economic and cultural divisions Japanese were experiencing. What the Japanese stumbled on in retaining and refiguring a residue from the past in the emperor was a timeless agent who could relieve capital of its inherent defects and remove temporal interruptions to the social order. It should be remembered that the Meiji state's slogan was enriching the nation, strengthening the military—which enjoined all to work and die for the imperial country (in other words, the emperor).

In modern Japan, there is little evidence that unevenness related to capital is acknowledged. Some thinkers (like Tanabe Hajime, in his work on history) saw the coexistence of different forms of historical time but provided no further explanation of the reasons for its presence. Moreover, the proliferation of combinations of the forms of Japanese and Western life that were joined in the country's modernizing process elicited responses from philosophers like Watsuji Tetsurō, who conceived of the matching as a deformation and insisted on them as having double but separate lives (*nijū seikatsu*), and Miki Kiyoshi, who envisioned them as examples of "living culture" or "everyday culture" (*seikatsu bunka*), which referred to how the past continued to live in the present and how the newly imported part of the present would become part of a living tradition. It is important to note that Miki, a former Marxist and later an adviser to the state, remained committed to a formulation redolent of the Marxian concept of subsumption. Similarly, although Marxists may have seen the presence of feudal remnants as freezing the development of capital and committing Japan to the permanent status of semifeudalism, what they called remnants were signs of uneven and combined development leading to the temporal figure of contemporaneous noncontemporaniety, which would stand as the emblem of both the normal temporal development of capitalism everywhere and a reminder of capitalism's incompletion. Watsuji was one of the few thinkers in the prewar period who demonstrated a partial grasp of the characteristic appearance of contemporaneous noncontemporaneity when he referred to the concept of a double life, which recognized the static copresence of received cultural components and domesticated Western imports. Although he saw this copresence as a natural result of Japan's encounter with the West and its subsequent modernization, he did not attempt to explain how and why it derived from Japan's embracing capitalism. None of these cases considered the materiality of the contradictions produced by uneven and combined development and its effects on Japanese life. This seems to imply that an unaccounted-for process everywhere spiritualized the material, with culture being invoked to denote time and temporality. In the case of Japan, the instrumentalization of culture may have derived from the country's initial experience of borrowing from China. In particular, Japan borrowed a written language and philosophy that were seen as additions to what had already been identified as the spiritual aspects of native life. But in capitalism the spiritualizing of temporality could well have been needed to resolve the material contradictions that uneven and combined development produced—which would have undermined the implementation of capital in societies that depended on such a strategy.

What capitalism showed as it migrated to different zones of the world, especially those outside Western Europe and the United States, was its capacity to adapt to local circumstances and customs to make the new social and economic program and its innovations appear compatible with older received forms of life, which it would eventually undermine. In a sense, Max Weber's acute observation of how capitalism was able to utilize certain forms of Calvinist Christianity, especially its conception of a calling obliging believers to serve their God with the utmost effort, was yoked to a presumed capitalist rationality that sanctioned encouragement to make it more adaptable and acceptable to certain regions of believers. This combination between religious faith and economic rationality became the inadvertent model for the rest of the world as capitalism expanded and established its production program. In Japan, the nativism of Hirata Atsutane fostered the performance of work as a ceaseless repayment of the blessings conferred by deities, mandating an identity between production and prayer. It might be said that this approach to make capitalism and the indigenous appear as natural couplings, if not actually removing the contradictions fostered by the new political economy in lands of its adoption, may have contributed to making it appear less wrenching and destructive. In Japan, nothing was more politically and religiously powerful in the Meiji period than the imperial association and alignment with the new political economy in inducing people to work and die for the country, that is, the emperor.

Such contradictions appear in the effort to attain full historical existence and the enlarged presence of a memory of the past preserved by archaic anachrony.[71] But memory of the past and dependency on it could only be a fictitious rescue operation. The real use of contemporary noncontemporaneity was to enlarge the memory of the present so it could free itself from "false recognition"—a pseudopast, or what Paolo Virino has called the "déja-vu." This downward slope into "false recognition" is exactly what occurred in the 1930s, with the turn from contemporaneous noncontemporaneity to noncontemporaneous contemporaneity. In the late Meiji period, the state was still encouraging the contamination of national history with the archaic narrative as if it were historical and punishing those who tried to separate history from mythology. The archaic represented by the emperor compelled the recalling or the pseudopast, forcing the recognition of it as if it were a retrieval (according to Virino) of a historical past believed to have existed and been lived. The illusory past of an indefinite origin for a land and people created by the deities of heaven and earth is always present in the act of "preserving" or "venerating" everything as it was.[72] "The 'past,'" Virino writes, "to be preserved and venerated (and this veneration's only requisite is in mimesis) is nothing other than the present." Moreover, it might be said, if I understand Virino correctly, the present is smuggled in place of something that has already occurred having been produced as an effect of anachronism.[73] It is hard to know what Virino considers a "real anachronism," since I have argued above that the archaic was the only real anachronism because the present that summoned it was bringing back something that had never existed as if it had genuine historicity. It could be proposed that the returning promised by the imperial restoration played this role in 1868, just as its proponents and later historians believed that they were referring to the present when they called for the return of archaic imperial authority.

What seems so important about the archaic figure of emperor and the anachrony it embodied of a pseudopast is its descent from a precapitalist temporal order. Japan's archaic prehistory probably resembled some version of the archaic formations Marx had classified in *Grundrisse*. Before the Japanese thinker and activist Kita Ikki became a fascist theorist, he wrote a book on the character of early or archaic communities in Japan in which he argued that they had a communal structure and emphasized equality, representing them as a form of "pure socialism."[74] In fact, Kita's book was a sustained attack on and rejection of the archaic myth that had obscured a thousand-year history to become the basis of constitutional theory in late Meiji Japan. Having an emperor who drew his authority from a mythology about the precapitalist era preside over a nation-state committed to capital accumulation imposed a contradiction on top of the other contradictions that capital was already continually producing. It would be difficult to find any other contemporary capitalist state whose political roots derived from what is still represented as a precapitalist agrarian communal order that is close to the country's origin and deities and for whose well-being the emperor continues to observe and perform ceremonies. But the projected allegory of archaism failed in its attempt to unify the opposites—a failure that appeared with the advent of capital and the event of historical factuality. Capitalism is a historical fact, despite its disavowal of its historical rise and development.[75] In the epoch of the precapitalist archaic systems, the absence of history prevailed and the conditions of possibility capable of explaining or accounting for the appearance of production experienced as history were inaccessible. In *Grundrisse*, Marx viewed the common systems of production found in all precapitalist societies, which referred to a consciousness that had not developed sufficiently to perceive that it inhabited part of a history and was thus incapable of identifying their historical character. He reasoned that the presupposition of labor belonged to the state and was "regarded as . . . divine presuppositions," rather than human.[76] Before then, it usually derived from the agency of divine intervention, as in the explanations of Japan's nativist discourse grounded in the archaic texts expressing the country's mythical history. The turn to agrarian nativism in the late Tokugawa period occurred when the "sprouts of capitalism" were beginning to surface, which inadvertently affirmed the dangers that turn posed to the settled social order and the need to return to an adherence to the origin.

Production was not seen as a result of historical conditions or experienced as such until the appearance of capital. With the coming of capitalism, production could no longer be described as deriving from divine agency (as authorized in the archaic narrative), since the process had become a component of capitalism. Marx argued that in the premodern archaic, the mode of production rooted in agriculture was seen to generate conditions outside of it from presuppositions external to its actual origins and development. In the early phase of capitalism and even afterward, the deployment of some form of subsumption and its reliance on appropriating from what remained prior and external to its production process from past modes of production were put into practice in capital's service. In the political realm, the refiguration of the Meiji emperor and national shrines exemplified this operation.

Japanese emperors since Meiji may have claimed their descent from mythic figures and deities as historically verified, but these claims were nothing more than fiction construed by the activists bent on seizing the jewel and arrogating absolute power for themselves. They were living the archaic imaginary narrative, which had its own vastly different historic origin. The singular linear direction demanded by a narrative of mythic origins (its necessary horizontal trajectory) could lead only to fascism in the end. Combining historical capitalism with an archaic myth embodied in an emperor or charismatic leader who enacted the drama of archaism in the present was an attempt to implant an absolute contradiction in the heart of Japan's modern capitalist society—a contradiction that would release "symptoms of morbidity." Italian fascism summoned the myth of *romanità* and transmuted the appeal to Romanness into a cult that, according to Emilio Gentile, "had the value of a mythic foundation for a fascistic politics looking to create a new civilization . . . one as solid and universal as the civilization of the Romans."[77] *Romanità* was a combination of the old and new Rome. Italian fascism was increasingly seen by domestic and foreign observers as a political religion devoted to worshipping the state and aggrandizing the image of Mussolini as larger than life and possessing rituals, symbols, and catechisms. Japanism (its Japanese equivalent) was formed in the 1930s, using the emperor and his unification with religious ceremony and governance. This process of sacralizing politics was evident in German society during these years, where myths, dogmas, rituals, and symbols pervaded everyday life. These myths and their enactment in rituals, symbols, and performances centered on the iconizing of Hitler and were drawn from a combination of remote medieval German legends and traditions and the divinization of the Aryan race and anti-Semitism. The Austrian historian Karl Polanyi wrote in 1935 that fascism had "advanced to that decisive stage at which political philosophy turns into religion."[78] In Italy, German and Japan fascism evolved into political religions, while in Japan an existing political religion based on a divine emperor was turned into political fascism. Guy DeBord, testifying to fascism's aptitude to produce "symptoms of morbidity," ultimately summed up fascism as a *technically equipped archaism*. Its decomposed *ersatz* of myth is revived in the spectacular context of the most modern means of conditioning and illusion."[79]

In Japan in the 1930s, this political logic of turning religion into fascism sought to make the present into the archaic past. In this process the present shed its historicity to realize the eternality of the mythic moment of origin as permanent present—what anthropologists like Ernesto de Martino and scholars of religion like Mircea Eliade called *in illo tempore* or *illud tempus*. Briefly, the proclamation of the restoration was a call to return to sacred time, not as a singular act (which would situate that time in history) but as a repeat performance (which would overcome temporality).[80] The appeal to a founding moment is directed against history. We know, for example, that the plotters of the coup and nativist drafters of the restoration proclamation turned to the archaic to bypass history and ensure that neither a failed restoration in the past nor a trace of shogunal authority would be included in planning the "great deed" of transformation. They considered Jinmu's foundation to be the beginning of a history that they would invoke against all subsequent history after the initial originary event. Eliade, who was also a fascist theorist, saw in this kind of repetition the annihilation of time and the welcome abolition of the historical, which he had excoriated as a pathological distortion of the sacred.[81]

The making of history, especially in capitalism, was little more than the constant repetition of the ever new. In contrast, de Martino envisioned the "dehistoricization of a critical moment" and its privileging of a "determinate moment of existence" that constituted a ritual coming from religion.[82] Eliade and de Martino had different views of history: the former insisted on ridding life of any preoccupation with history and on the "abolition of time through the imitation of archetypes," while the latter perceived in history the basis of human existence and saw even in ritual repetition an occasion for recovering history and "redeeming historical experience," which—through dehistoricization—offers a pathway to history.[83] The call to restoration in Japan (and perhaps elsewhere), committed as it was to bringing the past into the present to reenact archaic archetypes, unintentionally paved the way toward the use of forms of historical praxis. This may be one way to read Maruyama on the *basso ostinato* of the "archaic substratum" and how the timeless anachrony of the archaic chooses its time. This paradoxical possibility inheres in the repetition of the archaic myth, whenever the "determinate moment" appears. Even though myth and ritual share a common tendency for repetition, the summoning of the myth is unscheduled and thus unexpected and will always come with the difference expressed by the historical circumstances that have prompted it. This process was precisely what Tosaka identified in the 1930s when he pointed to the fictional past-form with which the state was seeking to replace the contemporary present. With the Meiji Restoration there was the perception that the flow of a linear chronology had departed from the way things should be, and there were attempts to return to the beginning to repair the temporal damage. Virino has argued that interruption provides the occasion to actually "stand within history as we are doing so," which resembles Stefan Tanaka's recent proposal for a "history without chronology." In fact, it is Tanaka's aim to supply history with the time that chronology has denied it.[84] In Japan in the 1930s, capitalism was the agent that rehistoricized the sacred moment of "that time" (origin) and emptied it of its capacity to negate becoming—which had been capital's principal vocation (the being of the now, not the becoming of the then). This is the manner in which "that time" is integrated into historical time, preventing us from standing within history. What seems to occur with the bonding of the archaic and fascism is that the former offers cover for the latter, which reveals the vast allegorical function it fulfilled in the making of an ideology called Japanism. When we know, as Marx perceived, that the communal form of one sort or another marked the economic and social life of early precapitalist formations, the archaic represents the precapitalist moment and provides a protective shield for the sanctity of private property—a paradoxical arrangement. Private property as original sin, according to Marx, came after the fall—that is, after the passing of communitarianism. The archaic and any effort to return to a fictive past (whether it presumes to claim some historical identity or is simply an archaic myth passing as history) are central to fascism, not simply ornamental effects. In short, fascism is inherent in capitalism and the political and social forms it can generate.

Since the archaic is derived from the precapitalist era that still linked economic activity to external circumstances like the presence of the divine, it was unable to see the real historical conditions involved in generating production. Its consciousness of time was comparably undeveloped, dominated by an extended present and an indefinite past usually consisting of a mix of myth, legend, memory, and some facticity. In contrast, the epoch of capitalism installed a principle of time and its accountancy, according to which the persistence of the past in the present could be recognized as contemporized (instead of passed and done with), thus positioning the past to consider and determine what constituted the noncontemporary. By the same measure, capitalism and the nation-state insisted on chronological linearity to synchronize and assimilate conflicting multiple temporalities unleashed by their constant appropriation of practices and institutions of the past that are now combined with new processes. Hence, contradiction appears in the effort (found in instances of passive revolution) to seek to achieve the possibility of a fully historical existence and a larger presence in the present's memory of experience. Put another way, the modern present was never transparent to itself, even if capitalism and the nation-state's place holding declared otherwise by insisting on the primary importance of the singularity of linear time and its incompatibility with the assertions of coexisting plural times. What historical materialism has overlooked in accepting the principle of linearity as the sign of progress, as Benjamin had warned in his "Concept of History," is precisely the congestion of times vertically stacked up in the present yet concealed until the occurrence of a moment of danger. Benjamin observed that history was not the site of empty time but "filled full with now-time (*Jetztzeit*). Thus, to Robespierre ancient Rome was a past charged with now-time, a past he blasted out of the continuum of history." In this way, the French Revolution saw itself as an incarnation of Rome that constituted a "tiger's leap into the past" and to reflect the same leap into history as "the dialectical leap Marx understood as revolution."[85] The event of Jinmu's state founding in Japan was brought to the now-time of the 1860s to merge with the restoration that incarnated the founder's great work, completed soon after the divine origin of the land. Here, restoration also promised repetition in the future if circumstances required it. The author of the proclamation of the restoration constructed an imaginary claiming historicity based on elements drawn from the earliest histories and nativist writings concerning the divine origins of the archipelago and the state foundation of Jinmu and made a recognizable narrative of it. The ideology was later called Japanism or simply fascism. In this regard, the subsequent history of the restoration in Japan sought to present a linear story line that would erase or displace all the contending discourses of the late Tokugawa period and their different notions of time and space. The alleged event thus joined the present and what Benjamin called the "now of recognizability," which happens only in a mythic story and must nevertheless be grasped as a memory "as it flashes up in a moment of danger," since the "past can be seized only as an image . . . at the moment of recognizability."[86] It is the "moment of recognizability" that counts, not whether or not the memory actually refers to a verifiable historical event. The past event finds its confirmation conserved in the present, fulfilled but charged with a new function to fuse the received with the newly constructed—as in fact, the Meiji Charter Oath proclaimed had been done in 1868.

Both principal factions of Marxism in Japan were complicit in this silencing of the several discursive and social-movement alternatives available in the late Tokugawa period. Only in significantly transfigured forms were some of the competing discourses able to survive in the new period, surfacing in the historical present to manifest traces of what they had been and stood for in a different historical era. But capitalism broke with its precapitalist predecessor by insisting on a new conception of time that announced the unevenness of contemporaneous noncontemporaneity and the possibility of combining temporally older survivals with the new practices. Installing a monarchal figure in the restoration who embodied the presence of archaic aura in what would become the heart of a modernizing society constituted both an affirmation of the new temporal regime and its absolute contradiction at the same time. Without capitalism's redefining of the contemporaneous as the privileged temporal tense, there would not have been any way to determine and identify the noncontemporaenous world of noncapitalism and the nonmodern. The noncontemporaneous in Japan not only called up the coexisting residue of precapitalism but also configured vestiges of the prehistoric archaic *illud tempus*.[87] This combining of the archaic and the capitalist modern seems to support Marx's observation that formally subsumed elements from earlier modes could exist alongside the advanced forms of capitalism. But by reversing the order to emphasize the primacy of the noncontemporaneous, the Japanese combination inverted the order of time and opened the path to fascism.

The archaism invoked by Japanese activists at the time of the Meiji Restoration summoned a mythic event of divine origins embodied in an emperor and the idea of restoring him to his rightful authority that would enable the inversion of historical time into a mythic repetition of cyclical recurrence. In fact, the historian Kan Takayuki has suggested that there is a remote resemblance between an "illusory communalism" (*genzō kyōdotai*), which Marx and Engels first proposed in *The German Ideology*, and the emperor system (*tennōsei*) or state Shinto used as a way for Japanese Marxists to approach the problem of emperorism.[88] What Kan saw in this kinship was an analog of the political religions of state authority in modernized societies, if not civil religions—a view not used by Marxists in their efforts to assess the role of the emperor.

The upshot was that both the feudal environment the restoration sought to overcome and the invocation of an archaism whose grandiose program recalled an origin before all history had implications the restoration plotters could not have foreseen. What must be acknowledged in this example and any similar ones is the repetitive historical experience that pasts are never fully extinguished and overcome: rather, their residues persist in presents other than those in which they originated. The result is a vertical stacking of presents filled with different times, which the contemplation of historical practice must confront to see how modern presents are crowded with contemporary noncontemporaneities waiting to be recognized and have their demands addressed.

Until recently, only fascists (not leftists) have been able to see this demand and use it for historical praxis. In 1930s Japan, the residues included various classes of people. There were peasants who, despite producing material for capitalist markets and being aided by new technologies, lived in villages connected by radio and newspapers to a wider national scene but who acted, and probably felt, as if they were still living under Tokugawa feudalism and had little or no sense of kinship with workers in distant and distrusted cities and their factories. There were also people who occupied the middle stratum who in the late 1920s and early 1930s began "learning to lose time."[89] They turned to what they saw as cultural moments when, they believed, things had seemed better than was the case in the present they inhabited. Intellectuals felt a strong nostalgia for discrete pasts, which produced an additional fantasy of noncontemporaneity—about the culture of Edo in the work of Kuki Shūzō, the shadows in architectural structures of an age without electric lighting recalled by Tanizaki Junichirō, or the work of self-conscious romantic writers such as Yasuda Yojūrō, with his sentimental and ironic veneration of the Japanese bridge and its embodied tradition of "ruin," "sorrow," and pathos, and of poets who reached back to the past for guidance in their present, with their quest for the "lost home" and ultimately a "return to Japan"—that is, the image of a more real Japan.

All this was accompanied by a bourgeois conviction that capitalism and the rationale for it were undermining tradition and its value but never led to a revolutionary anticapitalism. This familiar story discloses how the archaic and its claim of indeterminate time proliferates in material forms from remote pasts—whether condensed in architectural shadows or as surviving remains like bridges, temples, the Japanese house, and even customs allegedly unchanged for centuries—which are all able to adapt to and flow into fascism, offering the illusive security of transcendence of the past. In Japan the presence of the emperor made the archaic impulses and residues from the epoch of precapitalism look like a real noncontemporaneity when, in fact, a good deal of this imperial inventory had been invented in modern times.[90] Outside the large cities, Japan was still a museum of surviving feudal economic and social practices, resembling André Malraux's imaginary "museum" (musée imaginaire). Even after World War II Uno feared that custom and the retention of an older feudal mentality among peasants (that is, their way of thinking) would stand as a barrier to the implementation of democracy by the U.S. military occupation. Moreover, with commodification already saturating Japanese society in the 1930s and critics calling attention to that fact, the apparition of the archaic emerging from the recesses of a noncommodified precapitalist era provided a possible hedge against alienation. The recognition of contemporary noncontemporaneities (whether genuine or false) affirmed the preservation of a 'natural' way of life and even nature itself in a "magical way."[91] Ernst Bloch's reflections on Germany in the 1930s could apply just as well to Japan at the same time: "Thus the contradictory element is here, inwardly or subjectively, a muffled remnant, and it is equally in the times themselves, outwardly or objectively, and alien and surviving, in short a non-contemporary remnant. As a merely muffled non-desire for the now, the contradictory element is subjectively non-contemporaneous, as an existing remnant of earlier time in the present one objectively non-contemporaneous. The subjectively non-contemporaneous element . . . appears today as accumulated rage."[92] Yet this rage—including the false expressions of noncontemporaneity like the call to return to Japan, which referred to some pure past state contrasted with the now of an unacceptable present—could be used by capitalism as a distraction to offset and displace its own production of real contradictions.[93]

It should also be pointed out that the political-economic model of capitalism that shapes the organization of any society claims no history, only the cycle of repetitions of its processes. This means repeating the form of fascism inherent in those processes and its unchanging ghostly countenance, which is always ready to make unanticipated appearances like a revenant reminding the present of what must be done and sacrificed to make the machine right again. Most people in industrial societies occupy a timeless zone, a permanent present stretching out indefinitely toward an infinite horizon: their everyday lives are determined by the time of the working day that repeats itself endlessly until the economic machine breaks down and puts into question the unattended and unrecognized crises of a failed political and economic order. Hence, fascism thrives on economic crises produced by capitalism and seeks to correct capitalism and save it from itself, and fascism derives its own historicity from the event of the rescue mission. Theodor Adorno called this mission "the nightmare of a humanity without memory."[94] From their beginning, all capitalist societies like Japan were set up, especially in the industrial cities, under the principal sign of exchange—the negotiation between one party and another, swapping money for a commodity—which left no remaining record. In other words, the act of exchange is essentially timeless, which means it is without history. Once an exchange has taken place, it is removed from time. Many thinkers have reminded us that the institution of the factory and its systematic organization of production similarly functions as the place the amount of labor it takes to make a commodity and discipline the worker has already been calculated, but where the marking of time as such is absent in the actual production. The introduction and implementation of time study to estimate and determine the optimal amount of time required to produce a product led to the erasure of time because from that point on the worker's movements were routinized and automatically repeated in capital's production cycle. Where a country using the factory system differed from traditional societies was precisely in this erasure of time, whose continued presence capitalists increasingly saw as an irrational residue. Marx had observed in *Grundrisse* that industrial production reduced categories of feudal artisanal labor (like the time of training involved in mastering a trade or craft) into repetitive cycles that required little or no accumulated experience of the sort that was so important in traditional work. In this way, "concrete time vanishes" from the industrial scene. This emphasis on rationality and the course of rationalization is important because it overtakes traditional forms of production, eliminating the continuing necessity of exercising recollection, memory, and time as vital phases in the production process. The "divest[ing]" of memory leads to "conforming to what is immediately present," not being able to see beyond it, and reflecting "an objective developmental law."[95] In other words, the worker has been objectified and robbed of self and a reflexive history in which she can see herself and which she can possess as her own. This furthers the loss of autonomy and contributes to the permanent political immaturity that induces people to identify with the status quo and see it as the only model of life available to them. The move also explains workers' tendency to fuse with the collective ego—in other words, to subscribe to a tribal form of nationalism. Since fascism also derives its sense of time and memory from their absence in capitalism, it is thus free in societies like Japan, Italy, Germany, and even the United States to either resort to memories of what might once have existed and appeared as a residual trace of noncontemporaneity or to imagine a fictional temporality that must be situated in the present as a substitute for the vacated time. What the most recent manifestation of fascism shares with earlier historical episodes is this evocation of an affinity for the archaic and anachronic present (usually the same thing) as the present's temporal structure, whether it is Mussolini's Romanness; Hitler's thousand-year Reich; Japan's divine origins; or the "American jeremiad," the Puritan myth of origins of a new, exceptional civilization and the twilight of older civilizations abroad that had exhausted their productivity, together with the ceaseless advance into an endless frontier, pushing back the boundary of "savagery" and advancing imperialism and genocide in the name of that new civilization.

This long chapter first concentrated on the reconfiguration of the archaic emperor, cobbled together from the received tradition combined with new additions that would enhance the authority of both the figure and the new state—which the plotters of the return would serve as imperial retainers, or custodians (though they would actually hold power). Second, the chapter has tried to clarify the link binding the creation of the archaic emperor with the subsequent theme of the development of capitalism and fascism. Though this appeared an unlikely joining together, I have argued that it is generally characteristic of capitalism's aptitude to make what might be considered as rationally driven adaptations to local conditions, customs, and cultures to make the implementation of the new production system seem less disrupting and more natural. At the same time, such adaptations work to benefit capitalism usually at the great expense of undermining and often ruining those survivals of a received culture or making them look like unwanted remnants.[96]

CAPITALISM & FASCISM

Formation of Ideology

The singular figure of a mythic archaic founding event expanded into an ideology of archaism that became the political unconscious of modern Japan. It was used as an imperative to unify the people and the mystical national body in the memory of all Japanese and to secure absolute conformity and obedience. Through the production of texts that constantly repeated a narrative of Japan's origins and the divine mission bequeathed by the gods to their descendant, the emperor, the 1930s were drenched in evocations of the national body and the conviction that Japan was the sacred land of the gods. These texts included volumes claiming to prove Japan's divine origins with an assemblage of so-called facts that ultimately became the content of what is called Japanism. One of the earliest and most disputed books was Kiyohara Sadao's *Kokutai ronshi* of 1921, subsequently edited by the Home Ministry's Bureau of Shrines. This edited version became a source for or inventory of so-called facts related to the historical evolution of the national body.[1] Kiyohara's text is both a history of the idea of this mystical body from the Tokugawa period to his present and a collection of passages from histories by Confucianists and nativists from ancient times to the nineteenth century. The doctrine of Japanism included two principal critiques that cannot be separated from its ideological content: the first was the early criticism of fascism by the journalist and public intellectual Hasegawa Nyozekan, based on his assessment of the relationship of the political economy of capitalism to fascism; and the second was Tosaka Jun's broader reflections on the informing hermeneutic of fascism that so deeply penetrated the intellectual world (especially literature) and even newspapers with its "extreme foolishness" and absence of critical judgment.[2] Between Hasegawa's critique and Tosaka's scorching disassembling of Japan's ideology, I situate texts by Miki Kiyoshi, such as his 1935 work on the Japanese character and fascism (*Nihonteki seikaku to fuashizumu*)—a meditation on what it meant to be Japanese and the nature of the emerging fascism, which Japanists believed was compatible with the characteristics of Japanese thought. Miki was briefly a Marxist and wrote some influential articles on the humanistic dimensions of Marxism, but he became a member of the Shōwa Kenkyūkai (Shōwa Research Association), an advisory group to the politician and later prime minister Konoe Fumimaro. Miki died in prison at the end of World War II, like his friend Tosaka.

According to Hasegawa, writing in the early 1930s on the current situation, Japan had favorable economic conditions for the formation of fascism, which clearly resembled the experience of Italy and its development of capitalism. In fact, Hasegawa wrote extensively on how Italy and Japan had reached comparable levels of economic and political modernization.[3] He was one of the founders of the Yuibutsu Kenkyūkai (the Society for the Study of Materialism), and he saw himself as a positivist in the British manner—a perspective described by Tosaka (who was always ready with a critical assessment) as "bourgeois materialism." This is not to suggest that Tosaka disapproved of Hasegawa's writings but only to note that Tosaka believed that Hasegawa's "non-dialectical materialism" was closer to liberalism than to the more scientific historical materialism in the version of Marxism promoted by the Yuibutsu Kenkyūkai. Hasegawa left the society in 1933 in response to the state's accelerated attempts to curb the society's activities and censor its publications. In a series of critiques of fascism written in 1931 and 1932, Hasegawa argued that contemporary Japan was analogous to Italy at the time of the fascist takeover. But he also recognized that the name Japanism differentiated it from other contemporary ideologies that had similar developmental processes and political inclinations because of the effort dedicated to defining Japanism's exceptionalist character. Miki sought to distinguish Japan's characteristics from those of fascism (or Japanism). In contrast, Tosaka instead argued that Japanism was merely the Japanese version of the fascism that appeared elsewhere in the world and was part of a common global ideology. According to him, Japanism differed from Italian, German, and other variants only in its name—not in its claim to exceptionality. Hasegawa based his critique on an account of the circumstances of international economic failure and the implied warnings of increased social conflict that, he believed, explained the conditions that led to radical responses from both the left and the right. The Japanese left turned both to historical practice (interrogating the development of capitalism in Japan and the contradictions that undermined the economic and social order) and to philosophy (providing a materialist critique of ideology and the defense of science as put forth by the Yuibutsu Kenkyūkai). The Japanese right embraced an ideology that rejected history in favor of a religio-mythic narrative of divine origins and imperial sovereignty derived from it, a cultural history of the Japanese spirit, and the substitution of a precapitalist past for the present. Paradoxically, Maruyama Masao, usually associated with the left in Japan, wrote a remarkable set of essays in the 1970s on the "driving but unseen force of development of one thing after another" (*tsugi tsugi to nariyuki ikioi*) named *kosō*, the subterranean flow or undercurrent that structured history according to archaic archetypes.[4] Although Maruyama sought to criticize the reaffirmation of Japan's exceptional cultural heritage, his reliance on archetypes resulted in his unintentionally banishing time and abolishing history, which replaced historical temporality with a mythic stratum and its repetition of archetypes. At about the same time, Kobayashi Hideo produced a major work on the great nativist eighteenth-century exegete Motoori Norinaga, which sought to reaffirm the importance of the native language before it was changed by the adaptation of Chinese ideographs to make Japan's archaic oral stories readable. I comment below on what the interventions of these important texts on Japan's archaic legacy could have meant in the 1970s and early 1980s.

Reality and Representation

The struggle in 1930s Japan seemed to come down to a confrontation between materialism and idealism, and the central philosophical question of what constituted reality or actuality. To map the world of capitalism in the 1930s, we must see these terms as proxies for the opposed ideologies of idealism and materialism.[5] Moreover, the historicist crisis of the recent past (particularly the acknowledged production of historical excess) that revealed only history's inability to explain how the past has become the present failed to grasp the totalizing powers of the present, when it could no longer understand its own moment and how Japan had been set adrift from its past. The real problem was the inability of cognitive mapping to account for the totality of capitalism—the impossibility, as Theodor Adorno noted, of actually representing its complex magnitude. But this did not mean surrendering to the complete dominance of the commodity relation or to the final extinguishing of history and memory. Rather, the impossibility pointed to the need to constantly identify those moments and sites that continued to escape the penetration of the value form in social life.

The word for "reality" (*genjitsu*) was a compound of two ideographs, one (no longer written only vertically) that meant "appearance" and one that meant "real" or "actual." In contrast, the word for "actuality" (*jissai*) was composed of an ideograph designating reality and another that had several meanings: "time," "occasion," "meeting," "encounter," "dangerous," and "adventurous." It is important to note that *genjitsu* became associated with things as they are, not necessarily the real (or what was regarded as the real), while *jissai* implied movement and praxis. Ultimately, the two concepts were used to refer to archaism and actuality, and substitutes for knowledge were required to represent one's relationship to the capitalist totality or "stereotypy"—that is, a "misplaced concreteness . . . substitutes for knowledge" and the putative lived experience "of an actually nonexperienced world."[6] In short, the replacement of one abstraction for the real abstraction—the reification or objectification of social life—led to a conflict orchestrated by Japanists between purity and the chaos of mixing and difference.[7] As a result, the conflict came down to a collision between the abstractness of Western civilization (and its values of individuality and autonomy) and the spiritual values of archaic Japan (including those related to the time of the gods, the origin, the land, the masses that responded to such blessings by producing the means of subsistence for and the social reproduction of the race, and the pure experience of an ancient vision of existence).

Tosaka often identified *genjitsu* with phenomenology and the privilege it accorded to the phenomenal surface of things, whereas according to him the pursuit of the real required inquiring into circumstances and factors below the surface. He saw the everyday as the site of a materialized commonplace, housing the life of ordinary people and the commodities used in that life, and he contrasted the everyday with the extramundane claims of the lofty and the profound. This understanding of everyday life exceeded the scope of *genjitsu*, which was limited to grasping the surface of life. Its principal weakness, in Tosaka's thinking, was to make reality into a permanent status quo or even a false reality. Hence, Tosaka observed that the cognitive mode of apprehension promised by *genjitsu* acted as a code for idealist philosophers who envisaged reality at a higher plane of existence than at the level lived by most people in the everyday. Since *genjitsu* invariably emphasized the abstract over the concrete, it mistakenly sought to imitate the real—which displaced and even obscured the actuality of true reality or its concrete materiality, which he called its "thereness" (referring to Martin Heidegger's *Da Charakter*) and which was the location of the everyday. The purpose of Tosaka's critique was to show how people were led from engaging with the facticity and temporality of everyday life such as contemporary events like the seizure of Manchuria, mundane routines of their lives and their needs and interests or the nowness of the current situation that he subsequently defined as the content of his theory of history (which I discuss below). For Tosaka, like other materialists, the nowness of the present (what gave direction to history) was being obscured by a metaphysical conception of reality (*genjitsu*) that (as I show below) would locate the real in the archaic and fantasy of primitivism.[8]

In the cases of materialism and idealism, it was necessary to allegorize prior narratives to offer meaning in the present by explaining the crisis of the current situation in such a way as to disclose an adequate solution. Marxian materialists targeted the development of Japan's capitalism, contradictions in contemporary social life, like the growing economic problems produced by the depression, and the ensuing historical events and circumstances. In their view, the Meiji Restoration resulted in an abortive counterrevolution that in turn led to the establishment of an absolutist state centered on an imperial bureaucracy (the emperor's bureaucratic system [*tennōsei*]), according to the lecture faction, or to the beginnings of a bourgeois revolution that was yet to be completed, according to the Farmer-Labor faction. It is interesting to consider that the former faction's preoccupation with the emperor's bureaucratic system actually situated the faction's members in the same narrative social register of political dissatisfaction with the present used by the radical right, although their critical perspectives differed. This shared ground meant that both the left and the right seemed to agree that the problem of emperorism was institutional and bureaucratic, not obscured by the personalized figure of the emperor—which I believe was a major misunderstanding of the deep spiritualization of the politics inherent in the figure of the archaic.

The nationalist right turned to the myth of archaism and the national body (referring to the originating archaic political body and its governance) as the basic principles of Japanism. The problem posed by the contemporary was one of representation. This refers to what is known in contrast to what remains unknown, such as what lies beneath the surface of empirical reality and its complex configurations—which can never be fully grasped.[9] This contrast between known and unknown explains why the proclamation of the Meiji Restoration used the allegorization of a primary narrative based on the fundamental ideological units or ideologemes of the mythic story of origins—the smallest components we may call units that were woven into the ideology of Japanism to supply meaning in the contemporary context of the 1930s. The allegorization led to the construction of policy aimed at restoring a social system aligned with the requirements of archaism. By the same measure, the allegorized narrative provided the mechanism for social reproduction. Allegorizing required expanding the primary narrative to account for the occurrence of historical deviations such as the growing separation of subject from object and the increasing grouping of classes of people who have withdrawn from the objective realities of social life. The political right especially was concerned with representing what was unknown, even though rightists believed that they knew things other people did not. What the right wing imagined was a weakening solidarity of the collectivity and the accompanying loosening of ties of ethnicity. They seem to have misrecognized the impossibility of any unifying principle that failed to grasp and consider the totalizing reach of capitalism in social life. That failure necessitated both the return of the ethnic community to a narrative that realigned people with the national body, ancestors, deities, and emperor, and the acknowledgment of the blessings of Japan's origins. The Marxian left of the lecture faction faced the same problem in their efforts to represent an incomplete and partially unknowable capitalism (based on the assumption that it could reach completion), which was now permanently stalled by a Japanese-style rationality that insisted on Japan's exceptionality. The right seized upon the spectacle of unrestrained consumption and the curse of individualism that fed it as the reasons for the collapse of traditional values—all signs of a growing unevenness and the formation of a sociocultural configuration composed of combinations from past modes of production that had been fused to serve capitalist practices. Unsurprisingly, Miki's conception of "living culture," calling for a mixing of received Japanese social life and Western cultural imports, came close to resembling the Marxian operation of subsumption, which opens the way to uneven and combined development in its production of differences—recalling the comment by Fredric Jameson, in another context, that "the ontology of the present is an inventory of differences, rather than identities."[10] Even more striking was the resemblance of the idea of a "living culture" to the temporal figure of noncontemporary contemporaneity. But the left was convinced that the rise of fascism was due to the incidence of feudal remnants (manifested in the figure of semifeudalism) and attendant ways of thinking, which were seen as the principal barrier to the completion of capitalism in Japan. The remnants were seen as an anomalous temporal disorder, stubbornly standing in the way of the further development of capitalism in Japan. But the acknowledgment of the continued presence of lingering remnants that blocked capitalist progress also drew attention to the scandal of the fascists' offer to set things right by removing the present as a cause of the failure of capitalism's complete development—which would have left Japan in a state of permanent semifeudalism, economically, socially, and psychologically. Hasegawa, who focused on the evolution of an international order of nation-states and trade, attributed the coming of fascism to a breakdown of the international economic system and Japan's stage of medium- and small-scale capitalism. In his view, Japan suffered from uneven development, when compared with its larger competitors—which might have been another way of describing an incompletely developed or immature capitalism, although he did not consider the enduring feudal residues to be a major contributing factor.

The Japanist credo seemed to contain a distrust of capitalist excesses but not an antagonism toward capitalism itself, as Hasegawa explained. He showed how Japan exemplified middle- to low-level capitalism, which he believed is usually immune to the failures that accompanied more mature capitalism. The task before the right was to reduce the alienation of the collectivity by transforming the national narrative into an unconscious ideology. Here it is relevant to consider the theoretical reflections on ideology of Louis Althusser, especially his adaptation of Freud's conception of dreamwork. Althusser argued that ideology, unlike dreams, was an inversion of the lived social imaginary and that it was neither arbitrary nor cobbled together. In his rethinking of Freud, ideology also resembles the dream since both are unchanging throughout history and thus have no history—which is to say that both lacked the raw material of the specific social formations and its collectivities that framed existence. In Japan in the 1930s, for example, the frame for Watsuji Tetsurō's thinking emerged from what he called the specific relationship of climate to culture (fūdo). This relationship was unknowable but representable, although Watsuji presumed that it was expressed in its effects, and he argued that Japan's exceptionality derived from the mix of climates in the archipelago. This approach to ideology points to its workings in the concrete circumstances of individuals in the collectivity and of social classes, which are constituted to act as subjects in the workplace—that is, to its workings in everyday lives in innumerable affective and personal ways. When the primary narrative of restoration was allegorized into Japanism, it disclosed both the historical index of uneven development (without actually acknowledging it) and combinations of new and old practices that prompted this allegorization, the particular crisis that caused it, and its principal message—which was directed at realigning subject and object, as well as individuals and social reality, into an integrated whole. In this instance, realigning through the allegorization of the restorationist trope of national unity was an act of purification, ridding life of the jarring collisions between and fracturing of social relationships, cultural contaminations, and the contradictions between the old (Japanese) and the new (capitalism) so that people were forced to navigate the combination of the commensurable and incommensurable or at least suborn it to tradition. Subjects driven by such a political unconscious are induced to perform in the social division of labor, like work, as if it was their inviolate duty, and thus act as agents of production, exploitation, and repression without being told to do so. Interestingly, this theory of ideology prefigured the People's Republic of China's valorization of a similar practice in the 1950s and 1960s, which it called "watching yourself when alone."

In 1929, the cultural sociologist Seki Eikichi wrote that the view of values of "contemporary Japanism are greatly different from the philosophical values of national essentialists (kokusugisha) [of the Meiji period]). It has been recently discovered that contemporary Japanism, the special coloration of Japan's cultures heretofore, was not consciously made, but worthily affirmed in fact and place where it was unconsciously formed." Seki considered it a genetic inheritance [of the Japanese]. In contrast to Japan's culture of the past, "the special characteristics [of the present] are based on this new Japanese culture." His argument implied that a culture that had been formed unconsciously was rooted in organic naturalness, possibly even being dictated by nature, and would remain unconscious of the values it authorized and the mode of its inscription among the folk. His view was not far from Watsuji's valorization of climate and culture. Others would call this not culture but custom—which, Tosaka recognized, comes without saying where it came from or shows its historical identity. While predictably identified with political subjectivation, culture has appeared in bourgeois liberal states as well, if in a masked form so that freedom is redefined as the free market and the state is seen as its custodian. In the Japan of the 1930s, the inversion of social reality required making the present into an indeterminate distant past when subjects were more united with their ancestors, gods, and emperor—as if the subjects lived in the temporality of origins, where politics and religion would become combined. In fact, Japanism was a political religion that sought to overcome the economic unevenness that had been brought to Japan with capitalism and its social forms and that had thrown into disarray traditional values that bound the folk to their gods and ancestors. Marxists inadvertently reinforced this sense of fading traditional values with their criticism of the continuing existence in the present, with loitering feudal remnants blocking the completion of capitalism. The quintessential remnant was the emperor, who, far from blocking capital, was systematically used by the state to enhance its authority.[11] Yet it must be said that this Marxian view persisted well after World War II and the postwar reconstruction period in its continued use of the jargon of feudal remnants and the absolutism of the emperor system as if the Marxists were still in the prewar period. Seki never ceased to wonder how cultural sociology continued to emphasize the eternal, unchanging, and inherently special quality of Japanese culture, which he identified with the "basic spirit of the Japanese folk" "since state foundation"—that is, Jinmu's great work.[12]

Ōkawa Shūmei called for the beginning of a second restoration in a 1931 issue of *Kōmin shinbun*, a right-wing newspaper associated with an extreme populist patriotic association. His reason for the need of this restoration stemmed from his conviction that the Meiji Restoration had "snatched leadership of land and people from the hands of large and small lords who had intervened between emperor and the nation's people, [and] established a state that unified government and people and the four equal classes; internally it realized the basic principle of the mystical national body (*kokutai no hongi*), and externally it came to occupy a situation adapted to the form of the world. Sixty years after the collapse of the Tokugawa shogunate, today the Japanese people have continued the will of the imperial loyalists. Moreover, we must arouse anew samurai patriots from the 'rising people' (*kōmin*) in order to complete this intention." In other words, the Meiji Restoration had not gone far enough, and it was now time for the ordinary people to take charge and complete its unfinished business. Ōkawa further reasoned that in the Meiji Restoration, the ruler had brought the people relief from military oppression and the means of the state to honor them. "But the people of today have come to groan under the oppression of money." In fact, "a moneyed elite had replaced a landed elite and as a dark cloud darkens sunlight the people tremble most from mental anguish."

Here, according to Ōkawa, was the rationale for a second restoration: the need to move beyond a system that had come to produce only moneyed cliques. He argued that "the motto of this second restoration must be the 'rising of the people.'"[13] The problem that Ōkawa pointed to related to the question of capitalism and the already vast inequality it was producing as a condition of its law of uneven development—an unevenness that referred not simply to Japan's status in the global economy compared to that of advanced capitalist states like Great Britain and the United States but also to the widening economic distance between and within social classes.

This analysis of inequality was taken over by the writings of Kita Ikki, who had already specified that a revolutionary form from below was a necessary component of a second restoration, Ōkawa's "rising of the people," precisely what the first restoration—the Meiji—had purposely bypassed. Here, both the Marxian opinion and even the liberal left momentarily agreed with Ōkawa's assessment of the current situation, recognizing that the masses had been left behind by Japan's early commitment to capitalist development and that this had produced social inequality. However, they did not support Ōkawa's political solution, which was steeped in a virulent nationalistic fascism that had already begun to compare Japan with Benito Mussolini's Italy and Adolf Hitler's Germany. It is interesting to note the relationship between the materiality of capitalism's domination and failure and the fascist solutions—which on the one hand appealed to running the restoration again, but this time from below, and on the other hand sought to install a hedge against the permanent adoption of the autonomous subjectivity of an earlier era, using the fictional figure of a collective folk that was undivided by class and that resembled the folk's precapitalist forbears.

It was precisely this context that prompted Hasegawa to explore the relationship of Japan's political economy and the formation of fascism in its Japanist inflection and to turn to the contemporary model already at work in Mussolini's Italy. In his essays on the "Critique of Fascism," Hasegawa provided an account of how the political and economic circumstances were represented, which he used to explain the formation of a fascist solution and why the masses (whose members had been absent from the restoration and effaced by subsequent historical practice but later had become the working class of capitalist Japan) were now being seen as the principal agents of a second restoration but stripped of their class identity to assume a new status as an undivided folk. It should be said that the overlap between the Marxian left and the Japanist right has too often been overlooked. Yet, like other manifestations of the global fascist impulse, this overlap was not limited to Japan.

Hasegawa and the Critique of Capitalism

One of the best guides to understanding the confluence of capitalism and Japanist fascism in the early 1930s is the work of Hasegawa, who wrote a series of perceptive, informative, and critical essays about the political situation and the phenomenon of Japanism. However, it is possible to learn as much from what he did not or could not see or take seriously in the sociopolitical and cultural crisis stalking Japan in the 1930s. What I am referring to is his apparent inattention to the constant contemporary appeal to the importance of spiritualism in the mystifying iterations of the "Japanese Spirit"—what might be called its modernizing metaphysics, which, according to Guterm and Lefebvre, "only expresses the mystery of capital, the only foundation of all the mysteries of this society."[14] All human experience, ideas, concepts, events, views, and more are piled into an immense, heterogeneous accumulation of isolated and mixed elements. Nothing is forgotten or lost, and everything resides in one's consciousness—which is in a constant struggle with it: "Everything can be found here and not as moments in a totality," and "all successive formations persist within us—in chaos."[15] Hence, "'Spirit'—that favorite leitmotiv of conservative-revolutionaries and fascists alike—is the false, superficial, abstract reconciliation of this incoherent heterogeneity."[16] While spirit is the resolution of the chaotic mix, bringing all these isolated past elements together, it also momentarily possesses the capacity to unify a society that has been trying to understand its current fallen situation and is searching for a coherent way to reorder itself. We know from numerous examples in Japan, Italy, Germany, and elsewhere that fascism thrived on exploiting these disparate historical sediments of the capitalist crisis that contributed to making the unhappy conscious even unhappier. In the case of Japan, the capitalist crisis that Hasegawa sought to address was transmuted into a crisis of spirituality. Hasegawa believed that the current situation could be explained with an analysis of the circumstances of Japan's capitalism in the larger world's capitalist configuration. He discounted Japanism and its spiritual credo as insubstantial and having impoverished content, even though he felt obliged to describe it at the end of his article on political economy. Yet at the same time, he was able to recognize that Japanism appealed widely to people of diverse political opinions, although it seems to me that he could not explain why this was the case. He may have underestimated and surely misunderstood both the fact that Japanese spirit was an accumulated abstraction and its promise to allay the fears of insecurity among the Japanese petit bourgeoisie (especially the imminent threat of the destruction of all certainties). Yet Alberto Toscano reminds us that the antifascist model developed by Norbert Guterman and Henri Lefebvre in 1937 sensitively "embodied and embedded the role of history and temporality in all their unevenness, within contemporary ideology," which was also noticeable in the work of Ernst Bloch and Antonio Gramsci.[17] What this pointed to was the possibility of finding ways out of capitalism's totalizing process and the elimination of history demanded by value theory, those moments that continue to stand in the way of capitalism's relentless journey toward completion. In the 1930s and even after, I am convinced that the everyday was one of those sites that managed to evade the kind of thorough reification that Adorno and Max Horkheimer proposed in the 1940s, as both Lefebvre in France and Tosaka in Japan had already seen in their respective accounting of the everyday's successful escape from the totalizing domination of capitalism's real abstraction.

Hasegawa's essays were written for publication in the inaugural issue of the Marxian journal of the Yuibutsu Kenkyūkai, which state censors prevented from appearing (the essays were eventually published in other journals). What interested Hasegawa in Japanism was his recognition that it was not an "actuality of Japan's history," as such, but rather a product of world history that forced Japan to differentiate itself from other societies and obscure the role played by capital.[18] While concerns with the commodity form were absent in his considerations, he was able to show that the Japanese experience illustrated that capitalism's development followed no singular route but was always mediated by time, place, and circumstances. He also acknowledged that fascism constituted a worldwide political form, but he perceived that Japan's economic and social circumstances would alter fascism there in such a way as to adapt it to the country's historical and cultural experience. Specifically, Hasegawa proposed that Japanism in his day, an ideology that distinguished Japan and its people from others, could be explained only by using the history of the capitalist state. His interest in Japanism must therefore be understood as a part of his larger considerations of the relationship of capitalism to the formation of fascism in Japan. But in his articles on the appearance of fascism and its social and economic presuppositions, Hasegawa noted that fascism's reception in liberal states had become a "worldly reflex."[19] In time, fascism became the century's characteristic political ideology and program, lastingly tied to salvaging capitalism and preventing the working classes from breaking away from its hold on them by ridding society of cyclical failures and reliance on exploitation. According to Hasegawa, fascism in his time was a name used to distinguish bourgeois autocracy from other oligarchical and authoritarian political forms.[20] In fact, it is difficult not to conclude from Andrew Barshay's account of Hasegawa's political writings when he was associated with the journal *Warera* in the early 1920s that Hasegawa's critique of the state prefigured and must have mediated his later criticism of the formation of fascism in Japan in the early 1930s.[21]

In many ways, the course of Japan's gradual embrace of fascism had already been charted by Italy's fascist experience under Mussolini. Hasegawa and others would raise the question of the difference between Italy and Japan and point out departures taken by Japan, especially in its economic development. At the close of a long discussion of the forms of fascism, Hasegawa asked how circumstances in Japan would take away change and the developmental process in fascism as it turned to the specific nature of the development of Japanese capitalism.[22] He was concerned that Italian fascism was in the process of making unavoidable adjustments in response to undergoing a "steady deterioration in whatever ways." For this reason, he was convinced that in general worldwide fascism in the early 1930s must be seen as changing its quality and surviving in a new form called "cold fascism (*kurodo fuashizumu*)" or "legal fascism (*gōhōteki fuashizmu*)," turning itself into a functional process and emphasizing the command of bourgeois autocracy.[23] This new form had apparently replaced what was called "primitive (*genshi*)" or "original fascism" with its propensity for inflicting violence. Yet the new form continued fascism's opposition to social democracy. Hasegawa worried that if fascism failed to acquire the "influential status of legal fascism," it was destined to remain reliant on the "instrumentalization of violence (*bōryoku*)" of the bourgeoisie, "like the violent groups in our country."[24] Furthermore fascism would lose its original form and weaken into a functional form of bourgeois autocracy. This decline would represent the progression of fascism resulting from its separation from its original promise of enacting the possibility of a violent revolution—the principal aspiration of primitive fascism. Hasegawa concluded that the weakened fascism would continue to exist as a "traveling companion of a bankrupt capitalism."[25] In this way, it would become an "organic fascism" and abandon its original vocation as a revolutionary process conceived by Italian fascists for static legalization. But he warned that such a legalization of fascism offered no guarantee to reduce its violent tendency.[26] Hasegawa reported that the form of fascism that sought to replace the complications of politics and regulate the capitalist system according to its "fragilities was considered a progressive move" because it "oligarchized democratism" and introduced scientific planning.

Parliamentarians had thus lost the trust invested in them to direct the state, as he noted in the precedent set in England by Oswald Mosley, a rising member of the British Parliament who left that institution because of the political discord over labor, embraced fascism, and organized the British Union of Fascists in 1932. Hasegawa argued that a conscious legal fascism should pursue a political pathway that relied on parties rather than on the realization of rational planning carried out by "pure specialists" in the conduct of bourgeois politics, which meant understanding the necessities of a capitalist system driven by competitive interest. He was certain both that the contemporary Japanese bureaucracy was equipped to meet the requirements of scientific planning and that the dismal performance of political parties and capitalists resulted from "incoherent" relationships and fragmentation. To strengthen the capitalist system, he believed that a more specialized system of experts capable of regulating the "so-called financial capitalists, that is, oligarchic capitalists" had to be established. In a sense, Hasegawa was leaning toward a technocratically based fascism, similar to what was later developed by Miki. Hence, fascism became the special name for the ideology of worldly bourgeois autocrats, but that did not prevent Hasegawa from fearing the action of Japanese reactionaries who favored reconfiguring the original fascism of Italy, since they were troubled by misgivings about its formation in relation to Japanese society. The question he—Hasegawa—posed was how best could Japan's unique and exceptional circumstances accommodate the developmental processes of fascism. While this was a question that Miki later addressed, Hasegawa answered his own question by showing that Japan, with its favorable economic conditions of a medium-sized or small capitalist endowment, was the country closest to Italy in terms of economic experience. With this observation, he came close to describing Japan's developing capitalism as an instance of uneven development. He obviously saw this moment of medium- and low-level capitalism in Japan as a stage on the way to further development. But his immediate objective was to show that unevenness brought in its train some advantages that were unavailable to more mature forms of capitalism. This unstated observation implied that unevenness (manifested in medium- and low-level capitalism and marking not just late developers but the general circumstances that accompanied the adoption of capitalism) constituted reaching a stage under certain conditions in the general historical trajectory of capitalist development. What Hasegawa apparently ignored was any link to the idea of combined development, perhaps because that was too closely associated with Leon Trotsky or because it was already implied in the importation of capitalist procedures from abroad to work alongside older practices.

In a similar way, the Italian emphasis on the ideology of Romanness corresponded to the Japanese appeal to Emperor Jinmu's mythic founding of the state. What both countries shared was uneven economic development that drew its political authority from a fictive precapitalist past, as if to account for the deficit of lateness evident in the retention of remnants from prior modes of production to assure the present of both the continuity of a glorious past and a promising future. The historical problem may well have stemmed from the political and economic ambiguities of transformative events in Italy and Japan—specifically, that is, the change to Fascism in Italy and Japan's gradual drift toward the same solution arising from the incompletion of both the Risorgimento and the Meiji Restoration. Undoubtedly, the attempted inversion of past into present of the social reality that Hasegawa and other Japanese were living through in the early 1930s was an effort to alter the circumstances of the Depression. Japan's imperialist seizure of Manchuria in 1932 and the Depression (which led to the withdrawal of nations from international cooperation) opened the way to the formation of the fascist political imaginary. Moreover, Japan and Italy had a common political and cultural legacy that exemplified the Gramscian conception of passive revolution, which depended on the copresence of a remaindered premodern past that the state relied on to guide the present. Yet both countries confronted transformative events that showed the possibility of deadlock in the achieving of "restoration/revolution," thus risking slipping into a permanent impasse and showing the need to clarify that the transformations had not gone far enough. In Japan, the call for a Shōwa Restoration in the early 1930s signaled recognition that the Meiji legacy of unfinished business obliged the present to complete the unrealized ideals of the incomplete restoration and free the emperor from bureaucratic control. In Italy, the summoning of the grandiose figure of a Third Rome aimed to mobilize people for action in support of Mussolini's dictatorship.

Despite Japan's putative lateness compared to the capitalist countries of Western Europe and the United States, Hasegawa may well have misread the economic consequences of his time. He wrote that "while on one hand Japan attained rapid capitalist development, compared with the United States and the Chinese continent," on the other hand, in spite of Japan's success as a dominant capitalist productive system, its partially successful development was difficult to explain given the persistence of anticapitalism in the manufacturing sector and especially the unchecked "continuation of the characteristic cottage industries originating early in the Meiji period." Similarly the relations of property to tenant farmers often echoed earlier feudal practices. Hasegawa appeared to suggest that in societies with medium- or small-scale capitalism, when the productive system of capitalist semimanufacturing is compared to the failures of advanced capitalism that result from taking greater risks, fascism seems to appear in those circumstances where underdevelopment prevails.[27] But this view goes against the recorded experience of medium- and small-scale capitalisms that show they are scarcely affected by the downfall process that plague mature and high-scale capitalisms. Fascism constructs wall-like structures to protect medium- and small-scale capitalisms from failing and freezes the unevenness of the present, especially in those commercial and semimanufacturing processes that use hybrid modes of production. Frequently, these medium- and small-size capitalisms protect commerce and industry as a method of self-preservation, protecting themselves against the annihilation inflicted by large-scale capitalism. As a result, the smaller capitalisms are encouraged to enter into alignments with social democratic campaigns committed to rejecting the excessive liberalism identified with large-scale capitalism. Fascism is particularly opposed to liberalism's promotion of individualism and pursuit of absolute profiteering, financial absolutism, and so forth.[28] Here, Hasegawa praised common sense instead of philosophy and science in his approval of medium- and small-scale capitalisms like that of Japan, which seek to avoid the tyranny (bōrei) of large-scale capitalism, and he explained that it is for this reason that fascism successfully "gestates" in such places. It is hard to know from this passage whether he was expressing tentative admiration of fascism or criticizing it. However, in the face of the destruction of capitalism at the outset of the Depression, he appeared to compliment fascism because of its connection to medium- and small-scale capitalism. What may have explained his momentary sympathy was fascism's declared desire to save capital from itself, a move that seemed to have succeeded in the case of medium- and small-scale capitalisms. But it is also evident from his later texts, where he yokes the production of the Japanist ideology to Japan's uneven economic structure, that his view of fascism came to have a different hue.

To prevent development from moving toward the loftier levels of high capitalism, which would require taking on the risk of disturbing its international nature, medium- and small-scale capitalism would have to defend themselves by advocating forms of national regionalism (*kokkateki kakkyoshugi*). "The archaisms (*fukkoshugi*), like folkism (*minzokushugi*), nationalism, feudal ethicism (*hōken dōtokushugi*) and so forth" that accompanied medium- and small-scale capitalism in Japan were characterized by idealist attitudes based on the economic positions rooted in these forms of capitalism, which disclosed the "spirit of fascism." Here, it might be suggested, Hasegawa's understanding of the "spirit of fascism" fused with his view of the "Spirit of Japan," which he saw as an accumulated abstraction. While bordering on circularity, this explanation conformed to a rather crude theory of ideology employed by Marxism at the time, which was that ideology mirrored the economic and material conditions of its context. This was especially true of the lecture faction, whose members discounted the subjective nature of thought and ideology and saw the expression of thought as simply an instance of superstructural reflection.[29] The various archaisms, according to the lecture faction, were said to represent petit bourgeois perspectives on essentialisms that identified invented worlds, which usually looked backward to moments of imagined wholeness in a present wracked by socioeconomic fragmentation and a growing culture of lost hope. Hasegawa observed that while fascism opposed the materialism of early capitalism, at the level of medium- and small-scale enterprises, it professed to continue promoting the symbolic existence of such timeless figures as the deity (*kami*), the ancestral land (*sokoku*), and the folk and keeping alive among the people the relationship of archaism to the current economic situation. But if capitalism progresses to its monopolist stage of development, these symbolizations will be revealed as "abstract things." Yet the symbolizations of spiritual figures were already abstractions, even though they were supposed to represent immaterial cultural icons juxtaposed with the materiality of capitalism. In advanced capitalism they were employed completely consciously and cynically as expedient instruments of control. In effect, the attempt to deploy abstracted spiritualized cultural figures in the service of capital accumulation was not too different from the move to use the emperor to induce people to work and die for the country or Max Weber's linking of capitalism and Calvinist notions of a calling.

In 1930s Japan, fascism's strategy toward the processes of capitalism focused on getting an unsuspecting and unknowing middle class (which was by then a large group in Japan), to instinctively and unconsciously turn to a world of primitive beliefs and away from the materialism of consumption. In the Japanist ideology, this psychological campaign would lead to policies of installing in the present social relationships to a fictive communalism from the past as part of the larger effort to make the present into the past.

According to Hasegawa, there were probably many fascist intellectuals who consciously embraced and employed the mistaken ideas circulating among big capitalists that encouraged the acceptance of primitive beliefs and archaisms, but the ideas were still at the stage they only represented the articulation of key principles of a fascist formation yet to be organized. The symbolism of primitivity, popular among the "unenlightened middle class," was useful in recruiting members of the masses—especially petit bourgeois demanding order and farmers—which opened a way for fascism to become the ideology of the "unenlightened middle class," in which traditional ideas were deeply implanted. Pointing to the failure of bureaucracy to block the alignment between such a class and fascism, Hasegawa confessed "that the texture of Japan was conducive to the cultivation of fascism"[30] and that this made Japan a natural location for a fascist state. According to this extraordinary observation, the characteristics of Japanese thought made a natural couple with fascism—a view that was rejected by Miki, although Hasegawa, who later wrote copiously about Japan's characteristics, continued to hold it. Whether or not Hasegawa was right is an open question. But it is not the most pressing question, since it was liberalism rather than the traditional conservative and reactionary elements in Japanese society that ultimately offered the necessary accommodation to fascism. Yet Hasegawa may have been more wrong than right in overlooking the nature of capitalism in his account of the openness of medium- and small-size capitalism to fascism. Like many others, he attributed unevenness to lateness, which was less a problem than an uncertain grasp of capitalist logic as well as a convenient excuse. It should be stated that medium-and small-size capitalism contributed to the preservation of unevenness in its commitment to protecting and supporting the continuation of older, received practices, means of production, and even social relationships from the previous period. It was, I believe, this legacy that prompted the economist Yamada Moritarō to classify Japan as semifeudal and the working class as semi-serf. What Hasegawa also seemed to overlook were the facts that capitalism everywhere developed as a condition of producing uneven development (as if such unevenness were inevitable) and that the charge of lateness was as much an attribution of capital's own ideology in countries like the United States, England, and France as it was a description of societies in development that came chronologically later. Surviving remnants from the past are a problem that capitalism produces. In fact, it became the practice of advanced capitalism to classify latecomers as inferiors in a hierarchical relationship between advanced and underdeveloped countries, saddling the latter with the stigma of backwardness and the temporal task of catching up. Capitalism's capacity for uneven development reflects its way of strategically sacrificing some sectors for the advancement of others, a process that appears to have occurred even in those societies that have claimed advanced status and the completion of capitalism's development. Hasegawa's argument preceded a more thorough interpretation by the lecture faction, whose members proposed that Japanese capitalism had stalled and become a form of semifeudalism and political absolutism. Left liberals like Hasegawa also saw in Japan's incomplete capitalism evidence of a landscape cluttered with remnants from a prior mode of production. This is another illustration of political overlap, but this time the overlap is between Marxism and liberalism and is more multifaceted.

In a later text Hasegawa turned to the political problem of situating Japan among the world's nation-states, which by the 1930s began to witness the unwanted spectacle of increasing confrontations between states, and the inability of international organizations to constrain the antagonisms that were exacerbated by the emphasis on irreconcilable national differences. Here, he focused on the concurrent political and economic consequences produced by the conflict between the pressure for international cooperation and the demands of individual nation-states. This conflict paralleled that between mature high capitalism, which operated at a global level, and the national regionalism of medium- and low-scale capitalisms. At the heart of his analysis was his explanation of the appearance of a Japanist ideology—which was not part of Japan's long history, as its proponents claimed, but rather the ideology of an imagined reality that saw its content as real, inflected by contemporary world history but derived from the peculiar conflict-ridden history of the modern capitalist state. The absence of historicity in Hasegawa's analysis must be noted here, especially since its inclusion would have linked the development of capitalism in Japan to the Meiji Restoration.

The antagonism among states resulted from a system of production that was reflected in a particular political form, which in turn was necessitated by the conflict between demands of international cooperation and national interests, as well as by the present moment of world history and the specific history of national capitalisms. Because of this conflict, Hasegawa was convinced that the capitalist world had been splintered into many absolutist states, although it formed the possibility of attaining cooperation and unity. He believed that whatever unity Europe had known since the Roman Empire and the Middle Ages could be revived by the new system of independent states, which constituted an international order cemented by the communication and intercourse demanded by industrial development. While he was clearly referring to the unifying capacity of the world market, he was also convinced that the present moment was dominated by confrontation and collision among competing states and was thus more likely to foster a stronger feeling for one's home than to increase the likelihood of international cooperation. He portrayed an uncertain world order of capitalist nation-states in the process of withdrawing from one another, and starting in the early 1930s, this world was increasingly perceived as a dangerous place in which only the individual state could offer protection. In the 1920s, Japanese thinkers and writers had celebrated the benefits of cosmopolitan civilization and the harmonious chorus of humanity reflected in its member nations. It is worth noticing that Hasegawa recognized that in less than a decade, the state had become not only the principal subject of history and politics but also a form of a religion to be worshipped as an article of faith.[31]

In Hasegawa's view, the militarization of state structures demanded by isolated and absolutist states impeded the establishment of a genuine international unity and forced the states to revert to a "feudal, primitivistic" character centered on divided territorial states, even though modernity continued to embody revolutionary possibilities.[32] The development of international manufacturing helped emphasize the mechanization of production systems devoted to military armaments, thus serving nations rather than economies of personal consumption. Hasegawa readily acknowledged that the situation called for political strength capable of overcoming or finessing military demands, driven by the withdrawal of nation-states from international cooperation, putting the nation's interest above all other considerations and proceeding on its own. To offset this turnaround to nation-first policies, he proposed to offer a replacement system committed to peace rather than war. Such a system, he believed, would resemble the artisanal manufacturing process of the medieval guilds, which reflected localized forms of self-governing. Instead, the present had moved away from the sociopolitical model of a romanticized recovery of the Middle Ages and embraced the despotic authority of politics in the bourgeois state.

The bourgeois state remained a paradox for Hasegawa. On the one hand, he saw the modern state's response to "unpolitical free interventionism," created by the international system of manufacturing. Within these limits the bourgeois state had been able to establish an internal arrangement of order dedicated to trade and exchange. Yet on the other hand, he believed that the modern state promoted economic unity within traditional state-like territories or structures of free trade and was predisposed toward systems of unrestrained competition. An international arrangement of exchanges had evolved in the limiting system of collective independent states, whereby the exchanges denoted the international character of manufacturing, while the states viewed extreme autonomy as the principal unit of bourgeois competition. In time the juxtaposition of the universal and the particular produced an irresolvable contradiction, which (according to Karl Marx and Friedrich Engels in *The German Ideology*) the world market would universalize the particular (the political state) or the local would particularize the universal to lay the foundation for a world history not yet written. By the 1930s this contradiction had failed to materialize, and the world seemed to be heading toward separation, conflict, and another world war. It is not clear whether Hasegawa thought that the contradiction between individual states' interests and the desire for an international order represented the failure to achieve some expected ideal or whether he recognized in the contradiction a weakness that could be addressed and overcome. What he did not fully see in the spectacle of an environment wracked by vast contradictions was where he stood (and by implication where we stand) in relation to the concrete social reality of the time. While he probably assumed that it would be possible to develop some larger conception of society, he would or could not acknowledge that it was impossible to expect such a development at the time. Even so, as a liberal, he must have known that in the end all social facticity is invariably determined and shaped by society. Moreover, he understood the contradictory conflict between the contemporary world and one's home as a natural phenomenon, and he overlooked the generalized contradictions seen by others that worked to naturalize the prospect of war.[33] Hasegawa emphasized only the economic trajectory of capitalism without considering its related social corollaries, which included the narrative of the lived class struggle and people's efforts to alter contemporary circumstances. He had not yet succumbed to spiritualizing the material, in the manner of contemporary

Japanists, or occluding the material altogether as the content of social life. It also true that in the Japan of the 1930s, the spiritualizing of the material was performed by a number of people who were not Japanists but had other political and intellectual orientations.

Ultimately, the existing form of international union failed to prevent the collapse caused by state conflict in the world of capitalism, just as natural law proved ineffective in managing states driven by individualistic economic systems. Hasegawa compared the failure of internationalism (especially the inability of the League of Nations to prevent Japan's war with China) to that of the Holy Alliance (which had not succeeded in preventing the fragmentation of a larger international unity into emerging absolutist states).[34] Throughout his discussion of the widening gulfs among nation-states and the weakening of international organizations, Hasegawa kept returning to the argument that the problem was not the forms of the nation-states, as such, but rather the conflict and antagonism stemming from the forms of manufacturing required materials, the creation of markets, and the competition resulting from the assumed need for colonies.

Hasegawa recognized that the real problem was making the unit of states the basis of the international system of trust. However, he did not realize that the association between states and international systems in the world of capitalism did not constitute an "organic relationship" (like that of a part to the whole), a lesson he could have drawn from the collapse of the cosmopolitan ideal of humanity in the 1920s and Japan's involvement in that collapse. He did note that states like Japan, which claim unique conditions and requirements, are the first to go beyond whatever agreements they might have made with other states within the framework of international order. Japan was able to plead that its capitalism suffered from having been developed late and being of a medium or low scale, and that the country, still filled with scattered feudal remnants from the past, was forced to rely on the development of small enterprises, cottage operations, low wages, apprentice-style labor, and other survivals from an earlier mode of production. In other words, the persisting remnants introduced unique conditions that impaired the development of capitalist operations in areas where the past continued to undermine the making of profit for further reinvestment and expansion. Hasegawa insisted that these unique conditions represented an early stage in the developmental process of capitalism in Japan and that the requirements of its medium- and small-scale capitalist endowment had special needs reflecting these historical circumstances. Complicating matters, European nations could acquire colonies, which raised the unwelcome prospect of additional barriers to Japanese productivity. Absent in Hasegawa's thinking, however, was any reference to the relationship between imperialist adventures leading to colonization and the forms of massive dispossession of the conquered and sustained expropriation—a relationship that, by 1935, when Tosaka published his book on the Japanist ideology, had been acknowledged by a number of political and intellectual groups. Yet Hasegawa rejected the arguments made in Japanese pleas for special treatment. On the one hand, he realized that states like Japan acted with the international cooperation of imperialist countries, and on the other hand, he noted Japan's tendency toward tribal territorialism and regionalism.[35] Japan's actions reflected its effort to reach a higher stage of capitalism, while its tendency seemed to be a throwback to an earlier form of agrarian regionalism, which had led to its present desire to expand agricultural production. Agricultural-based regionalism belonged to the late nineteenth and early twentieth centuries, and it had been overcome by the drive to achieve the stage of high capitalism that could no longer be realized. This situation led to a series of contradictions among the quest for high or advanced capitalism, international cooperation, exclusionary internationalism, and the pressures exerted by statism and nationalism (including the inconsistencies produced by the retention of feudal residues). The principal contradiction between internationalism and nationalism was formal and internal to high capitalism, while the matter of feudal residues was based on the unique conditions of Japan's transforming capitalism. This entailed both the distinctive features of class that "reflected feudal components that remained (fixed) in the industrial system" and the requirements of political forms that represented its superstructure, the structure of state machinery, and so forth. Hasegawa was persuaded that it would be difficult to disregard movements only because of their unsuitability to defend one's household with the state machinery. Because a highly developed and advanced capitalism would still require political strength in the context of an unevenly developed Japanese political economy, it would risk losing the distinctions from the Western legal experience that characterize modern tendencies in law, morality, and religion. The result would be an atavistic reversal and a return to a naturalized medieval spirit.[36] Hasegawa observed that in Japan, not only did capitalism exist alongside feudal remnants, but capitalism could not overlook these remnants and indeed often deliberately supported their survival by putting them to use in service of its own productive process. Here, I believe that both Hasegawa and the Marxists misunderstood the nature of the remnants under capitalism and the unevenness they signified. In fact, not all of the remnants were useless, but the peculiar politics of the remnant promoted by the lecture faction seemed to conceal this point. In the 1930s, examples could still be found of precapitalist economic practices mixed with newer techniques and put to work for capitalism, which was exactly the "uneven and combined" development designated by Marx. Exploitation from precapitalist modes of production could still be carried out in the service of the capitalist economy without undergoing much change. As Marx wrote in *Grundrisse* (which was not available in Japanese at this time), "capital takes what it needs and can use." Village economies were not immediately broken up when the Meiji era began its drive toward economic growth, but were encouraged to retain their cottage industries and keep people on the land until large-scale industries could begin to absorb their inhabitants for labor. In Okinawa, older property relationships were reinvented to maintain the production of sugar until the colonization of Formosa (now Taiwan) in 1895 and the establishment of a more modern and technological system of production. In Okinawa and the countryside of the main islands, Korean colonial laborers were imported to work in rural areas under the most extreme forms of exploitation, just as women in Okinawa were forced to assume responsibility for cultivating the fields when the men were sent to the Pacific Islands to work in extractive mining.[37] Yet it is also true that a good part of the countryside continued to use feudal forms of land tenancy until after World War II. Focusing on the problem raised by a landscape strewn with remnants from the feudal past, Hasegawa complained that the bourgeoisie in Japan would not be able to overcome the stubborn lingering of feudal political forms, yet acknowledged that it was a task that had to be faced and eventually achieved along the road leading to a higher level of capitalist development. Starting late, Japan had been unable to complete such tasks as dissolving the capitalist state's several guild-like organizations (except for the military), fearing that it would not be possible to escape being drawn into feudal ways of thinking in the course of dealing with practices that reflected feudal attitudes. In other words, the responses to the demands of the new frequently involved relying on the old—which in some cases, but not all, might lead to new configurations and combinations.

Here, Hasegawa seems to have been troubled by the presence of barriers posed by feudal remnants, which seemed to be evidence of the permanent incompletion of Japanese capitalist modernization—a view favored by contemporary Marxists like Tosaka. But the remnants that Hasegawa believed might interfere with the development of capitalism could in fact be used by being subsumed to capital's productive agenda. Old practices could coexist alongside new innovations produced by capitalism or joined to them in such a way as to produce combinations that could facilitate the continuing reproduction of uneven development. This was the economic counterpart of the political route followed in a passive revolution (which is how I understand the Meiji Restoration)—in which elements of a precapitalist or feudal past are used to create a new arrangement of political order and authority. Hasegawa was also implying that the state and those empowered to rule could not or had not entirely rid themselves of feudal attitudes. Still, the backward drift toward fascism was explained not by the retention of feudal elements alone but by a combination of capitalism, the persistence of surviving remnants, and a religio-mythic ideology centered on an archaic origin that had never existed (along with its contemporary embodiment in the allegedly divinely descended emperor).

Hasegawa observed that the unique character of Japan's medium- and low-scale capitalism would distort the development of imperialism in two ways: it would focus on the development of social forms of agrarian economy, and it would risk undermining any nationalism founded on an ideology of such capitalism. It seems that here Hasegawa was arguing that capitalism had to be founded on the expansion of the manufacturing sector and the formation of an urban industrial working class, and that a putative capitalism based on agriculture would not lead to a proper modern nationalism. He argued that the first way would convey an old feudal idea, while the second would reflect the contradictions of capitalism and the uncertain relationship between industry and agriculture. Furthermore, the first way would have to juxtapose a singular, anarchic, small country–ism (Japanism) to a capitalism based on a general bourgeois rejection of commercialism, advocacy of urban centrism, centralization of power, internationalism, and so forth. That way corresponded more closely to championing all the things its opposite had rejected (in other words, Japanism advocated everything that capitalism rejected, even though it was not anticapitalistic). The differences produced between two opposing contradictions were found in a capitalism that followed its international impulse, as opposed to reversing course and echoing the Tokugawa policy of seclusion, although now Japan was clearly linked to the rest of the world. Advocates of reversing course called for Japan to have self-support and self-sufficiency, separating its nationalist capitalism from the larger arena of international regulations—and presumably from the world market, placing it under supervision of medium and small capitalist institutions. Hasegawa recognized a possible difficulty: concentrating on the internal aspirations of the capitalist system while failing to develop a viable rational means of protecting the system from collapse. In their zeal to eject capitalism, the agrarianists (*nōhonshugisha*) pursued a utopianism based on the human spirit and action. Nationalism, under the flag of anticapitalism, proposed changing the masters of capitalism, an impossible plan that aimed to make capital more secure by reducing its scale. Hasegawa maintained that all nationalism would lead to was more anticapitalism, even though nationalists did not intend to interfere with the operation of capital. In short, political motives would dominate national interest and confine Japan's economic development to the level of medium-low-scale capitalism, which rejected international cooperation and unity and favored the agricultural sector.

At this juncture in Hasegawa's account of the conflict between the two perspectives on capitalism in Japan, he turned to the question of Japanism. Convinced that the two perspectives were the principal pillars of the capitalist empire that was at the point of confrontation between a philosophy of scientific politics and action and the imminent collapse of capitalism under the threat of an agrarian-based anticapitalism, he recognized that contemporary anticapitalists were responsible for fostering the recent upsurge of Japanism.[38] It is difficult to know whether the defenders of the scientifically rational position included more than a handful of high-ranking politicians or bureaucrats and people with business interests, but it is clear that those who rejected the bourgeois ideology represented a larger and more populist group of farmers of all sorts, large numbers of petit bourgeois constituencies like small shop keepers and office and service workers fearing disorder and the imminent collapse of the socioeconomic edifice and workers' lives. The main reason for their attraction to Japanism was that their ideological representations were steeped in virulent forms of organic nationalism sanctioned by tropes that in turn recruited from the mystical arsenal of mythical history and could easily be aligned with fascism. At its heart was a pervasive agrarianism that still resonated with the political culture of the precapitalist past. What most distinguished the anticapitalist perspective from its internationalist adversaries was the awareness that Japan in the early 1930s was experiencing the unevenness of a temporal divide (contemporaneous noncontemporaneity), with a large part of the population living in conditions that were still close to those of the prior age in spite of the presence of different presents. Yet it was precisely the no-time of the mythic tropes that recalled an origin of state foundation, embodied in the "Spirit of Japan," that convinced people to believe that they could overcome the temporal divisions forced on them by their present and instead inhabit a divine and timeless order free of discord and travail. Here, it seems to me, is the perfect example of the working of ideology, whereby the solution to a disquieting social reality in an everyday present is projected into its reverse in an indeterminate but undisturbed past that has been summoned to replace the troubled present. But the inversion does not apply to the real conditions of people's existence, only to an illusion of them—an ideology, quoting Louis Althusser, representing "necessarily (an) imaginary distortion . . . [between] the relations of production and the relations deriving from them."[39] Hence, what is inverted are the real conditions of existence that are embedded in production, exploitation, and repression (in fact, in the division of labor itself)— the real relations that constitute people's lives but in an imagined relation to them. Japanism sought to transport Japan and its inhabitants into a precapitalist mythic realm by claiming a timelessness presided over by the emperor (who already claimed immunity from the ravages of time) and near to the national deities. In this timelessness, there was no differentiation between work and worship, which was materially expressed in devotion to the gods and ancestors who had blessed the Japanese. Ideology thus fosters the illusion of disidentification—in the case of Japan, seeking to remove agents of conflict by remaking all classes as Japanese or, in the wording of the native ethnographer Yanagita Kunio, *jomin* (ordinary people). In Japanism, we see the tropes and story line of the Meiji Restoration proclamation reallegorized and reconfigured to meet the exigencies of the moment (the crisis of capitalism, to use a term from the interwar years).

But Hasegawa explained the worldly character of Japanism by using a passage from the writings of Houston Stewart Chamberlain.[40] What interested Hasegawa was Chamberlain's assertion that since "Roman times the state had functioned as a religion and for the Jews, religion was the state. But even today, when soldiers rush into the battleground crying out it is for religion, that is the state."[41] Hasegawa pointed out the religious power of Japanism and its capacity to appeal to a wider population than the petit bourgeoisie. Japanism was able to draw on the resources of Japan's archaic cultural origins—like the first so-called histories and the story of the divine origins of the islands—as well as both the obligation to repay such blessings (through reproduction by cultivating the land) and the fact that Japan was the first country to have received the "spirit of language (*kotodama*)." As implied by Chamberlain's statement, the tendency for culture and religion to connect makes Japanism a civil religion, more committed to maintaining social solidarity than to upholding strictly religious observances. Yet as it could be argued (and was by Kobayashi Hideo), it was the gift of language inscribed in poetry and early imperial proclamations that unified the Japanese with their natural environment—that is, with nature itself. Hasegawa saw Japanism (not the "Japanism of other countries") in other countries around the world, not just in island countries of the "Orient." Japanism was not just a reality of history but a product of world history, which could be explained from the formula of the history of the capitalist state. Here, Hasegawa was referring to the formation of bourgeois states and the contradictions between the nongovernmental development of the international character of manufacturing, mediated by noninterventionism, and the sovereign nation territorial state-like limits that were not bound to the international developmental order. He compared the modern state system with its Roman and medieval predecessors to show how the predecessors had avoided such strong contradictions, while the modern system had become entangled in them.[42] He saw a profound difference between a time in which single isolated states formed their economic systems according to their own needs and the era in which an international system developed and mechanized the system of production, which entailed manufacturing for international economic life rather than producing for the economic life of a single state.[43]

According to Hasegawa, all of what appeared to be an anticapitalist shell (a term used to refer to the trend toward a greater emphasis on the thought and action of scientific politics) reflected the response to treat Japanism reasonably, which meant rationally. After all, it was a fact that Japanism was a modern phenomenon with no connection to archaic exemplars, even if it often employed their authority. The ideology of Japanism appeared in a more or less completed form in the early 1930s. It was already seen by critics like Hasegawa and others as a principal force opposing the development of a mature internationalist capitalism and capable of speaking for all the groups that advocated returning to medium- and small-scale nationalist capitalism and its temporal unevenness that combined remnants of the feudal past with the new operations of capitalism—thus reproducing the temporal structure of contemporary noncontemporaneity initiated by the Meiji Restoration. Japanism immediately showed its indebtedness to and the strength of a reservoir of tropes provided by the restoration's proclamation in its determination to bypass Motoori's interpretation of the godly way, a religious imperative allegedly transmitted from the origin. This meant that it was not the same ideology envisioned in Motoori's understanding of the "way of the gods," even though it (like the restoration proclamation) clearly implied such a relationship and its late feudal heritage.[44] In Hasegawa's reckoning, the temporality of a Japanism from the feudal period (nativism) differed in class composition from its modern avatar, which meant that thinkers like Moto-ori and the nativist scholar Hirata Atsutane were addressing samurai and merchants as well as artisans and village leaders from a lower social stratum. But for Japanism to appeal to a wider audience, it was necessary to dilute all the extreme limitations and exclusivity of earlier nativist thinkers. In contrast to the earlier views, Japanism had paradoxically sought to attract support from a broad array of social groups, including self-governing agrarianists, anarchists, autocratic types, and fascists. Its success in recruiting such a mixed bag of supporters was attributable to its ability to avoid being too closely tied to fixed rules of action, standards of life, or even principles.

Leslie Pincus has explained that Hasegawa "identified the cultural means by which the dominant classes in Japan endeavored to link the interests of subordinate classes to their own." She is right to point out that under the regime of uneven development the Japanese bourgeoisie had already incorporated "bourgeois forms of social and cultural life" into Japan's society and appeared to have no direct relationship to persisting feudal legacies, in contrast to the petit bourgeoisie, farmers, and even working classes.[45] But at the same time (and even before Hasegawa published his critical texts on fascism), Japanese artists and writers had begun to appropriate older forms of expression capable of conjuring up images of a discarded past now put to work in the present to invite Japanese to see their true selves. These older cultural forms (embraced by the bourgeoisie) produced a compensatory nostalgia for the immense cultural loss by revisiting those sites in the past that were increasingly identified with the essence of a vanishing identity. Pincus suggests that while Hasegawa saw "sterile forms and superseded forms" as significations of "reactionary nostalgia," the petit bourgeoisie saw them as promising an escape from disorder and a reified everydayness—an escape that only the return to an indeterminate moment in a distant past could achieve because it ensured a return to home and belonging.[46] Yet members of both the elite and lower classes supposedly could see themselves in these simulacra of forms, emptied of their lived history, which indicated that Japanese were already leading the double lives envisioned by Watsuji: they were accepting the contradiction of noncontemporary synchronicity as if it was compatible with everyday life in Japan. But it was not, and we must consider Watsuji's conception of a double life as merely an attempt to head off possible conflict between the subaltern and ruling classes by recognizing as the status quo the equivalence of traditional or customary social life and the new bourgeois version. What seemed to be at stake was how to assimilate the claims of customary social life lived by the subaltern masses before they became a dangerous challenge to the established political leadership. Hasegawa was quick to insist that Japan was not a feudal society but a bourgeois one.[47] He also insisted that the society confronting artists in his present "was not a feudal structure whose immediacy remained in contemporary Japan," but rather one that had been "completely bourgeois-ized, a society that followed the several forms of advanced bourgeois culture on the surface and formally . . . it was a Japanese life produced from the surface-like composition of bourgeois society and Japanese who lived within a superficial bourgeois culture."[48] Nonetheless, the society was still not feudal. But this did not mean that feudal residues had disappeared with capitalist modernity and were absent: in fact, they existed throughout the nascent manufacturing enterprises of 1930s Japan. But bourgeois culture fantasized a hybrid existence that sanctioned the simultaneous coexistence of "being dazzled by neon signs and dreaming of the hand lamps of feudal times."[49] This is what I believe to be Hasegawa's most important observation, which called attention to the contemporization of noncontemporaneity in the everyday, signaling the temporal dominant of Japanese life under the regime of uneven and combined development. Here, the remnant, which Marxists had viewed as the insurmountable barrier to capitalism's completion, exemplified the functional instantiation of formal subsumption, whereby residues of the past are appropriated and reconfigured to serve a different present. In fact, this was the principal role played by Japanism and its arsenal of tropes signifying the origins of Japanese culture, which would be the authorizing resource and image for all subsequent historical reminders that art and culture might recall. Pincus suggests that Hasegawa was convinced that fascism (which, I might add, he identified with Japanism above all) fed off such remnants as they were inscribed in the interstices of a bourgeoisized society. But in fascism, the temporal order of contemporizing the past was inverted to the noncontemporization of the present. It is important to notice that this hegemonization of bourgeois culture both recalls Gramsci's conception of how passive revolutions open the way for culture to redefine the political and lead away from liberalism to fascism and suggests the extent to which Japan in the 1930s mirrored the Italian example.

Despite Hasegawa's optimism about the benign, contentless character and wide popularity of Japanism, two years after his article was published, official discussions were inaugurated to consider methods "for rehabilitating thought criminals throughout the empire." Former socialists like Akamatsu Katsumaro began to warn against the persistence of "dangerous thoughts," referring especially to communism and to liberal education's emphasis on individualism that had spawned ideologies that must be countered by a "third ideology" like Japanism.[50] The sociologist Takata Yasuma had already formulated what he called his conception of a "third history" that would overcome the weaknesses of both materialism and idealism, and by the 1930s he had become a strong advocate of a Japanist social science aimed at emphasizing the special characteristics of Japaneseness and countering the injuries inflicted by what was believed an exaggerated and mistaken acceptance of class as a primary category of social organization and productive social relations as viable principles of social determinacy. Like many of his contemporaries, Takata sought to replace class with the category of the folk, a task he considered the proper vocation of social science. In 1932, Tsukui Tatsuo, his contemporary and a fellow sociologist who was well acquainted with Italian fascism, called the Japanese national body the classic archetype of concreteness. He proposed the "annihilation of the anti-Japan character of capitalism and statism" and advocated proclaiming that "the emperor for the Japanese is the beginning and end. Without exception, if the emperor is thrown out, there must be his (immediate) return."[51] In short, existence for the Japanese was impossible without the emperor. Yet already in the early 1930s, Tosaka was publishing the essays that would become *Nihon ideorogiron* [The Japan ideology], which would systematically dismantle the Japanist credo in its many manifestations.

Hasegawa clearly failed to appreciate the dangers of Japanism and minimized its toxic nature, since he was persuaded that this nature was not worthy of serious attention, given that its content was unbelievable and even absurd. Perhaps in those early days of Japanism, he could not yet anticipate that it would have a threatening future. This discounting of the content of Japanism as trivial reappeared later in dismissals of the ideology put forth in the "Overcoming the Modern" symposium of 1942, which advised that Japan was too reliant on Western conceptions of modernity and the time was ripe to overcome this dependence for a more Japanese conception of the modern, even though a great many young men, according to a later account by Takeuchi Yoshimi, went to their death because of them. It might be argued that Japanism's lack of a viable content, cobbled together from archaic religious tropes and cliches, made it dangerous. Most Marxists of the time shared this distrust of ideology and expressions of subjective consciousness, relying on the rejection of ideology by the Comintern and Second International, which explicitly attributed ideology to suspect subjective superstructural impulses that automatically reflected the base's material interests. Hasegawa was snared in the privilege accorded to economistic explanations. Unlike Japanists such as Tsukui and Takata, Hasegawa may well have discounted the important advocacy of a new foundation for Japan—which may not have led to the creation of a new man and woman, as Giovanni Gentile proclaimed had happened in Italy. But in Kita Ikki's program, a new order was seen to transform the folk into a new Japanese, now assigned as direct partners with the emperor in the reconstruction of the archipelago.[52] This idea of a mobilized populace directly aligned with the emperor dated back to the Meiji Restoration and Saigō Takamori's ill-fated attempt to change the course on which the new state was embarking. Such a move, according to Dylan Riley in his study of European fascism, was more about the identity of social relationships than about property and the redistribution of wealth.[53] But in the end no strategy for overhauling Japanese society appeared; the roles of the ruling classes and bureaucracy were only reinforced. Hence, the ideology of Japanism was more material and practical than just some evanescent set of reflections of the economic infrastructure and could claim that revolutionary change was coming—even though, like all populist-inspired promises, it merely replicated the system of political power at hand that it had pledged to replace. Hasegawa was more committed to showing the role played by the several forms of capitalism and the conflict between inter nationalist and nationalist strategies of development—which, he would come to believe, brought Japan to war—than he was to the promises of a jingoistic Japanism that look backward to an indeterminate past to guide the present.

Japanist fascism brought attention to the importance of the archaic and uneven temporalities that appeared to be crowding and filling the present. This was precisely what Bloch, commenting on Nazism in the 1930s, identified as the surfacing of the specter of the nonsynchronous and what Tosaka renamed "primitivism." Bloch saw in the relationship between the formation of the Nazi movement and the Nazis' successful manipulation of the surviving remnants from the past what he called contemporary nonsynchronicities. He observed that "not all people live in the same now. They do so only externally, through the fact they can be seen today. But they are thereby not yet living at the same time with the others."[54] The remnants contain an earlier element, and when they collide with a different present, this element invariably interferes by promising a new life in the untimely zone although it "hauls up what is old." Bloch was convinced that Germany's masses "streamed toward it" to get out of a contemporary present that seemed intolerable to them. According to him, Germany was more modern than atavistically traditional, since most people had been socialized into the social relations of production and recognized the centrality of capitalism's organization of the economy. In this regard, the struggle ignited by a crisis was between capital and the bourgeoisie on one side and labor and the proletariat on the other side, and it was about the consequences and demands of modernization and how the contemporary present should be constituted. The struggle revealed concerns about everyday life, which was being left behind by the failure of capitalism to fulfill the aspirations of the present and change its course.

In the 1930s, Japanese thinkers like Hasegawa and Tosaka were already aware of the growing divisions within the social order brought about by capitalist modernization and exacerbated by the Depression, and of the increasingly severe plight of the folk and the residues of the past persisting in the present that were symptomatic of contemporary noncontemporaneity. These factors made it easy for such thinkers to see in Japan's turn to fascism a kinship with the contemporary German experience. But Japan's march toward capitalist modernization had started later than Germany's, and because Japan's capitalism was medium- and small-size, there were still large areas of the country where labor had not yet been brought into capitalism. A comparison of the two experiences of capitalist development would show that Japan was not simply chronologically later than Germany but also that Japan's adaptation to capitalism was more condensed and selective. This left many regions more or less outside capitalism's orbit even in the 1930s, leading to a collision between unchanging custom (the timeless) and the time of the workday and its demands. Added to this was the question of how much change Japanese were obliged to experience in a short period of time. The interwar period was filled with sweeping changes in the style of life, such as the transformation of the cities into modern environments with all the conveniences of modern living made possible by capitalist consumer commodities as well as the changes in social relationships demanded by the relations of production.[55] In the countryside, changes came more slowly. But it was the countryside that was considered the repository of traditional cultural values that were still actively observed (in particular, the religious beliefs centered on Shinto), and it was there that organic (folk) nationalism and fascism were most tightly connected.

Throughout the interwar period, critics regularly expressed anxiety about the effects of Japan's multiple cultural imports from the West on people's lives, which remained embedded in the practices of a received native culture. Moreover, the growing critique of foreign thought, which Ōkawa described as a form of mental colonization, was early recognized by the state, which responded by rounding up Communists, Marxists, socialists, and even liberals and subjecting them to an often grueling process of recanting their beliefs—which led to their confessions of (tenkō) conversion, which usually demanded the rejection of modern Western ideas and conceptions of life for the return to more nativist Japanese forms as a necessary step in following the ideological imperative to return to Japan. Unlike Germany, Japan did not follow a path to contemporary nonsynchronisms. Instead, because of the concentration, selectivity, and compressed duration of its development, Japan remained closer to its noncapitalist past, as evidenced everywhere in the persistence of remnants, beginning with the restoration of the emperor. Many critics of the fractured cultural scene in 1930s Japan addressed the problem of mixed temporalities. The difference between Japan and Germany was reflected in their respective fascisms: In Germany, the "mythical enchantment of the soil" was not sufficiently "archaic to recall . . . archaic conditions, communal property or common land,"[56] whereas in Japan the valorization of gemeinschaft and traditional village structure and life was a staple among Japanist social scientists like Takata and others who claimed personal familiarity with village life. In Japan some thinkers complained about the sacrifices made by people in the Japanese countryside for the development of the cities in the late 1920s, but there was nothing like the intense estrangement between Berlin and the countryside in Germany and the desire for the Heimat (homeland) and a sense of belonging to it. The plaintive call for "a return to Japan" was the Japanese analog to the German quest for belonging, but this call probably occurred more often among intellectuals and culturalists (bunjin) than among ordinary Japanese.

Despite its promotion of "one country-ism," Japanism was opposed to internationalism in name only. But the idea of a Japan-first "one country-ism" did not necessarily clarify its content. Japanism appeared to be a coherent enough doctrine whose content consisted of archaism and myth, but its point was to make it seem to be and say all things to all people. For writers like Hasegawa, it resembled a vague declaration of support for cultural myths. The reliability of the textual evidence for this supports that this was assembled by the Shrine Department of Compilation under the title *Kokutaironshi* (A history of the development of the national body). Because the creation of the book was entrusted to a ministry department, scholars were confident that the work was a history of the evolving content of Japanism. However, they had reservations about its accuracy.[57] (In fact, the history resembled the narratives constructed by Hirata Atsutane in the nineteenth century.) The *Kokutaironshi* used terms from the materials and diverse claims found in histories from the eighth century, which were largely taken as holy writ, yet despite the similarity in content, the book's message was quite different from that of the histories—as of course were its audience and time. The book focused on the announcement in the *Nihonshōki* (Chronicles of early Japan) that "there is the land of the gods in the east and it is called Nihon." After the appearance of this announcement in the book, the intellectual content of Japanism never strayed from the claims that Japan is the land of the gods and the country is their divine creation. The single purpose of the *Kokutaironshi* was to clarify Japanism through the use of that announcement, and the text concluded with the present time, asserting that the fundamental character of the country since antiquity had remained contemporary and unchanging: "Japan's antiquity comprised of the Great Eight Islands, called Oyamato, . . . a country of . . . self-sufficiency . . . one of agriculture, reed plains, a land of abundant rice."[58] Nothing fundamental had changed since these origins, making antiquity identical to the present and closing the vast temporal gap between the past and the present. This move of imposing the past on the present undoubtedly implied the existence of the historical—which, as in the restoration proclamation, meant going back to the origin to restart history. According to the book, which was produced in an industrializing society, Japan remained rooted in the soil, supported by a false consciousness that mythologized an identity that was first disclosed and never changed after that. This world of ancient forms has no place for class but only an imagined timeless community and nature unconnected to urban life, a sort of native exoticism: "Foreigners have called [Japan] . . . the 'land of the gods,' the 'ancestral country,' the 'country of rites and rituals,' the 'country of true gentlemen,' and so forth. The principal authority of this country is the emperor, proclaimed as a descendant of the sun goddess, as well as in the words of Jinmu *tennō*, the first human emperor, since he was a grandson of Amaterasu *ōmikami*, he was an *arahitogami*, a visible deity or living god, that is, the emperor. The way of the gods is following the traces made by the gods. Formally speaking, since Japanese are descendants of the gods, it can be said that they learn the speech and conduct of the ancestral gods."

The text declares itself to be the newest expression of "Japanist thought" for the twentieth century, even though it scarcely changed the wording from its most primitive sources and proclaimed that nothing had changed since the time of origins. The text is no more than an abbreviated version of the classic nativist expressions, cobbled together by scholars of dubious reliability—such as the Shinto legalist Kakehi Katsuhiko, who was noted for supplying religious myths to bolster the foundation of political fascism.[59] Kakehi was apparently an enthusiastic supporter of Japanism and endorser of the *Kokutaironshi*. According to him, "the basis of our national body (*kokutai*) illuminates all things as expressions of (the great living spirit of heaven and earth and the most deep and true feelings). Amaterasu ōmikami of the world confirms the ideal of eternality of Takamagahara [the plain of high heaven] by making primary this Japanese spirit; it becomes the spirit that over the ages realizes this ideal of the skills in Japan of the heavenly descendants." Then there was Anesaki Masaharu, a distinguished scholar of religions who refrained from relying on the "words of deformed people" quick to jump into "strange dancing" and "hand clapping on shrine platforms." He cautioned that the substance or essence of the national body was not the eternality of the heavens and earth or the imperial lineage of ten thousand generations. Rather, the true essence of the national body is based on Amaterasu's governance of Takamagahara and the transmission of its great virtue to Japan and the goddess's imperial descendants. Anesaki advised that if virtue resulting from the growth of heaven and earth is practiced, the dignity of heavenly rule becomes expressed in the divine character of the supporting heavenly deities, which is the basis of the national body: the gods make Takamagahara appear among "those who reside in this heavenly place and bestow this sacred virtue on them to guide the conduct of affairs in the present that become the activities of the human world"—that is, "the descent of heavenly descendants. It advanced to become the founding of the state by Jinmu *tennō*."[60]

According to Hasegawa, there were large similarities and few differences between these writers and the army of other scholars concerned with defining the national body as anchored in the eternality of its archaic precedent. In 1937, the narrative was repeated in the officially compiled and issued *Kokutai no hongi*. Hasegawa was concerned to show that such rhetoric was not only characterized by its repetitive enunciations but also to point out its emptiness, specifically the absence of any substantive content apart from the endless reiteration of the religio-mythic cadences of the archaic past in the twentieth-century present. Like his contemporary Tosaka, Hasegawa saw the archaic as simply the transmission of a legendary explanation of a primitivistic land called the country of gods—that is, the putative divine origins of what came to be known as Japan. As an origin narrative, it was cast as an explanation of the creation of the world and was compared to the American practice of teaching the Bible's version of creation in the public schools—until the Scopes trial of 1925 questioned the veracity of that version, which was promoted by evangelical churches. The Scopes trial was a reflection of the widening gap between rural and urban society, and the defense of creationism was in part a stand against the withering of small-town America in an era of industrialization and secularization in the cities. Hasegawa, perhaps mistakenly, discerned in the American teaching of creationism a narrative similar to the circulation of the myth of Japan as the land of the gods, which was at the heart of Japan's origins. In both cases, he proclaimed, there was no long development or history, as such, nor could it qualify as genuine thought (shisō). He argued that since the narrative of the land of the gods showed no sign of historical development or thought process it was only a "legendary, primitivistic belief."[61] For this reason, Japanism was able to dogmatize a "single country absolutism" that could encompass anarchism, national socialism, fascism, proletarianism, and other ideologies.

The idea of Japan first, a unified, single-country absolutism, one that often sought to identify the nation-state as a single family, does not mean that the rural-urban division in Japan disappeared: instead, it remained as the source of tensions that were ready to explode under certain circumstances. In 1929, Yanagita Kunio published his classic work on the city and countryside in Japan, in which he lamented the great sacrifices inflicted on rural Japan in favor of augmenting urban industrial growth. While Japanism may have resonated with this and other accounts of such disparities, its ambitious exceptionalist claims of divinity for the whole nation in contrast to all other nations at a dangerous time in world history, the specter of national withdrawal, and the appearance of political totalisms exceeded the limits of the rural-urban divide. With no specific content apart from its repeated retelling of the story of national origins, Japanism made itself available to any political perspective capable of attributing its particular program to the beginnings of the country. In this sense, Japanese became a sort of empty signifier into which virtually anything could be poured. The fact that it was nothing more than form was recognized early by the enthusiasts of a political party whose enhanced name (Dai Nipponshugi) added to the ideographs for Japanism (Nihonshugi) the ideograph for great (dai), indicating that it was either the Greater Japanism Party or the Great Japanism Party. The name thus implied the party's breadth of coverage and appeal. Hasegawa ironically commented that only a political party would add *dai* to *Nipponshugi* to indicate the principal spirit of its general plan. But he also recognized that although many Japanists hesitated to call themselves by that name, many of them favored "reject[ing] the old thought of a dependent Japan." He wondered where the intellectual origins of Japanism were to be found:

"As for our national body, since its beginnings it has been organized on [the basis of] one body, not two between spirit and things, that is, ethics and economics. This model is illustrated in the Ise Shrine (*taibyō*)."[62] The inner shrine symbolizes divine spiritual miracles, the outer shrine material revelations; Amaterasu of the inner shrine is the manifestation of fairness and justice (*kōmyō seidai*), Toyouke ōmikami of the outer shrine, [the manifestation of] national events, [the] maintenance of value, the manifest god of production who creates (generates) and grows all things in the national territory. The two shrines show that . . . spirit and matter should not be considered as separate, just as morality and ethics are indivisible and Ise is one shrine. It is said that this is what realistically instructs the system of the national body.[63]

While Hasegawa was well versed in the textual bases of the Japanist credo and how it was able to mask or even displace the problems of contemporary capitalist production by focusing on the creation by the deity Toyouke ōmikami of all things of cultivation and growth, it must have been difficult for him to conceal his disbelief and his fear of the damage this kind of mythic tale was capable of wreaking in the conditions of the time. The tale diminished both history and human labor, as it recalled in the 1930s the precapitalist world that attributed production to divine intervention. Yet despite his disbelief, the encounter with the power of myth in shaping minds seemed to have had a profound and lasting effect on him. In his incredulity and mistrust of an ideology that had no content, he discovered a vocation that would last a lifetime: he subsequently spent a good deal of his energy in writing on the true nature of the Japanese character, as if doing so would wash away the mental scars that Japanist thinking had inflicted on a generation.

The archaic figure and discussions of the national body were rarely associated specifically with production, and when such a linkage was made, it was through the identification of a morality (*dōtoku*) and economy exemplified by the Ise Shrine. But it is worth remembering that the archaic form evoked only the world of precapitalism, despite its protean utility in fashioning an ideology that aimed to eradicate Japan's dependency and inferiority in the 1930s. The importance of the archaic figure for capitalism lay in its precapitalist neutrality. I am referring to the fact that the archaic, even in its most intense articulations, raised no barrier or opposition to capitalism. Indeed, it embraced the unity of morality or ethics with economics, and the religious beliefs' underpinning of this union authorized it. For the archaic, morality and the economy were one and the same thing, not two that were opposed to each other—as they have appeared in modern capitalism. Moreover, the archaic, during the precapitalist era, remained silent on the nature of the economy, which hadn't yet been conceived as an independent domain, apart from random remarks on the relationship between production and growth to the deities responsible for generating socially reproductive practices. The *Kokutaronshi* describes Japan as a land of "self-sufficiency . . . one of agriculture, the country of the reed plains, a land of abundance." This ancient description reflects the preoccupation of nativists in the Tokugawa period who saw agrarian production both as a means of social reproduction and as a way to repay the deities of heaven and earth for the blessings they had bestowed at the time of creation on the land and its people. The land was called [*aohitogusa*], a word associated with the luxuriant, diffuse, and dense growth of rooted blue-green grass in the act of creation and the nature inhabited by living and growing things. This people later became the masses Japanese fascists sought to mobilize as an organic folk collectivity. When Hirata and his rural followers began to restore the identity of work and worship, making the pairing explicit and literally ideologizing it in the early nineteenth century, this intervention was directed at the observation that the separation of morality and economics was already under way. It was this understanding of the archaic form that was evoked in a twentieth-century society dominated by the industrial rhythms of capitalism. But the mode of relationality was cast within a framework of exchanges ruled by a divine emperor (more like a priest-king) who communicated regularly with the national deities and his imperial ancestors—all of whom were descendants of the sun goddess. We must thus see the archaic implanted in a modern capitalist and technologically expansive society not as a deterrent to either but rather as a displacement of the contradictions between capitalism and a timeless imaginary (in which these separations and distinctions had not developed). It was, I believe, precisely at this point that the archaic figure could strengthen the impulse toward political fascism. Some thinkers in the 1930s such as Tsukui worked to supply the archaic with a new economic foundation called national socialism (*Kokkashakaishugi*) and pointed to Mussolini's Italy as an example to consider following.[64] Tsukui identified his conception of national socialism with Italian fascism and discovered in Italy's autocratic leadership a similarity to the imperial politics of Japanism. "By not unconditionally branding fascism as reactionary," he proposed the importance of "considering the profound truths contained within it." Tsukui was convinced that fascism in Italy became the politics of Mussolini, while "in Japan, it was imperial politics that correctly conformed to fascism."[65]

Tsukui was one of the most verbal among the many Japanists in the 1930s who monotonously repeated mantras dedicated to exceptionalizing the divine endowment as expressed in the mystical concept of the national body that in turn was identified with the divine origin. Thinkers like Tsukui sought to provide the form of archaism with content by advocating a Japanized socialism. To this end, Tsukui resuscitated the idea of national socialism as conceived by Takabatake Motoyuki a decade or so earlier to offer Japanism a new direction and eliminate its dependence on vulgar and secular socialism. "Japan's national socialist movement believes absolutely in this spirit of the national body," Tsukui proclaimed, referring to "one lord [and] all the people (*ikkun banmin*)." National socialism was to be a Japanized socialism and the Japanese people's spirit to be different from similar spirits in other countries. This singularly majestic spirit, limited to the Japanese people, is an existence which it is not possible to obliterate.[66] Despite Tsukui's intention of supplying content where there was none, his mode of expression echoed the rhetorical circularity of Japanism and displaced the supposedly new message. In much of the Japanist discourse, it is possible to discern the linguistic presence of the restoration proclamation of 1868 and behind it the logic of the archaic chronicles. But in its form of archaism, Japanism's expansive narrative exceeded that of the restoration proclamation and was able to appeal to a diverse constituency of groups ranging from agrarianists opposed to capitalism to monopoly capitalists—in other words, to groups that had not existed in 1868. The figure of the archaic had the capacity to conceal the uneven socioeconomic positions occupied by capitalist monopolists, socialistic anticapitalists, and agrarianists who opposed urbanization and manufacturing. The archaic's power of appeal to persuade people to look away from the dangers of unevenness derived from its religious authority and association with the timelessness of the origin as a guide in Japanese life. It would thus be a mistake to overlook the support of the financial clique (*zaibatsu*), which included many ardent and "enthusiastic disseminators of the emperor system mythology."[67]

If, as Tsukui argued, Japanism was based on the premise of fascism's politicized scene of synchronic nonsynchronicity, this was because Japanism reversed the order of time and resituated the noncontemporaneous and nonsynchronic archaic at the head of the chain of temporality.[68] This move mirrored the inversion of a scheme (attributed to Gramsci) that initially contemporized the past, turning it into one in which the past took precedence over the present to produce the figure of a noncontemporaneous present that is the past. Japanism's reliance on the auratic archaic form promised liberation from any accountability to history, whereas the marshaling of mythic exemplars worked to rid both the present of the scourge of historical deformation and the country of its contemporary dissatisfaction with modernity. But the dissociation from the modern did not mean a break with capitalism. Japanism instead enshrined an unenvisioned future that could be reached only by harking back to a historical imaginary origin that became a model to be implanted in the present. In other words, according to Japanism a present past would unlock the path to the future, which was precisely what restorationists sought to do by evoking the archaic even as the new Meiji state endeavored to become modern.

In the end, Hasegawa's critique did not go far enough: it stopped when he began to prepare to dissociate himself from the radical left of materialist Marxism of the Yuibutsu kenkyūkai. His analysis of artistic and cultural production, linked to his "Critique of Fascism," seemed to prefigure this decision and allow him to begin moving beyond describing the relationship between culture and fascism and closer to the bourgeois elitism he had once disparaged. Unlike Hasegawa, Tosaka followed the original critical route and observed the deep roots of the dominant forms of cultural expression and the sociohistorical mediations in which it was embedded. As I show below, Tosaka addressed some of the same problems that prompted Hasegawa's critical quest, especially those associated with the claims of artistic autonomy and literary neutrality. It is well to recall that Barshay has demonstrated that beginning in 1933 (not more than a year since the last part of his critique was published), Hasegawa began "to turn back" on himself and "to unwind." What this meant was his repudiation of "any association that could possibly link him, in official minds, with the illegal Communist party."[69] His earlier preoccupation with class struggle migrated toward considering the importance of developing the "integral state" and working for the necessary and "communitarian forms" which would fulfill the imperative of greater social solidarity.[70] It is interesting to note, if not unintentionally ironic, that this move must be seen in his criticism of Japanism to become both the force of national integration and the rhetoric that ceaselessly advised the folk to "return to the archaic," which for Hasegawa meant the "return to Japan." But this time, according to Barshay, the "cause of the state was the cause of the life world," which were now unified, having been once separated. To realize this new ambition, Hasegawa, like Miki Kiyoshi and other prominent intellectuals, joined Konoe Fumimaro's research apparatus, the Showa Kenkyūkai and the state.

But even before Hasegawa hurriedly turned away from his critique of the state to embrace it, he showed signs of what would be his subsequent change of direction. We must tease out of his discussion on art in his "Critique of Fascism" how he arrived at reasoning already implied in his detailed discussion of the relationship between Japan's low- and moderate-scale capitalism and fascism. To this end, it is not surprising that the discussion on art focused first on the relationship of artistic and cultural production and the characteristic perspective of social classes. On the one hand, he wanted to privilege the expression of an art that was what he described the "most strong art," and not kitsch—an art devoted to capturing the real.[71] But the problem with this desire was that he was able only to typify a weak and mediocre art capable of satisfying the low taste of the petit bourgeoisie, and he could not exemplify truly great art, apart from identifying some of its well-known masters (Leo Tolstoy and Michelangelo). He sought to explain that weak art was motivated by its unreality, appeal to sentimentality, and romanticized themes driven by commodification and commercial motives. But apart from vaguely proposing that it is "living reality," presumably stimulated by the artist's feelings that are "similar to natural feeling" and the concretizing of action in the reality of everyday life, he remained uncertain about whether only great artists are capable of reproducing (*saigen*) the real.[72] It might be the artist's connection with "historical change," seeing it unfold before being perceived by others, that authorizes his prescience or sense of grasping the real. But it is never mere imitation. Great art, for Hasegawa, apparently appears undistinguishable from the work of great artists, who, in a circular way, signify "the words of mysterious intuition." Whether art is the work of recognition, intuition, or insight, it must be restored to concrete reality.[73] In other words, the artist or other producer of culture must be endowed with some magical insight to rise above the constraints of social class and history and create a reproduction that is intimately capable of expressing faithfulness to the real.

Although Hasegawa's shifting attitude toward the state appears to imply an uncertainty in his thinking about Marxism and liberalism or an ambiguity in his considerations of history and artistic or cultural neutrality and autonomy, it is difficult to square the seemingly sudden shift with his capacity to identify contradictions and antinomies. I am not convinced that Hasegawa inadvertently produced any contradiction, nor do I think that he believed he had inadvertently done so. What he appeared to be particularly interested in offering was an account that would offset the claims of fascist art, reveal the consequences of that art, and contrast it to "art that most resembles art (*mottomo geijutsu-rashii geijutsu*)."[74] It should be noted that he remained committed to seeing art and culture as reflecting history, but at the same time he recognized that the historical was largely driven by oppositions—which, paradoxically, meant that it was possible for each different view to claim to accurately reflect history and realize the real. But that would only produce multiple versions of the real, a kind of liberal pluralism of art, and would never realize some kind of totality. He seemed to view poetry differently: "The poetry of love is not an artistic reproduction of the life of love, it is itself the reality of love's life."[75] In the age of the *Kojiki* [Chronicle of ancient history], the earliest recorded text of the origin and Japan's earliest emperors. he proclaimed, "the reality of social life and artistic life were harmoniously united." When the artist has lost contact with contemporary reality, art becomes a fragment of a not fully discerned social crisis or simply entertainment for the masses. "In the late feudal [era]," he wrote, "a stimulation based on a premonition of the breakup of the military life produced Bakin's romantic literature, which was like Kipling's imperialist literature; but these were remarkable cases and art soon became extremely impoverished. The widespread circulation of poorly expressed articles of writing repetitively commodifed by the capitalist system was the art of the petit bourgeoisie and lower middle class, whereby repeating feudal content became the central trend in Japan's mass culture, publishing and cinema. This was fascism in art."[76] It also explained Hasegawa's verdict that "fascism in art was a denial of art by artists."[77]

Hasegawa's view of contemporary art and consumption was premised on the misconception that Japanese society, especially the urban classes, had been bourgeoisized. He pointedly complained that the petit bourgeois and lower middle classes had a seemingly inexhaustible appetite for art that reproduced the feudal past and was created by cultural producers who did not necessarily share their taste. The petit bourgeoisie should have known better, he charged, and the artists had no particular emotional commitment to the feudal past since they were bourgeois modernists.[78] In fact, these producers of culture had "departed from feudal forms" and had made the necessary transition to the process of bourgeoisization that he had seen as the dominant structure of Japanese society. It must be recalled that Hasegawa was convinced that Japan was no longer a feudal society, even though he acknowledged that feudal elements were still present in the struggle of the country's small and medium scale capitalism with the operations of high capitalism. Moreover, the feudal elements acted to preserve the peculiar system of underdeveloped semicapitalism. He knew that fascism was bred in such an environment afflicted by political, social and economic crises, which worked to further accelerate and reinforce the attenuation of feudalist content and forms. Yet he wondered why artists chose to portray not real contemporary society but the passed feudal past. What struck Hasegawa as an apparent anomaly or unexplainable contradiction nevertheless persuaded bourgeois artists to pursue a path that led to their refusing to portray the reality of modern bourgeois life. It is arguable that artists saw what Hasegawa failed to recognize: that the temporal dominant of contemporary Japanese society was the mixed time of contemporaneous noncontemporaneity. I believe that his enthusiasm for capitalist modernization was misplaced here, since even the urban classes in Japan could still see themselves in the representation of a passed feudal past that persisting remnants constantly fortified. Unanticipated material and psychological effects of living in a time of great uncertainty, accompanied by the additional challenge of coping with mixed times with their respective temporal regimes obliged Japanese to navigate through a difficult contemporary landscape. Hasegawa was persuaded that this observation that undermined everyday life and imposed new demands on it was ratified by the capitalist success of art and other cultural forms that provided avenues of escape from the present (such as literature, popular historical accounts, and films) that were preoccupied with portraying the feudal past. For Hasegawa, cinematic portrayals of medieval sword battles (*chanbara*) may have signified the collapse of aesthetic standards, but it also underscored his failure to grasp the character of popular culture in the everyday life that capitalist modernization brought in its wake.

Hasegawa also had trouble understanding what prompted artists to turn away from contemporary capitalist reality and toward the feudal past. He saw the opposition to the capitalist rejection of the feudal mode and life as an empty "daydream" and artists' efforts to promote a change in contemporary everyday life as an ill-conceived attempt to conceal a fascistic tendency.[79] This opposition represented a disapproval of both capitalism and contemporaneity, if not also of the historical that he had seen as key to reproducing the real. In his view, this opposition was nothing more than a kind of fascistic attitude to art, and instead of reinterpreting the history of the forms that art pursues in history, the artists relied on "borrow(ing) the history of the past."[80] Hence, the feudalistic content of their art was drawn from their own limited historical knowledge, which they used to serve their opposition and not to confront the reality of everyday life.

The problem, Hasegawa believed, was one of class. Classes like the lower middle class, petit bourgeoisie, and proletariat embraced an art and culture that looked to an imagined feudal past. He was aware that the feudal elements still persisting in the capitalist system had no appeal to the "middle strata (*chukansō*)" and that it was "natural that the dregs of the feudal systems stopped" at this class boundary.[81] He explained that the feelings and attitudes of the lower middle class were driven by the recognition that these people had no other choice but to view themselves from the perspective of feudal elements, especially "in their evasion from the current situation of their lives and in their class-like movements." "This strata," Hasegawa wrote, "from the standpoint that it is industrially feudal, it is psychologically feudal and thus feudal in its artistic alignment with Fascist art," which laid the foundation for subsequent commercial development.[82] Fascist art—in the forms of novels, radio programs, and films—endeavored to represent lived petit bourgeois reality and became the "unconscious power" filling the consciousness of the lower middle class that prevented them from seeing beyond the immediate sphere they inhabited. This brings us back to Hasegawa's initial engagement with the possibility of producing great art and the dangers that threaten to undermine that possibility. He acknowledged that great art is created by artists who somehow are able to rise above both the constraints of class and the imperatives of history, and who thus possess some mystical quality that enables them to capture the real. But his defense of artistic autonomy and its distance from popular culture was at the heart of a bourgeois conception of social order and subjectivity, which used art and culture to differentiate those who were in a position to know from those who (like the members of the lower middle class and workers) were not and who showed this by their shallow command of the components of bourgeois life and the ease with which they succumbed to bad art. The problem with lower middle-class popular tastes, Hasegawa implied, is that they couldn't tell the difference between what they liked and good art. At the same time, this valorization of bourgeois culture insisted that the formation of genuine value in art required the creation of an autonomous sphere of art and culture separate from politics, one in which political considerations were absent or had been eliminated in the making of art. While Hasegawa conceded that the artists who produced popular art were not necessarily committed to a feudal past and were fully bourgeoisized, he saw in their work and its popularity among the lower classes a dangerous intrusion into Japanese social order because their art inspired a flight from reality that led to fascism. In fact, Hasegawa defined fascism as a denial of art, which suggests the depth of his concern about the challenge fascism posed to the bourgeois social order he was defending in this critique of art. His critique was not only an attack on popular culture but also a denunciation of a deceiving art that he saw as the "dregs" of fascism, serving a political purpose, which he considered capable of undermining the informing principle in the production of great art that would unsettle the division of mental and manual labor by transforming the relationship between politics and culture. Hasegawa was convinced that if such artistic commodities like novels, movies, and magazines were looked at directly along with the fateful failure and indifference of the lower-middle-class movements in the present, this reality would disclose the historical story lived by the masses. Hasegawa argued that fascist art had lured the masses away from the reality in which they were living, increasingly separating them from history.[83] What is interesting about this charge is that he was already saying in the early 1930s that fascism was recruiting its supporters principally from the lower middle class by inducing them to turn away from their lived reality through the consumption of cultural commodities that provided them the false security of an imagined past. It is also interesting to note that in his now classic essays on nationalism and fascism in Japan, Maruyama ratified this interpretation of fascism's class composition until the military coup of February 1936, after which fascism's leadership and direction came from the military, semi-feudal bureaucrats, business, and intellectuals.[84] Hasegawa's account is limited to the 1930s. But he failed to recognize that fascism would be largely taken over by the middle stratum he had designated as "bourgeoisized" and by intellectuals who, like him, came from that stratum. Yet it should be noted that when he defined great art as capturing and concretizing the reality of everyday life, he was pointing both to the centrality of the relationship between culture and politics and to a sense of the actual, even though he left the realization of that sense to a form of magical thinking. Miki and Tosaka would return to the problem of how to reconfigure actuality in a temporal environment dominated by the figure of a braided past and present.

ACTUALITY &
THE ARCHAIC MODE
OF COGNITION

The Critique of Japanese Fascism
and the Promise of Living Culture

If Hasegawa Nyozekan saw in Japanism both a content lacking substance
and a form lacking stability, the philosopher Miki Kiyoshi went further:
he separated the claims of Japanism and its deformation of the character
of Japanese thought to contemplate what might be considered an authentic image of the Japanese thing (*Nihonteki na mono*)—that is, Japaneseness.
Miki addressed what he saw as the principal defect of Japanism, which was
its claim to ownership of the Japanese thing. Unlike Hasegawa, who was preoccupied with the relationship between the lower middle class and Japanism and their connection to Japan's medium and low form of capitalism,
Miki seemed less concerned with addressing the ideological attractions
of Japanism than with identifying the true character of Japanese thought
and liberating it from its Japanist appropriations. The difference between
these two friends stemmed from the fact that Miki, unlike Hasegawa, was
a member of the Kyoto school of philosophy (in fact, he was undoubtedly
one of its most impressive students), and his training was responsible for
his interest in the larger questions of philosophy—which in turn led him
to consider Japan's historical mission in the world rather than the details of
contemporary social and economic developments. When he wrote "Japanese
Character and Fascism" in 1936, he saw that Japanism could easily slip into

fascism. However, he appeared more concerned with the authentic character of what he called Japanese thought than with the peril posed by fascism. Miki ignored the historical as a way to separate Japanese thought from a fateful encounter with fascism. But taking Japanese thought out of history permitted him to exceptionalize it, which made it even more receptive to fascism. Miki, like Hasegawa, became deradicalized and, by the end of the 1930s, served Japan's integral state throughout the war.

In the year before Miki published "Japanese Character and Fascism," Tosaka Jun published his major critique of Japanism, "Japan Ideology" (*Nihon ideorogiron*), which demonstrated the principal role played by liberal culture in bolstering Japanese fascist ideology. The two philosophers had a close relationship, and Tosaka acknowledged that after Miki returned from Europe, where he had been exposed to Marxism and Martin Heidegger's new existential phenomenology, Tosaka might have been one of the first people who turned to the left as a result of Miki's influence. "For me," Tosaka confessed, Miki "was a very important senior colleague (*senpai*)," but "he had become a humanist, I am a materialist." Despite Tosaka's dedication to Miki, he began to distance himself from Miki's humanism, adding that Miki had not embraced a "materialist historical view," which, for Tosaka, meant that his friend had departed from historical materialism to adopt a "relativistic historicism." In fact, he considered Miki's conception of history as instantiating an idealistic hermeneutic discipline, and he saw "Miki as a philosopher of meaning, a scholar of thought."[1] Even though Miki had been involved in Marxism and produced notable essays on Karl Marx's humanism in the late 1920s that were savagely attacked by the Marxian historian Hattori Shisō, Tosaka looked on these essays as a continuation of Miki's 1926 work on Blaise Pascale. In Tosaka's view, Miki was concerned with philosophic history (*rekishi tetsugaku*), which took him away from the world of material history and mediations. The difference between Miki and Tosaka and Miki's avoidance of materialism may explain his silence on domestic issues (especially those relating to contemporary political economy and the privileging of culture and thought), which drove him to separate the character of Japanese thought from fascism. Moreover, the importance of Miki's passion for philosophic history revealed the ambiguity and restlessly driven changes in his intellectual commitments, especially his move away from criticizing fascism and toward affirming its rationality. Behind these changes was Miki's early valorization of humanism and its capacity to change and progress, which ultimately resulted in his faith in technology or *poiesis*, the human aptitude for making.

While friendship and a philosophic attitude that led them to address contemporary life linked Miki and Tosaka, they maintained a tense critical relationship, sharing an intellectual challenge of the uncertain but, at the time, vital project of defining the relation between culture and politics. Nothing seemed more compelling to prewar intellectuals in the 1930s in Japan and elsewhere in the industrial and modernizing world than the need to determine whether contemporary circumstances demanded new cultural forms capable of reshaping the political landscape or required a new politics to overcome a historical crisis resulting from capitalist modernization. This question confronted industrial societies and spilled over into their colonial domains. Resolving the question would surely result in a redrawing of the boundaries of the cultural realm. The Depression compelled thoughtful people in many places to analyze the spectacle of economic, social, political, and cultural contradictions that capitalist modernity had unleashed but contained for the time being. Throughout the decade there was widespread agreement among thinkers and writers that they were living in a time of crisis that required immediate attention.

In a 1932 essay titled "A Philosophical Explanation of the Consciousness of Crisis," Miki joined other observers to call into question the vast economic and cultural unevenness that had resulted from Japan's capitalist modernization. Marxists were already pointing to the persistence of unwanted remnants from the feudal past, while people of a more liberal persuasion complained about the effects of late development and the prospect of an incomplete modernization as a consequence of the social and economic policies of the early Meiji era. The high-water mark of this crisis was reached with the production of discourses on culture that envisioned a relationship to reshaping politics in a spatiotemporal configuration, in which the lived contradictions appeared to have already been inscribed in the texture of Japanese life. But there was also a crisis in the multiple ruptures, unanticipated discontinuities, and unevenness that characterized everyday existence and the observably different but coexisting presents that people were compelled to live in at the same time. Japan shared this experience with other societies in the 1930s, as was clear in Hasegawa's discussions on capitalism and fascism and the accompanying recognition of a growing separation of modes of cognition from what was happening in everyday life—which revealed the urgency of finding for them adequate, concrete forms of representation. Capitalism rapidly adopted concepts like culture, representation, and modernity, mobilizing them as mediations in a sociopolitical environment marked by the ceaseless generation of new forces of production and social relations that only increased divisions and conflicts. One response was the quest for lasting and stable forms of representation endowed with the capacity to arrest the fragmentation produced by the ever-changing world of capitalism. Another was the proposed reunion of everyday life with art, but this was an illusory fantasy, dramatized by Yasuda Yojūrō in his program of modernity as "irony," as well as the shared "coincidental" ground of "modernism" and "fascism" his movement and many other cultural groups occupied. The irony referred to the prospect of appearing modern but not yet quite so, since traces of a more traditional life were still available and being lived in the 1930s by writers and artists. At the same that writers and artists seemed to be pledged to modernism, they were willing to support the forms of an arcane and often irrational archaism that Japan's fascism had promoted. Miki condemned Yasuda's romantic faction as "opponents to the present," dedicated to an "opposition not to a limited reality but rather an unlimited one" and viewing the real as "narrow" and "petty."[2]

Modernism was a broad cultural movement devoted to exploring new forms for their own sake—especially in art, architecture, and philosophy (which eschewed realism in favor of abstraction and rejected the certainty of reason). As Raymond Williams once said of literary modernism, it was produced in the large, urban, industrial centers and viewed its local experience as universal. If it was disposed to discount history and its own antecedents and adopt a rigorous formalism that appeared to ape science, it used the past through the techniques of reconfiguration, rewriting, revision, parody, and incorporation of what it considered to be the timeless and useful. Driven by the ceaseless quest to make and celebrate the new, modernism often risked appearing to be part of capitalism's never-ending production of new commodities for consumption and its abstraction of social relations and reality. Furthermore, fascism saw achieving a new form of politics as the way to unburden the present of the political failures of the past. Antonio Gramsci had already suggested that when liberal politics begins to show signs of faltering, it ceases to share political leadership with new groups and moves toward fascism. Modernism and fascism agreed on the impossibility of representing a historical object or set of events already mediated by social abstraction that prevented people from seeing it directly. They also agreed that in the 1930s society was witnessing the detachment of fixed forms of representation from prior modes of existence. Where capitalism prevailed, representation became an unsolvable problem since it faced the demands of capitalism's reason and its claims of having received a culture of reference, which was steadily being shunted aside to a world of irrationality and ghosts. In 1930s Japan, a prominent discourse on aesthetics seemed committed to retrieving the concrete and immediate and to aspiring to displace a politics embedded in abstract exchange. Speaking directly to fascism's distrust of contemporary politics, this discourse had already announced its verdict on all political attempts to break the logic of reified existence. Both modernism and fascism thus participated in the struggle to find a mode of representation that could master the fundamental abstractness of what was occurring. Both were obliged to appeal to some form of presentation and performance that promised relief from the constraints of the dominant socially mediated abstractions of value and relentless fragmentation. With fascism came the attempt to flee politics (which was anchored in unworkable representational categories) by calling for the unity of an organically whole folk community as a natural order—the dream of Japanist fascism.[3] Modernism, like fascism, rarely entertained the possibility of eliminating capital and private property.

In most cases, literary and artistic modernism were pledged to searching for a way to unite art and everyday life. But what tied modernism to fascism was their shared desire (for different reasons) to rescue an aura that was no longer accessible (if it had ever been so). This meant not rescuing the aura's antecedents or the past but identifying and affirming the value of the timeless in culture—as the critic Kobayashi saw in thirteenth-century Buddhist sculpture, which was no longer bound to its historical moment of creation but was accessible for all times (thus, some modernisms use the past). Often this quest led to the espousing of myth and the construction of a semblance of nature. In the Japanese case, the origin was espoused in place of the historical. But according to Miki, the goal of the effort to revise the relations between culture and politics by installing the former in place of the latter was to promote technology, which quickly evolved into making war. While Miki saw the way forward in a liberal culture and the retention of private property, Tosaka believed that this would eliminate liberalism, since that was a compromised solution and already complicit with fascism.

In "Japanese Character and Fascism," Miki asked but did not answer a question: "has fascism come to Japan?"[4] Others (including Hasegawa, whose essays Miki had read with approval) had been writing on the subject for some time. In fact, in 1933 Miki had co-authored a proclamation with Hasegawa that protested the Nazis' burning of books. In the case of Japan, the political intensity of the 1930s had shown the extent of fascist activity and the growing presence of the Japanist ideology, capped by the young officers' mutiny of February 26, 1936, and their call for a Shōwa Restoration. Nearly seventy years after the Meiji Restoration, the growing demand for its completion came to a head in the mutiny of officers about to be sent to Manchuria. The plotters sought to bring about a restoration of direct imperial authority to a people's emperor, ridding the country of political party leaders and financiers. The idea had been circulated more than a decade earlier by the fascist theorist and activist Kita Ikki and prefigured even earlier by Saigō Takamori, who died defending what he considered to be the true goal of the Meiji Restoration and whose life was romanticized by the writer Hayashi Fusao in 1940. Miki was aware that fascism had begun to occupy an influential place in Japanese political society, and its signs could be seen everywhere. In contrast, Tosaka viewed the officers' mutiny as a symptom of "circumstances" leading to occurrences in the "form of a hysterical explosion of one section of society against another."[5] Miki located the roots of fascism's recent growth in Japan in social and economic conditions driven by changes in the global situation of the time.[6] He wrote that "world historical determinants" were capable of enflaming and spreading from one region to another—for instance, moving from Europe to the United States and eventually Japan. At this moment Miki was most concerned with the relationship between Japanese thought and fascism, particularly how the former seemed to provide a favorable climate for the latter's reception and expansion. Fascism, he argued, thrived on the character of Japanese thought and without arousing any concern could find and slip into a place within any given philosophy or thought by appearing to be a real representation of Japaneseness. Fascism had entered Japan in such a way that it seemed not to have arrived yet. Masked in Japaneseness, it was barely noticed, and when detected it was considered too weak to matter. The relationship between Japanese thought and fascism gave Miki an opportunity to define the character of Japanese thought—especially its apparent openness (which could lead to fascism, among other ideologies).

This sudden and seemingly invisible relationship led Miki to ask what there was about Japanese thought that made it so welcoming to a political import—that is, what inherent methodological weaknesses made Japanese thought susceptible to such an overpowering outside influence? He was convinced that the answer lay in the absence of historically philosophical reflection in Japan. In his view, an argument must always be based on an actual historical view. What Miki meant was the actuality (jissaiteki) of historical practice, which led to action (kōiteki) or praxis. Miki pointed to a tradition

of Chinese historical writing that looked to the past with the aim of draw-
ing useful political and moral lessons for the present, "strongly showing
the actual tendency that history constituted a mirror." However, the power
of that writing was inferior when compared to the power of a historical
view in the West that was both scientific and sensitive to history's developmental unfolding and its connections with the rest of the world. Japan
could benefit from following actual historical practices in China and the
West, but Miki noted that the prominence of nationalist history in Japan
and other societies had an undesirable "reactionary meaning."[7] As a result,
contemporary Japanese thought had lost its focus on historical consciousness and sacrificed its capacity to see history as the development of connections within the broader world. In this sense, Miki was thinking about
the project of history along the lines of an encompassing Hegelian world-
historical scheme. What troubled him about a loss of historical consciousness was the resultant failure to differentiate one epoch from another and
establish proper criteria for judging the differences among epochs. Specifically, he wondered how an event like the Meiji Restoration would be seen
from the perspective of the wider world if world history in Japan was abandoned for a narrower nationalistic history. The lack of this kind of historical
perspective in contemporary thinking about the "Japanese thing" choked
off any capacity to recognize, in its absence, fascism's distrust of history
and preference for the indistinct vagueness of the distant archaic. In fact,
what drew fascism to Japanism was their common distrust and rejection
of history. The apparent defect in Miki's account was a failure to provide an
adequate historical explanation of how and under what conditions Japanese thought had developed. But what remains a puzzle in this account
of the different traditions of historical practice was his silence on the current historiographical debate among various Marxian factions about the
development of Japan's capitalism. If the debate showed anything, it was
the methodological sophistication that Miki admired in Western historical practice. But his neglect may have been prompted by differences with
some of the debaters like Hattori, who had been one of the severest critics of Miki's earlier Marxian essays.[8] And like Hasegawa, Miki was already
moving away from his earlier radicalism. Even so, Miki was right to consider the necessity of historical consciousness and its capacity to facilitate
qualitative distinctions among the plurality of historical times. Proponents of Japanism regarded the restoration of the archaic as a burdensome
but necessary step in historical differentiation—particularly the ability to
make comparative judgments. "Many learned people lack a method," he

complained, citing "Japanists who, consciously or unconsciously, overlook contemporary Japan" in their single-minded preoccupation with an image of an archaic past. The foundation of this conceit, which came from an overdetermined Japanese nationalism in the 1930s, was a failure to understand that history was concerned with development and that it was never solely preoccupied with the past but always obliged to consider the present as well.[9] In this respect, Miki was expressing a philosophic argument that had been articulated by some of the more conservative members of the Kyoto school of philosophy. These included Kōsaka Masaaki and Kōyama Iwao, who were already arguing for the vital importance of the present in historical thought. Miki insisted that it was unnecessary to follow the nationalist bent of Japanese thought. Moreover, he responded to Japanist claims of a special character by discounting altogether any inherent "special characteristics" in Japanese thought. He was particularly concerned with disputing Japanist assertions that what was considered as Japanese thought and fascism shared a kinship, which implied that there was little difference between the two. According to Miki, the problem lay in employing an idea or practice that had not survived its own time or that did not belong to a different and outmoded empiricity, and he pointed here to the classic description of anachrony as the attempt to extract a distillation that had escaped capture from the phenomenality of things.

For Miki, the Japanists' assertion of a "special character" had no basis in fact. Accordingly, such assertions expressed nothing more than a feudal attitude that belonged to a past historical time and that ran counter to what he identified as the Western thing—that is, the modern. Here, I believe, Miki made a crucial distinction between the archaic that belongs to a past historical age and its proper time, even though the archaic was constructed from mythic stories found in the ancient chronicles. And he argued that the decision to use the archaic outside its own time made archaism into a mode of cognition that was no longer constrained by its temporal moment and was available to address any present. Hence, he saw archaism as a form of cognitive apprehension or mapping of the terrain of any temporal moment, which it would guide by restoring forgotten archaic exemplars to the present as a condition of a new start and a time now liberated from any damaged and disabling history. Moreover, the content of the archaic was limited to Japan by its culturally specific referents. Archaism functioned to organize the lived experience of everyday life, becoming a political unconscious that was automatically evoked by the "shadow of the emperor," which was cast everywhere in contemporary daily life.[10]

Tosaka later called this archaic mode of cognition the "archaic phenomenon," which was seemingly rooted in common sense that, like the force of custom, required no explanation. He was referring to Miki and moving beyond the cognitive mode to its phenomenological presence. Miki was particularly sensitive to this distinction between the archaic past and the the capacity of archaism of the present to show that the appearance of capitalism represented the passage into modernity. That passage required paying attention to identifying differences in the historical stages of modernity's development rather than appealing to some folk characteristic that had no empirical reality. The apparent resemblance between the archaic past and the present archaicism, he remarked, was quintessentially expressed in the conversion of the archaic into archaism, which he characterized as pretending to be something it was not that aimed at distinguishing the importance between the two even though (like many Marxists, especially historians participating in the debate on Japanese capitalism) he acknowledged the significant presence of large numbers of remnants from the past in contemporary Japan. It is possible that, if necessary, Miki was willing to conflate the archaic with the feudal since the former's claim to timelessness made it possible to imagine the former subsuming the historicity of the latter. However, this was a move that neither Hasegawa nor Tosaka was prepared to make.

Miki's fixation on the present grew out of his early decision to think through the consequences of contemporary eventfulness to gain a proper understanding of the charged conjuncture of his times and to form a strategy for policy and action. He saw himself as a philosopher with a vision of world history in which humans were in a world-historical existence.[11] These twin concerns and the actions they dictated further showed his emphasis on the importance of actuality and how it anchored his outlook. He was particularly concerned with the widely held view that a crisis existed in the 1930s and the articulations of anxiety about the state of the human condition by diverse writers and thinkers. The crisis had begun in the 1920s, but its pace accelerated in the early 1930s when the Depression spilled over into international discord, as Hasegawa had described. The first stop in Miki's intellectual trajectory was an attempt to construct a philosophical anthropology grounded in materiality rather than religiosity. His brief encounter with Heideggerian existentialism introduced him to the role played by history, both in its theorization of alienation and its existential conceptualization of a hermeneutic demand to address the question of self-understanding in the current human condition. Yet it is also true that

Miki's quest to find an adequate anthropology that related human contemporaneity, being there (*Dasein*), and a thereness that he identified with everyday life as the place where people lived out their routinized lives and worked. But this preoccupation with finding such an anthropology led Miki to address the troubling exigencies of the historical moment, which was fueled as much by the conjunctural force imposed on Japan and the gathering storm of global and regional events that led to full-scale economic failure and an evolving totalism—a storm likely to be resolved only by war.

Miki's involvement in the conjuncture underscores its importance as a common determinant of the 1930s that nonetheless was experienced differently by countries like Germany, Japan, and Italy. What brought the countries together also accounts for their differences from one another. For example, Japan had a diachronic history from the Meiji Restoration to fascism that was mediated by the archaic, while Germany and Italy followed different historical routes, even though they also saw using timeless myths as the way to overcome the disappointments of the historical present and make things right again. All three experienced capitalism in the 1930s within the larger framework of the effects of economic depression, and all three decided to withdraw from the world to attend to national interests, a strategy that Japanists called Japan first or "one countryism" for all and that, as shown above, drove Hasegawa to despair.

The present that supplied empirical authority for Miki's identification of a pivotal contemporaneity (the arena of actualization) convinced him that philosophers should pursue a practical calling, a decision also made by Tosaka when he turned his philosophy toward assessing the everyday. But Miki believed that philosophy's purpose was to guide the incipient liberal endowment in Japan, which he believed was on the verge of collapsing in the chaos of the crisis.[12] He recognized that the growth of capitalism in Japan had proceeded rapidly, that it was based on liberal thinking that had not yet had adequate time to mature. The problem, he said, citing Émile Durkheim, was Japan's failure to achieve full development of individualism and liberalism, which were needed to broaden the scope of society. Despite experiencing rapid economic growth, Japan remained a comparatively narrow society that was less constricted by the persistence of feudal remnants or the feudal legacy of the Meiji Restoration than it was by an ideology of fascism suitably adapted to the contemporary stage of the Japanese capitalist development.[13] In this view, Miki agreed with Hasegawa's earlier assessment of the adaptability of fascism to Japanist discourse. Miki also suggested that there were "many people in

Japan today" who "frankly acknowledged that Japanism is fascism."[14] But he clung to his distrust of the persistence of the feudal reminders in contemporary Japan, residues from a prior age unevenly distributed throughout the country. He reasoned that these remnants indexed the insufficient growth of individualism and liberalism, undermining their chance to become political and moral factors prominent enough to counter the Japanist affinity for fascism. In a dire forecast of things to come, he argued that Japan's special character would eventually verify that one of the most advantageous conditions for the triumph of fascist rule in the nation was the extent to which the "feudal thing" would be able to morph into the "Japanese thing." Here, of course, was the subsumption of the feudal into the archaic, or their conflation into the unified figure of the "Japanese thing" that erased their previous identities. Rejecting the view that feudal remnants made Japan unique, Miki wrote that "today, Japanism is fascism," but he explained that the problem is neither the "feudal thing" nor the "Japanese thing" in itself but a much broader perspective.[15] He could accept the fact that the formation of Japanese born in Japan meant that they possessed specific characteristics derived from the land and people. But he also recognized that the components that went into the making of Japaneseness had evolved through a history of borrowing from other cultures, beginning with China and expanding to the West. And he recalled that the philosophy of wholeness informing the theory of fascism owed a great debt to Georg Hegel, neo-Kantians, Ferdinand Tönnies, and Heidegger, among others. Miki proposed that although the West was characterized by individualism, Japan was dominated by a sense of wholeness and the idea of a formless form. Throughout their nation's history, Japanese had been able to assimilate different kinds of learning and influences from abroad, as if they possessed a natural flair for importing the content of foreign offerings but not the forms containing them. This borrowing was particularly true of Japanese society in the late eighteenth and early nineteenth centuries, when Japan predominantly assimilated Western philosophy and science. Even xenophobic nativist scholars like Hirata Atsutane, who separated themselves from earlier borrowings from Confucianism and Buddhism and emphasized the purity of Japaneseness, flirted with Christianity and acquired a knowledge of its main texts: Hirata probably translated the portions of both the Old and New Testaments that he inserted into the Shinto doctrine of life after death, with not even a hint of acknowledgment.[16] In this example, the "Japanese spirit" was designated as both the "form of formlessness" of Japan's cultural essence and the reason for the country's progress.

The capacity of the Japanese throughout their history to absorb cultural components from the outside suggests nothing more than the figure of a sponge, but the difference is obvious since sponges have form. It is hard to know from Miki's writings whether the Japanese Spirit was some sort of inflection of the Hegelian world spirit or a disposition inherent in Japan's ethnic collective to create a culture of combinations. Miki used the term to mean both.

The active formlessness that Miki discerned in the act of Japan's habitual appropriation from foreign cultures led him to practice a kind of formalism and reinforced his distancing from the historical. In his consideration of Japan's long tradition of cultural borrowing, Miki presents the act as if it were an irreducible element in Japanese thought and character and remained outside of history and its mediations. The formalism of "formlessness of form" authorizes an unfixed ground that constantly shifts, removing the assurance supplied by structure and forms. Formless form, which often appeared to be merely random content, risked producing cultural deformations and anomalous syncreticisms exemplified by Hirata's explanation that people no longer needed to fear death or being sent to a place of permanent pollution since they would inhabit the invisible realm found around cemeteries and continue to live their lives as they always had. The absence of history in the formless has been detached from the original concrete foreign life from which it was appropriated and made to conform to a context alien to it, pitting abstraction against cultural concreteness. Yet as I show below, the justification for what was named cultural life expressed a kind of ungrounded liberal pluralism and consumerism. It should be noted that this formless form put Miki on a dangerously shifting intellectual ground, which led to the fascism he was trying to criticize. He was apparently referring to the production of plural discourses in the late Tokugawa period—all of which, in one way or another, showed some contact with foreign ideas. The strength of formlessness, he explained, lay in its capacity to seek out and take over other forms for use because it had no fixed original form to prevent its ceaseless gathering up of foreign information. According to Miki, this appetite for borrowing the content of other cultures raised the status of tradition and in fact defined it. Yet at the same time he was dismissive of those who valorized the beauty and charm of traditional Japan's culture because they failed to recognize that it had been produced under historical conditions that no longer existed.[17] It was clearly impossible in modern Japan, Miki argued, to actually construct "a pure Japanese style . . . by rejecting Western-style architecture, when such production is considered," "we come to feel uneasy." "The beauty of pure Japanese architecture knows the beauty of wood grain." But in modern Japan, the construction of structures like apartment buildings, factories, and public buildings is constrained by the social conditions of contemporary life and cannot ignore Western architecture to pursue a pure Japanese style. In a sense, Miki was pointing to the replacement of wood and bricks by concrete and cement. If Western-style architecture is adopted, its ornamentation requires Western-style paintings. Japanese have been taught that elegance can endure, with the use of such aesthetic terms as *aware*, *sabi*, *wabi*, *shiari*, and *yūgen*, all bequeathed by the past. But, Miki asked, is it possible to secure peace of mind when today's young people are addicted to what they view as the greatest pleasures of modern entertainment: movies, recordings of Western-style music, and the literature of the self? Miki valued traditional culture but saw a troubling sign that it was generating problems for contemporary Japan because of its meretricious linkage of the past and present.[18]

Still, it was the perseverance of the formless form that explained Japan's successful adaptation of its diverse borrowings from abroad. This was exemplified by Japan's experience in adopting capitalism. Miki suggested that Japan's taking over of the whole machinery of capitalism from industrialized England after the Meiji Restoration was not an act of pure imitation, as many contemporary critics claimed. Rather, Japan's successful adaptation to the new economic system was mediated by internal practices, which even before the restoration had been tending in the direction of capitalism. Miki was referring, of course, to the Marxist historiographical debates on the nature of capitalist development in Japan, which located the "early signs of capitalism" in the late Tokugawa period. Miki attributed this development to the "many holisms," group collectives that constituted a factual presence (*genson*) that in turn spurred capitalism to develop rapidly.[19] He argued that it was the formless form that distinguished the Japanese character, which absorbed foreign elements and combined them into a mix of incommensurables. It is possible to see in this mixing of elements from different cultures a resonance with capitalism's processes through the exercise of ceaseless but unplanned subsumption of forms, whereby economic, political, and cultural elements are taken over and coexist with appropriations of forms of practice from older modes of production to serve the new capitalist agenda. Yet the difference between the two forms of absorption lay in the fact that only one took over what had been near at hand from an earlier history. Miki chose to see the operation of combining incommensurable practices as the manifestation of the Japanese Spirit. He viewed the operation as an abstraction, empowering the essentialized formlessness to incorporate components from other cultures and make them work in Japan, and he did not seem to recognize that he was reconfiguring an appropriation in the same way the Japanese had been doing for ages.[20] This was the spirit's path to Japan's progress, a strategy enabled by the absence of specific fixed forms that might block the appropriation of foreign importations. But Miki realized that this had been shaped by the archaic moment in which it had formed. This association with the "archaic phenomenon" meant that the Japanese spirit's formless form of borrowing already implied at its origin the presence of an authorizing formlessness capable of appropriating from foreign cultures. Takeuchi Yoshimi later read this as a "structure of unlimited receptivity for use," and (as noted above) Maruyama Masao identified it as the *kosō*—the "archaic stratum" or *"basso ostinato,"* the deeper rhythm, extracted from the ancient histories, running through and determining Japan's history of cyclically withdrawing from and reentering the world.[21] According to Miki, the characteristic Japanese appropriation from other cultures often resulted in the reconfiguration of adopted material to fit the new environment and efface its original identity. This presumably undercut the merciless accusations of imitation since even before the Meiji Restoration and pointed to the power of recognizing use-value and its role in Japanese history, which led Miki to revisit the nature of history and the production of culture.[22]

After suggesting that the tradition of borrowing from other cultures persisted in Japan, Miki returned to considering history's vocation as principally concerned with the pursuit of change and development. The folk, he declared, are not only biological objects but also historical subjects since they are changeable, living creatures: "Insofar as they are humans born and bred in society, they must also alter their humanity according to the changes in society, [changes] ranging from feudalism to capitalism."[23] Since the Japanese character is a formless form, it is the proven way to produce a new characteristic or culture in keeping with the current changes in society. Here, Miki recognized the need to envision the birth of the new Japanese, a Japanese that combined their received culture with imports from abroad, which he believed was possible because the formless form of culture can produce only the diversity of "opposing ideas, practices and forces at the same time."[24] The genius of the formlessness of the Japanese spirit lies in its receptivity to external cultural and intellectual adoptions that increased the changeability of Japan's character and led to growing differences in Japan's character.[25] Miki wrote that it was to the credit of the ancestors of the modern Japanese that from the beginning they recognized the logic of appropriating (and the resulting eclecticism and synthesizing) of such diverse components as Buddhism and Confucianism, which led to the coexistence of various cultural adoptions. He believed that this type of combining incommensurables was at the heart of the Japanese character. In this respect, he cited approvingly the philosopher Watsuji Tetsurō's conception of stadialization (*jūsōsei*)—a vertical strata of periods or layers of time imposed on each other, a figure close to Miki's accumulation of different cultural moments that coexisted in some larger frame. But Miki later rejected this model for the Japanese character, which was continually developing a "new type of culture" once he recognized that it could no longer "sufficiently follow the form of the traditional culture of the past," a recognition that made it difficult, if not impossible, to ignore the challenge posed by Western culture and abandon the prospect of assimilating it.[26]

With this formulation, Miki was able to invert the archaism with which Japanists had valorized Japanese culture and assert that the archaic now provided a justification of difference. The inversion converted what had been a static culture unchanged since the origin's fetishizing of sameness and purity into a process of ongoing change and increasing difference. This resituated the archaic in a place once seized and colonized by archaism, which had emphasized the centrality of an exceptional culture of sameness that defied the threat of difference by remaining unchanged and static. Here was what Miki meant when he had proclaimed that the problem in Japan derived from the aura of sanctity attributed to the classical period— in fact, to ancient times. He argued that the adulation of antiquity meant that it could never be added to, since doing so would undermine its claim of uniqueness. Even though uniqueness was considered a "special thing" for the Japanese to pursue if it was concerned with character, Miki was convinced that uniqueness in itself was without value, unless the principle of antiquity was employed to sanction changes.

Miki thus recognized the flaw in the logic of Japanist fascism that refused to grant utility to foreign imports selected for assimilation. The reactionary conservatism of recent fascism, adhering to the form of the past, had "vainly rebuffed foreign thought and . . . separated itself from the dignity of the Japanese spirit." Not only did he reject the Japanist monopolization of the "Japanese Spirit" by redefining it, but he also responded to the contemporary emphasis on culturalism (*bunkashugi*) as a substitute for politics by proposing that 'living culture' (*bunka seikatsu*) was constituted of heterogeneous elements drawn from different cultures, thus arguing that it is the nature of Japaneseness to endeavor to study foreign countries to impart new forms to Japan's culture."[27] Yet it is important to note that he emphasized the primacy of culture rather than that of politics in the heated environment of the late 1930s. Miki saw the possibility of realizing this goal in his conception of "living culture" that he devised in the late 1930s. Living culture was a temporal model that embodied the noncontemporizing of the contemporary (showing the role that noncontemporaneity was assigned in mediating and shaping the contemporary) rather than its reverse (contemporizing the past, as seen in mature forms of capitalism). The reversal reflected a process that privileged the noncontemporary over the contemporary, whereby a nonmodern or noncapitalist society was positioned to appropriate new components for use from modern cultures and subordinate them to the society's older practices. This notion resembled Miki's description of how Japanese drew material from other cultures to create a Japanese version of it based on eclecticism, synthesis, and the assimilation of foreign things in the received culture of the "Japanese thing." This model also informed the explanation of the mystical *Kokutai no hongi* (published in 1937), or how Japan had adopted cultural elements from India, China, and the West and subordinated them to the Japanese character.[28] Miki had no sympathy for the bureaucratic academics who had compiled the *Kokutai no hongi* and little to say on the subject of the archaic myth. Yet his conception of living culture and the *Kokutai no hongi*'s acknowledgment of assimilating and subordinating external acquisitions to Japaneseness seem to share a kinship. Needless to say, the *Kokutai no hongi* represented the most extreme expression of Japanism and was intended to draw the folk to encounter and identify with the sublime of the archaic myth of origins, principally through the instrumentality of what Alan Tansman has called the "magic of language" and the "spirit of words" (*kotodama*). In this respect, Kobayashi's turn to the archaic in the postwar period was in fact a return, since his purpose was to resuscitate the centrality of the "spirit of words" originally uttered in oral stories before their captivity in Chinese ideographs. Through this kind of instrumentalization, the mystical text sought to vocalize the archaic myth through repetition, enabling the masses to hear (if not grasp) the words' spirit.[29]

In Miki's conception of living culture, it is possible to perceive the turning of capitalism's inclination for contemporizing the noncontemporaneous into its opposite, which subordinated the contemporary to the noncontemporaneous. For him, history centered action, actuality, and production that reflected the human capacity to constantly make and re-make the present, leading to continuous changes and increased differences driven by contingency. The historical present was laced with differing moments of the past that rubbed against the contemporary in a process that required actualization to address and manage the resulting tensions of temporal unevenness. In effect, action meant braiding past and present together. Actuality supplied Miki with an occasion to engage with the immediate present and survey the surviving remnants of a precapitalist age that crowded the contemporary landscape in the 1930s and represented a vanished social formation. In the 1930s, most (though not all) Marxists repeatedly highlighted the survival of feudal remnants in the capitalist present, seeing in their countrywide distribution a major force blocking the completion of capitalism and thus the transition to a socialist revolution, as well as condemning the Meiji Restoration to permanent incompletion and the new nation to a frozen state of semifeudalism. Miki would have agreed with such views and the resulting dim forecast for realizing a completed capitalism under present conditions. But unlike proponents of the vulgate version of Marxian thought, he was more concerned with the process of cultural production that was rooted in historical action and that offered immunity against congealing commodification—which, like feudal remnants, had become a shell emptied of creativity and set adrift when it lost contact with the concreteness of its originating time. Achieving the prospect of "living culture" promised to give older components from the past not only a new time but also a new function. Miki assigned the task of counteracting the ravages of commodification's inexorable process of social abstraction to this "living culture" because it offered the newness of vital creativity and the promise of true social relationships between people, instead of the deadening effects of objectification, nonrelationships, and self-estrangement. At the heart of the new time and space of living culture was a dedicated commitment to seek out and incorporate the difference represented by appropriating from the outside what was useful as the guarantee of continuing change and development. For Miki, this sense of the different, embodying what he believed would introduce new use-values, was the work of the true character of Japan conveyed through the agency of the "Japanese spirit" and that spirit's definition of history's purpose. Despite Miki's avowed separation from Marxism, its traces remained in his association of use-value, difference, and the making of history. It is at this juncture that Miki distinguished the temporality of modernization (*kindaika*, which he associated with the nineteenth-century development of the capitalist society and state, starting from the Meiji Restoration) and that of active contemporization (*gendaika*, which had a form similar to that of modernization but was of a different character, centered on the "current situation" [*jimu*]).[30] Here, Miki was conceptualizing the moment of the present and its requirements for praxis.

Miki's efforts to envision what he called living culture as a genuine alternative to the commodity form's tyranny bonded cultural creativity to the abstractions of commodified life in such a way that the former was supposed to overcome or at least restrain the excesses of the latter. What he may not have noticed is that "living culture" was already an accumulation of abstractions. In any case, this fusion of irreconcilable elements produced a vast cultural mix with coexisting temporal heterogeneities and subordinated the new from the outside to the received old of the inside. Like many of his contemporaries, Miki was drawn into discussions of how to determine what constituted concrete reality in a world saturated with the commodity form and dominated by abstract exchanges. The result was the sovereignty of value and the elimination of its history. For Miki, the real (*genjitsu*) referred to actuality—which, in authorizing human action, implied a practical present.[31] "What we call real life," he argued, "is the active everyday life."[32] In this formulation, the actual world was identified with the everyday, and specifically with the situations humans find in daily life. But here he ran into an aporia: even though he saw no incompatibility between actuality and history, he appeared troubled by the noticeable distance between everydayness and history. The actions in the former were rarely visible in the latter, and the latter was seldom mirrored in the former, which meant that the two spheres of activity remained distinct from each other. According to Miki, "the historical is creative, revolutionary, whereas everydayness is customary, the natural. . . . Everyday action is not seen in historical practice and it cannot be said that everyday humans are historical people."[33] Moreover, history was filled with eventfulness and charged with the task of extracting meaning from that eventfulness and the principle of reason behind it, while the everyday was dominated by endless repetition, routine, and a scarcity of events. The distinct temporalities that marked the two spheres led to a potential for conflict. Miki unsuccessfully tried to eliminate this potential by proposing that the everyday should be considered as the basic presupposition of the historical—which would throw it into the category of the world historical—even though he recognized that "everyday humans are not world historical beings."[34] This entailed imagining the everyday as contained in the framework of world history, with the everyday's own time replaced by the time of the nation-state. It also annexed the everyday to the time and history of the nation, even though Miki proposed that daily life was actually the source of historical time. Moreover, it risked making the everyday complicit in Japan's fascism at home and imperialism elsewhere in Asia. The aporetic nature of this distance between everydayness and world history (especially the place of the nation-state) came from the effort to fuse the differing temporalities embodied in an "original historicality"[35] (the everyday) and the world historical plane of history. Closing the cleft between conflicting spatial formations would supposedly bring the now of everyday life into alignment with the more abstract principle of Japan's world-historical mission. Yet doing so would fail to bridge the disparity between a history that moved forward and led to imperial acquisition and the circularity of everyday life. Miki sought to solve the problem of combining the rhythm of circular time that dominated everydayness with history's linearity by relocating a shared eternality in a new kinship of what might be termed the eternal now in the timeless domain of an endless present.[36] This strategy would later find a place in Maruyama's definition of the "archaic stratum."

The everyday actuality and an abstracted historical narrative devoted to the nation-state could not easily, if ever, be connected: what was experiential and composed of memory (the everyday) differed from history, since both were absent in the constructions of historical narratives. The desire to fuse different temporalities into some sort of alignment meant incorporating unassimilated residues and remainders into the framework of the nation-state to make unwanted remnants of passed pasts disappear. In the end, none of this worked for Miki, even though he had hoped to eliminate the frictions caused by noncontemporaneous contemporaneity by subordinating the everyday to the larger spatiotemporal chronotope of Japan's imperial world-historical mission. In "living culture," he had apparently invented a figure of time that closely resembled contemporary noncontemporaneity. In this way he recognized that the everyday, though a site of action, was less actualizing than history was, and thus he revised his earlier view to satisfy the requirements of Japan's world-historical mission. By that time he was already at work for the state. As a result, the everyday either remained outside the historical or acquired its meaning by uniting with world history—though that meant the everyday was at risk of losing its identity and becoming nothing more than the shadow of world history. Although Miki did not participate in the 1942 Kyoto conference on Japan's world-historical mission, it seems clear that his attempt to contain the everyday in the larger arena of world history constituted a dramatic departure from his earlier reflections on the autonomy of everydayness.

As a national narrative, history pointed to the singular and unique, while everydayness consisted of averages and the commonplace: it had rhythms of repetitive routine that could never be identified with history and that occurred in another zone of temporality. In his effort to link the everyday and world history, Miki posited a shared ground that indicated an originating historical consciousness that was both the source of history and a sense of historicality that would steadily mature (*zeitigen*, *kairos*).[37] But creating this shared ground was like building an impossible bridge of dreams between different temporal and spatial zones that could never be joined. The proposed maturation signified only a level of continuing mixing and collisions of uneven temporalities between the everyday and world history, which together would be forcibly homogenized into a smooth narrative succession that supposedly illustrated the inevitable maturation of time. At this point, Miki appears to have had no choice but to sacrifice the temporality associated with the sentient claims of everyday life—affect, experience, and memory—to the abstraction of a worldly narrative movement and allow history's meaning to be revealed. In this way, he inadvertently transported the everyday back to its original remaindered status and location. However, this opened the way to recognizing the existence of differing and distinct temporalities belonging to the separate spheres of everydayness and world history, as well as of the imperative to pursue historicality from within the zone of everyday life rather than from outside it. When Tosaka later took on this task, he eliminated the category of the mission of world history as an unnecessary barrier to securing access to the everyday, history, and its time.

Yet Miki's preoccupation with the present and the current crisis ultimately drove him to the idea of commitment and the immediate experience of the self within history. He also turned toward the problem of all presents (which entailed the interaction between received cultures that had fallen into abstraction) and the nourishment supplied by the reception of foreign influences (whose coexistence with living traditions promised to regenerate the present). Around the same time in the late 1930s when Miki embraced the concept of "living culture," the theme of everyday life had become a compelling issue in popular discourse and the subject of research devoted to measuring the quantitative changes occurring in daily life that spurred the development and introduction of new techniques to facilitate greater efficiency. These discussions and research into daily life focused on how contemporary Japan had effectively acquired a two-tiered society, as a result of the coexistence of different and incommensurable components. The writer Tanizaki Junichirō discounted the figure of the new culture houses of the 1920s in an essay, "Inei raisan" (Praising shadows), in 1931, while others like Tanigawa Tetsuzō considered the idea of a two-storied life to be foolish, and still others attested to the impossibility of living with an undigested replication of Western civilization that clearly worked against the "discipline of communal living."[38] Notwithstanding such complaints, the continuity of doubling what Watsuji called double life had become a fact of life, particularly in the cities and the circumstances in which women found themselves living in modern Japan.

Miki believed in the possibility of using older cultural elements of the past in configuring a new culture. However, the reliance on older cultural elements to guide the unsteady present stood in marked contrast to the 1920s idea of cultural living (*bunka seikatsu*), with its uncritical fetishizing of the new urban Western ways—especially its excessive commodification in the cities that Miki later described as a form of colonization. Cultural life must be distinguished from living culture because it was a consumption campaign inaugurated after World War I to induce people, especially the middle class, to buy and consume new household products and other commodities imported from abroad. Living culture, which was conceptualized in 1930s, focused on the argument that Japan had no choice but to experience a mixed culture. Miki blamed the consumerist fad of cultural living for its emphasis on nothing but commodities such as new household labor-saving devices as well as on new forms of popular pleasure and entertainment—in short, for superficial frivolousness and the dangers it posed in its enthusiastic encouragement of accepting the external and the surface to the neglect of a "true living culture" with its interiority, depth, and substance. Miki was speaking mainly of life in the cities, and although the new commodity culture penetrated into the countryside, he remained silent on the rural-urban divide. Cultural living was tainted by the dye of Europeanism and Americanism and illustrated the challenge involved in retaining the perspective of Japanese independence. At the same time, he cautioned against the recent strategy of advising independence that was endorsed by a self-complacent anti-foreignism because much could be still learned from the West through the mediation of the received tradition. Convinced that his present was the moment for Japan to undertake to what the West had to offer to avoid falling into the trap of militarism, he believed that this task required both assessing the limitations of foreign cultures as a condition for imagining a new living culture and also looking back at and surveying the utility of the legacy of the Japanese tradition.

It is important to understand how Miki differentiated between the core of living culture and its 1920s predecessor, cultural living: "The postwar boom after World War I which came with new housing and labor-saving devices seemed to have grafted imported innovations on received traditional practices of daily life." However, "living culture" was not even a problem of culture, since true culture "reflected the domain of spirit and different civilizations."[39] What distinguished "living culture" (especially in the context of contemporary Japanist announcements of Japan's irreducible uniqueness) was its positive and progressive attitude toward life in contrast to the morbidities unleashed by the illusive fictions of the mythic imaginary. Here, Miki was clearly appealing to the German conception of general culture (*allgemeine Kultur*) and the English idea of culture—each of which, in its own way, implied a process leading to the formation of cultivation. Thus, culture in Miki's thinking referred to the acts of human production and working on nature. He thought that living culture as a form of production encompasses the transformation of life accompanied by a kind of will to culture and did not simply refer to importing things to be imitated. In essence, living culture was the working through of his idea of history as actuality, redefining history's mission as constantly combining incommensurate practices from past and present moments to repeatedly reaffirm the dominant temporal order of contemporizing its other—that is, the noncontemporaneous.

The mythographers of Japanism supposed that everyday life in Japan was cultural rather than merely natural, and thus filled with vestiges from the past that managed to persist in the present. According to Miki, "there are words we are unable to neglect and they are not things we have produced for the first time but were transmitted to us from some distant past of the folk. And we are born within these traditions."[40] He was confident that traditions were not left behind in the past but are continually moving, changing, living things. He argued that the doubling of life in contemporary Japan had actually first been perceived in the late Tokugawa period by the thinker Sakuma Shōzan, who came up with the recommendation (appropriated from China) that Western science and technology be combined with traditional Eastern moral philosophy (*tōyō no dōtoku, seiyō no gakugei*). After that combination, Sakuma believed, the Japanese still needed to acquire a new philosophy to make up for the congealed apathy among contemporaries for whom the old is no longer adequate.[41] This passage suggests that the combination would in time lead to the further evolution of traditional philosophy as it interacted with imported science and technology. It also expressed Miki's conviction that philosophy should guide both culture and politics, as a means of resolving the division between the two. Tradition, he reasoned, was distinguished from the remnants because the latter were simply surviving traces of passed historical cultures—whose remaining residues are reanimated and often refigured in the present but drained of content and function, leaving only the empty husks of their form to survive in a different time. Tradition thus came to signify the persistence of vestiges from the past that lived on and functioned in a present different from the time of their origin. The past unceasingly continues to permeate humanity, entering a demand to be understood to find a place for itself. And the act of transmitting the past can be accomplished only in the present, where traditions are activated in the encounter with the new and external. Following Heidegger, Miki held fast to his view that the past was the bridge between the present and its future.[42] The point of his discussion of tradition was to distinguish it from the traditionalistic claims noisily made by contemporary Japanists, whom he faulted for their appeal to the unrational and their commitment to archaic myth, which confused genuine traditions with concocted claims of traditionalism. Miki also accused contemporary Japanists of overlooking the role played by actuality (the concrete real) and failing to recognize how creativity is produced. Japanese fascism, Japanism, remained encased in the archaic myth of origins and the supposed divine creation of Japan and its people, which bequeathed the mystical nation's political body (kokutai) to future generations. Hence, "tradition is not able to truly live as tradition where there is no actualization."[43]

Individualism and liberalism occupied the center of Miki's concept of the cultural living program in the 1920s. Insofar as it remained important for the development of a national living culture, it was necessary to "conquer" "the feudal remains" to permit "individualism and liberalism to retain their significance."[44] Women especially, he noted, seemed to crave the culture of commodity exchange and consumption and the lifestyle provided by Westernized household labor-saving devices—that targeted urban middle-class populations and symbolized the importance of a new, materialist lifestyle including radios and new architecture, pleasures, entertainment, and clothing in contrast to Miki's loftier notion of living culture. The reason for this, he believed, was that women were even more subjected to feudal leftovers than men. Yet cultural living could be considered only as a stage in the larger and longer process of realizing living culture, a process reflected in the growth of material culture and the economic process from feudalism to capitalism. The effect of linking liberalism and individualism to modern material culture would be to use both to achieve goals that were in fact neither liberal nor individualistic. To contend that a living experience would not terminate in the recuperation of liberalism did not necessarily lead to a reversion to feudalism but rather the realization of a form of cooperativism as the foundation of a new living culture.

For Miki, cooperativism promised the production of "social discipline," since he had come to believe that contemporary society (like capitalism) was deadlocked as a result of the "abuses" inflicted by "individualism, liberalism, and rationalism."[45] Culture must be "cooperative" and "public," or it could not exist.[46] According to Miki, culture invariably equaled folk production, the proletariat, the masses, and the people and was thus always collective, communal, and directly opposed to ideals of living culture. Modern ideas (especially individualism) needed a system to gain control, and liberalism worked to undermine "social discipline among the nation's people."[47] Cooperativism presented the prospect of attaining wholeness and discipline capable of uniting people to move beyond the dangerous currents of self-interest that accompanied the older "cultural living," with its attraction to foreign material goods (but not ideas) and endless consumption of commodities. Miki's appeal to holism (zentaishugi) bordered dangerously on fascism and appeared to be a paradoxical turn in his thinking. But it is essential to recall that from the beginning he had emphasized the importance of social cohesion in Japan. "That Japanese society came to exist as a comparatively closed social order," he wrote in 1935, "was probably fortunate for the development of a holistic outlook. Fascism is not, in essence, a feudal ideology but rather one that conforms to the stages of contemporary capitalism."[48] The problem, as he saw it, was the intractable opposition between individualism and a holistic collectivity that was the foundation of Japanese social cohesion—which was capable of sealing the breach between the inherently closed nature of the latter and the necessary widening of openness of the former.[49] I believe that the cooperativism Miki favored, spawned by a newly revised living culture, could not be differentiated from uniformity. Japan, he explained, remained relatively inferior to other societies because its modernity had not developed historically and its liberalism, imported from outside, had proved inadequate to meet the country's needs. Basically, the nation lacked an ethical endowment capable of controlling and regulating the population without recourse to the threat of coercion by state-initiated violence. What was needed was an ideological apparatus positioned in such a way that it could get subjects (shūtai; not shinmin [imperial subject]) to perform their duties to the state voluntarily and effectively. The Meiji slogan of enriching the nation, strengthening the military never qualified as a doctrine to elicit voluntary cooperation, since it was issued from above as a command of the state. If liberalism had not rooted itself in Japanese society, as Miki believed, history led him to posit the existence of the "space of Asia" within the Greater East Asia Co-Prosperity Sphere as a modern example of the cooperativism of living culture. "The day on which the Orient is formed," he advised, "is the day on which the 'world' is formed in its true meaning."[50] An Asia directed by Japan would announce the true beginning of world history. This gesture came close to authenticating Gramsci's earlier proposition that when liberalism exhausts its productivity, it inevitably passes into fascism. Miki consciously sought to distance himself from the Japanese version of fascism (if not from its more rational forms, especially expressions of poiesis). However, his understanding of Japan's imperialism led him to imagine a social order just as fascistic as the Japanist version, consisting of an imaginary gemeinschaft [communal] capitalism that fused technological nationalism with a cooperative based on an organist folk—in other words, fascist totalitarianism under a different name. Perhaps paradoxically, but not ironically, Miki referred to the state apparatus he had disparaged as "bureaucratic fascism."[51] He failed to give a political name to his explanation of why Japan had turned to holism and fascism, and he provided only some observations about historical immaturity and the weight of tradition. Much of his description of liberal political development also matches Gramsci's concept of passive revolution, as applicable to the Meiji Restoration. But the restoration was an unplanned seizure of political space and time and was decided on at the last possible moment, and not by history but by individuals acting with no real political principles except for a vague call to return to a nonexistent origin (what Takayoshi Kido called a farce in one act), foreshadowing the way Japanese modernization ultimately evolved into fascism. Miki never really recognized the role played by unevenness, even though he was aware of the operation of combined development—which, in his conceptualization of living culture, implied the existence of unevenness, as disclosed in the historical immaturity of Japanese development and its dependence on appropriations from foreign sources.

The Archaic Phenomenon

Tosaka notes in his now classic study of ideology, "The Japan Ideology" (*Nihon ideorogiron*), that for him the main conflict to be resolved was always that between philosophic idealism and materialism—not any materialism, but one defined as dialectical in contrast to other materialisms. Behind this conflict of intellectual positions, it is possible to glimpse an even deeper dualism: between reason (or, as Tosaka put it, modern "scientific" logic) and what he considered to be unreason (he regarded the archaic as the embodiment of unreason). It should be noted that Tosaka saw in ideology an abstraction capable of encompassing the entirety of the social formation, reaching all levels of social relationships throughout the political order, economy, and culture. For him, ideology worked to suppress and even efface what constituted the lived reality of the moment through which Japanese society was passing. He was convinced that ideology appeared widely and in diverse guises, disciplines, and intellectual and cultural activities—from recondite philosophic texts to daily newspapers and films, which served as proxies capable of carrying particular ideological messages that targeted a specific group or class and reinforced a conception of the real that he believed had no relationship to concrete contemporary social existence. As a Marxist, he believed that the foundation of a social order that authorized ideology and its spread was commodity exchange, which generated diverse substitute accumulative abstractions. These disguised what Alfred Sohn-Rethel much later called the "real abstraction,"[52] but which Tosaka could only imply. Tosaka saw both neo-Kantian philosophic idealism and its privileged theory of epistemology as the principal means of abstracting thought and experience, which found expression in a number of disciplines like philology and literature. What Tosaka seems to have inadvertently uncovered, despite the limitation under which he was working, was that the Japanese society identified by the exceptionalist claims of the "Japanese spirit" or "Japanese thing" had been produced by commodity exchange as much as by the social class system that was often its carrier. Here, I believe, is where Tosaka most disagrees with Miki—who along the way also acknowledged the relationship between fascism and capitalism, but who seemed to avoid probing it further and even proposed later (during his government service) an Asian form of capitalism. Perhaps more importantly, Tosaka (unlike Miki) was able to detect that cognitive faculties of the Japanese had been historically conditioned by the epochal transition to capitalism, which constituted an all-encompassing "social synthesis."[53]

Tosaka recognized that fascism had not been derived from finance capitalism and its class interests and that the origin of liberalism in Japan had not been connected to economic activity. He believed instead that the Japanese liberal experience could ultimately be attributed to the mystfications of the Japanese spirit. In fact, terms like the Japanese thing and the Japanese spirit represented special characteristics that defined the exclusivity of Japanese reality. The content of Japanese reality apparently was signified by ordinary terms like the "state," "folk," "race," "economy," "politics," and "culture," yet Japanese relatively differed from those terms as they were used elsewhere in the world by virtue of their unique derivation and particularity in the Japanese context and the way they informed the Japanese spirit. Tosaka questioned the utility, relevance, and suitability of terms like the "Japanese spirit," whose use gives the status of spirituality to the substance or essence of things. Accordingly, he was convinced that, "to call Japanized reality a particular Japanese spirit, that is, to abstract a Japanized reality as a particular spirit, makes it possible to see the symptoms of mixing in our spiritualism is connected to Japan."[54] Tosaka went on to charge that the abstracted "Japanese Spirit" was enthusiastically embraced by fascists, who ultimately used Japan as an abstraction of superiority opposed to internationalism. He wondered how reasonable it was to look upon things as expressions of a particularistic "Japanese spirit," which fascists increasingly equated with the "Japanese reality of the situation."[55] In this regard, the concept of a Japanese spirit was made into an abstraction, inasmuch as it appeared everywhere and was made to represent a broader reality to which all kinds of things in their apparent flight from concreteness were reducible, due to that reality's capacious spirituality. Tosaka thus recognized that the autonomy of Japanese reality was based on the country's independence and separation from the international sphere. This characteristic of a spiritualized Japanese situation was not only prior to the international sphere but was also positioned to sublimate itself to it—that is, to a single principle of an abstracted Japanese reality. But Tosaka saw in this move only an older common "theoretical trick" (toriku) of nationalist fascists and the most "representative of social fascists," groups whose members resorted to abstracting the "situation" of reality under the shapeless cloud that was the Japanese spirit.[56] While Tosaka never explained the necessary conversion from the reality of the dominant exchange commodity system to consciousness (especially its capacity to include the entire range of social reality through the mystification of substitute abstractions), he came close to doing so. In his critique of ideological proxies, he saw epistemology and idealist philosophy underwriting such disciplines as philology, literature, journalism, and diverse cultural activities and the possibility of glimpsing in them the silhouette of substitute forms of knowledge that concealed the originating and absent real abstraction. The real danger this posed was the revelation that fascist Japan was grounded in an accumulation of fictions.

I believe that Tosaka was the most committed defender of Enlightenment thought that Japan had produced, from the time of his appearance in the late 1920s to his imprisonment in the late 1930s, when he was initially forbidden to write. He died in prison at the end of World War II, having apparently scratched out on his cell wall his solidarity with Rosa Luxemburg and her last days. *The Japan Ideology* is the quintessential statement of his passionate lifelong defense of the values of the Enlightenment throughout the darkest days of interwar Japan.[57] It is also his sharpest criticism of the unreason that he believed had seized the Japanese intellectual world in the years that witnessed both the formation of fascism and the beginning of World War II. In many ways his critique of unreason and irrationality anticipated Georg Lukács's great 1962 *Destruction of Reason*: Tosaka condemned the same tradition of German *Lebensphilosophie* that Lukács criticized. Lukács saw his method as an exercise of reason, while Tosaka had earlier named his the logic of scientific criticism.

Using Marxian analysis, Tosaka developed what I would call a deep hermeneutics of suspicion (a term he would undoubtedly have rejected) that, through a long analytic trajectory, disclosed how epistemology and philosophic idealism had successfully and successively concealed themselves through an overdetermination of proxies (cultural and political forms) that worked to reinforce fascism. It did so "first," he wrote at the end of chapter 11 of *The Japanese Ideology*, "with metaphysics, then interpretative philosophy," which came down to the hermeneutics of philology and finally "literature-ism," all of which overlapped with each other.[58] This was Tosaka's singular model of a steadfast commitment to concealing "modern idealism" in contemporary Japan.[59] His pursuit of the concealed itinerary of idealism in this text is consistently unsparing and rigorously steeped in logic, and he risked repetition to ensure that he had clearly made his point. I cannot help admiring this breathtakingly sustained exercise in philosophic critique (rarely equaled in Japan even today) that was aimed not only at his former teachers at the Kyoto Imperial University, with whom he was able to maintain friendly relations, but also at the famous Kyoto school of philosophy. Tosaka regarded philosophic idealism as the core of the Kyoto school and the philosophic choice of the Japanese bourgeoisie, and that idealism became the principal idiom used to provide authority for the fascist ideology of Japanism.

Yet the strength of Tosaka's ideological critique was also its weakness. If logic broke through the veil that concealed philosophic idealism, the materiality of history also remained out of sight—notably, often in his own writings. His privileging of the philosophic idiom over its historicity might have explained the reasons for both idealism's concealment and its dominance. While this appears to be a paradox difficult to explain, what is clearly manifest is how little Tosaka engaged in the contemporary historiographical debates over the development of Japan's capitalism, as well as his dedication to liberating historical time from consciousness and relocating it in the materiality of the workday of daily life—which, it seems, he could have presented as an alternative to the automatic linear narrative embraced by the contributors of the 1930s historiographic symposium on the development of Japan's capitalism. But Tosaka might well have been prompted to reject any practice of historical discourse founded on a progressive linear narrative form that in turn was centered on the unit of the nation-state, since the use of such a discourse risked reviving the claims of nationalist exceptionalism rather than supporting the international division of labor and the abstractions of national culture over daily work. In the end, his historical explanation of fascism in Japan resembled the lecture faction's position in the famous debates, especially regarding the principal role ascribed to feudal remnants—which, in fact, derived from the findings of the historiographical dispute. Another possible explanation of Tosaka's rejection of the historical discourse described above might be attributed to his intellectual socialization in the formalism of the neo-Kantian philosophy that he later sought so strenuously to discredit. Tosaka relentlessly emphasized formal logic and the formalism of scientific criticism (which invariably bracketed the historical), instead of focusing on capitalism's history and the mode of structuring that history imposed on lived social reality. In effect, he frequently seemed to have abandoned the historical present for the indefinite temporality of philosophy, almost reversing Marx's recommendation to abandon philosophy for history. In fact, Tosaka never addressed the question of the historicity of philosophic idealism itself—especially the source of its abstracting aptitude, which it had effaced as a condition of a formalistic presentation that had been stripped of its mediations to appear as unvarnished truth. In this respect, philosophic formalism shared a kinship with the abstraction of the value-form produced by exchange value and its increasing disavowal of and separation from the domain of history (that is, the domain of labor, in the service of use-value). With his near fetishization of a formalistic scientific critique, Tosaka ran the risk of seeming to endorse the view that production resulted from value and circulation rather than from the activity of living labor in the making of use-value.

Nevertheless, Tosaka's scorching critique brilliantly ripped the covers off idealism and showed it to be an ideological illusion of reality—especially the ground it claimed authorized social reality but that in fact only further distorted it. This was probably as far as a philosophy about philosophy could go without taking a detour into history. Yet it would be a mistake to conclude that Tosaka had failed, since he was one of the strongest thinkers among his contemporaries and one of the bravest in his stand against the forces of Japanese fascism in a dark time—bravery for which he paid with his life. In fairness, it should be said that his philosophic critique engaged what he considered to be the principal problem haunting contemporary Japan, which was its avoidance of historial explanation, and that he demanded, like an unyielding and impatient nemesis, a final resolution of the seemingly irreconcilable conflict among the real, the given, and the actual. In doing so he provided the necessary index of the specific historical present that had society in its thrall. This opposition played out in the conflict over the respective claims of idealism and actuality, or the claims of the substitutes they had accumulated like the crisis of spirit (in the space of culture) and the politics of time, with its attendant challenge to the status of history faced by Japan and other industrial capitalist societies in the 1930s: did understanding the immediate moment require a historically informed accounting or a complete rejection of history in favor of a template based on an untimely and timeless past to replace the crisis-ridden present? Tosaka's response was to propose the primacy of the time of lived everyday reality under capitalism. This was a reckoning with time itself, which Heidegger had called for earlier, instead of the timeless transhistoricality of an eternal origin that claimed to exceed all history as the condition of the fascist imperative. Tosaka attempted to reanimate the echoes of Marx and Friedrich Engels's concrete critique in *The German Ideology* of the Hegelian valorization of the heavenly over the earthly in a different time and place on the other side of the world.

In a 1936 article titled "The Growth of Japan's Fascism" (*Nihon fuashizumu no hatsuiku*), Tosaka announced that "what everybody probably sees and hears first is the cultural guidance of bureaucratic fascism issued from the top."[60] Like Miki, Tosaka considered the question of how to control cultural production to be the crucial problem of the moment, but the two men had different political perspectives. Miki believed that the people (*minshū*) created culture, but he seemed reluctant to claim that they saw themselves as reliable subjects capable of taking responsibility for that creation. In contrast, Tosaka saw in the fascist state's administration of culture an instrument of oppressing the people by robbing them of their agency to create culture, which ultimately removed their entitlement to subjectivity. Given Tosaka's observation and Miki's silence, it is worth noting that many writers on fascism inside and outside of Japan have recognized that Japan did not experience a mass movement mobilized by fascist political parties (and complimented Japan on having avoided such a movement), in contrast to Nazi Germany and fascist Italy. But it seems clear that many thinkers and writers who experienced the everyday in the 1930s knew that Japan's bureaucratic fascism had no need of a mass movement precisely because the country's population had been largely depoliticized into greater subjugation. In this regard, Japan was in fact a classic instance of reverting from modernity to archaism as the effect of desubjectivation of the populace. The state's control of culture and cultural policy produced an obedient population at the same time as oppressing its members.

For Tosaka, the issue was the subordination of everyday life to intense bureaucratic regulation, thus verifying the extremes of possible domination implicit in Max Weber's thesis on the modern bureaucratic vocation to control everyday life. Tosaka also recognized in this bureaucratic effort to subordinate the everyday to the state and thus assimilate it to the desire to diminish, if not eradicate, whatever temporal and spatial autonomy the everyday had been able to retain. He was also aware of the corresponding subordination of politics to culture, an effort that employed cultural production in the service of political demands to suppress dissent and criticism. This effort was not simply the inversion of cultural production into a disguised politics of time expressed in fascism: it was also a thorough fictionalization of culture intended to replace a model that had supposedly evolved from Japan's historical development into a modern capitalist society. In short, the aim of this inversion was to deny modern history and the culture it had fostered by what Tosaka was fond of calling the camouflage (*gisō*) of idealism. Sanctioned by the state, cultural discourse attempted to lessen the incidence of social conflict by implanting an image of a more culturally unified and integrated social order no longer divided by the state and everyday life according to class, gender, sexual differences, region, and so forth. Much of Tosaka's critical practice revealed his nuanced understanding of this accelerated turn toward cultural discourse and how it failed to supply the suppression promised by camouflaging. He had already detected the grounding of culture in an ontological view of the world, according to which existence was replaced by its derivation and ontology became a stand-in for philosophy. It was in this moment of intellectual discovery that Tosaka began to identify a new vocation for philosophic reflection in the lived experience of everyday life—notably, the centrality of the workday of capitalist Japan. His position dramatically contrasted with that of people who were pursuing a spiritualistic history, grandiose cultural narratives of a glorious premodern cultural past. Historians like Nishida Naojirō and Hiraizumi Kiyoshi (author of the paradigmatic 1927 "Marrow of History" [Rekishi no kotsuzui] formulated a new framework for the perspective of a spiritual and ultranationalistic cultural history of Japan before the modern age students would follow in the succeeding decade). Nishida was a Kyoto historian whose 1932 "Introduction to Japan's Cultural History" (Nihon bunkashi josetsu)[61] turned his attention to cultural achievements in the Muromachi period (1336–1573) and the construction of Zen gardens, concentrating on the rock garden in Ryōanji and its exemplification of a culture dedicated to self-centeredness and introspection. Nishida was also a member of the state-sponsored Research Institute of Japanese Spiritual Culture (Nihon seishin bunka kenkyūjo), under whose auspices he brought out a number of nationalistic works that moved the study of Japan's early, premodern culture away from political and economic history and toward the contemporary situation. The same could be said of Watsuji's historical writings.

Tosaka was even more suspicious of remote transcendental preoccupations that obscured social reality through a strategy of displacement and dissimulation, as seen in his critiques of philosophers such as Nishida Kitarō, Watsuji, and Takahashi Satomi. Tosaka believed that philosophic hermeneutics mistakenly sought to penetrate the recesses of a hidden order of meaning rather than engage with the immediate surface challenges posed by contemporary material reality. He argued that instead of seeking access to the deeper meaning of a hidden order, hermeneutics should investigate what lay behind the immediate surface of contradictions and thus identify the capitalist forces generating those contradictions. His conception of history flattened time and assigned it to the surface, rejecting both any assumption of meaning or a deep hidden order in which it remained housed. This, I believe, was Tosaka's response to the view of history that informed the historiographical debate focused on explaining the development of capitalism in Japan, which should have concentrated on the effects of capitalism on the lived now-time of the everyday instead of searching for its beginnings in the Tokugawa past.

Given Marx's commitment to a practical materialism, it is not surprising that Tosaka saw the study of history as a way of intervening in the concrete present; in fact, he was convinced that the historical perspective was the only one available. Using this perspective entailed embracing Marx's conception of historical time (now designated as history's content) and assuming the necessity of considering it alongside capital's structuring of everyday life to identify the historical exits it might offer. The everyday might appear to be the same from one day to the next, but it had the capacity to produce differences. Tosaka believed that time and space had been captured by capitalism and made into new categories for organizing people and their social relationships to serve capitalism's agenda of accumulation. Implied in this view was the conviction that contemporary Japanese bourgeois society made considerations of recollection, time, and memory (that is, historical consciousness) meaningless, which prefigured Theodor Adorno's conception of a society dominated by timeless exchange and lacking both memory and history. As a result, Tosaka was induced to start not from the concept of history but from its experience of the everyday, which he saw as a practical present that grounded the character of politics. Practice was inscribed in the routines and traditions that constituted the experience of everyday life. And that life defined the force of an accumulated lived historical time, which had remained overlooked or ignored as a history produced by the everyday. In this way, Tosaka's conception of historical time upended the view that history was unidirectional and linear. Instead, history yoked the past to the present and produced stacked layers of everydays that appeared the same and embodied routines and traditional practices that the layers imposed on each other. This new view was crucial because it made accessible an inventory of everyday times in a sort of palimpsest, creating piled times of experience that linear progression would have left behind or ignored. For Tosaka, the inventories come from times past but are themselves not past: rather, they are always present because they are read from the perspective of the present. The figure of the palimpsest makes the whole historical inventory accessible, which means that historians can detect political possibilities that had either gone unnoticed or been seen merely as part of a heritage of accumulated routines.

Tosaka felt that the most important question was why historical time had become so compelling in the present. Of course, that had a good deal to do with historians' concentration on the present and their blurring of ideology and social reality. Moreover, Marx's histories were entirely focused on the structure of the present (what I have called the historical present), which called attention to the unacknowledged retention of the past in the present and the fractious relationship between different temporal claims. Apparently prompted by the need to rescue historical knowledge from scientific dismissal, idealism's metaphysical transcendentalism and abstraction of national narratives that had been removed from the routines lived in the everyday noticed only the absence of the contemporary living conditions and the history that would explain their dire circumstances. As Tosaka saw it, the problem was how the present was situated in a historical time contemporaries were living. It is my contention that historical practice had invented a historical time suitable for dating the national narrative based on the temporal rhythm of nation and capital, and I believe that this explains why historians have shown so little interest in the question of historical time apart from resorting to chronology to mark the unfolding moments in a linear narrative of progress. Tosaka's sense of vision comes from the presentness of today—from the character of the now that generates autonomous forms of the contemporary value system. He used *seikaku* to denote character, which could also refer to the disposition of a time or perhaps even to its zeitgeist (a word he did not use), as long it retains a secular sense of meaning. This character could not be considered without taking into account the space of everydayness and the materiality composing it, as Tosaka had argued in an earlier essay titled "On Space."[62] Moreover, it is not permissible, he warned, to measure the value system embedded in the "realities of today with the categories of tomorrow."[63] This is because the present has announced its kinship with a period's character (invariably meaning a political disposition), and in so doing has drawn attention to the relationship between the part (the relationship between historical periods) and the whole (the totality of historical time). The work of today must be done today, and tomorrow's work will correspond to tomorrow's necessity. Tosaka was convinced that he had found the proper "law of perspective," since the present determines what must and can be done before and what comes later.[64] It is only in the present (the today) that history can be done. If, as Tosaka supposed, the present appears to be the "time of our life," a seeming timeless duration of endless routines and repetitions required by work, the everyday provides the location of "history's mystery"—a view recalling Marx's accusation that Hegel used the term *mystification* and its implied imperative of demystification.[65]

Tosaka's discussion of history and everydayness included an obvious appeal to the model of the commodity (or the actuality of the conduct of custom, which resembles the "skin" that covers and conceals what is beneath it), whose mysterious form managed to conceal from view the principle of historical production.[66] In this process, labor is transmuted into abstract value and the pursuit of surplus value, which is made to appear natural and timeless when in fact it is unnatural and filled with real time. A deeply embedded unhistorical and abstracted figure of everyday life, like the commodity form, now needed to be unveiled by restoring the content of its concrete conditions of existence. The reason for this move, according to Tosaka, derives from the fact that the solidity of history is concealed, like the commodity, throughout places in society but that cannot remain hidden any longer. In this way he saw the present as miniaturized in the today (*konnichi*) and showing its shape in the time of now (*ima*). Tosaka's conception of the "accent" might be read as the agent but it more likely functions as a microcosm representing the whole of history. Tosaka was projecting the centrality of the everyday onto the making of history's time. As a result, the present (now seen as the "realm of necessity," not a utopian "possibility") must be the starting point for the rehistoricization and actualization of all pasts in the present moment—which is the site of planning and organization of what comes before and what is to follow.[67] This demands that "practical work, all historical narratives, [and] all human action must begin with the present," which is every today.[68] This meant that each day brought freedom and thus an opportunity for change, depending on both "necessity" and the political disposition to act. The importance of this conception is its presentness, the now-time of everyday life, rather than a Heideggerian future that leads toward death.

In spite of the regularity of ceaseless routine and common experiences and occurrences in each day, Tosaka maintained that days must be separated from each other, and he distinguished each day from what preceded and followed it, recognizing its inescapable dailyness yet acknowledging that the everyday still housed the substance of historical time that would disclose the mystery of time's difference. To uncover the mystery, it was necessary to focus on the importance of the content of everyday life—not on the form of the nation and its fixed narrative of a plotline, which Miki was committed to pursuing. Here, Tosaka clearly distinguished between the nation and the everyday, and he sought to shift the focus of history from the former (form) to the latter (content). Tosaka saw the historical time of the everyday as the only possible history, because it was about the ordinary, common, and familiar and was grounded in the concrete details and reality of the lives lived by most people, which he contrasted with the eventful, extraordinary, and uncommon world of national history (which nobody actually lived or experienced) and its entrance onto the stage of world history. The implied reversal would entail the primacy of larger-than-life abstractions represented in world history and national narratives, in which the everyday remained eventless, if not invisible, and the lives of ordinary people remained silent. In Tosaka's theorization, historical time was compelled to conform to an order that permitted no exchanging of today for tomorrow or yesterday. Work never waits, because people must work today out of fear that tomorrow will be worse if they do not. The present is always today, and history must always be practical—a time and place of praxis, capable of realizing the difference resulting from the logic of dialectical interaction between the everyday present and the totality of historical time but not grand utopian schemes of anticipation and expectation. It should be recognized that this conception of historical time as history's content sharply contrasted with Miki's effort to explain everydayness as the source of history and then his subordination of everydayness to the forms of world history and the nation and their shared conception of linear progression.

I believe that Tosaka was proposing a conception of the historical present to replace the borrowed dominant phenomenological conception of time, based on consciousness from the domain of experience and memory with a concept of time founded on the lived reality of a bodily temporality, since the living body always takes place in the present. It is thus the immediate present that contains the "kernel of the crystal."[69] He warned that this dependency on a conception of time rooted in consciousness reduced historical time to a mere representation of time, that is, a phenomenological time that has robbed life of its claim to historicity and specificity. Here, I believe he was referring to the reliance of historical practice on the form of the narrative and the unfolding of the nation's story or plotline, informed not by time but by a chronology that dated significant changes and moments. When Tosaka argued that time was the fundamental content of history (not of form), he acknowledged that historical practice was usually reduced to telling the story of the nation-form. It seems possible to suggest that he saw form as an abstraction that determined what would be included and what would be left out of the kind of story historians were

committed to telling. It would not be unreasonable to assume that for Tosaka, who recognized the historical division between mental and manual
labor, manual labor had become abstracted because of its association with
commodity production and exchange, as indicated by Marx's observation
that not "an atom of use-value could be found in the commodity," which
reflected the idea that labor was contained in the commodity through "exchange abstraction."[70]

The example Tosaka would have had identified of the importance of
history's content of time appeared in his decision to equate the everyday
with the time of the workday and the creation of abstract labor power,
which referred to the calculation of the labor and time used in making a
commodity to determine the worker's wages, and which meant that the
worker sold labor power and was entirely separated from the commodity
and its exchange. The aspect of the content that time shapes history was
reflected in the recognition of the larger framework of uneven time, which
governed capitalist social life and production and which was validated in
his acknowledgment of surviving feudal remnants in his present. These
remnants blocked the further development of capitalism and consigned
Japan to occupy a permanently indeterminate world of semifeudalism. In
the case of the former, abstract labor and time evolved from the disregarding of commodities as values that facilitate exchanges. In the case of the
latter, the lingering remnants of the past intervened both in the historical time of capitalism and in the way it operated in production, as well as
shaping the rhythms of social and political life. For Tosaka, this content of
time—which corresponds to what might be called content as form—was
the appropriate form through which time would be expressed in any given
present, a form that did not exist before and would not last into a future.

In fact, Tosaka asserted that the historical is the last principle, beyond
which there are no other temporal referents to rely on. Time can rely only
on history, especially not on the principle of temporality and its openness
to eternality (which comes from nowhere). History is thus its own time
and cannot employ the time of phenomenology, metaphysics, or science.
Tosaka named this principle of historical time the everyday.[71] This naming acknowledged the perspective of the everyday as the character of the
real, a response to idealists who saw in their conception of the real the path
to a hidden order of meaning embodied in the illusion of the atemporal archaic (rather than in the actuality demanded by attention to the immediate
moment). For Tosaka, the everyday also constituted a unit of analysis that

he believed was superior to the nation-form because it was composed of the time in which people actually lived and worked as well as of the family, which he had already recognized had been transfigured into an "archaic phenomenon." The everyday present embodied the condensed meaning of historical time: it was both the site of necessity and flexibility, encapsulated in the today and made visible in now-time. A conception of the today that epitomized the present shared with it the concealed principle of understanding that it—the everyday—constituted the only possible meaning of the historical. For Tosaka, as I suggested above, the historical was nothing more than the time of work in daily life and the oppressive conditions under which that work was carried out. He did not subscribe to the grandiose fantasy of world history to which Miki and other Kyoto thinkers subordinated the everyday, burying its identity, or to the nation-form that putatively originated from world history only to disappear in its shadow. Instead, Tosaka presented a concept of history that not only rejected the conventions of historical representation and units of organization but also was one that he believed was the only possible way of envisioning the historical (the lived reality of time of the worker or proletarian, who was the principal agent of history). This conception was not about history and its narrative form, which Tosaka discarded, but about the subject of historical time—that is, the conception was related to his certainty that history could not be separated from its time, which defined history. History was historical time, and thus he was right to imply that historical studies had ignored this vital and necessary observation about the historical process. The secret of historical form was that it had no form but the content of time, which would determine the proper form in its own historical time. For Tosaka, the historical time's kernel (its secret) was the everyday. This clearly was a gloss on Marx's view that the inversion of Hegel's dialectic would reveal a rationality within a mystical shell. Tosaka insisted that time must be divided to keep it from becoming mere temporality and something other than history, and he believed that the quantifying and measuring involved in taking minced slices from the content of time came close to making historical time look as if it was nothing more than chronology. What saved Tosaka's conception of time from slipping into mere chronology was his locating the source of historical time in the everyday, especially that portion consumed in abstract labor in the workday.

What seems so important and original in Tosaka's meditation on historical time and the principle of everydayness is that his conception of history reflects not a distorting form but a living content. When he identified historical time with the lived reality of everydayness, reducible to a single day, he positioned its content in such a manner as to draw its own form from within itself in the figure of character or disposition, which invariably is politically marked.

Accordingly, "the character is the category that grasps content with respect to content and not form," and "in historical time, the unity of various characteristics made into a modality is differentiated and parsed into periods possessing various characters."[72] Tosaka added that periods embody differing characters or dispositions (forms). What is important manifests itself in moments of change that occur in periods because of the "quality of their *character*," not the reverse—which would refer to the successive change from one period to the next. "For this reason," he asserted, the movement of character "is the opposite of periodization in the natural sciences. This difference originates solely in the fact that *historical periods come from their own historical contents*," a fact conveyed through the content's form rather than a linear, evolutionary movement from one status to the next on a scale of improvement.[73]

If form (which I am using as a synonym for character) calls attention to the means by which content will be shaped, it also suggests it has been produced by history itself. For Tosaka, this creates form:

> [This] is like the maturation of the fig that falls by itself when time ripens from the tree of history. When they fall, people must unerringly receive [figs] in hand. [A fig] is only good if people discover a definite or fixed character within history. But how they receive this ripened fruit [and whether they use it] skillfully for their present depends completely on the character of people themselves. It is like saying that it relies on the character of the body of all the people. How their character is tied to the character of history—to the period. The problem is like returning to their historical sense.[74]

Still, Tosaka worried about what actually caused the maturation of the fruit of the tree of history, or what actually determined the nature of a characteristic of a period in historical time. He introduced the role played by politics (in turn driven by social relations and material forces of production) as in the rising of classes, and the time of the workday marking form, which he saw as bound to character. In taking hold of the characteristic of the period, he advised, "the basket (*ran*) called class is necessary," wording that suggested the meaning of a homonym: "rebellion" (*ran*) and, he continued, it is politics that character reflects, not cultural history that fails to achieve periodization.[75] It is possible that he was suggesting that material economic and political conditions are involved in moving and changing history, while culture retains a reflective and subjective status that prevents it from producing consequential changes leading in turn to shifts in periodization. It should be recalled that he located history's secret in the existence of character, which referred to politics mediated by social relationships and the "material forces of production," which stamped its imprint upon experience to create historical difference, its "heterogeneity."[76] In any case, politics derives from the matrix of material relations and forces of production that results in fixed forms, which are the source of the various characters in history. Within the framework of historical periods, the correspondence of the form and the character of contemporaries are affected by politics in ways that culture would not affect them since they are members of classes.[77] Class thus mediates between people principally because material conditions of existence produce a classification of society's inhabitants according to their socioeconomic positions. Through the exercise of what Tosaka identified as the formation of form (*Formbildung*) and a period's capacity to change form (*Formweschel*), with a new or different configuration within the totality of historical time, the present is made to stand (as if metonymically) for all presents—including, presumably, past presents—since the particular present of the now of today accents all historical time.[78] This, he announced, is the focal point of historical time. Yet all of it is compressed into the present of a single day, which (here Tosaka echoes Heidegger) contains the three temporal moments (the past, present, and future of historical time's structure that are concentrated in every present), "and thus the principle of today, the principle of everydayness, uniformly governs historical time. This, precisely, is the spirit of history."[79] Yet this move treated the present as the zone of temporal unevenness (even though Tosaka did not identify it as such), inadvertently prefiguring Frantz Fanon's "zone of occult instability."

There is no causal linearity in Tosaka's scheme of historical time, but there may be a geometric configuration or circularity, which one of his former Kyoto teachers, Tanabe Hajime, proposed in his lectures of 1940 on historical reality (*Rekishiteki genjitsu*). Even though Tosaka acknowledged that the series of periods in historical time could be aggregated into several stages of historical time, resulting in their dialectical interaction, he said nothing about the direction of the movement of historical time and did not differentiate between the modern and premodern epochs. He described discrete periods as comparable to living bodies following something like a life cycle that brought them to an end, to be regenerated in another live body. This was not an organicist view but one of a dialectical process of refiguration and periodization, which saw the various epochs interacting with each other in a dialectical succession. Yet at the same time, each epoch was partitioned off from the others, constituting a continuity of diversity (in which each period, however diverse, functioned as a historical individual) and referring to a part while simultaneously calling attention to the totality. Tosaka continued to insist that time's rhythm was dominated by sporadic jerkiness and probably unexpected leaps, instead of being a continuous flow associated with linear temporalities or a rhythm suggesting the effect of a montage rather than a progressive narrative's linear continuity. It may be added that his conception of historical time was animated by contingency, reflecting the unfixed surface character of content. "The constant repetition of the same act though in a different day"—whatever the act might be (even drinking tea)—lies in the crystallized core of historical time.[80] And the failure of history to reveal that the form he had first equated with historical time is now disclosed as the principle of everydayness, which is really the mystery of history.[81] Each day makes no guarantee but offers the possibility of new practices that leads to differences among days. It is almost as if he was saying that everydayness simultaneously constituted both the content and the form of history.

In this inquiry into historical time, Tosaka thus argued that philosophic idealism had thrown up a number of cultural and political forms to convey a conception of reality that he considered to be deformed because of the forms' departure from the lived reality and time of everyday life. Of course, this was consistent with his rejection of the real, which did not disclose a genuine, lived reality but displaced it to a false reality that he associated with things as they are, the status quo, or the distraction of the archaic and induced people to ignore what was happening in their contemporary everyday in support of the authority of the unquestioned customary or a nonexistent fantasy. Tosaka's criticism of philosophic idealism included the practice of historical narrative. In his penetrating analysis of the mediations concealing philosophic idealism, he discovered that the real problem was its production of and reliance on the primacy of form. What he seemed to be concerned with—his conception of historical time as content—was both the possibility of new kinds of historical practice and the need to criticize another instance in which idealist philosophy was concealed by the privilege accorded to form. It also suggest that Tosaka's emphasis on the primacy of content was a response to Miki's concept of an ambiguous formless form.

Tosaka's theorization of a material history grounded in the present and the now-time of the today mirrored the impact of Lukács's meditations on the significance of the present's immediacy for history, which shadowed his reliance on Marx's concrete historical practice. Like Lukács, Tosaka saw in the problem of the present the certainty of history, which in imperial Japan had been systematically bracketed and distanced by philosophy's emphasis on substantiating its theoretical approach in unmediated contemplation that would only produce an unreasonable chasm dividing the subject and object of knowledge. This view constituted the core of Tosaka's assault on idealism. When Kyoto philosophers like Kōyama, Kōsaka, and Nishitani Keiji turned the spotlight of philosophic reflection on the analysis of the present, it was either to situate the present within the global framework of Japan's world-historical mission or to discard the present in favor of an as-yet-unimagined Japanese modernity no longer yoked to imitating the West. Missing in these considerations of the Kyoto school of philosophy that called for an overcoming of a modernity made in the West was the crucial process of mediation that Lukács identified in any philosophic analytic encounter with the present of the sort that Miki and Tosaka pursued. Failure to pursue this course that would account for the mediations in the development of a historical process would only result in prolonging the state of pure immediacy and doom the prospect of carrying out a deeper analysis of reality. Moreover, to overlook the role played by mediations in social analysis could only repeat the same experience of immediacy that invariably confronts ordinary people of bourgeois society. In this sense, the summon to return to Japan or to the archaic was really a call to return to the same. The Marxian historian Hani Gorō, an energetic participant in the historiographical debate on the development of Japanese capitalism, early condemned a spiritualist historical discourse that was committed to finding the timeless "marrow of history" and was preoccupied with essential cultural values that were unchanging and eternal, frozen emanations of the past. Hani's move to allegorize a late eighteenth-century past for use in his present was a way to address the contemporary historical problem and gain access to the proscribed actuality of the present, which he described as "our own historical existence."[82]

It is understandable that the challenge posed by Tosaka's theorization of historical time and its practical consequences remained unmet, given the political environment of the time. The Marxian debates on Japanese capitalist development were already under way, and many historians had entered the fray. Most of the leading participants were limited by the ideological and intellectual constraints imposed by the Comintern and its vulgate version of historical materialism. The silence suffered by Tosaka, who did not subscribe to such dogmas, persisted through the post–World War II period, becoming something of a habit since survivors of the older Marxian factions often used the same language when they returned to prior issues, as if the war had changed nothing. Part of this indifference may have been the result of Tosaka's radicalism and his uninhibited frontal attack on the received conventions of historical practice, including both bourgeois and Marxian historians and their fixed attachment to the sovereign form of linear development of progressive stages in the narrative of capitalism and the nation-state. Conservative historians either resorted to rejiggered versions of a Japanist account of national history—usually relying on the discourse of cultural exceptionalism later called discussions on the Japanese (Nihonjinron)—or threw themselves into the safe arms of a remote cultural history, usually of premodern periods that had no visible relevance to the post–World War I order. Both moves came down to the same thing: sneaking in the older Japanist-inflected idiom under the cover of forms of cultural discourse and history.

In fact, Tosaka's scheme of historical time struck at the heart of historical practice, whether bourgeois or Marxian, in efforts to describe Japan's capitalist transformation. His most significant intervention was to substitute the everyday (which he saw as time, everywhere) for the nation-form as the unit of historical inquiry. The reversal of the order of procedure (beginning with content—that is, historical time—rather than with form) was revolutionary in its implications. It apparently unsettled his Marxian colleagues before and after the war since it invalidated the received perspective, which had worked progressively from form to content, or linearly from transition to transition. The reversal of order that he advocated meant starting from the everyday present (the time of our lives, as he put it), which housed the content of history's time in the details of everyday life lived by ordinary people. Here, he departed from Lukács, who followed the standard historical practice of privileging form and the developmental narrative of the nation, which in turn preceded the content that filled the form to provide a fixed plotline of progressive linearity that had rarely, if ever, been called into question.

According to Tosaka, this order of thinking began with a fixed form (whether of Marxian stages of development or of liberal-bourgeois linear progress) that necessitated the creation of historical content capable of validating the predetermined claims of this form, especially its forward movement and rhythm. A narrative in which form precedes and prevails over content engages in a kind of trompe l'oeil, in which the form is seen to evolve from the content despite the fact that the content was made up to fit the form. Tosaka argued that the form, though external to the content, was used to mold the shape and direction of content and to fit a chronology based on the irreversible unfolding of history from one year to the next. By choosing to start with the content (exemplified by the synchronic temporality of the now of the present everyday) and placing it at the head of the signifying chain, Tosaka rightly pointed out that only the content could produce the form capable of capturing and conveying content, which, as stated earlier, he initially called the character or disposition of a period or event and which resulted from mincing or parsing, that is, differentiating a particular slice from the totality of historical time. Jean-Paul Sartre had also recognized the distortion in the version of Marxism that abandoned dialectical interaction in favor of understanding real temporality projected by the lure of progress promised by bourgeois modernizers. For Sartre, this detour reflected Marxism's surrender to the idea of time that was derived from the actual processes of the capitalist economy, which sought to represent history as an inflection of production, the redistribution of capital, and so forth—in short, capitalism's temporal accounting of its movements, or the global circulation that represented a phase of social development. But Sartre also recognized that this trajectory was noticeably different from what could be produced by the dialectical determination of real historical time, which constitutes the true relation of humans to the past and future. I believe that he correctly distinguished a history marred by capital's account of time and attributed to both Marxian and bourgeois historians the creation of confusion from accepting the process of production in place of the dialectal interaction of humans, which constitutes the correct model that is capable of explaining the history they made. The interpretive power of this strategy based on capital's time informed nearly all national narratives and even biographies of individual people. Finally, I would point out that Tosaka's model of historical time closely corresponds to the temporal figure I have proposed as characterizing the uneven and combined development that accompanied the politics of passive revolution. It is possible to resituate this particular form of contemporary noncontemporaneity within the framework of his notion of content in historical time. Tosaka's theory of content filled with the historical time of the present everyday remained undifferentiated, but it still allowed for differences to appear in its several periods. It could be argued both that capitalism created uneven time and the need to combine what was retained from earlier practices with its new innovations and that this strategic combining showed not only how capitalism developed and expanded but also how it installed the permanency of uneven time wherever it established its productive processes. The appearance of the figure of contemporary noncontemporaneity was the appropriate form of the content of historical time in the epochal period of capitalism: it came not from outside of historical time but from within it, inflecting the unevenness of historical times and the accompanying politicality of new material relations centered on the present and condensed into the smallest unit of such unevenness (that is, the single day of everydayness). The inversion of this temporal figure, which sought to privilege the noncontemporaneous past over the contemporaneous present, dramatized fascism's illusory and deceptive representation of time in its political effort to forcibly invoke the mythic and archaic and resolve the crisis in the present. This reversal aimed to dematerialize time and language by respiritualizing them.

It should also be noted, in this connection, that a distinction must be made between Tosaka's discussions of history and its concept, on the one hand, and the actuality of doing history (that is, historical practice), on the other hand—a point on which he remained silently unhelpful. Much of this discourse on historical time and content was expressed in the abstract idiom of philosophy and logic, and he offered no examples of what he was discussing. It became evident he was constructing a critique of historical practice without moving on to the next stage of showing how his concept might be operationalized. Because he saw this discussion as part of his overall critique, which the text of The Japan Ideology invokes from beginning to end, he apparently saw no need to go beyond describing how to write a history that privileged content over form in an abstract mode that often appeared to recuperate the language of the philosophic idealism he was criticizing. His criticism of history was of a piece with the broader critique of Japanist ideology. Moreover, it was related to his effort to uncover an idealist hermeneutics (a theory of interpretation) that could replace the logic of historical explanation and the materiality of the historical present expressed in the "thereness" (Da-charakter) of the everyday of now-time, with its objectivity leading to practice.[83] According to Tosaka's reckoning, this hermeneutic move had been made by Watsuji Tetsurō in his study of climate and culture (Fūdo). Watsuji had shown that the division between subject and object was overcome if one considered that people (for example, the Japanese) live in a specific climate but do not experience it as something felt objectively or external to themselves but rather experience it personally since they are within it. This experience represents a form of individual understanding that comes from entering the climate (say, cold weather) because the outside does not experience anything. According to Tosaka, Watsuji argued that when weather is collectively experienced, it is experienced by the group that understands itself in its "human between-ness" (that is, a "community of the same") and is linked to a place called Japan and its climate in what Stolz described as "culturally specific intersubjectivity."[84] In short, Watsuji believed that climate determined both the nature of the coherence of a national community and the making of Japan's particular and exceptional culture. In this regard, the separation of subject from object was ostensibly overcome, along with the materialism of an external, objective existence, freeing cultural history of the constraints imposed by the charge that it lacked material grounding.[85] Moreover, that separation dissolves the separation of present from past and removes the emphasis on the privileged perspective of the historical present (an emphasis that Tosaka particularly criticized) and opens the way for Japanists to use exemplars of the archaic past to guide the troubled and crisis-ridden present. Tosaka was convinced that a hermeneutics founded on the principle of the identification of climate as culture was designed not only to repudiate historical materialism (indeed, history itself) but also to exchange philology for history and an indefinite and abstract past for a concrete present. In Watsuji's world, nothing seemed to change except, perhaps, the weather.

Although Tosaka rejected philosophic idealism because of its excessive metaphysical impulses, he recognized that its influence persisted in the hermeneutic that proposed to discover the world of meaning, which classically exemplified instances of interpretation that exchanged the "order of reality maintained by the actual real world of the present" for an atemporal hidden domain of meaning.[86] His explanation of this temporal and spatial switching recalled Marx's critique of Max Stirner's ghostly nonplace or spiritual history that descended from heaven rather than earth. Contemporary metaphysics, Tosaka argued, is "nothing but a philosophy of interpretation" extracted from philology.[87] But he acknowledged that on its part isolated facts depend on interpretation and cannot exist without it and that interpretation on its part needs a basis of facticity. He saw a problem in the way that interpretation drifted away from meaning based on facts and toward meaning for its own sake, so that meaning ended up occupying the place of fact. The past designated to replace the reality of the present was the realm of the archaic, a place without space or time. Thus, it was a dream-like construction of a world of meaning that defied reality. The whole interpretive switch from actuality to a ghostly unreality was an orchestrated sleight of hand that resembled a shell game. Tosaka saw that contemporary bourgeois philosophy rested on the separation of the pursuit of meaning from facticity to produce a contemporary reality in which interpretation replaced the actual world. "The real world is diminished," he wrote, arguing that interpretation was now used only for the convenience of meaning.[88]

What interested Tosaka was the wider hermeneutic strategy produced by this philosophical reversal and its philological special coloring, which supplied the means of evading the realistic treatment of facts. He was particularly mindful of the trick of idealist philosophy that made the exchange of meaning in the immediate reality appear to be reasonable. Yet he understood that philology was not necessarily fated to provide only a groundless buoying up of a timeless meaning in a fascist cultural ideology, like Japanism: rather, there were plentiful examples of its broader explanatory utility. Liberal scholars of classic texts had imparted a national history founded on archaic texts that permitted no real division of time and whose temporal remoteness provided an excuse for them to ignore the actual problems of contemporary history and life. If philology could be said to deal with history, it was a history contained in the most distant archaic texts—which, though they had nothing to say about the contemporary conditions of Japan, had been repositioned to offer an interpretive template to guide the present and all subsequent history. For Tosaka, a philosophy of interpretation that leaned exclusively on the excavation of meaning from ancient words and texts produced by and relevant to a remote and inaccessible past risked falling into abstraction. Furthermore, he recognized that while philology was not necessarily destined only to support the grounding of a timeless order of meaning, its recent appropriation compromised its utility and practitioners. The decision to deploy classical studies to understand the problems of the present transformed the scientific discipline of philology into an ideology he called "philologism" (bunkenshugi).[89] Such an ideological application of philology mirrored Marx's observation of the way a vampirical capitalism prioritized dead labor over living labor. Where philology foundered, despite its claim of explanatory neutrality, was in its willingness to supply services to "various forms of reaction on an international scale necessarily derived from the content of capitalism itself."[90] The principal defect of philology lay in its effort to take words for things, thus eliminating the necessary space between them and making the referent and what it referred to one and the same thing. This effacement of the distinction between word and thing was made possible by removing philology from inquiries into the historical-linguistic substance of language, at which point etymology became an inadequate form of historical investigation. Implied in this removal was the revival of the nativist philology of eighteenth-century thinkers like Motoori Norinaga and the members of his school, who had already established the identification of mind (*kokoro*), word (*kotoba*), and thing (*koto*), the identification of person, referent, and the surrounding environment of the authorizing national land created by the gods (which was indistinguishable from the archaic language of the Japanese of that originary time). The identification of word, and thing—coupled with the elimination of the spaces among them—conferred on the language the divinely ordained "spirit of words" (the mystical power that the deities of heaven and earth had bestowed on Japanese, making it a divine language). The identification was important since both referent and reference were rooted in the divine land and its environment, with the community and the land united in a collective voice that spoke through the spirit of language.

The mystical nature of the language was thus one of the principal characteristics that Japanists attributed to Japan's culture, an attribution that Kobayashi later refined in his important postwar book on Motoori. It should be noted that Kobayashi was Tosaka's chief adversary before the war. Throughout his critique of archaism, Tosaka insisted that the classics could not function as a substitute for history and could provide no basis for addressing and resolving the problems of the present. The vast gap between classical categories and current logic meant that the ethics of the past could not be applied in the present. Tosaka was criticizing Watsuji and the contemporary morality of Japan, which had been sought to authorize the contradictory claims of a timeless ethics, presumably derived from the archaic origin and freed from history to curb the social excesses of capitalist modernization. If class categories were to be translated for the modern present, he argued, it must be recognized that neither the original form nor its successors could ever be reproduced. This is because history is never completed. Yet such a translation was precisely what Japanists advocated with their notion of a "spirit of language" that never changed because it was complete at its origin.

Tosaka's observation that metaphysics, the philosophy of interpretation, and literary-ist philosophy shared the same bourgeois idealist ground derived its force from the "smell" of "philologism" and its valorization of the archaic.[91] His attention to the role of philology in this network of disciplinary linkages (especially the aligning of philology with philosophy) had been prompted by philology's abundant interpretive talent for singularly focusing on the remote past. He noted that philosophy's descent into philologism and an excessive emphasis on meaning turned it into a philosophy of meaning that was primarily devoted to interpreting the world. Here there is a hint of the similar route taken by Valentin Voloshinov, a Soviet linguist and member of Mikhail Bakhtin's circle who authored a classic Marxian text on language in the 1920s. In response to Marxism's "predictable mechanistic materialism," Voloshinov concentrated on the verbal in its dialogic and social interactions among speakers. Tosaka's reflections resembled this earlier work not only in his agreement with Voloshinov's excoriation of the abstract objectivism that dominated linguistics and separated language from its act of achieving ideological fullness, but also in the absence of any consideration of the encounter between speaker and interrogator. The subsequent failure to account for the dialogic moment in the formation of language resulted in even greater abstraction, which further reduced the presence of speech. This abstraction arose from the primacy accorded to the convention that "has determined the whole course of linguistic thinking," whereby reflection on language was "formed over the concern of the cadavers of written languages."[92] In this way, philologism—which always addressed the finished monologic utterance constituting the "ancient written monument"—concluded it should be considered as the "last word."[93] Thus, a dead, written, and alien language became the true and only description with which thought has been continuously concerned. Here, the model of a dead language that informed the philological perspective calls to mind once again the prioritization of dead labor over living labor. This point was not lost on Tosaka, whose astonishment at the attempt to summon the archaic past as a suitable guide to the immediate present echoes the passage that Marx, in *Capital*, volume 1, describes the seizure of the living by the dead. Moreover, Tosaka regarded the dominion of an interpretive theory based on fragmented remnants of texts in an ancient language as little more than limited traces of an alleged origin of the land and reflections on it. What Tosaka seemed to focus on was how philology was made to guide contemporary interpretations of journalism, everyday life, and literature, as well as on how dead forms of utterance could be used to shape the conditions of the living in the same way that dead labor had come to dominate the circumstances of living labor.

Faintly echoing Voloshinov's critique of philology, Tosaka saw the discipline's alignment with literature as similar to literaturism (*bungakushugi*), the process whereby the self is released from all social and historical entanglements capable of explaining its character, which permits the ideological sovereignty of self-consciousness valorized in first-person novels (*shishōsetsu*) and, according to Katsuya Hirano, "rooted in the bourgeois ideology of individualism."[94] As Tosaka saw it, this was a form of extreme aestheticism and art for art's sake. Philology, he announced, had early won its independence from linguistics. It had moved toward concentrating on the deciphering of ancient texts but had gradually refined its purview to become a form of philosophic methodology claiming to address questions of the present. Hence, "Philology reduced itself into an interpretive logic of contemporary cultural expression and general classical studies, separate from linguistic studies and philosophy . . . to be thought of as a philosophic method bringing actual meaning to general contemporary existence."[95] Philology had evolved from linguistic philosophy to confront the outside. This move toward interpreting the world beyond words and concepts required understanding techniques that could open the way to interpretation and whose philosophical basis was hermeneutics in the narrow sense. But he noted that this hermeneutic kernel was still tightly constrained by its original function: to analyze the meaning of words and the content of archaic texts. Tosaka commented that philology managed to erase reality itself in its release into a dream world.[96] The embracing of fantasy referred to the imaginary of German Romanticism and its retrospective mourning of and "deep affection for a world that had passed."[97] In place of this romantic nonplace, substitutes were made to recover histories of the past that had been effaced (resulting in grief over its loss), or even the vague image of a secret Japan. However, in Tosaka's estimate hermeneutics was never able to overcome its original philological impulse.

In his essay on philology, Tosaka followed the evolving materialization of hermeneutics, especially in the German philosophic environment through to Heidegger. Tosaka settled on reducing the tradition to phenomenological reflection, where, because of its bracketing (*Entfernung*) of the historical outside (society, politics, and the economy), hermeneutics replaced the vacated space and its absent history with being. What seemed particularly relevant to my study is Tosaka's recognition of the way philology became the basis for thinking through "social phenomena and institutions in situations that rely on it": it sought to exempt itself from the same history. He was specifically referring to the problem of philology's random and "unsystematic appreciation" of the current situation in Japan.[98] This digression into the vagaries of philology attracted a disproportionate amount of attention because it led Heidegger to upholding the figure of the archaic and its valorization, which alleged that the archaic showed what the present should look like. It also suggests why Heidegger was so enthusiastically embraced in Japan: he showed how interpretive philology could liberate itself from the concreteness of historical linguistics and even the historical present, subsuming itself to philosophy and a culturally higher level of activity. Tosaka argued that philology had lost its original ties to historical linguistics and could not avoid appearing to be a "burlesque or cartoon" that could only generate nonsense and slipped into the status of a caricature that he called "philologism," indicating that it "has lost its concreteness."[99] In this connection, he pointed to Watsuji's attempt to realize a pure philosophy and to extract anthropology's core, free from historical mediation and rooted in the Heideggerian concept of being as the final remnant of phenomenology. In the end, the allegedly pure philology based on the founding meaning of words is not pure at all. Rather, it is contaminated by a philosophical perspective grounded in being and turns to the application of classic texts to understand the actuality of the present. Tosaka considered this move a crime (tsumi). Its consequence was to purvey a philosophic meaning that was unqualified to address and resolve an actual problem in contemporary reality and was based on circumstantial conclusions recruited from an "unconscious hypothesis and bad faith."[100] This strategy of using classic texts from a remote and irrelevant past (or the archaic itself) to guide the present had no apparent limit, and its practice was widespread among dissatisfied nationalists and fascists, as well as scholars of China and Buddhist priests who were intent on explaining the current situation by way of ancient India. Tosaka focused his critique on the unsuitability of using the archaic to grasp the contemporary scene. He juxtaposed the reasonableness of modern logic to the irrelevance of (and irrationality of using) premodern ways of thinking embodied in archaic texts to pilot the present. He saw in the reliance on archaism a dangerous assault on the heritage of the Enlightenment and the rule of reason.

I have suggested above that the archaic had become a form of political unconscious in modern Japan, a legacy of the Meiji Restoration that had been transported well into the postwar years. It associated the world of origin with the permanent offer of returning to its unchanged and archetypal model if the present appeared to have lost its way. It was a yearning driven by a desire explicitly to "go backward upstream." It must have seemed like going back to a home that had been left a long time ago—perhaps even the lost home of Kobayashi or Orikuchi Shinobu's distant shores of those "who rarely come." It was always there, waiting to be summoned. The 1930s in particular were drenched in calls for a return to Japan, reversing the course of temporal flow to go backward upstream. But like Marx, Tosaka was determined to make sure that the dead could no longer seize the living. After all, "The Ideology of Japan" was primarily concerned with the grip of the archaic on contemporary life and of the dead on the living, holding the present hostage to an indeterminate past that was being portrayed as a time before time. By the 1930s, this backward-looking temporal frenzy had reached such a level of saturation that it appeared to have captured and colonized the Japanese consciousness. Moreover, Tosaka always related his preoccupation with the status of archaism and philologistic interpretation to his analysis of history and time. He had already noted that philologism was related to the project of continuing the flow of history upstream to the archaic moment, which inevitably explained nothing. History for the Japanese was moving backward, away from the modernity of the West, and thus it was like a river whose direction had been changed, though not away from capital. Tosaka was pointing to the futility of a logic that if it was not absolute nonsense at least sought to reverse time to reach an impossible origin and use it to resolve the problems of contemporary capitalist society. Of course, this was the function of restoration and its inseparable kinship with the archaic. Tosaka not only questioned the reversibility of time's movement from forward to backward, but he also criticized the use of causal linearity as an explanatory strategy. His discussions of the archaic were ultimately concerned with the distorted figure of time that had banished history. It was as if the temporal structure of capitalism that had contemporized the past with the present had been turned into a temporal edifice in which the past archaicized the present.

Tosaka concluded that a general account of words did not explain things. First, the "mechanism of archaic thought" depends on a close relationship between language and an ancient form of logic. This relationship suggests a reliance on mediating archaic utterances that functioned as totalizations, like *mysterion*, the unspecified, concealed, or *mystic*, unspeakable; *mythos*, telling, narrating; *epos*, epic, poetry; *logos*, reason. But he added that this relationship has no place in modern logic.[101] Using words as explanations implies that the things to be explained are productions of a developed society that is not committed to reversing the "flow of history," an operation that prevents history from explaining things. Proponents of philologism are guilty of bad faith or at least an unconscious intention that seeks at all cost to move the argument back upstream to the archaic. And second, philologism could never be the basis for understanding the actual problems of the present. Tosaka asked whether the classics have any meaning and discounted their relevance because the archaic was only a temporal referent, transmitted historically to the present. He concluded that using the archaic to solve problems would be "foolishlessly useless" because it returned the problem of the present to the remote and indistinct past for guidance, making that past a reactionary force. This was a case of conflating the archaic with the production of an ideal when it had not been conceived of in this manner until much later, long after its epoch had passed into history. The archaic is thus nothing more than a historical product of a determinate moment.[102] Third, the archaic model does not constitute a logic since it is only something that can be logically considered in the present, not on its own terms in its time. Tosaka acknowledged that different classics from Greece, China, India, and elsewhere have had their own forms of categorizing or organizing knowledge, which is no less true of the uncivilized (*mikai*), who still possess forms of categorical logic characteristic of noncivilized peoples. But he was quick to add that such logics have no semblance to the logic in current use among civilized nations today. He was proposing that the logics of earlier eras (especially the logics of the archaic and primitive peoples) were limited to their time, place, history, and social development and—most important—inapplicable to the present.[103] Fourth, the archaic must be translated, but the translation should never be confused with the original. Tosaka seems to have been advising that translation in the most literal sense of the word should be limited to transposing the sentences of one language into the sentences of another. Yet that would mean that the act of translating involved the introduction of culture, which risks serving philology in finding inappropriate cultural solutions for actual contemporary problems. In this way, translation reflects its character as not an original work.

Tosaka was convinced that translation could be important in showing the operation of logic among comparably developed contemporary societies. He did not consider using translation to be simply a technical problem because such societies had already entered the capitalist realm, were familiar with the worldly idiom of exchange and production, and shared skills and structures as well as a socioeconomic ground based on the international division of labor and the world market. Even if the societies had local differences, they also shared a temporality implanted by capital to standardize its operations on the global level. Tosaka asserted that translating the same thing from one language to another is not actually translation but an example of exchange and reception.[104] Under these conditions, which Hasegawa had already outlined, Tosaka argued that it was no longer relevant for Japanese to proclaim that foreigners could not understand the "Japanese Spirit" and that the Enlightenment had been cut short in Japan. Such views reflected an old principle of trying to translate different orders of logic used by those who still insisted on applying the logical systems of ancient China and India. He emphasized that replacing a contemporary capitalist society with a remote archaic configuration and a nonexistent past was violating time according to the changed rhythms of historical development, since there was no bridge between the two worlds of the premodern and modern. In brief, Tosaka was complaining that it is not possible to employ traditional systems of logic to account for meaning in modern societies. But he accepted the possibility of adopting the content of an original Buddhism into the cultural content and idiom of the present. He took as his example a work by Watsuji on ancient Buddhism and highlighted the importance of how Watsuji had used a historical example rather than resorting to an archaic myth of origin, as so many contemporaries were encouraged to do, which required translating the categories of ancient Buddhism through a familiar and accessible modern logic. But Tosaka warned that it would be perpetuating a fraud to translate the living present into the archaic because doing so would undermine or even eradicate the present's active practical logic. That is why a translation must always be just a translation. Yet he seemed to imply that a translation between two vastly remote and different worlds would forever remain unintelligible unless, as Watsuji's work on ancient Buddhism suggests, it was made available in an idiom that a present-day reader would understand, which in effect would make the text contemporary and perhaps original. The difference between Watsuji's strategy and what archaists were promoting was that the former advocated contemporizing an older text in the logic of the present for present-day readers, while the latter did not since the archaic texts were considered sacred and inviolable. Watsuji was coming close to recommending the contemporization of the past that reveals the uneven temporality of capitalism—a temporality that always seeks to appropriate components of received past modes of production by making them appear to be contemporary and available for immediate use. In this example, Tosaka indicted philological philosophy for its uncritical support of idealism and its blindness to a living logic by adhering to a dead one—in contrast to some forms of philosophy that recognized the need to employ a living logic. Tosaka believed that the problem exemplified by this operation of interpretive or hermeneutic philosophy lay in that philosophy's capacity to criticize philology by exposing its tricks even while using its explanatory value. He saw in the disclosure of this critical philosophic aptitude the possibility that it might be more widely and beneficially applied in contemporary Japan, given its unlimited opportunities to criticize the Japanist ideology.[105]

In this connection, Tosaka encountered yet another requirement of philosophic idealism and the metaphysics of interpretation that encouraged him to revisit the status of literature. Literature and its wide reach in society were never far from his thoughts. He was particularly concerned about the worrisome trend leading to the separation between politics and literature (and culture in general). He approached the problem by addressing the recent calls for the establishment of a formalistic literature, or literature for the sake of literature. What troubled him most about these calls was the potential effect on Marxian literary production. Even though Marxian authors tended to be skeptical about current literary phenomena, he conceded that no real difference existed between writers leaning to the left and those leaning to the right.[106] At the heart of this preoccupation to maintain the separation of literary production from politics was the fear that anti-Marxist rhetoric of critics like Kobayashi would persuade most literary writers that they should ignore all considerations apart from the creation of art for art's sake. In this attempt to return to something like pure literature, Tosaka perceived the disregarding of any consideration of society and history associated with idealism, especially in the phenomenological orientation that had become an article of faith in the Kyoto school of philosophy. This effort to isolate literature reflected the character of a society committed to abandoning a totalizing perspective in favor of one that consisted of discrete but separate spaces and moments of consciousness, a perspective that he believed had led to a crisis of understanding and culture.[107] The "literaturization" (bungakushugi) of philosophy was similar to the process that transposed philology into philologism, and it was yet another instance of the ongoing process of disregarding political and social realities that was common in fascist cultural policy and that resulted in the virtual colonization of philosophy by literature, obliging philosophy hereafter to use literary categories.[108] As I suggested above, literaturization was based on the assumption that the individual stood alone, a sovereign self, and on the presumption of self-consciousness as the sole source of the individual's decisions, choices, and courses of action. For example, in many first-person novels the protagonist is always the hero of his own life. When bourgeois idealist philosophers turned to literary criticism, the literary dimension—not the philosophic one—prevailed. And it was left to the readers to decide what attitudes to take toward literary philosophy, while professional philosophers remained silent on the subject. The process of literaturization resulted in the consciousness of an autonomous literaturism positioned to shape political expression that Tosaka called "literary liberalism."

Tosaka believed that the crisis in Japan, ignited by a worldwide emergency, was expressed in the language of liberalism. But it should be noted that Japan, like other societies, used mediations derived from its own experience of the historical present to help it understand liberalism. Seeing Japan's bourgeois philosophers as both the most vocal defenders of the liberal idea of freedom and the self-appointed custodians of that idea, Tosaka was persuaded that they had from the beginning misunderstood the concept. He observed that his fellow philosophers (many of whom had been trained in the Kyoto school of philosophy) as well as liberal thinkers like Kawai Eijirō erred in thinking that the concept derived from the German understanding of the idea of freedom, which was usually explained in the lofty language of transcendence. Some of Tosaka's contemporaries—like Nishida Kitarō, whose philosophy Tanabe once described as a religious-like temple—even saw in this conceptualization of freedom the possibility of a romantic exit from the mundane world or an escape to a higher plane on which they could separate themselves from the sphere of everyday mediocrity and the distortions of partisanship. Tosaka considered these views of freedom to be wide of the mark and to consist of a series of simplistic misunderstandings, since the freedom of which these people wrote derived neither from philosophy nor from literature—even if it was appropriated by both disciplines. Their definition of the term was not in fact associated with the freedom of individual will or the belief of identifying a proper knowledge of freedom. Their error, Tosaka claimed, came from their failure to take into account the practicality required in discussions of freedom, such as how freedom informs the everyday life that these thinkers seemed so intent on transcending. Tosaka argued that their writing about freedom was all empty talk with no precision or substance, no matter how sincerely they cared about freedom.

According to Tosaka, the advocates of liberalism failed to acknowledge that freedom developed from economic relationships and political action, both of which depended primarily on practical considerations—the nego-tiation of exchange in the former case, and the distribution of power in the latter case. He added that historically liberalism had been articulated in the form of economic freedom, and capitalist development was presumably premised on its necessity. This was not the freedom of the post-Hegelians whose sight remained fixed on heaven rather than on earth. Economic free-dom produced political liberalism, which was eventually included in the combination of politics and economy represented by modern liberal politi-cal economy. In Japan, Tosaka asserted, the original character of liberalism was not understood, a neglect that bordered on a denial of common sense and resulted in an ongoing inability to grasp the ideology as economic and political categories. Moreover, he added, economic freedom was not practically affiliated with philosophy, literature, or culture. Indeed, free-dom was described as totally separate from the political field, especially after liberalism had been linked to literature and lost its original identity. The outcome was the disappearance of political freedom, which Tosaka de-scribed as having had an especially short shelf life in Japan. Freedom did not vanish, but it was imbued with a new meaning when it was combined with culture to make a hegemonic cultural freedom the only acceptable definition of liberalism.

Hence, what once had been denoted as political freedom had been su-perseded by a cultural freedom that provided a license for activities that had nothing to do with either politics or economics. Liberalism's penchant for having plural interests had opened a door to the ideological dangers implicated in a metaphysics of ideal cultural forms and their claims to en-titlement and eternality. Tosaka uncovered in fascism a partnership be-tween economics and culture that resulted in eliminating any concern for meeting social and individual needs. This recognition allowed him to iden-tify fascism as the true heir of liberalism, validating Gramsci's view of the process by which liberalism ends in fascism, even though Tosaka would not have known about the work of the Italian thinker. While fascism would invariably acquire different content in different places, mediated by local and cultural circumstances, Tosaka was convinced that its appearance was linked not simply to the present moment, but rather to the longer epoch of capitalism through the conveyance of liberalism. He also believed, like Gramsci, that fascism would remain dormant but inscribed in the interstices of liberalism, ultimately leading to its substitution, like the ghost in the ma-chine. But this ghost was no metaphor. The replacement of political liberalism and freedom by culture was intended to depoliticize the intellectual world and divest it of its critical political practices, insisting instead on the separation of culture and politics. It may well be that this separation was more extreme in Japan than elsewhere, but it characterized most fascisms of the period. Moreover, it worked to erase the original political content of liberalism and create a world imagined by the petit bourgeoisie, as Tosaka emphasized would happen when political categories were transfigured into cultural and literary ones. Hasegawa's reflections on the relationship of art and fascism in the early 1930s had prefigured this observation. The most dramatic transformation of liberalism, according to Tosaka, appeared in the changes in the use of such familiar terms as "restoration." The word had once been used to call for a historic return of imperial politics, but it now referred to the restoration of art or literature. While politics had come to be associated with the human (that is, humanism), the change blurred the narrow boundaries of factionalism and asserted that there was only a subjective bonding among humans, which would override mediating objective criteria that had always produced social divisions. Here was a clear indication of fascism's distrust of representative politics and its desire to rid society of all forms of representation that might contribute to fomenting division and conflict. Tosaka repeatedly complained that terms without any referential connection to reality (like "folk," the "collective body," the "Japanese spirit," and the nation's "political body") were being widely used and signified the unconstrained freedom of culture that now occupied the space vacated by politics. Behind this strategy of abandoning concrete political freedoms for something called cultural freedom, as if they were separate values, lurked an organic national collective that would soon speak in a unified voice. Tosaka perceived in these changes the subjectivization of anthropology and the end of philosophy, a danger he undoubtedly detected in Miki's thought.

Tosaka had already called attention to a crisis of culture, which enabled fascism to come forth to relieve it through the enunciation of cultural policy. But cultural policy in the mid-1930s was only concerned with underscoring the increasing confusion of thought, and appearance of intellectual disunity. What he named the distraction of fascist cultural policy that promised to ease the cultural crisis also inadvertently raised the question of what had brought that crisis about.[109] For Tosaka, the crisis of new meaning was the genesis of the cultural crisis, returning to his principal critique of interpretation theory. And that meant that the call to lessen the crisis of culture became a crisis itself. The problem Japanese society confronted was not only the lowering of intellectual standards but also the threat posed to cultural skills and thought. Tosaka referred to this lowering of standards as a form of willful "ignorantization," which was guided by an ill-informed bureaucratic leadership bent on stamping out genuine critical thinking. He was particularly concerned about the processes of emptying words of concepts and separating linguistic forms from any relationship to material referents. While there was no way to avoid using language to communicate, he argued that fluctuating artistic expressions and every-day regulations should become standardized and organized materialist categories.[110] His critique aimed to restore and increase concreteness in place of the present's propensity for abstraction. The issue for him was not just the nagging persistence of interpretation through which information and knowledge were mediated before being conveyed but also the domi-nance of the theory of interpretation, which had come to prevail during the 1930s.[111] The literaturization of philosophy was another instance of the phe-nomenological bracketing of the external world of politics and econom-ics that fascist cultural policy favored and promoted. Tosaka renamed this process "literaturization" (bungakushugi), according to which philosophy was either obliged to use literary categories or literature would subsume other disciplines and speak for them in a literary voice.[112] He noted that daily newspapers now used this approach.[113]

Tosaka classified Japanism as a Japanese inflection of the larger ideo-logical phenomenon of fascism found throughout the world in the 1930s. As a system of thought, he judged the Japanese version of fascism as the most deficient because its principal categories were related to telluric ref-erents native to Japan and its myths of origins, culturally mediated modes of agriculture, the way of the gods, a divinely descended emperor, the spirit of language, and so forth. Japanists felt confident that in using these ref-erents, they were making up for the contemporary absence of "common sense" (soshiki) found throughout Japan. In fact, the referents were a re-sponse to Japanism having pushed Japan and its exceptional national in-ventory into the cellar of intellectual respectability, where the sources of its breath were being oppressively crushed. Japanists used cell-like units called ideologemes) to complete a list of the referents that would restore "common sense."[114] Yet their list was intended to help them recruit the folk who supposedly would see themselves in that list and grasp its "direct connection" to their everyday life. But in reality the items on the list had nothing to do with the folk's everyday life.[115] The weakness that Tosaka un-covered in this approach was its reliance on an ideological discourse rooted in the claims of national essence, a discourse now expanded by what could be described as injections of archaicism. To construct a more inclusive na-tionalist system as a barrier to the effects of the worsening international economy and its diminished stock of contemporary categories of national-ism, Japanists incorporated absolutistic, ancient nativist categories to pre-sent a less threatening image of contemporary circumstances. The use of this kind of categorical archaism today, Tosaka emphasized, had no logi-cal relationship to categories of practice in everyday life.[116] Revisiting an earlier theme, he noted that because archaic categories have only a phil-ological function, they are nothing more than acrobatics performed on a wide scale. He argued that it was necessary to pay close attention to and critique the many philological categories that were being linked to present-day archaism, although most of them were derived from Tokugawa-era na-tivism (*kokugaku*).

Tosaka detected a singular sentiment in an emotional perspective that ranged from Orientalism (*tōyōshugi*) or Asianism (*Ajiashugi*) to Japanism. It seemed to him that the spectacle of so many movements sharing one cultural affect could disclose a political kinship that accounted for their si-multaneous appearance. He discounted their collective contents as "unpro-gressive" and "completely filled with trash."[117] Yet he could not help taking their messages seriously as objects of criticism, because variations derived from Japanist archaism in the face of the crisis of Japanese capitalism were links in the chain of a world in crisis. The imperialist "trumpet sounds of the Manchurian and Shanghai incidents were nothing less than its unmis-takable effects."[118] He saw this route to self-renewal that led to imperial ad-ventures (especially its nationalistic stridency), which declared a national crisis that led reactionary ideologies to demand that hereafter the Japa-nese word for Japan must be read as *Nippon* and not *Nihon*, where the slight difference in pronunciation was considered "dangerous thought."[119] Even though Japan was aligned with Hitler's Germany and Mussolini's Italy in the late 1930s, some Japanese saw Japanism as totally different from the ideologies that had developed in the West and were convinced that it was not a form of fascism. Japan was perceived as having reached its present situation principally because of an excessive reliance on imitation of the West and because of the inability of the masses to "grasp the essence of the Japanese spirit" as a "self-awareness regarding Japan's political body *kokutai*."[120] After World War II and the U.S. occupation, Japan began to be seen as an exemplar of successful modernization, and Western—especially American—scholars no longer considered it to be a fascist nation. In fact, social sciences in the United States had in the immediate postwar period discounted the utility of the term *fascism* and considered it meaningless, a kind of prefiguration of the later announcement that ideology had come to an end. However, Japanese Marxists continued to believe that the refeudalization of the Meiji Restoration, emperorism, and fascism cast a shadow over postwar society.

Despite specious comparisons with the West and claims of exceptionalism based on a divine archaic origin and the superiority of the nation's political body, Tosaka considered Japanism as simply a variant of idealism produced by fascism.[121] He explained that this idealism was extended to certain aspects of society, since the ideal infiltrated socioeconomic mechanisms. The historical conditions that produced Japanist fascism were not reflected in its ideological discourse, in spite of the materialistic circumstances involved in its formation. This was a departure from the vulgate version of Marxism that explained ideological production as mirror-like reflections of the real and pointed to new possibilities of understanding ideology as something more than a surface phenomenon. Even though Japanism is an idealist form of thought (and a particularly deficient one), from the beginning it possessed a basic ideological nature, almost as if it had emanated from the earth itself. In *Shisō to fuzoku*, Tosaka explained that "thought is able to acquire the appearance of bodily reality in society by grasping the form of custom" that conceals its presence. Custom manages to hide the thought deeply buried within it, and the Japanist ideology similarly hides the commodity.[122] Although it is probably conceivable to argue that Japanism cannot be defined because of its timelessness, others have claimed that it has no substantive content. But committed Japanists like Minoda Muneki, described by Nishida Kitarō as a "rabid dog" who put forth the proposition that it is all things, declared that Shinto's "godly way" (*kannagara no michi*) is all-encompassing, including past and present as well as East and West.[123] According to Tosaka, the real import of Japanism lay in the material historical conditions accompanying that claim—conditions it remained silent about but that showed the way to the political development of monopoly capitalism—in contrast to Hasegawa's earlier affirmation of the standstill consequences of medium- and small-scale capitalism. Significantly, this difference of high-level and medium-low scales capitalism was clear in the relationship between monopoly capitalism and imperialism: the former concealed the many contradictions in its domestic policies through the exercise of state power, while relying on the pretext of promoting a policy directed at resolving these disparities on the international level, although in fact it only further exacerbated them. Hence, fascism became the political mechanism to recover the power of the state machinery, taking advantage of the fears of the petit bourgeoisie and the expansion of the middle class imposed by certain domestic and international political conditions. In these circumstances, the Japanese state was able to exploit middle-class anxieties by circulating the threat of political crises at home and abroad. It seemed particularly successful among those who had lost faith both in the dictatorship of the proletariat and in the undisguised rule of the bourgeoisie. Fascism seized upon the illusion that the crisis harmed the interests of the bourgeoisie while continuing to support the expansion of finance capital.

What caught Tosaka's attention was the observation that Japanism had emerged from the "essence of imperialism"—namely, the execution of imperial wars and the military consciousness informing that execution.[124] Although fascist militaristic consciousness was a worldwide phenomenon in the interwar period, once it was aligned with Japanism, a preexisting military group became available to achieve the move to an aggression organized by an elite "authoritative military occupational corps." Here, Tosaka was referring to a military tradition dating from the Meiji Restoration, when what had been conceived of as a defense against foreign imperial designs on Japan became an instrument of imperialization. The existence of a military consciousness was a necessary precursor of the militarist nature of Japanism. Putting the whole nation under arms in World War II was a result of the restoration, which itself was seen as a continuation of the military system of remote antiquity. Moreover, Tosaka argued that the consciousness of the militarist clique—which was not merely an occupational group but a privileged status whose authority derived directly from the emperor, as commander in chief—was part of the very essence of Japanism.[125] He rejected as misguided contemporary depictions of the modern military as a successor of the former samurai class (now described as nonhereditary neosamurai [*shin bushidan*]), a notion that once again bound an indeterminate feudal past to the present. Tosaka also frowned on the ethos of Bushido (the way of the samurai), which the modern military and even the Japanese folk were said to follow. But he saw the use of Bushido as just another way to claim that the Japanese ideal military system was that of a whole nation under arms.

One result of this use of Bushido was to characterize the military as relying on farmers, who constituted its social base and to whom the defense of the realm was entrusted. The peasant army drew its recruits from the rural middle classes of agricultural and fishing villages, notably among people who had medium-size farms. These folk came from the upper rural class and were seen as the custodians of agricultural village life. The military treated them as local elites and added them to its ranks, accompanied by large numbers of their tenants. Tosaka was aware that this class was closest to Japan's feudal heritage, and he recognized that agricultural cultivation had been the economic core of feudalism. He also recognized that this group still embodied traces of older relationships and modes of thinking and conduct. But he perceived a vast difference between a historical feudal system, like the previous Tokugawa political order, and a feudal ideology no longer bound to feudal institutions.

Tosaka looked upon the dominant feudal ideology inculcated in farmer-soldiers as a form of an accidental restorationism. Yet it was apparent that Japanists were using the call for this unification of roles to set the stage for a return to agrarianism. He believed that in his day the meaning of the term for restoration constituted a serious contemporary problem, since it prolonged the existence of a consciousness favorable to the revival of the feudal system, which in turn avows it to be "nothing more than an indistinct" term signifying different meanings.[126] One of those meanings had already been articulated by Marxists in the lecture faction in their interpretation of the Meiji Restoration as an aborted revolution or one that never happened that had resulted in refeudalization. Tosaka proposed that the current emphasis on familism used its fascistic manifestation and most mature meaning. He knew that Japan had always had some sort of family system, and he believed that its evolution during the Tokugawa period was a key part of the social formation at the moment when feudalism had reached its most mature form. He noted that it was this family system, not some older variant of it, that Japanists were seeking to revive in the present, along with its inseparable associations with the feudalism that had produced it. Here it is possible to see the unintended irony in the Japanists' effort to empty the restoration of its sponsorship of a political and social transformation after 1868 while they simultaneously committed themselves to the return of a feudal regime as a replacement for the restoration that had overthrown that regime. In this way, the restoration, which once had heralded the arrival of a new imperial state, became synonymous with the ambiguous extension of feudal consciousness.

Paradoxically, capitalism in Japan appeared to be moving toward reproducing some vague form of the feudal system of the past in the promotion of small and medium-size enterprises and preserving an agricultural base, which contrasted markedly with the prevailing monopoly capitalism that at its highest level of development had produced the Japanist ideology as a shield. The anomaly of a restorationist consciousness seeking to replicate feudalism in the heart of a capitalist society was thus the result of primitivizing that society. I believe that Tosaka was one of the few theorists anywhere in the world who identified fascism's powerful impulse toward primitivization, a kind of return to the barbaric simplicity of a time before time that preceded even the archaic moment so assiduously acclaimed by Japanists. We must see Tosaka's recourse to the primitive as a way of reducing the archaic to its fundamental barbaric characteristics, which he believed, remained at the heart of Japanese society. For him, the primitive also conveyed the recessive character of Japan embodied in the Japanist ideology of his day. Tosaka recognized in this ideology an absurd tendency to primitivize a country that had already developed into a complex contemporary capitalist society governed by material necessity. But he was referring not to the primordial ooze but rather to an unnamed moment before the organization of the mythic origin and the time of Jinmu's state founding. Thanks to Walter Benjamin, we know that the cultures we praise and prize are the productions of a barbarism that is kin to primitivization. Tosaka acknowledged that in the realm of ideology and ideas, the notion of primitivization offered what might be described as relief from both time and history and that it, like restoration, was timeless. While there may have been a superficial resemblance between archaism and primitivism, they were not the same: the latter was rooted in the social consciousness of people in farm villages and the rural middle class, representing the ideal of primitivizing the complexities of social life and reducing society to the simplicity of basics. In this regard, primitivization, which, for Tosaka remained the earliest primal state of human community, had only the slightest resemblance to what might be called the nonmodern or antimodern attitudes (usually associated with people in the countryside who lacked a command of modern logic). But these states of premodern agricultural life were relatively advanced in organization compared to the primal. Tosaka reported that Tachibana Kōsaburō, an agrarianist and theorist, was said to have considered the mechanization of the countryside as a nonrevolutionary imposition of a form of development that led only to destruction. The nonmodern (or antimodern) was directly related to objects in the contemporary material world but was described by the word denoting primitivism; yet at the same time the association of primitivism with the contemporary countryside remained only a most ideal desire among agrarian conservative elements. Both restorationism and feudalism had begun as idealized movements, and they emerged from time and history: they could develop no further in the present except as ideological figures of desire that promoted antimaterialism in a society already deeply committed to materialist life. The function of this return to feudalism was to give the Japanist militarist clique an opportunity to reinforce the authority of the fusion of soldier and farmer (*heinō itchi*) and support the corresponding economic imperative (founded on agrarianism) to put the whole nation under arms. Agrarian fundamentalism may have been rescued from the status of a remnant because of the Japanists' effort to return Japan to an earlier form of agrarianism that had prevailed in feudalism and persisted in capitalism.

Tosaka's view that restorationists in contemporary Japan had turned to an abstracted and idealized form of feudalism must be situated in the context of the broader Marxian historiographical discussion of the development of capitalism in Japan. In the 1930s, the lecture faction had adopted a thesis that explained Japan's stalled capitalist development as a result of the persistence in the present of surviving feudal remnants. This thesis was classically enunciated by the economist Yamada Moritarō, who argued that Japan's development was frozen in a state of permanent semifeudalism. This explained the historiographical quest to document Japan's beginnings in the late Tokugawa period and the transmutation of the Meiji Restoration from an incipient bourgeois revolution into the reactionary agency of a refeudalized and absolutist political state. As I mentioned above, Tosaka never participated directly in the historiographical debate about the development of capitalism in Japan, but his remarks on the feudalization of consciousness might be seen as an indirect comment on the role played by the remnant in retarding capitalism's development and freezing society into semifeudalism. It should be noted that semifeudalism implied the existence of remnants and residues from the past without enumerating them. It also constituted half of something else (in this case, capitalism), placing Japan in the category of latecomers to capitalist development and not viewing it as an instantiation of an exceptionalized Japanese-style rationality, which is how Yamada saw it. He had not, as such, identified any feudal remnants in semifeudalism and had thus concluded that semifeudalism worked against the completion of capitalism. Yet this seemed to ignore the emperor and the institution of the imperial house (the un-named paradigmatic remnants), unless it was a safe way to call attention to both without actually saying so. With Tosaka the emperor and imperial household were identified through the proxy of a generalized emperorism.

In Tosaka's analysis, Japan had reached the state of monopoly capital-ism, and he undoubtedly had some trouble agreeing with an assessment that attributed to feudal remnants not only capitalism's incomplete devel-opment but also (in the eyes of Miki, for example) the source of fascism. But Tosaka's rejection of the lecture faction's view was not total. He was able to retain the belief in the existence of a remnant by dematerializing that remnant—a process that in fact probably reinforced it. The demateri-alization of the remnant could be linked to the mythic figure of emperor, through a form of allegorizing because he was not just a monarch but also a divinity, not just a human body but also a spiritual and immaterial force. It was the relationship between two revenants signifying a dematerialized spirit or ghost of the remnant that stood in the way of Japan's moderniza-tion. In this way, Tosaka managed to maintain both his fidelity to the lec-ture faction's view and his belief in the unevenness that diverted Japan's political and economic maturation into monopoly capitalism. By stripping feudalism of its material associations—which required removing any re-lationship between it and a specific historical institution, abstracting and idealizing feudalism into a neutral figure—Tosaka could imagine how Ja-panism could bypass the restoration as the overthrow of the Tokugawa and paradoxically directly link a conception of restoration relieved of its histo-ricity to feudalism and its reduction to primitivization.

Earlier in *The Japan Ideology*, Tosaka had presented the effort to provide a scientifically critical perspective on "our present existence, especially toward the philosophic idealism of our time and all its social and cultural applications" (which represent the word and spirit of the cultural world) as the informing principle of his materialist project.[127] The rationale for re-jection of the claims of literature's sovereignty over philosophy and other disciplines was the conviction that a "philosophic consciousness or even consciousness of life in one direction appears as literary consciousness and in another as political consciousness."[128] Tosaka was always suspicious of the immaterial nature of what he called "phenomenological time," and that suspicion ultimately drove him to see the everyday concreteness of routine and work as the content of history.

Nonetheless, Tosaka was unwilling to minimize the importance of the primitivizing of consciousness and thinking that, he argued, was most active among the farmers and others who lived in rural villages: in time, their views were adapted by the middle class and Japanists. Tosaka was especially critical of the susceptibility of the petit bourgeoisie and its proclivity to embrace mystical notions such as fortune-telling, especially faith in medical nostrums (chiryō) and the delusions kindled by the troubled consciousness among the bourgeois middle class. He observed that ordinarily the flight to mysticism might be what Japanese considered to be an ideology of the military, owing to its base in farms and villages. And he concluded that this kind of mysticism was not really an appropriate option since it and modern mechanized warfare were a bad mix because the military had to rely on mechanization.

Convinced that rural people with medium-size farms constituted the backbone of Japanist militarist consciousness, Tosaka noted that this social class also represented Japanism's greatest expectation and success, as it promised, so it was believed, Japanism's most trustworthy source of support. Japanese farming villages had a daily consciousness that came from a commitment to agriculturalism (nōgyōshugi), and when bonded to the national history, that was transformed into "agrarianism" (nōhonshugi) in a way reminiscent of an earlier time when agrarianism was viewed as the moral foundation of the nation. But this bonding was in actuality an attempt at revitalizing a feudalist ideology, which had seen the reestablishing of agricultural production as the basis of the feudal mode of production in the heart of a capitalist society. However, as Tosaka noted, there was a fundamental difference between a historical feudal system that had existed in the past and a feudal ideology in the present Japanese society: the bonding derived from the demand for the "unification of soldier and farmer," rather than from the past. At this juncture, Tosaka revisited the status of restorationism and concluded that an "ambivalent" conception of restoration was part of a feudalist ideology.[129] And the most persistent characteristic of such a restoration was its close emphasis on and identification with the family system. The movement toward a reverse-course restoration that would seek to revive a discarded feudal ideology signaled nothing more than a process of primitivization that was to be achieved not in the realm of empirical material existence but in the realm of thought and ideology. This would permit one to remain in the contemporary world while dreaming of and yearning for a feudalist restoration. Here, Tosaka perceived that an ambivalent and abstracted restorationism that sought to reinstate a feudalist consciousness constituted the key aspiration of Japanism. In this case, that meant inverting the historical restoration to connect it with the process of primitivization, idealistically reducing feudalism to a primitive state and increasing the petit bourgeois opposition to technology, mechanization, materialism, and rationalism while upholding its delusional religious consciousness and occult beliefs. It is interesting to note that this middle-class ideology, which opposed the general fascist valorization of technology found elsewhere, was welcomed into and served Japanism.

Yet Tosaka also acknowledged that the parochial spirituality animating the rural middle class and its members' devotion to mysticism prevented the class from meeting the requirements of Japanism to become a more representative national constituency. He proposed that the spirituality practiced by the rural middle class could no longer remain and would have to be replaced by restorationism, thus transposing spiritualism into a political concept capable of producing a civic consciousness that conformed to a worldly political ideal. This meant redefining Japanese spiritualism to meet the criterion of some universal or global standard relating to a common civic consciousness and ridding spiritualism of the elastic "ambivalent restorationism" that produced the primitivization and centrality of the family system.[130] Tosaka observed how the military common sense and the agrarian fundamentalism of the rural middle class had bonded with the institution and apparatus of emperorism, which he defined as the "spirit of the Imperial Way" (*kōdō seishin*) materialized in emperorism. This bonding would provide the necessary condition for unification that would enable Japanism to become the expression of fascist political authority.[131] Yet this spiritualism could claim no universalism or even a connection to civic consciousness and was as parochial and irrational as the mysticism and religious delusions attributed to the rural middle class and petit bourgeoisie. At the end of *The Japan Ideology*, Tosaka stated that the purpose of the work was to assess the role of the emperor and capitalism, and he pleaded he had no space to address the problem. It is also true that writing about the emperor at that time was a dangerous occupation that could easily lead to imprisonment or worse. But he might have pointed to the Meiji slogan of enriching the nation, strengthening the military, which obliged the population to work and die for the emperor (that is, the nation). This explanation was later glossed by the novelist Natsume Sōseki in *And Then*, where he shows contempt toward businessmen and the instrumentalizing of working as a key to financial success.

Tosaka considered the family to be the most basic unit of archaism, and he could show both how ideology functioned at the level of policy related to everyday life and how familistic ideology was connected with capitalism and its cell-like but all-important commodity. He sought to demonstrate how the restorationist trope reconfigured the dominant form of political consciousness in the 1930s and determined the reorganization of social relationships and the structure of political authority. It is thus not surprising to see that he chose to employ the model of commodification to explain the conceptual figure of archaism and its vast functional reach. If, as Marx had explained, the commodity form had its own temporal trajectory that (through subsequent fetishization) banishes its historicity, the family unit is positioned to act similarly and fill the role of the archaic in the wider Japanese totality. The archaic had originally referred to a distant time, but once it was transformed into archaism, it became a timeless ideology without history or place. One of the fundamental demands of archaism was to invert the register of the temporal order by placing the past (the nonsynchronous model of origins) ahead in the present to reshape the character of government. It was believed that through the smallest and most basic unit of the social, it could be shown how contemporary life could be remolded into a fictional form, supposedly enabling it to revive the timeless paradigmatic arrangement of relationships from an indeterminate past.

The occasion for Tosaka's examination of how the archaic phenomenon played out politically and materially—especially how the family unit was employed to buttress archaism—was the complex and somewhat confused legislative initiative in 1934–1935 that sought to solve the problem of prostitution. Tosaka's examination led both to his excursion into the prehistory of a timeless primitivism and its fundamental form of familism and to his discovery that behind the issue of whether public prostitution should be allowed or made legal loomed an issue that had little to do with prostitution. He concluded the legislative initiative was nothing more than an expression of the archaic phenomenon.[132] The proposed legislation was ostensibly prompted by official concern that if a widening of prostitution were permitted, it would damage the morality of the family and possibly undermine health and hygiene, as well as the "beautiful manners and customs" of the Japanese tradition.[133] Tosaka was certain that the owners of private brothels were voicing the view held by a majority of the members of the Diet, which supported the maintenance of a private licensing system of brothels. In the end, the dispute came down to identifying anyone who opposed private licensing of prostitution under the influence of "materialist thought" imported from the West. He saw that private brothels related to capitalism's drive to accumulate money, which had less to do with family morality than with the sanctity of private property and the continuation of profit for the owners. It was therefore impossible to separate the privatization of prostitution from the moral sanctity of the traditional "family system of our licensed prostitution," which its defenders claimed had endured for three hundred years or even "three thousand years," concluding that the "necessity of the prostitution system" actually derived from Japan's "beautiful manners and customs."[134] The proposed legislation reinforced the system of licensing instead of abolishing it.

Tosaka saw the absurdity of the debate, during which the advocates of change were said to "proclaim a . . . secrecy about the national ethnic spirit," which showed that the real issue had to do with the importance of bringing together members of the proletariat and farmers to reconstitute them as the figure of an undifferentiated folk. This effort was apparently directed toward maintaining some sort of unity in the face of a family system that was widely acknowledged to be facing hardship and even imminent collapse, which explains why brothel owners could confidently exploit the logic of the folk character of Japanese social life. Yet in their exaggerated effort to achieve a unified folk in the present by linking it to an image drawn from the feudal past, the proponents overlooked the temporal difference between a folk consisting mainly of peasants in Tokugawa-era Japan and a society chiefly composed of industrial workers and farmers, a difference that stretched ideological fantasy beyond the bounds of credulity. Tosaka also pointed out that the defenders of prostitution argued that the family system had always supported licensed prostitution by reinforcing low wages and constraining labor power. He conceded that the drive to preserve licensed prostitution was one of the most passionate illustrations of restorationism or archaism in contemporary Japan. He also noticed its patent pointlessness in trying to conceal transparent private interests that had nothing to do with the family system.

Yet the situation was probably far more desperate than hitherto recognized. To say that the family system was a bulwark of licensed prostitution worked ideologically to keep wages low and limit the power of labor. The idealized family system was also a way to reduce reported levels of unemployment because it overlooked the large numbers of people who were actually unemployed but were counted as employed within the household. In an ironic gesture, Tosaka asserted that the truth of ideological declarations that the family system was the principal representative of the essence of Japanese society was cast into doubt by the population statistics gathered by Tokyo's statistical bureau, which had begun to determine that the size of families was shrinking and that increasing numbers of people registered as belonging to families were in fact living separately from them. The statistics showed that the traditional family system was declining, "telling a story that it [the family system] was moving and individualizing."[135] The statistics also showed that Tokyo was increasingly made up of migrants who had recently moved there from the countryside in search of work. In short, the data exposed the existence of the family system as a phantom. An interesting observation, made not by Tosaka but by Hani and others, was that rural Japan was witnessing a similar process, with declining households and the disappearance of whole villages. Tosaka did note the decline among rural households and concluded that deterioration of the family system had become a national problem.

Despite the changes revealed in the data, most Japanist ideologues failed to acknowledge the diminution of the traditional household. Instead, they focused on the increase of a "detestable individualism."[136] Tosaka thought that the idealization of a traditional family system when it was gradually declining was impelled by the desire to see in it the solution of social problems plaguing contemporary Japan—notably unemployment and poverty. The collapsing family system worsened those problems, leaving family members to support themselves or swell the ranks of the unemployed. This was particularly true for women, whose expulsion from disintegrating households accelerated the drive for women's financial independence that had started in the late 1920s. Tosaka was convinced that the large numbers of women who daily commuted to Tokyo for work or schooling provided an accurate index of this new independence, and he suggested that economic hardship and unemployment made it possible for women to become financially self-reliant modern women. Here he was concerned with explaining what lay behind ideology—in this case, the viral anti-individualism of the Japanists' view of the traditional family system—but his explanation was derived not from some excessive reactionary consciousness but rather from an effect "reducible to the archaic phenomenon," in which restoration was considered as "the model of archaism."[137] While Tosaka stopped short of explaining the relationship between restoration and familism, he must have seen that the centrality of familism for Japan was preserved because of the restoration. In fact, he saw the problem for Japanist proponents of familism was the collision between capitalism and feudalism, since Japanese monopoly capitalism was far from being dominated by individualism (although the early signs of it were present). Tosaka understood how Japanists linked the family to this earlier form of individualism, which had produced the contradiction that now made individualism appear to be the reason for the declining family system. His account underlined the necessity of returning to the feudal order and thus the principle of familism. However, he made this observation without explaining how such a temporal reversal might manage to reach that passed moment, although he implied that it would happen because of the restorationist dynamic and the conviction that the archaic phenomenon was unlimited in its possibilities. Japanist ideologues either failed to see the contradiction in ascribing the current collapse of the family system to an individualism that had accompanied an earlier form of capitalism now passed or, as Tosaka proposed, were deluded into believing that the blurring of contemporary monopoly capitalism would encourage the interpretation that it was anticapitalistic.[138] Actually, both might be true.

In regard to the movement of history, Tosaka argued that there should not simply be a restoration that always seeks to return to a distant antiquity, which almost suggests a form of the "restoration/revolution" congruent with the passive revolution that Gramsci had envisioned. Because of the relation between the idea of the so-called restoration and variant idealisms or ideology, no matter how modernized a precapitalist society becomes, it is still capable of bringing to the surface manifestations of progressivism—as exemplified by the Meiji restoration of imperial governance, which was followed by some quite radical innovations. Here Tosaka implied (though he did not actually state) that the Meiji renovation, coming in the shadow of the restoration, had moved to combine progressive components with inherited received practices from the past and thus qualified as an instance of either "restoration/revolution" or passive revolution. He may have had in mind the radical model of the French or Russian Revolution, and he was surely aware that these past examples contrasted with the current situation and its preoccupation with the Japanese family system and the evidence of its decline. Ultimately, the obsession with the family system and its use by Japanists as a model for the reorganization of society that sought to oppose the authority of rational social science was propelled by an arbitrary and random consciousness that used regulationism (tōseishugi) as a way to maintain capitalism. This was oddly contradictory, since for Japanists regulationism referred to an approval of rational social science, though Japanism supported capitalism at all costs. This concern with familism and the formation of an ideology of the family system resembled nothing more than an ideological attempt to revive as a template for the present something of the spirit of Tokugawa feudalism and its hierarchical and closed system of social constraints. The concern was an attempt to make of the present a huge repository of remnants. At the same time, Tosaka argued that this atavistic effort was less concerned with the problem of the family system or households than it was with providing a model for the organization of state and society.[139] What he had difficulty understanding was why such archaic phenomena were invariably aligned with reaction, when even the Meiji Restoration had produced progressive transforming changes.

Tosaka thus grasped archaism as the principal historical trope informing fascist political and social organization in 1930s Japan. It is important to recall that archaicism had a double meaning: it was both a process of return and a historical archaic time. He saw in its use the state's effort to reduce individualism as a necessary condition for leaving the modern present to return to the fundamental social unit at the core of a feudalism that the Meiji Restoration had overthrown. In his view, this desire to reembrace feudalism was not only a sign of a conservative and reactionary consciousness but also an expression of the movement to a return to a "positive archaic phenomenon in the present."[140] While he could approve of certain types of archaism, such as the return to the classics in the European Renaissance and even to a certain extent in the Meiji Restoration, he believed that the state's current efforts to install an older family system in the heart of a modernizing capitalist society represented a further "turning away from the authority of rational social scientific consciousness" and an attempt to exert greater control of capitalism through the excuse of preserving it.[141] The relevant tactic was to increase the centralization of state management of capitalism. He explained that the tactic was presented in a rough form with a content haphazardly thrown together. State policies of imposing older forms of familism were an obscenity. It is for this reason that familism will appear most markedly as a type of archaic phenomenon. Yet it was not sufficient to say that familism was only part of archaism. More correctly, it had become part of primitivism. Censorship meant that Tosaka was unable to criticize the imperial institution, but not necessarily the bureaucracy over which it presided. Thus, he used the bureaucracy to communicate his view of the emperor as a primitive, precapitalist emanation. While the institution that he called into question bore a vague resemblance to Rousseau's ideas of a social contract, Tosaka was quick to add that it was different from the sort of primitivism associated with natural law and naturalism. He reasoned that this Japanese version of primitivism was related to conditions that could not be disrupted by altering its fixed content with any replacement generated by history. If at first it was archaic, it was also radical and extremely primitive. In the exchange for a history of human culture, primitivism extended the uncivilized horizon indefinitely into a timeless zone of barbarism.[142] Japanist ideology juxtaposed the family system to the individualism associated with modern Western societies. Theoretically, this pairing was reduced to returning to the older more general categories of *Gemeinschaft* and *Gesellschaft*, which were based on the move from involuntary to voluntary relationships: the former was an idealization of precapitalist social organization, and the latter was first and foremost a Western aspiration based on individualism. This use of categories derived from German social science collapsed history, since it did not account for how community was actually transformed into society.

This return to the model of premodern primitivism was prompted by what Japanists saw as the need to guide bodily sentiment and sensation reflected in the traditional sentimentalized emotionalism (*nasake*) about love between parent and child, which amounted to "unconditional domination."[143] Yet behind these expressions of unrationality and antirationality, Tosaka identified the authorizing principle of "mystery," or the "mysterious" (*shimpishugi*). In addition, he saw the descent into the unrational as a move toward "exoticism," which constituted the "primitivization of theoretical function" that in turn determined the primary nature of social relationships and showed that the idea of familism was based on the strength of a metaphor for society. In this way, the family was fashioned into a microcosm that called attention to and represented the larger social formation—a relationship that paradoxically resonated with the receding echo of precapitalist neo-Confucian theories of the relationship between nature and society, if not also with the principal social unit informing the hierarchical order of things in the Tokugawa feudal system. This meant reducing human relationships to the most basic and primitive level of family or clan, in which all authority was vested in the patriarch.

Tosaka was correct to see this exchange of social models as only a functional or instrumental archaism, since it referred to the original human community or a state of nature that preceded the emergence of the archaic myth, and not to the world of the gods and the first emperor, Jinmu. In other words, first came humans and myth, and later came the Japanese. In this connection, primitive familism was thus presented as existing prior to archaic organization and becoming its apparent source. It was the most extreme form of primitivism: a dark world, completely of the earth, under-ground, violent, and driven completely by unmediated intuition. Yet since Tosaka considered this form as a throwback to a primal nature, he con-cluded that it was used by the modern Japanese state in a tropic theoriza-tion derived from the ideology of "familistic primitivization" to produce a political outcome that established state and society on the basis of a fabri-cated historical metaphor.

If primitivism made familism indispensable, the principle of mystery that corresponded to this familistic primitivity required a psychological sense of religious feeling, which mysticism supplied. Tosaka noted that the religious sense provided by mystery and mysticism and the psychological anchor for this conception of familism reflected the primitive emotional-ism associated with the clan and the particular locality over which specific tutelary deities presided. While the idea of returning to this archaic model of local territory and particularistic religious practice and emotionality in the midst of a modern capitalist society made no sense, the same might well be said of the figure of the emperor—especially since such religious feelings were ascribed not to individuals but to the larger social collective. If the first characteristic of contemporary familism was primitivization, then the second was mysticism, which was accompanied by primitive reli-gious feelings for the clan and its tutelary deities. This return to the origins of such beliefs as animism and the creative powers of the earth necessitated a system of totemic worship linked to an agrarianism of simple production and reproduction.[144] Here Tosaka risked coming close to stepping over the boundaries of censorship and being censored since he was referring to the religionization and particularistic regionalization of the family. In his ren-dition of the most archaic narrative, certain "great men" were deified as the "material" embodiment of meaning, serving as the foundation of a prim-itivized familistic religious formation.[145] This belief vaguely prefigured the restorationist idea that conflated religious ceremony and governance (saisei itchi), if primarily more for political than religious purposes. I believe that Tosaka was unraveling the origins of the imperial family in some dis-tant past and explaining its derivation from primitive familistic religious practices that had continued in the modern era. Here was the fundamental contradiction: all primitivization appeared as nothing more than a form of modernization that a developed, modern capitalism had produced for and by itself. In other words, all of Japanism's folkic and spiritual mani-festations were found in familism. The summoning of primitivization was only a repetitive, noisy incantation that signaled the complete abandonment of historical reflection in favor of an antihistorical and reactionary conceptual form that had no relevance to the modern society it was supposed to serve. This was possible through the act of orchestrating a systematically emptying out of the received national culture and reducing it to an exceptionalizing national essentialism (*kokusuika*), which created a new traditionalism dedicated to jettisoning Japan's actual historical traditions in favor of a neonativist fantasy pathway to fascism. Distinguishing between tradition and traditionalism was absolutely vital for grasping this fascist strategy, which sought to erase the crucial difference as a necessary condition for making the historical present look like the ahistorical archaic past.

At the center of the contradiction, spawned by an archaism that meant restorationism, Tosaka identified the problem in the reconstruction of a new national narrative that harked back to the content of the mythic histories of the seventh and eighth centuries found in the archaic chronicles like the *Kojiki* and *Nihonshōki*. He was particularly concerned with the contradiction of the contemporary common sense of a national idea in which the appeals to these histories were formulated and produced in his present by the archaic principle of restoration in the broadest sense of the word, which would simultaneously convey the two meanings of archaic and restoration in a single word (*fukko*). For Tosaka, the current version of this archaicizing pattern stemmed from the idealist notion of the primitivization of contemporary society. Despite the vast temporal distance between the archaic stratum and Japan's modern society, the mythic history of origin (that is, the archaic restoration dedicated to renewal) claimed both an authority of a principle that exceeded history and a constant presentness, thus producing an antinomy between its unbound timelessness and any encounter with the historical boundaries of contemporary society. In these circumstances, Tosaka argued that a reactionary restorationism could never be more than an intellectual and emotional ideology. Primitivization or the archaic (Tosaka used these terms interchangeably) could conform only to the realm of ideas, not to current actuality. But this did not prevent an ideological masquerade from circulating, like the commodity form, and penetrating every nook and cranny of society and culture. The problem was temporal, since it resulted in the elimination of time and history. The Japanist effort to advance a conception of sovereign nontimelessness in the archaic, as expressed in restorationism, was an attempt to conceal the contemporary temporal order of capitalism by installing a primitivistic family system. What this transfer accomplished was the construction of a temporal contradiction. The irony in this move was that capitalism's belief that it was eternal and characterized by a past without history was undermined by the restorationist decision after 1868 to posit the "opposite historical category denoting 'ancient times' (korai)," which cast capitalism back into a finite historical process as a stage—although previously its historical categories had transcended time.[146] It is true that the original political economic defense of capitalism saw it as both natural and eternal. As far as I can determine, Japanists never acknowledged the historicity of capitalism, even though the Meiji Restoration used capitalism to posit its own external category of eternality to overcome the contradiction between historical time and timelessness. It is possible to imagine that the program to replace the present with an indeterminate archaic past was part of the Japanist strategy, since Japanism's steady support of capitalism implied that it had always existed. But this strategy could not have been implemented without reversing the temporal order of unevenness, which required positioning noncontemporaneous contemporaneity ahead of contemporaneous noncontemporaneity. Even though Tosaka never explicitly argued that the Japanist promotion of the past in the present was an attempt to conceal time, this view can be inferred from his critique of the logical impossibility of suppressing or concealing the historical development of capitalism: acknowledging capitalism's existence would collide with the Japanist effort to restore a precapitalist archaic presence in the present that attributed economic production to the divine (which was not yet able to envision the occurrence of this history). In fact, it was Marxism that forced the issue by insisting on the fundamental historicity of capitalism, a view reflected in Tosaka's observation that the present stage of capitalism led people to believe that it was transhistorical. But like all economic systems, capitalism unfolded in stages, and it was the Meiji Restoration that provided the impulse to unwind the history concealed by claims of eternality. Moreover, the contradiction was doubled, since restorationism could not separate itself from the historicity of the restoration, nor could it free itself from the interchangeable associations of the restoration or the blurring of differences between restoration and the archaic. It is important to recall that the restoration was simultaneously timeless, archaic, and a historical moment: Jinmu's timeless founding of Japan and the historical formation of the Meiji state were based on Jinmu's accomplishment, which only a divinely anointed emperor could bring together. In the end, Tosaka was convinced that the archaic was a worthless category that had appeared under the worst circumstances "to construct a nationalistic essence organization" to expressly counter the contemporary internationalist category (commonly referring to European and American thought). It "was a nativist and absolutist category," and its most "distinctive feature . . . is that it had no utility in today's real life."[147] But Tosaka was also right to note that archaism, not the emperor, was the principal cause of driving the prewar society toward fascism.

EPILOGUE: DÉJÀ VU

Postwar Japan was shadowed by its dark decade of the 1930s. During the American experiment to transform an entire population socialized in fascist conformism into a democratic community, the unfinished business of the recent past remained patiently passive and unseen yet present. But after the Occupation ended in 1952 and the Americans left, assuming the position that Japan was more valuable as a capitalist client in a Cold War American imperium than as a transformed autonomous social democracy, the unresolved problems of that dark decade rushed through a metaphorical floodgate to swamp the partially implemented reforms and drown its remaining aspirations to make way for a different future. The swift replacement of many of the Occupation reforms revitalized the unwanted residues of a past unwilling to disappear, becoming the permanent historical furniture in the structure of the long postwar, a temporal category authorizing its chronological measure. In a similar way, the critical discourses of the prewar period passed unnoticed into either a stale national narrative of predetermined Marxian stages of development or a narrative that gauged progress by global economic success in the form of growthism. Along with the great democratic experiment, the encouraging acuity of prewar criticism and the resistance of thinkers like Hasegawa Nyozekan and Tosaka Jun were forgotten. The Occupation left an enduring trace, as if it had been a transition that would end only in a moment that never seems to come. But this trace was overlaid on an already existing hybrid culture, which Miki Kiyoshi might, had he lived, have heralded as an exemplar of his conception of living culture and Maruyama Masao would have seen as evidence of the workings of the *basso ostinato* or "archaic stratum," a subterranean historical rhythm whose intensity had varied between moments of openness (or change) and those of closure (or withdrawal) since ancient times. Both thinkers highlighted the persistence of repetition and remnants and the periodic combining of newer and older elements in the constant remaking of culture in Japan's supposed rebirth or second coming.

According to the well-known story an army of occupation, led by well-meaning disciples of the reformers of the U.S. New Deal, was dedicated to remaking the Japan that had been created during the Depression. The occupiers' ambitious aims included rebuilding a destroyed industrial infrastructure to revive capitalist production and equipping the country with a new political order securely established as a genuinely social democratic order. The Americans drafted a new constitution that clarified what the U.S. constitution really was: a relic sanctioned by an eighteenth-century slaveholding elitism that already had outgrown its functional utility by the end of that century. The new constitution imposed on a defeated Japan was more progressive than its predecessor, the Meiji Constitution of 1889, its anachronic retention of the emperor, now in putatively symbolic form, recalling the Meiji model, which it was supposed to replace.

It seems paradoxical that while the United States embarked on a vast postwar program to reconstruct war-torn economies (including those of its former fascist enemies like Germany, Austria, and Italy and that of a former colony like South Korea), American plans for the renewal of Japan appeared far more ambitious, as if that country needed a total makeover from the ground up. The Americans apparently believed that Japanese society had to be rid of the traditional scourge of feudal remnants, whose survival had eased its path to fascism and undermined the growth of capitalism. Ironically, Supreme Commander for the Allied Powers General Douglas MacArthur's uncommon use of the word "feudal" sounded odd and closely resembled the language of Japanese Marxists. U.S. postwar involvement in Germany and Italy could be explained not by positing an incomplete modernity in those countries but by referring to the interwar economic crises that occurred there (as well as in Japan), which could be fixed by postwar economic means. In contrast, the political renewal in Germany and Italy was largely left to the citizens of those countries, although in Germany there was close oversight by the Allies. In contrast to Japan, neither Germany nor Italy had constitutions drafted by a foreign power imposed on them, nor did they experience other deep reforms intended to alter matters of religious belief, social behavior, and education. There seems to have been a crucial difference between the U.S. response to Japan's postwar recovery and Americans' attitude toward the other defeated nations.

Because Japan's fascist history was thought to have been the result of a legacy of feudal residues, the country was seen as having been stalled in a state of historical backwardness, and thus it was not eligible for much in the postwar treatment designated for more advanced European states. But it should be noted that Marxists of the lecture faction continued to use the language of feudal remnants to describe Japan's current political situation, as if war and defeat changed nothing. It is hard not to see in this scenario the phantom figure of a historical stagism with a linear trajectory (not necessarily Marxian) and the teleology of progress as a criterion that, though not acknowledged, was used in evaluating the occupied countries. It is also conceivable that the U.S. view of Japan might have been bolstered by contemporary social science, which focused on defining indelible national characteristics. However, it is equally possible that Americans introduced the cultural relativism of the social sciences (especially anthropology) in the belief that societies are capable of change—with the help of the United States, in the case of Japan. In any event, Germany and other defeated countries did not need a complete makeover based on a model of the social and political experience of the victors. In contrast, Japan was considered not only wayward but also backward and apparently in need of a different approach. Such assessments invariably depend on who is making them and are often accompanied by evaluations of what constitutes examples of advanced and backward societies. For example, the modernizing makeover of the developing world during the Cold War was a continuation of imperialists' long-standing habit of calling such makeovers not modernizing but civilizing. This makes it even harder to understand why Japan was treated as it was in the Occupation, when it was clearly industrialized, modernized, and imperialized. Direct links were forged between the Occupation reforms and a subsequent textbook model of modernization centered on the Japanese experience that was exhibited for emulation by the unaligned and underdeveloped societies of the former colonial world and its new nations. This was the case not only in the postwar decades: the successful occupation of Japan was revisited as a model as recently as the Iraq War, when the United States again engaged in nation rebuilding.

It is notable that the American view of Japanese history had a close resemblance to earlier Japanese Marxian interpretations, which sought to explain the late development of Japanese capitalism and its being stalled at an immature stage as consequences of the crushing weight of surviving elements of the feudal past in its modernizing process. It is ironic that the emperor and the imperial bureaucratic apparatus that the Occupation rescued and retained for the future its leaders were busily imagining had been the most important feudal remnants in the prewar Marxian critical appraisals. The American Occupation was inspired in part by high-minded aims and grandiose ambitions to remake a defeated Japan into an exemplar of political equality and capitalist economic proficiency. The American occupation was pledged to redeeming its failed uncompleted modernity from the ground up, what Maruyama called a new beginning of modernization, the first having been the Meiji reforms after the restoration. The new start required a new set of values, many of which came from America (though they were not always in practice there), to transmute a folk socialized into feudal and hierarchical conformism into a modern, rational, and informed citizenry. Yet a question remains: when did defeating an enemy become the occasion for nation building and a total modernizing makeover?

In retrospect, it seems important to emphasize the difference between the Americans' occupation of Japan and their practices in Germany, Austria, South Korea, and elsewhere, inasmuch as the Occupation aspired to make the Japanese utterly different from what they had been. However different the local historical and cultural experiences were in the countries the United States partially or totally occupied after the war, those differences do not account for the amount of disparity in their treatment. The Occupation too often came close to resembling something I have commented on: the mad workings of H. G. Wells's protagonist in *The Island of Doctor Moreau*, who sought to transform lower orders of life into humans. This Occupation removed Japan from the world in which it had recently played such an important role, as if it had been transferred to another register of occupancy like the older status of Tokugawa seclusion or a new status as a charter member of the new American imperium, reinforcing its, America's, own avowal of exceptionalism. More to the point is the fact that in the vast historiography of the Occupation produced by Americans there is rarely any mention of the fact that at the same time when Americans were trying to reshape Japan and the Japanese there were other military occupations in Germany, Austria, and other countries. In any event, the American experiment in Japan was interrupted in the late 1940s, with Cold War geopolitics and the sudden shift of power relations in East Asia— announced by the Communists' victory over the Nationalists in China and the outbreak of the Korean War. These events led the United States to reconsider its future role in the region. Leaders of the Occupation altered its planned reforms, changed its direction, and substituted Japan for Nationalist China as America's principal ally in the Asia-Pacific region. The United States continued to work to restore Japan's capitalist industrial structure (which benefited greatly from the Korean War), but it put the brakes on Japan's democratization process by easing up on the punishment of wartime leaders and reinstalling some of the members of the prewar imperial bureaucracy in positions of power. At the heart of the political reforms was the imposition of a new constitution written by Americans. This gave women the vote, pledged Japan to renounce the maintenance of military forces, and retained the emperor—now defined as the human symbol of the unity of state and people, whereas before he had claimed absolute authority based on divine descent from the sun goddess at the time of the origin, created and implemented by the deities of heaven and earth.

Postwar Japan was led to revisit its prewar past and recover some of its key components, resulting in what has increasingly appeared to be an instance of déjà vu. The key component that brought the immediate past into the present was the decision to retain the emperor and the imperial household. It is still hard to understand why the decision was made to retain the emperor and exempt him from all responsibility for the war. While the final decision belonged to MacArthur, some U.S. officials had already proposed that retaining the emperor would avoid bloodshed, help in the struggle against communism, and ease the task of modernization. But there were many more Americans and people in its allied countries who opposed it. In any case, the retention of the emperor resulted in repositioning him and the archaic aura he embodied in the midst of the allegedly new democratic polity. It also opened the way after the end of the Occupation for the return of elements of prewar politics, including some that recalled aspects of Japanist fascism such as the annual celebration of National Foundation Day (*Kenkoku Kinenbi*), commemorating the founding of the state by Jinmu, and the controversy over Japan's national anthem (*Kimigayo*), which enshrines the emperor and his military associations—thus sanctioning attacks by right-wing thugs against critics of the emperor. The refusal to hold the emperor (together with government officials in charge of everyday life before the war) responsible for the war spared him from going to trial and effectively disallowed any reference to him during the subsequent war crime trials. This made it possible to resuscitate the political culture of the prewar era, despite the putative safeguards of the new constitution. The state's decision long after the Occupation ended to finance the public spectacle of Emperor Hirohito's funeral was probably illegal but contributed inestimably to the enhancement of the imperial figure, as did the publicity as he lay dying. It is difficult not to see America's complicity in assisting the return of the archaic.

Actually, both Japan and the United States benefited: the Japanese retained their emperor, now constitutionally assigned to the role of a symbol, and the Americans gained an ally, constitutionally committed to nonaggression in a controversial provision that is still being debated seventy years later. Moreover, the Occupation cracked down hard on the Japanese left, in the context of the emerging Cold War, and allowed the Liberal Democratic Party to have what now seems to be a permanent grasp on power. The Occupation thus ensured that there would be no viable political competition, involving the CIA in stabilizing the party's electoral position and using a number of independent private foundations (like the Asia Foundation) to purportedly assist in normalizing Japanese political society.

In this connection it might be useful to recall the argument of Paolo Virino about déjà vu. The return of antiquity (*fukko*) that accompanied the restoration of the emperor also led to the return of the anachronistic phantom or pseudo past as if it were retrieving an infinitely repeatable historical past believed to have once existed. This was the meaning implicit in *fukko*, a term used to denote both restoration and the archaic—both of which were temporalizing states, capable of being in and out of time. This illusory past of a timeless origin was always availably present in the acts of preserving and venerating. According to Virino, "the past" that is "to be preserved and venerated" through mimetic performance is nothing more than the present itself, "smuggled in place of something that already happened."[1] He argued that the real anachronism was a real fiction (in some respects, not unlike a real abstraction), something that had never really existed yet was founded on the conviction of its genuine historicity. Thus, the archaic figure of the emperor is the auratic living embodiment in the present of a pseudo history that in turn is validated by its putative origin in a precapitalist temporal order. One of the reasons proposed for retaining the emperor was the appeal to the claimed long historical continuity of the imperial genealogy, which goes back to its origin and the myths associated with it. What is historically certain is the origin of the institution in a precapitalist agrarian order intimately tied to religious rituals performed by an emperor or ruler, who acted as the mediator between humans and deities to beseech the gods for abundance and tranquility and to validate his own claims to authority. At the time, these religious acts were undoubtedly indistinguishable from governance, which meant that religion and politics were unified (*saisei itchi*). The reinstallation of such a figure in a highly technological and rational capitalist society that was embarking on a great democratic experiment was not only a classic anachronism but also a spectacular historical anomaly.

The new Japanese constitution retained aspects of the Occupation's democratizing program by guaranteeing people rights rather than imposing duties on them. This was in contrast to the Meiji constitution, which had imposed duties on subjects. The constitution also vested sovereignty in the popular will instead of in the monopoly of a divine emperor. But recoding the emperor into the symbol of the state and unity of the Japanese people opposed the democratic dispensation. Returning to an archaic imperial institution and at the same time seeking to weaken it by removing its source of divine legitimacy created an insurmountable antinomy in the national consciousness. Moreover, the emperor's former custodianship of religious rites and rituals, which were also political functions, connected the source of his rule with the unseen realm of national deities and ancestors—an empire of spirits and gods to which territory visible to all was added only later. Some of the rites still conducted are arcane reenactments, such as the emperor spending a night in the Ise Shrine and sleeping and apparently having sex with the sun goddess during his enthronement ceremonies. But who would know? The Occupation retained the convention of calling the monarch "emperor" even after Japan at the end of the war had been forced to forfeit its former empire in East Asia, which obliged the emperor to return to the invisible domain where real power remained.

The emperor's reign was measured in imperial time, which coexisted with world standard time (capitalism's time), the maintenance of a convention that signified that even the most rabid, anti-Western Japanist in the prewar period would never deny the importance of capital. The calendar that Japanese still use counts the years beginning with the start of the current emperor's reign. The ideology of archaism was regenerated as a postwar civil religion in which the emperor's exercise of his traditional role, based on the identity of ceremony and governance, was in large part made to conform to the demands of secularization. By endorsing the principal Japanist ideologemes—which centered both on embracing the imperial institution and the archaic associations surrounding the figure of the emperor and on auraticizing that figure—the Occupation contributed to and even enabled (inadvertently or not) the filtering of the claims of uniqueness and exceptionalism into daily life in present-day Japan.

The presence of the emperor in the public domain was reinforced by publishing works about being Japanese, a trend that began anew in the

1970s. These books focused on the unique nature of Japan's culture and almost invariably linked this uniqueness to the emperor and imperial origins, evoking images of art, culture, ethnicity, and language. Publishing and the mass media collectively acted as an unofficial state apparatus to convey this cultural ideology, reminding Japanese of their identity and birthright. The figure of the emperor, the imperial family, and its auratic archaic appearance was diffused throughout public space. In recent years, this campaign to keep the ideological presence of the emperor before the public was enhanced by revitalized Shinto associations like The Japan Conference (*Nippon kaigi*),[2] which played a major role in Liberal Democratic Party politics, as well as by an expanding constituency of adherents and even a smaller brigade of foreign admirers whose favorable scholarship on Shinto and the emperor has been used to support the image of the imperial institution. Cultural support is supplied by state sponsorship of a building (resembling a mausoleum) dedicated to the study of Japanese culture (*Nichi bunken*), unsurprisingly located in Kyoto. While this state cultural institution has a different name, its activities often recall those of comparable institutions in the 1930s such as the Research Center for the Study of the Japanese Spirit.

One critic of the imperial institution, the independent and great sinologue, Takeuchi Yoshimi, proposed that the emperor functioned as a kind of metonym of Japan, bringing to mind the ruin of a classical Greek statue without arms or legs that, even in its ruined incompleteness, was still capable of standing in for the whole of ancient Greek civilization.[3] He also observed that contemporary Japanese society thus contained "any number of miniature emperor systems" that were undistinguishable from the "hamlet communal order," the archetypal agrarian village that provided the foundation of the imperial institution. This observation closely resembled the perception of Gilles Deleuze and Félix Guattari that fascism derived its strength from microcosmic structures, or what a Japanese historian called its grassroots. Takeuchi put it best when, in the 1960s, he identified the emperor system with the natural environment, which reminded the Japanese that they had a feudal and perhaps fascist legacy and that miniature emperor systems were embodied in every "blade of grass and tree leaf" of Japan. He also reminded the Japanese that the emperor system was like a lizard: even if its head is cut off, its tail continues to wiggle.[4] The remnants of the country's feudal heritage were so pervasive in Japan that the intellectual Yoshimoto Takaaki was encouraged to propose that the masses (by which he probably meant the agrarian classes) had been "effectively absorbed into the emperor system."[5] He was likely referring to the consciousness of the communal system in relation to the ideological structure of the modern emperor system forged at the time of the Meiji Restoration. In the late Tokugawa era, villages had been increasingly undermined by the penetration of the capitalist market economy into the countryside, so it is not surprising that the crisis-ridden premodern communal order had been incorporated into the newly invented ideology of the imperial system. As a result, the new imperial ideology expressed, among other things, the living consciousness of the communal order's experience of this crisis—which meant, according to Kan Takayuki, that the imperial system remained implanted in the unconscious of the village community and farm household, solidifying the relationship of the peasants and farmers to the imperial house. The restoration sought to resolve this socioeconomic crisis of the late Tokugawa years by superimposing the restored emperor, who embodied the contradiction between the archaic and the new political beginning, on a communal order destabilized by the forces of capitalism. Thus, the restoration and the emperor provided a necessary solution to the social, political, and economic problem of the moment, but the imperial institution's lasting vocation (which stood above any conflict) was committed to resolving this contradiction.[6]

The imperial institution functioned as a magical metonym calling attention to the totality, and it became impossible to separate Japanese culture from the institution. The archaic thus remained ever present in both the part and the whole. As an archaic sign, a symbol, and an embodiment inseparable from the imperial countenance and titular head of the Japanese nation, the emperor was positioned to secure the people's acceptance of existing political arrangements and to enlist them (without their consent), as Motoori Norinaga had insisted in the eighteenth century. This was achieved by attaching people's feelings about their local community, which thereby became identical to the Japanese community and state. Combining the domains of the social and political and making them interchangeable made it possible for a social act to become a political one and vice versa. The political theorist Bertell Ollman argued that people were thus encouraged to identify the form of rule under which they lived with the Japanese as a social and ethnic group, and they were persuaded to act politically as if they were a social group and to act socially as if they were a political totality.[7]

Kan recently reinforced these observations about the saturation of the imperial image in daily life, when he argued that the imperial figure infiltrated every aspect of everyday life and dominated the environment like a permanent eclipse. In addition, given the emperor's ubiquity in Japanese society, his figure functioned like the omnipresent commodity form. Kan showed that in daily life, every Japanese encounters the emperor's presence—what Kan called the emperor's shadow—in countless ways, though people are not aware of their relationship to an archaic emperor. The aura of the archaic shadows their environment as much as the miniature emperor systems nestled among the "blades of grass and tree leaves" throughout the country. Japanese at least are always aware of living in the calendar time of the emperor's reign, as well as in the normative capitalist time of business and work. Moreover, imperial time occupies a part of the everyday time of Japanese as well, through family genealogies and rituals of reverence for ancestors, shrines, religious holidays, the emperor's birthday, marriages, deaths, national symbols, and the acceptance of the emperor in every hamlet in the country. The archaic countenance commands the everyday, even if people are not cognizant of the persisting and pervasive shadows in their everyday lives.[8] What appears to be a promise that the shadow will always remain available for reanimation and reactivation is guaranteed by the presence of certain committed forces like Shinto groups centered on the emperor's religio-political authority, nationalists aligned with right-wing thugs, and a bureaucratic apparatus that has never ceased to act in the emperor's name.

Neither Miki nor Tosaka was able to see how the presence of the archaic emperor filled the everyday lives of the Japanese. Tosaka saw the everyday not as a forgotten remainder of modernization but rather as its primary accomplishment. In his view, the proper vocation of philosophy was to turn away from the dreamworld of a transcendent idealist metaphysics and focus on material life and the everyday. For Miki, the everyday was the site of renewal throughout Japan's history, where the new was received and adapted. Yet for Miki and Tosaka, to have not thought about the ubiquitous instantiation of the archaic shadows casting its dominant pall over Japanese society does not necessarily mean that its recognition never occurred to them. In the political environment of 1930s Japan, people could not write much about the emperor before attracting the attention of the censor or the police. Even in today's Japan, people often risk their lives if they criticize the emperor. It is not surprising that some of Japan's most gifted thinkers did not take that course. But it also suggests the possible operation of a strategy of intentionally displacing by thoughtful people critical of the imperial institution and the state a complex belief system, expressing the work of a cultural politics deeply rooted in an unconscious that encouraged denial of the emperor's importance by ignoring the reminders of his presence and the extent to which submission to the archaic institution had been so fully incorporated. Whether the emperor possessed real political authority, owing to the divinity he was said to embody, or instead had acquired a new symbolic status, the persistence of this archaic figure in a modern, industrialized society continues to offer the promise of resolving the contradictions and disorder produced by the temporal unevenness, colliding oppositions, and irresolvable antinomies that have been present in Japan throughout its long cultural history and its recent capitalist modernization. The archaic Japanese emperor was seen as the only figure capable of bringing opposites together: the archaic that he embodies (that is, the national origin) ensures the constant achievement of unity and community. Hence the aura of the archaic requires the persistence of the emperor—who is its vehicle of expression and the mark of both Japan's modernity and its effort to complete a capitalism that will never be realized anywhere. The emperor is permanently juxtaposed to the moment of a realized origin and state foundation that will never change.

It is in this context that we must briefly consider texts by two of modern Japan's most eminent intellectuals and critics, which discuss the return of the archaic in the 1970s: Maruyama's *Kosō* (1972) and Kobayashi Hideo's *Motoori Norinaga* (1978–1982).[9] Maruyama was an active participant in postwar discussions on political subjectivity and Japan's political modernization and the author of a major book on the history of political thought, the subject he taught at Tokyo University. Kobayashi was a literary critic and editor at Shinchōsha, who wrote on a wide range of subjects dealing with Japan and the West, and he was a principal participant in the 1942 symposium on "Overcoming the Modern." Both thinkers were extremely well versed in Western and Japanese thought. Their texts represent a return to the archaic, and they appeared when (as noted above) publishers turned to issuing books on being Japanese and the exceptionality of Japanese culture. I do not think that either author was affected by this fad, since both had started to think about their respective subjects long before they produced their contributions to the return to Japan discussions. But there can be no doubt about the effect these texts would have on Japanese opinion, as their ideas worked their way down to more popular publications.

It is my contention that both Maruyama and Kobayashi turned to the question of the archaic as a way of treating it metaphorically and thus ridding it of its previous negative associations, while simultaneously retaining some of the positive associations for their immediate present and an uncertain future. Most importantly, they shared not only the decision to bypass the centrality of origin and its relation to the imperial genealogy but also the choice to see in the archaic a way to return to the present. While each in his own way valorized the present, they differed in their view of its importance. Maruyama may have been more inclined to explain the changes in his outlook resulting from his wartime experiences than Kobayashi was. The latter appeared to provide no special reason to write on Motoori, apart from reminding readers that he, Kobayashi, had paid a visit to the home of the eccentric nativist ethnologist Orikuchi Shibobu, who advised him to start with the *Kojikiden*, Motoori's great exegeses on the *Kojiki*.

Maruyama wrote a long prefatory essay in 1984 that reflected on the experience of the past and explained his shift from concentrating on more recent political texts to turning to the archaic texts—the chronicles and subsequent writings throughout Japan's history—to record the mix of myths of origin and the accompanying narratives of historical events. He had described the patterns of *kosō* he had been able to extract from the chronicles as a prototype, but now he saw them as the figure of an archetype.[10] The change signified a move from seeing the archaic as a singular and static type to grasping it as a type that would repeat itself through time. The configuration whose "first form" Maruyama had discerned that was repeated time and again in Japan's subsequent history appeared in the opening pages in Motoori's *Kojikiden*: "From antiquity down to the present, there has been good and bad in the world . . . which does not differ from the meaning of all the deities. . . . In the periods of time and conditions within the world one thing after another changes from good events to bad events; the reason (*kotowari*) for this relies on the original intent of these deities."[11] This pattern expressed in the text, a continuing repetition in history, corresponded, as I show below, to Maruyama's view that a repetitive rhythm coursed like an underground river—the archaic stratum like the musical figure of *basso ostinato*—through Japan's history, oscillating between Japan's opening and closing to outside influence and change and transforming Motoori's principle of the godly intention of the change from good to bad.

The wartime experience provided Maruyama with a way to describe the repetitive historical patterning in Japanese history in terms of regularized shifts between moments of openness and those of closure. The key was provided by the Meiji Restoration, which appeared to him as a double image in which Japan's history moved from the long night of Tokugawa seclusion (*sakoku*) to a restoration that opened Japan to the outside world, cultural contacts, and change. Maruyama saw this shift in the opening of Japan by the United States, which he made into a metaphor for the new configuration to describe its repetitive occurrence in both Japan's modern history after 1868 and in the long period before then. The constraints on and loss of personal freedom during World War II (already reported by To-saka) recalled for Maruyama an "intellectual seclusion" that persisted to Ja-pan's final defeat.[12] According to Maruyama, Japan had known three major moments of opening: the first was in the sixteenth century, with the com-ing of Christian missionaries and the formation of Southern barbarian (*Nanban*) culture, a product of Portuguese trade from the south (known as the southern barbarian trade); the second came with the opening of Japan and the end of the Tokugwa shogunate resulting from the Meiji Restora-tion; and the third was the closing down in the 1930s with fascism, which led to war, defeat, and the Occupation. Maruyama believed that this last opening was yet to be completed, and that at the time he wrote it was too soon to know what its final results would be. But he was confident that the political system, ideology, and structure would not be destroyed but replaced by a new democratic arrangement. Moreover, he was certain that the growth of the economy had become more important than political is-sues. A curious way of expressing his confidence was to say that it did not matter to him whether or not there was an emperor, since the emperor was no longer a problem. While it is hard to know what exactly Maruyama might have meant by so easily discounting the role of the emperor in Japanese society (which had recently been retained by the Occupation), it seems clear that the figure of the archaic loomed larger than the emperor in his thinking. In other words, he implied that the emperor had become an empty vessel. What seemed most vital to Maruyama was that Japan remained open to cultural contacts and change—which, for him, finally "touched upon the suitability of the word *kosō* and the beginning of the struggle to think."[13]

Maruyama thus used his conception of the archaic stratum to think through the first chronicles to find a basis for a distinctive and last-ing historical consciousness in the story of origin and the ancient politi-cal state, with its divinely ordained imperial genealogy. Despite Motoori's encompassing concept of reason and his acceptance of a style of specula-tion and narration that corresponded to the first divine intention in the age of the gods, Maruyama was convinced that the myths did not end the possibility of history once the compilation of materials was completed but would continue in a particular "rhythmic flow" through the continuing accretion of several aspects of the development of historical consciousness.[14] In other words, the first chronicles were the principal source that authorized and enabled the formation of a coherent Japanese historical consciousness. By extracting the flows directly from the first chronicles down to the present, meaning was revealed in the continuum of historical accounts that came after the chronicles.[15] The archaic stratum is clearly derived from the method of using Chinese ideographs in the earliest myths. Within the accounts of the creation were three basic verbs that served as the foundation of expression: *tsukuru* (to make), *umu* (to give birth), and *naru* (to become). The latter two were the principal categories of the philosophy of hermeneutics used by Japanism.[16] From the Shinto thinkers of the Tokugawa period to the nativist proponents of the Japanese spirit, there was no lack in the philosophy of Japanism or hermeneutics, as noted in chapter 4, in the use of the basic concepts of *umu* and *naru*. According to Maruyama's reading of Motoori, the concept of *tsukuru* related first to the human capacity of making things, later to the changes in things, and finally to fabrications: in English he put it, "first is to be born, secondly is transformation and thirdly is completion." *Naru* evolved into the category of *nariyuki*, the course of events making historical consciousness possible. For Maruyama, the three categories did not necessarily guide each present, but their presence ensured the possibility of change or closure and "historical optimism" through the realization of change.[17] That optimism was announced by "one thing after another (*tsugitsugi*)," the energy that produces the trend of the times (*ikioi*) or their conditions (*nariyuki*), reminding readers that the late Tokugawa loyalist Yoshida Shoin believed that even though Mencius had acknowledged that the way of the sages had not yet formulated the idea of *jisei* (trend of the times), it was an exception when the ordinary people of society once uttered the word to show their intention, implying that the idea was already available in Japan.

Hence, the constant presence of this possibility of change in every present disclosed the structure of the archaic stratum, a view that I believe echoed Miki's earlier observations that change functioned similarly, to enact the shift from the old to the new, using restorationism as a standard (since the word also denoted archaism). At another level, Miki argued that change led to friction with the idea of progress, since that came from the future. Absent from the core of the archaic stratum's historical image were both the future and the past, which had definitively passed. As a result, the archaic stratum was nothing more than the time of the present, mirroring Japan's aptitude for esteeming the present. Maruyama saw *kosō* as capable of producing change yet at the same time setting up constraints to change—which seemed to illustrate for him the pattern of alternating between opening and closing in Japan's long history. He claimed that this idea of the archaic stratum derived from an early work by Henri Bergson on society, but it also resembled views circulating during the Cold War that pitted open democratic societies against closed authoritarian ones. In his consideration of the archaic stratum's patterning, Maruyama wanted to show that the repetitive moments of opening and closing in Japanese history reflected a historical optimism, as evidenced in the *Kojiki*'s inaugural use of such terms as *tsugitsugi nariyuku ikioi* (one after another the course of events change). As *kosō*, it had a linear trajectory of "creative increase," not of progress: it was neither an eventually achieved objective or a consciously purposeful movement of individuals. If evolution was seen as unlimited adaptation, the "mysterious" matching of affinities appeared. According to Maruyama, "the making of the core of the historical image in the archaic stratum came neither from the past nor future but from the now."[18] This meant that Japan's historical optimism was a result of favoring the now of the present. Since the past is created by the act of retrospectively looking backward at unlimited traces, it is concretely situated in the now, not in the then, and it is idealized because of the process of becoming and birth. The past is thus contemporized anew (or made present). The present has no completed past, and the future is nothing more than the act of starting out from now fully supplied with vitality from the past. Maruyama seemed certain that if the utopia of the future failed to impart meaning and an objective to history, the distant past has no reason to become a standard for history. He was referring to the archaic aptitude for creating good and bad times, change, and stasis.

Maruyama argued that while Motoori had conceived of the present of now time, the now was actually space that moves itself, linked to the "eternal character of the future": it showed the Japanized "eternal now" (*eian no ima*), or the sense of the permanence of the now (*ima no eian*).[19] He added that the idea of an eternal now had become the viewpoint of Japanism that sanctioned action. For Maruyama, the character of what he considered the moderate reforms of the Meiji Restoration that brought about, over time, a larger revolution was inherent in the logic that privileged the time of the now. Even though the restoration called for the restitution of a nonexistent past in the present, it came from the present rather than the past or future. The restoration merely reflected the identity of the now with the putative archaic. It is interesting to note how closely Maruyama's valorization of the now follows Tosaka's meditations on historical time and the now of the present, even though Maruyama's text never cites Tosaka. For Maruyama, the archaic was none other than the present time, a view that provided him with a way of distancing its association from the historical effect of the past's domination of the present, thus affirming the promise of the present's dominance of the past. Reforms initiated by the Meiji Restoration followed the model of the Enlightenment's conception of the now, which the restoration coupled with the idea of having the deities take credit for the deeds, presenting the pattern of the archaic stratum. But when activists in the late years of the Tokugawa era had seized the jewel (the emperor), they had also seized the deeds of the gods. More importantly, the act preceded the adoption of the Enlightenment model. Maruyama never freed himself from the aura of the archaic claims of uniqueness. Instead, he substituted a unique present for a unique origin and declared his desire for a new beginning, as noted above, that sought to retrieve the liberalism that had led to fascism and war through a logic that managed to validate the déjà vu of postwar Japan.

Unlike Maruyama, Kobayashi sought to redeem the archaic. If Maruyama's logic aimed to free the archaic of its negative association with Japanese fascism for a new present, Kobayashi aspired to purify the archaic of its archaist deformation (that is, historical contamination), avoiding the wrong turns offered by history and returning to the archaic's true course, as originally figured in the ancient chronicles. But in following an earlier rejection of history that he had never abandoned,[20] he risked restoring those components of the archaic that had led so easily to its prior distortion. In this regard, he remained focused on the archaic and its sense of elegance (*furi*)—what might be described as the "ancient manner" to make possible a new present, which will appear to be concretized in the ages after antiquity, becoming not successive imitations but rather the product of individuals who had mastered its essence.[21] The reason for this certainty could be found in the vigor and style of ancient words that were never flimsily placed in the textual body of the *Kojiki*.[22] Following Motoori's exegesis, Kobayashi was convinced that the ancients had been able to differentiate between true and meaningful words, which were substantial, and meaningless words, which were not: the former were probably seen as more concrete and felt by the "heart/mind" (*kokoro*) as reflecting the real, while the latter mirrored the corruption of language and the distortion of the real, which Kobayashi undoubtedly saw as abstraction or an exhausted echo of an earlier debate. The contamination of language also referred to the entry of Chinese into Japanese and even the domination of Chinese, through the Japanese adoption of Chinese ideographs, and (in Kobayashi's postwar present) to the flood of Americanisms and the Japanese eagerness to Japanize their sounds to make them appear Japanese. Here, Kobayashi disclosed the point of his discourse on Motoori, as well as the importance of language (in this case, Japanese) and the enduring relevance of the archaic for all ages (especially his present), and the imperative of realizing what he called a "language commune" (*gengo kyōdōtai*).[23]

For Kobayashi, the archaic was the time of origin and the age of the gods, who eventually came down to earth to bestow on the Japanese people the heavenly gift of language. He was particularly concerned with the long tradition of theories about the beginning and development of Japanese literature. There was a consensus that the original source of that literature was ancient religious prayers (*norito*) that accompanied written imperial proclamations. This view was derived from a conjecture made by Orikuchi from Motoori's *Kojikiden*, which Kobayashi rejected as "unskillful" because it held that the interpretation was decided only after the appearance of writing.[24] Kobayashi also recognized that Orikuchi and other interpreters had not shown any belief in the figure of the spirit of language or the material design (*aya*) of words—that is, the use of Chinese ideographs, which were shaped to resemble the object to which they referred. In his reading of how surviving ideographs (*ji*) were buried in new years' writings in the Chinese manner to provide the key with which to enter the world of archaic words,[25] Kobayashi was apparently pointing to the most archaic or earliest extant ideographs, whose approximation of the objects they represented as words appeared closer to the real thing than was the case with later ideographs. Hence, the real source of Japanese literature must be found not in writing but in the earliest signs of the presence of the "spirit of language" even before there were written words (that is, before the adoption of ideographs seeking to represent the things they referred to). Instead, he proposed that the origin of language resided in vocal utterances that prefigured writing. As a result, Kobayashi was convinced that the source of literature lay in the ineffability of the "spirit of language" and its miraculous presence in expressions of recitation before the act of writing.

Accordingly, the strength of the "spirit of language" was exhibited in the formation of words necessitated by the occurrence of yearly ritualistic ceremonies that required fixing prayers (*norito*) to prevent them from being lost. The first spoken words related not only to events that people experienced but also to events lived and performed by the ancients. It was precisely because people could feel, see, and hear that separated the experience of ancient existence from later historical efforts to recover it in written words. The past that does not exist apart from spoken words is the reason why historians cannot manage to deal with the past.[26] Kobayashi proposed that where the "spirit of language" was zealously defined as coming from mouth to mouth, life in villages would be centered on politics. Poetry and prose, he noted, were never separated from religious ceremonies and observances. He acknowledged that while this order of life was timeless, its existence could not be dated. For the folk of antiquity, this practice probably began with the formation of social life, when the gods came down to earth to bestow heavenly words on people who honored the deities. These may have been prayers, while the words for honoring the gods were imperial proclamations—a fact that conflated religious ceremony and governance. In this context, Kobayashi suggested that the people of antiquity had no sense of or use for history, because the yearly recitations were repeated and there was no separation in terms of conduct between religious and governmental ceremonies.

In his discussion of the "spirit of language," Kobayashi also included Motoori's observation that the presence of that spirit appeared in the creation of the postposition particles *te, ni, o, wa,* and so on, which constituted the guiding determinations that made "connecting" possible. Motoori claimed that "it was the unusual and strange 'spirit of language'" that was the foundation of the Japanese language's uniqueness and that allows it to connect our lives to each other's lives and people to energy and work.[27] The central importance of the postposition particles for Motoori and, perhaps, Kobayashi was their capacity to determine the connectedness among people and between people and their surroundings. This sense of connection was the core of Kobayashi's notion of a community that he called the "communal language." Kobayashi described the postposition particles as "working" and "action" words that, through "force" (*iki(h)oi*) and "labor" (*hataraki*), resembled the "words" of the "thread of life" or "chain of beads" (*kotoba no tamanō*) and determined the "connections among us" formed by the "strange spirit of language."[28] With Motoori, the power of relating to things transmitted from the mouth of humans in ancient times who had not yet acquired the art of writing meant that the first words written down were words of proclamation, since they were needed for the inclusion of prayers before songs. Such proclamations honored the *kami* in public and could not be read or written in the Chinese style of *kanbun*, like the things of everyday life. Yet a long time passed between the first recitation of a proclamation and the first composition of a narrative.

For Motoori, the act of reading poetry and narratives (once they had appeared) meant only reading expressions of the national language: "Reading the *Kojiki* by way of imitating it as much as possible is an extremely natural fact."[29] This practice of reading through imitation had been proposed by Motoori, and it pointed to the inviolability attributed to sacred texts that should be read only in such a way as to foreclose any chance of interpretation, which could change what the text conveyed. The relevant texts were typical imperial proclamations and rescripts, whose readers were advised to imitate the text only as an exercise in literal recitation that required no interpretative intervention. In this account, there was no difference between the poems of the *Manyō* and the stories of the *Kojiki*. Here, Kobayashi turned to eliciting the flavor or taste of the things that had constituted the life of the ancients in an attempt to record and thus "assess the *fumi*, manner of ancient things" found in the ancient chronicles that were no longer available to sight and hearing. He was particularly concerned with becoming able to capture the form of a life that had passed and to penetrate its world of things that had colonized the everyday of remote antiquity. His technique was to appeal to the *fumi* and *furi*,[30] a nuanced range of the sense of taste, of the *uta* (songs) said to have been bestowed by the deities, two signifiers capable of simultaneously emitting different meanings—such as the divine manner, sensations, elegance, countenance, flavor, touch, and feeling—through an imaginative empathic entry into the material existence of these distant lives. Access to the true world of "ancient conditions" (that is, "ancient facts") need not rely on the imitations of the Enlightenment since it can be found in the *Kojiki* through grasping the *furi* of "ancient words" (that is, the sensation of meaning).[31] If it is not possible to approach them directly, Kobayashi believed that they could be approached indirectly through experiencing their sensation, as if one was seeing and hearing: "like holding antiquity in [one's hand]." Kobayashi was proposing the use of a modern interpretative hermeneutic to enter the interiority of time and lives out of reach—a process that almost looked as if he was offering a momentary reliving or reenactment of ancient life. Yet the purpose of this hermeneutic was to make such understanding available as a guide in the present. His notion of the archaic sensibility guiding daily life and its capacity to inhabit the present came close to Maruyama's identification of the archaic with the now. But after Kobayashi noted that it was important to know how to close the distance between the observer and this remote time, he warned that the past could not be approached from an external perspective, even though the songs had opened a way to enter the intentions and gestures of ancient things.[32] While he remained silent on who could make this journey to the archaic in the real present of the now, I suspect that he included neonativist ethnologists like Yanagita Kunio and Orikuchi, who also had a low opinion of history—which they replaced with the acts of seeing and listening to the folk until they began to really think about the folk's lives—which the folk would gradually reveal although they would not necessarily relate their thoughts to an outsider. Hermeneutics is invariably constrained by its assumption that the observer and the observed must share some cultural experience or horizon, despite the temporal distance separating them. According to Kobayashi, one must know the body that has lived and the diversity of human experience within one's self. Knowing the body means that it has been "touched by words," because Japan has been the first country with the "spirit of language." In the end, this gift from the gods, that is, the spirit of language, enabled Kobayashi to embrace the idea that identified Japanese as a "communal language" that the ancients had created.[33] For him, true words touched people deeply and produced personal expressions that registered on the face and could be read by like-minded other members of the language community.

In a sense, Kobayashi was persuaded that the ancients saw words as agents of action and believed that "ancient words" (*furukoto*) and "ancient facts" or "things" (*furugoto*) were virtually interchangeable. The belief in a "communal language" is rooted in trust in reason, which is a sign of meaning embodied in the material design of words. If there is no link to the "ligament" of language, there will be no "communal life."[34] Kobayashi was persuaded that entering an established language order was like entering a natural environment, an enclosed landscape of words and syntagma connecting the folk into a community. But this order was not something imparted by somebody, as if that person had made it by hand. I would suppose that environment, in this instance, refers to something that is directly connected to the Japanese heart/mind. In fact, he believed that this language environment was like the body. Because language and its spirit are possessions of Japan, they are common property, a shared wealth called language that is supplied to communal life. But this kind of ownership is not like gathering personal or private property, something paid to us in the form of language. It is interesting that Kobayashi made language a common currency, making speakers of a communal language into a collective, while the fact that the language is owned by all in common is a guarantee of the collective's permanence—which is a strangely material form of communalism. Kobayashi kept returning to the connection between a collective ownership and the spirit of language of the ancients, which ensured the production of the communal language that is closest to the body and constitutes an environment and elegance from which one is never separated. In seeing that the movement of the "spirit of language" followed the ancients, who sang about their feelings, Kobayashi argued that they deeply believed in the country that had been given that spirit, a country that has enhanced and fixed the myriad words of the poets.[35] Kobayashi emphasized the reciprocity in the language and the lineage (*uji*). The flavor of the ancient words was reflected in the ancient intention, which remained fastened to elegance and has reappeared repeatedly since antiquity. His return to the archaic was a celebration of a hermetic and closed world that he believed was still available to contemporary Japan since it was ageless.

Kobayashi's return to the archaic resembled the earlier effort to implant the past in the present, but without the stridency of a toxic ideology devoted to mobilizing people into readiness for war and destruction. Even so, Kobayashi's critique was a replay of the nativist discourse (*kokugakuron*) of the late Tokugawa period, which had been directed at freeing Japanese culture and sensibility from the domination of Chinese thought and language. And by extension it seems that the critique might have reflected Japanese experiencing the second round of a dominant Americanism in the postwar period, the first being in the cultural infusion of the 1920s, or perhaps all foreign influence, a virtually driven imperative to turn history back into nature. In this respect, it was both antiforeign and antihistorical. While it is not clear who and what Kobayashi was targeting, it could have reflected the influx of Americanisms flooding into the language and the spread of American popular culture. What Maruyama and Kobayashi shared was an unquestioning acceptance of a timeless recursive logic, which suggests that it made less difference to Maruyama if it was a historical consciousness that remained unchanged throughout Japan's history or for Kobayashi a way to express his indifference to the actual historicity of the ancient texts for what they were able to yield of the beginnings of Japanese literature. Maruyama's conceptualization of *kosō* contains an echo of Miki's formlessness, whereby the oscillations of entry and withdrawal cancel out fixity. In contrast, Kobayashi reanimated the logic of philology (which Tosaka's relentless critique sought to undermine) in his view that language began before writing, in the godly gift of the spirit of words.

Where Maruyama and Kobayashi agreed was in their disregard for history, time, and change, although Maruyama's path tilted toward a finally completed present ironically resonated with the Marxian critique of the feudal remnant and capitalism's incomplete development, and Kobayashi valorized the ancient countenance presented in the action of words. In the end, they shared a quest for a new beginning that had been seen before, time and again. And they both seemed to evoke the unchanging figure of remote antiquity in a society in which the noncontemporary still prevails over the contemporaneous and is always poised to reshape the present rather than be shaped by it.

NOTES

Preface

1 Benjamin, *Origin of German Trauerspiel*, 194.
2 Not all the thinkers who contributed to this discourse used the conceptualization of "real abstraction," but most were concerned with the mystifying relationship of capitalist abstraction and ideology. The idea of real abstraction was worked out by Alfred Sohn-Rethel in *Intellectual and Manual Labour*. It was, among other things, a critique of the artificial division between mental and manual labor, which Marx and Friedrich Engels had already raised in *The German Ideology*.
3 Marx, *Grundrisse*.
4 Roberts, *Philosophizing the Everyday*, 16 and 21–23.
5 See Walker, *Marx et la politique du dehors*, 23–55, 145–75, and 369–93.
6 See Tombazos, *Time in Marx*, 5–6.
7 Tomba, *Insurgent Universality*, Historical Materialism, chap. 1.
8 Benjamin, *Arcades Project*, 470. For a fuller explanation of this historical practice, see also N7a,1 on the same page.
9 Benjamin, *Arcades Project*, 857.
10 Benjamin, *Arcades Project*, 462.
11 Benjamin, *Arcades Project*, 463.
12 Benjamin, *Arcades Project*, 846.
13 Ross, *L'imaginaire de la commune*, 1–18.
14 Marx, *Capital*, 1:91.
15 Adorno, *History and Freedom*, 253.
16 See Max Horkheimer's view in Benjamin, *Arcades Project*, 471.
17 Benjamin, *Origin of German Trauerspiel*, 24–25.
18 Benjamin, *Origin of German Trauerspiel*, 24–25.

Chapter 1. In the Zone of Occult Instability

1   Allinson and Anievas, "Uneven and Combined Development."
2   See also Osborne, *Politics of Time*, ix–x and 1–29.
3   This is the principal theme of Antonio Gramsci's essay *The Southern Question*.
4   Marx, *18th Brumaire of Louis Bonaparte*, 15 and 17.
5   Thomas, *Gramscian Moment*, 136.
6   Thomas, *Gramscian Moment*, 147; see also Gramsci, *Prison Notebooks*, 2:232.
7   For an exemplary account of the morphing of Chinese nationalism into nativism and fascism, see Clinton, *Revolutionary Nativism*. Clinton's book was one of the first to show that fascism was not limited to European claims of exceptionalism but was capable of taking root wherever capitalism established its production agenda. Alberto Toscano's forthcoming book *Late Fascism* makes the case for studying fascism in the context of the broader world and conjunctures that nourished it. See also Finchelstein, *A Brief History of Fascist Lies*, which importantly focuses on the fascisms of the Global South, including Mexico and other Latin American countries.
8   Traverso, *New Faces of Fascism*. This work is in keeping with the grand tradition of historiography of fascism by making it appear as an exclusive endowment of Europe and mentioning the rest of the world only to register the panic waves of otherness signified by Islamophobia. The idea of "post-fascism" seeks to have it both ways: it refers to something that is after fascism yet still resembles it, while making sure to convey that it is not the same as the historical antecedents of fascism. Thus, it is fascist but not fascism.
9   Thomas, *Gramscian Moment*, 147 and 155–57.
10 Thomas, *Gramscian Moment*, 200.
11 Gramsci, *Prison Notebooks*, 3:378. See also Gramsci, *Further Selections from the Prison Notebooks*, 349–50.
12 See Tansman, *Aesthetics of Japanese Fascism*, 14; Miki, *Essensu*, 269–86.
13 Adorno, *Minima Moralia*, 151. Adorno proposed that theory must engage "cross-grained" and "unassimilated material," "blind spots," things that had been forgotten and had fallen by the wayside, and "admittedly anachronistic" items to go beyond the rectilinear historical dynamic and provide "flashes" of "undreamed" historical experience (151).
14 Osborne, *Politics of Time*, x.
15 Osborne, *Politics of Time*, 5.
16 Osborne, *Politics of Time*, 16.
17 Osborne, *Politics of Time*, 17.
18 Fanon, *Wretched of the Earth*.
19 Du Bois, *Souls of Black Folk*, 2.

20   Fanon, *Wretched of the Earth*, 159.

21   Benjamin, *Arcades Project*, 842–43.

22   Jameson, *Geopolitical Aesthetic*, 155.

23   Sartre, *Search for a Method*, 91n9.

24   Trotsky, *History of the Russian Revolution*, 7. Trotsky's theorization in this
regard went further to figure a global chronotope of capitalism, with
combinations of space and time that would, he believed, shape world
history. The concept of the chronotope is from Bakhtin, *Dialogic Imagination*, 84–258. In the chronotope defining a specific space-time relationship mediated by a particular historical conjuncture, time is spatialized
and "thickened," while space is temporalized by being subjected to the
rhythms of capital's movements.

25   The letters exchanged by Marx and Zasulich and his unsent letters to her
are in Shanin, *Late Marx and the Russian Road*.

26   Bloch, *Philosophy of the Future*, 140–43.

27   Bloch, *Heritage of Our Times*, 62 (emphasis in original).

28   Bloch, *Heritage of Our Times*, 62.

29   Geoghegan, *Ernst Bloch*, 109.

30   Ross, *L'imaginaire de la commune*, 1–18.

31   Marx, *Capital*, 1:91.

32   Bolz and Van Reijen, *Walter Benjamin*, 48.

33   Benjamin, *Arcades Project*, 388.

34   The above quotes are from Benjamin, *Arcades Project*, 403–5.

35   Benjamin, *Arcades Project*, 857.

36   Benjamin, *Arcades Project*, 389.

37   Lukács, *History and Class Consciousness*, 158.

38   Benjamin, *Arcades Project*, 403, 404.

39   Bolz and Van Reijen, *Walter Benjamin*, 46.

40   Benjamin, *Arcades Project*, 392–93 and 460.

41   Benjamin, *Arcades Project*, 462.

42   Benjamin, *Arcades Project*, 470.

43   Tosaka, *Zenshū*, 4:136–40.

44   Benjamin, *Arcades Project*, 475.

45   Benjamin, *Arcades Project*, 435.

46   See Thomas, *Gramscian Moment*, 131.

47   Benjamin, *Arcades Project*, 471.

48   Benjamin, *Arcades Project*, 473.

49   Benjamin, *Arcades Project*, 883.

50   Benjamin, *Arcades Project*, 884.

51   Benjamin, *Arcades Project*, 476.

52   Benjamin, *Arcades Project*, 942.

53   Benjamin, *Arcades Project*, 436 and 942.

54   Marx, *Capital*, 1:103.

55   Benjamin, *Arcades Project*, 944 (emphasis in original).

56   Benjamin, *Arcades Project*, 470–71.

57   See Thomas, *Gramscian Moment*, 176.

58   The quote comes from Balibar and Wallerstein, *Race, Nation, Class*; emphasis in original. I am indebted to Steve Edwards's unpublished paper "Time's Carcase" for this observation and note 11.

59   Bloch, *Heritage of Our Times*, 110 and 109 (emphasis in original).

60   Murray, *Mismeasure of Wealth*, 16. It should be noted that the work of Moishe Postone, in his now classic *Time, Labour and Social Domination*, cleaves to the centrality of value theory and risks emptying Marx's work of all history—and despite Murray's disposition toward value, Postone still manages to leave space for both the social and history.

61   Marx, *Capital*, 1:91. "We suffer not only from the living but from the dead. Le mort saisit le vif."

62   Morfino and Thomas, *Government of Time*, 18.

63   Tanaka, *New Times in Modern Japan*, and *History without Chronology*, 27.

64   Watsuji, "*Zoku Nippon seishinshi kenkyū*," 377–78.

65   Japan had withdrawn from the world in the early seventeenth century and remained in self-imposed isolation until the so-called opening of the country (an event called *kaikoku*) by Commodore Matthew Perry in 1853. The Tokugawa policy of isolation was called *sakoku* (closed country), and its afterlife implied a psychological mind-set that led to closed minds.

66   Rancière, "Concept of Anachronism," 34. See also Ramizi, "Anachronism and Its Histories."

67   Rancière, "Concept of Anachronism," 35.

68   Rancière, "Concept of Anachronism," 46–47.

69   Rancière, "Concept of Anachronism," 47.

70   Marx, *18th Brumaire of Louis Bonaparte*, 15–16.

Chapter 2. Restoration

1   Allinson and Anievas, "Uneven and Combined Development," esp. 474–85; Thomas, *Gramscian Moment*, 136.

2   Thomas, *Gramscian Moment*, 147; Gramsci, *Prison Notebooks*, 2:232.

3   Tōyama, *Meiji Ishin*, 19–20.

4   Tōyama, *Meiji Ishin*, 20.

5   Tōyama, *Meiji Ishin*, 20.

6   Tōyama, *Meiji Ishin*, 21.

7   Tōyama, *Meiji Ishin*, 20.

8   I thank Gavin Walker for alerting me to this function.

9   Rancière, "Concept of Anachronism," 21.

10   Gramsci, *Selections from the Prison Notebooks*, 59; see also *Prison Notebooks*, 3:257.

11   Thomas, *Gramscian Moment*, 145–57; esp. 154.

12   Gramsci, *Prison Notebooks*, 3:252.

13   Davidson, *How Revolutionary Were the Bourgeois Revolutions?*, 316.

14   Gramsci, *Prison Notebooks*, 2:207.

15   Davidson, *How Revolutionary Were the Bourgeois Revolutions?*, 317; Gramsci, *Prison Notebooks*, 3:232.

16   Gramsci, *Further Selections from the Prison Notebooks*, 277; see also 374–75.

17   See Waite, *Nietzsche's Corpse*, 83; Karatani, *History and Repetition*, 1–25.

18   Tierney, *Tropics of Savagery*, 82.

19   Tierney, *Tropics of Savagery*, 82.

20   Tōyama, *Meiji Ishin*, 25–26.

21   Although the origin and development of an imperial authority predated the beginnings of feudalism in the twelfth century, since that time—and especially during the nearly three hundred years of virtual imprisonment in the imperial palace in Kyoto under the Tokugawa shogunate—the emperor must be considered to be a survivor of feudalism and a feudal remnant.

22   Tōyama, *Meiji Ishin*, 51.

23   Davidson, *How Revolutionary Were the Bourgeois Revolutions?*, 318.

24   Davidson, *How Revolutionary Were the Bourgeois Revolutions?*, 319.

25   Quoted in Davidson, *How Revolutionary Were the Bourgeois Revolutions?*, 319.

26   Engels, "Einleitnung zu den Klassenkampfen in Franrkreich" [Introduction to class struggle in France], quoted in Lowy, *Politics of Combined and Uneven Development*, 28.

27   Lowy, *Politics of Combined and Uneven Development*, 29.

28   The concept of historical trope is from Jameson, *Marxism and Form*, 6–10.

29   See Najita, *Ordinary Economies in Japan*; Hirano, *Politics of Dialogic Imagination*; and Tsuneishi, "Rice and Coal." These studies underscore the development of new economic forces and social constituencies aligned with the participation of the populace.

30   Tōyama, *Meiji Ishin*, 162–63.

31   Engels, *Peasant War in Germany*, 56.

32   A good deal of the lecture faction's historical practice appears to have been driven by the need to use absolutism to explain the failure of the Meiji Restoration to reach a revolutionary stage, leading to the rise of fascism as its final outcome. But here, Marxists were constrained by their adherence to stage theory, which deformed their narratives and punctured expectations of its development to a stage of capitalism from which to inaugurate a revolution to pass into socialism. These expectations were derived from an abstracted historical process, comprised of stages of which a more mature capitalism, having eliminated feudal

remnants with the requisite conditions, would signal the right moment. It was a Marxian response to a time that seemed to offer the political prospect of realizing a revolutionary outcome. This explains the necessity for a stage theory driven by a transition from feudalism to capitalism as the model for another transition yet to come: that from capitalism to socialism. But it was found that historically revolutionary movements did not work according to this template.

33 Tōyama, *Meiji Ishin*, 162.

34 See Hirano, *Politics of Dialogic Imagination*, 69–103 and 144–235; Harootunian, *Uneven Moments*, 73–173.

35 I am referring to the Sanrizuka struggle in Chiba Prefecture over land designated by the state for a new airport in Narita, and the surfacing of its entrenched tradition of the nativism thinking of the Hirata school, and the farmers' persisting slogan that agriculture was the basis of Japan. See *Kaishi suru fukei*. See also Fukuda Yukie, *Sanrizuka andosoiru*. Both works show the importance of preserving the ancient village and are informed by the sense of an unconscious communal body (*kyōdotai*) that is ready to appear when aroused by a turbulent time that challenges its continuation.

36 Marx and Lenin, *Civil War in France*, 65.

37 Irokawa, *Culture of the Meiji Period*.

38 Tōyama, *Meiji Ishin*, 329; see also 37–39. I am also guilty of having followed this convention in Harootunian, *Toward Restoration*.

39 Tōyama, *Meiji Ishin*, 39.

40 Tōyama, *Meiji Ishin*, 210–11.

41 Tōyama, *Meiji Ishin*, 163.

42 Tōyama, *Meiji Ishin*, 164.

43 Fujita, "Seimeiron," 3:382. It should be noted that Takasu was a prominent participant in the formation and extension of the Japanist ideology of the 1930s.

44 Tōyama, *Meiji Ishin*, 225–26. See also Mitani, *Meiji Ishin o kangaeru*, 203–4. It is worth noting that the title of Mitani's book (in English, "Thinking the Meiji Restoration") resembles that of François Furet's 1978 *Penser la revolution Française*.

45 Mitani, *Meiji Ishin o kangaeru*, 205.

46 Mitani, *Meiji Ishin o kangaeru*, 204; K. Inoue, *Bakumatsu Ishin*, 155.

47 I. Inoue, *Ōsei fukko*, 334.

48 Tōyama, *Meiji Ishin*, 226. See also Mitani, *Meiji Ishin o kangaeru*, 203–4.

49 The paradox is that many of the theorists of restorationism who acted and even died for the idea (like Maki Izumi, Hirano Kuniomi, and Ōhashi Totsuan) were from lesser domains and had serious differences with those from major domains like Satsuma and Chōshū. Most of the former group never lived to see the Meiji Restoration.

50　Tōyama, *Meiji Ishin*, 166.

51　Tōyama, *Meiji Ishin*, 167; I. Inoue, *Ōsei fukko*, 166–95. See also K. Inoue, *Bakumatsu Ishin*, 152–54.

52　Mitani, *Meiji Ishin o kangaeru*, 204; Tōyama, *Meiji Ishin*, 231.

53　See Mitani, *Meiji Ishin o kangaeru*, 284, for a rational explanation that posits a natural kinship between the "feudal character" and "archaic character" but does not account for the historicity of the former or the mythic nature of the latter.

54　Yasumaru, *Kindai tennōzō no keisei*, 178–79.

55　Yasumaru, quoted in *Kindai tennōzō no keisei*, 178.

56　See Kan, *Tennōsei ronshū*, 1:13.

57　Quoted in K. Inoue, *Bakumatsu Ishin*, 155.

58　Saigō, quoted in K. Inoue, *Bakumatsu Ishin*, 155.

59　The above quotes and discussion come from K. Inoue, *Bakumatsu Ishin*, 155.

60　Yasumaru, *Kindai tennōzō no keisei*, 177; Kan, *Tennōsei ronshū*, 1:61–80.

61　Tōyama, *Meiji Ishin*, 164.

62　In Yasumaru, *Kindai tennōzō no keisei*, quoting Iwakura Tomomi, 176.

63　Suzuki, *Ishin kōsō to tenkai*, 3–4.

64　Yasumaru, *Kindai tennōzō no keisei*, 176.

65　I. Inoue, *Ōsei fukko*, 333. All of the above quotes are from the Proclamation.

66　Harootunian, *Things Seen and Unseen*, 391–92. For the role played by Miki and his restorationist texts, and how the figure of restoration was reduced to the syntax of action, see 379–89.

67　Harootunian, *Things Seen and Unseen*, 393. All the above quotes are from Iwakura's writings on the idea of restoration.

68　Foucault, *Order of Things*, 330.

69　Yasumaru, *Kindai tennōzō no keisei*, 17. It is also important to recall the postwar period's important discussion about the status of subjectivity, in which Japan's leading intellectuals implied that was absent in the general public in the prewar period, where they were subjects of the emperor but possessed no individual subjectivity. This suggests that since the Meiji period their population was fundamentally unpolitical, kept outside of acting in the political sphere.

70　Virino, *Déjà Vu and the End of Theory*, 48.

71　Virino, *Déjà Vu and the End of Theory*, 26–50.

72　Virino, *Déjà Vu and the End of Theory*, 52.

73　Virino, *Déjà Vu and the End of Theory*, 53.

74　Skya, *Japan's Holy War*, 110–28.

75　Virino, *Déjà Vu and the End of Theory*, 161.

76　Marx, *Grundrisse*, 472.

77　Gentile, *Struggle for Modernity*, 60.

78   Polanyi, "Essence of Fascism," 360, quoted in Gentile, *Politics as Religion*, 37.

79   DeBord, *Society of the Spectacle*, 110.

80   Virino, *Déjà Vu and the End of Theory*, 175.

81   Eliade, *Myth of the Eternal Return*. In this book Eliade condemned what he called "the terror of history."

82   Virino, *Déjà Vu and the End of Theory*, 177.

83   Virino, *Déjà Vu and the End of Theory*, 179.

84   Tanaka, *History without Chronology*.

85   Benjamin, "Concept of History," 4:395.

86   Benjamin, "Concept of History," 4:391.

87   Virino, *Déjà Vu and the End of Theory*, 189.

88   Kan, *Tennōsei ronshū*, 1:4 and 1:16–18.

89   Bloch, *Heritage of Our Times*, 101.

90   See especially Fujitani, *Splendid Monarchy*.

91   Bloch, *Heritage of Our Times*, 107.

92   Bloch, *Heritage of Our Times*, 108 (emphasis in original).

93   Bloch, *Heritage of Our Times*, 109.

94   Adorno, *Critical Models*, 339.

95   Adorno, *Critical Models*, 339.

96   My thanks to Carol Gluck for this observation.

Chapter 3. Capitalism & Fascism

1   Kiyohara, *Kokutai ronshi*.

2   Tosaka, *Zenshū*, 5:86–87. See also Tansman, *Aesthetics of Japanese Fascism*, 14.

3   Hasegawa, *Hasegawa Nyozekan senshū* (hereafter HNss), 2:292. I have also consulted a biography of Hasegawa (Barshay, *State and Intellectual in Imperial Japan*).

4   Maruyama, *Maruyama Masao shu*, 10:3.

5   See Jameson, *Geopolitical Aesthetic*, 3, 9–84 (esp., 10, 25, and 49).

6   The quotes are from Toscano, *Late Fascism*, 81–82, forthcoming.

7   Toscano, *Late Fascism*, 82, forthcoming.

8   As I show below, Tosaka's materialist critique of the idealist Japanist ideology echoed Vladimir Lenin's classic philosophic work of 1908 (*Materialism and Empirico-Criticism*), even though their contemporary targets differed.

9   For this discussion of representation and allegorization, I have relied on Jameson, *Allegory and Ideology*, 1–48.

10   Jameson, *Allegory and Ideology*, 44.

11   Seki, in Kawamura Nozomu, *Bunka shakaigaku gairon*, 2:216–17.

12 Seki, in Kawamura Nozomu, *Bunka shakaigaku gairon*, 2:218.

13 Seki, in Kawamura Nozomu, *Bunka shakaigaku gairon*, 2:233–35.

14 Guterman and Lefebvre, *La conscience mystifiee*, 173, quoted in Toscano, *Late Fascism*, 88.

15 Guterman and Lebfevre, *La conscience mystifiee*, 140, quoted in Toscano, *Late Fascism*, 88.

16 Toscano, *Late Fascism*, 88.

17 Toscano, *Late Fascism*, 91.

18 *HNSS*, 2:366.

19 *HNSS*, 2:279.

20 *HNSS*, 2:292. See also Barshay, *State and Intellectual in Imperial Japan*, especially the discussion of the two phases of fascism in Hasegawa's analysis of fascism (193–202).

21 Barshay, *State and Intellectual in Imperial Japan*, 163–86.

22 *HNSS*, 2:292.

23 *HNSS*, 2:290 (both quotes); see also 324–34.

24 *HNSS*, 2:290.

25 *HNSS*, 2:291.

26 *HNSS*, 2:291.

27 *HNSS*, 2:293.

28 *HNSS*, 2:294.

29 *HNSS*, 2:294.

30 *HNSS*, 2:294. See also Barshay, *State and Intellectual in Imperial Japan*, 191–201.

31 *HNSS*, 2:366.

32 Tosaka later extended this argument to claim that contemporary Japan had already reverted to this primitive state of feudalism. See chapter 4 for the argument.

33 *HNSS*, 2:368.

34 *HNSS*, 2:369.

35 *HNSS*, 2:373.

36 *HNSS*, 2:374.

37 Matsumura, *Waiting for the Cool Moon*, chap. 7.

38 *HNSS*, 2:376.

39 Althusser, *On the Reproduction of Capitalism*, 183.

40 Hasegawa is quoting from Houston Stewart Chamberlain who was an English-German political philosopher who was described as a "racialist" and whose theories have been charged with "influencing" Nazism.

41 *HNSS*, 2:366. This quote is from Hasegawa of the Chamberlain passage.

42 *HNSS*, 2:366.

43 *HNSS*, 2:367.

44 *HNSS*, 2:376.

45 Pincus, *Authenticating Culture in Imperial Japan*, 242. I am indebted to Pincus for her brilliant account of fascism and art and how culture shaped politics.

46 Pincus, *Authenticating Culture in Imperial Japan*, 242.

47 Pincus, *Authenticating Culture in Imperial Japan*, 242. See also HNss, 2:401–2.

48 *HNss*, 2:401.

49 Quoted in Pincus, *Authenticating Culture in Imperial Japan*, 242.

50 Ward, *Thought Crime*, 103–4. Seki quote from Kawamura Nozomu, *Bunka shakaigaku gairon*, 2:239. See also Hoffman, *Fascist Effect*, 38–88.

51 Seki, in Kawamura Nozomu, *Bunka shakaigaku gairon*, 2:239. See also Hoffmann, *Fascist Effect*, 38–88.

52 I am referring to Kita, *Nihon kaizō hoa taikō*. An English translation of this text appears in Tanka, *Kita Ikki*.

53 Riley, *Civic Foundations of Fascism in Europe*, xv–xxxii.

54 Bloch, *Heritage of Our Times*, 97.

55 For more on the circulation and spread of capitalist commodity culture in the interwar period, see Silverberg, *Erotic Grotesque Nonsense*.

56 Bloch, *Heritage of Our Time*, 49–50.

57 *HNss*, 2:376.

58 *HNss*, 2:377.

59 See Skya, *Japan's Holy War*, 185–225.

60 *HNss*, 2:377–78.

61 *HNss*, 2:378.

62 *Taibyō* could also refer to the imperial mausoleum.

63 *HNss*, 2:379.

64 See Hoffman, *Fascist Effect*, 69 and 86; Tsukui, *Nihonteki shakaishugi no teishō*, 94–112.

65 Seki, quoted in Kawamura Nozomu, *Bunka shakaigaku gairon*, 2:241.

66 Seki, quoted in Kawamura Nozomu, *Bunka shakaigaku gairon*, 2:241.

67 Seki, quoted in Kawamura Nozomu, *Bunka shakaigaku gairon*, 2:238–39.

68 Tsukui, *Nihonteki shakaishugi no teishō*, 5.

69 Barshay, *State and Intellectual in Imperial Japan*, 202.

70 Barshay, *State and Intellectual in Imperial Japan*, 202.

71 See Pincus, *Authenticating Culture in Imperial Japan*, 243–44.

72 *HNss*, 2:396.

73 *HNss*, 2:389.

74 *HNss*, 2:390.

75 *HNss*, 2:393.

76 *HNss*, 2:396.

77 *HNss*, 2:407.

78 *HNss*, 2:407 and 401.

79   *HNss*, 2:402 (emphasis in original).
80   *HNss*, 2:406.
81   *HNss*, 2:406–7.
82   *HNss*, 2:406–7.
83   *HNss*, 2:407–8.
84   Maruyama, *Thought and Behavior*, 25–83.

Chapter 4. Actuality & the Archaic Mode of Cognition

1   Yoshida, *Tosaka Jun no tetsugaku*, 61–62.
2   Arakawa, *Miki Kiyoshi*, 168–69.
3   Tansman, *Aesthetics of Japanese Fascism*, 84.
4   Miki, *Essensu*, 232.
5   Tosaka, *Zenshū* (hereafter *TJz*), 5:40.
6   Miki, *Essensu*, 232.
7   Miki, *Essensu*, 234.
8   For a detailed account of Hattori's complex critique (which principally
      focused on his conception of the "basic experience of workers," which he
      considered to be an extension of his bourgeois philosophical anthropol-
      ogy, and which led him to condemn "Miki's philosophy as substantially
      anti-Marxist"), see Iwasaki Chikatsugu, *Nihon Marukusushugi tetsugakushi
      josetsu*, 124–42.
9   Miki, *Essensu*, 237.
10   Kan, *Tennōsei ronshū*, 1:276.
11   Miki, *Essensu*, 320.
12   Miki, *Essensu*, 240.
13   Miki, *Essensu*, 240–42.
14   Miki, *Essensu*, 242.
15   Miki, *Essensu*, 244.
16   Miki, *Essensu*, 243. See also Harootunian, *Things Seen and Unseen*,
      142, 148, and 150.
17   Miki, *Essensu*, 238.
18   Miki, *Essensu*, 239.
19   Miki, *Essensu*, 240.
20   Miki, *Essensu*, 243.
21   See Miki, *Essensu*, 336.
22   Miki, *Essensu*, 248.
23   Miki, *Essensu*, 249.
24   Miki, *Essensu*, 251.
25   Miki, *Essensu*, 251.
26   Miki, *Essensu*, 249.

27   Miki, *Essensu*, 243–44.

28   For an analysis of the language of this mystical text, see Tansman, *Aesthetics of Japanese Fascism*, 153.

29   Tansman, *Aesthetics of Japanese Fascism*, 156.

30   Arakawa, *Miki Kiyoshi*, 149, still embodied older relationships and modes of thinking and conduct.

31   Hayden White borrowed the term of the English philosopher Michael Oakeshott and explored its utility for historical practice. See White, *The Practical Past*, 3–24.

32   Miki, *Essensu*, 210.

33   Miki, *Essensu*, 212.

34   Miki, *Essensu*, 211.

35   Miki, *Essensu*, 218.

36   Miki, *Essensu*, 215; see also 218.

37   Miki, *Essensu*, 229; see also 230.

38   "Seikatsu bunka ni suite," 416–35.

39   Miki, *Zenshū* (hereafter MKZ), 3:384.

40   *MKZ*, 3:385.

41   *MKZ*, 14:357.

42   *MKZ*, 14:308.

43   *MKZ*, 14:310.

44   *MKZ*, 14:388–89.

45   *MKZ*, 14:270.

46   *MKZ*, 14:366.

47   *MKZ*, 14:338.

48   Miki, *Essensu*, 240–41.

49   Miki, *Essensu*, 240.

50   Miki, *Essensu*, 272.

51   Miki, *Essensu*, 253.

52   Sohn-Rethel, *Intellectual and Manual Labour*, 20.

53   Sohn-Rethel, *Intellectual and Manual Labour*, 7. The term "social synthesis" was used by Sohn-Rethel to describe the commodity exchange system.

54   Tosaka, *Nihon Ideorogiron*, 117. I used the Iwanami edition of this work (which is a magnified version) since I found the size of the printed ideographs in *TJZ* too small to read. A translation of this work by Robert Stolz is forthcoming.

55   Tosaka, *Nihon Ideorogiron*, 119.

56   Tosaka, *Nihon Ideorogiron*, 119.

57   It should be noted that in the mid-1930s Tosaka had the idea of creating an encyclopedia of scientific knowledge for ordinary people, a project worthy of the Enlightenment.

58   Tosaka, *Nihon ideorogiron*, 233.

59   Tosaka, *Nihon Ideorogiron*, 233.

60　*TJZ*, 5:42.

61　Sir George Sansom's *A Short Cultural History of Japan* was modeled after this popular book.

62　For Robert Stolz's fine translation of sections 1 and 4 of this important work, see "On Space (Introduction and Conclusion)," in Kawashima, Schäfer, and Stolz, *Tosaka Jun*, 17–35.

63　*TJZ*, 3:102.

64　*TJZ*, 3:102.

65　*TJZ*, 3:101; see also 102.

66　*TJZ*, 4:271.

67　*TJZ*, 3:102.

68　*TJZ*, 3:101. For Stolz's translation, see "The Principle of Everydayness and Historical Time," in Kawashima, Schäfer, and Stolz, *Tosaka Jun*, 12.

69　*TJZ*, 3:101. For Stolz's translation, see "The Principle of Everydayness and Historical Time," 12.

70　Sohn-Rethel, *Intellectual and Manual Labour*, 6–7.

71　*TJZ*, 3:71.

72　*TJZ*, 3:98. For Stolz's translation, see "The Principle of Everydayness and Historical Time," 8.

73　*TJZ*, 3:98; my emphasis. For Stolz's translation, see "The Principle of Everydayness and Historical Time," 8.

74　*TJZ*, 3:99.

75　*TJZ*, 3:99.

76　*TJZ*, 3:98; see also 99.

77　See *TJZ*, 3:102. It should be pointed out that Tosaka's view of the interaction between class and culture, in this instance, was less developed than Hasegawa Nyozekan's grasp of the relationship. It should be recalled that Hasegawa identified petit bourgeois tastes with a popular culture of romantic escapism and worried about its effects.

78　*TJZ*, 3:101.

79　Stolz, "Here, Now," 134–40.

80　*TJZ*, 3:101.

81　*TJZ*, 3:101.

82　Hani, *Hani Gorò rekishi ronsha sakushuū*, 1:45.

83　*TJZ*, 3:262. For Stolz's translation, see "On Space," 26–35.

84　Stolz, "Here, Now," 143.

85　Stolz, "Here, Now," 144.

86　Tosaka, *Nihon Ideorogiron*, 25.

87　Tosaka, *Nihon Ideorogiron*, 216.

88　Tosaka, *Nihon Ideorogiron*, 219.

89　Tosaka, *Nihon Ideorogiron*, 24.

90　Tosaka, *Nihon Ideorogiron*, 26.

91　Tosaka, *Nihon Ideorogiron*, 36–37.

92   Volosinov, *Marxism and the Philosophy of Language*, 71.

93   Volosinov, *Marxism and the Philosophy of Language*, 72.

94   Hirano Katsuya, "Dialectic of Laughter," 186.

95   Tosaka, *Nihon Ideorogiron*, 37–38.

96   Tosaka, *Nihon Ideorogiron*, 43.

97   Tosaka, *Nihon Ideorogiron*, 42.

98   Tosaka, *Nihon Ideorogiron*, 50–51.

99   Tosaka, *Nihon Ideorogiron*, 48.

100 Tosaka, *Nihon Ideorogiron*, 52.

101 Tosaka, *Nihon Ideorogiron*, 54.

102 Tosaka, *Nihon Ideorogiron*, 55–56.

103 Tosaka, *Nihon Ideorogiron*, 57–58.

104 Tosaka, *Nihon Ideorogiron*, 59.

105 Tosaka, *Nihon Ideorogiron*, 60. It should be noted that his criticism of phi-
     lology did not go as far as a recommendation to throw the baby out with
     the bathwater. Which meant that he still saw some value in the discipline
     of philology after his scorching criticism.

106 Tosaka, *Nihon Ideorogiron*, 224–25.

107 *TJZ*, 5:66–67.

108 Tosaka, *Nihon Ideorogiron*, 226.

109 *TJZ*, 5:66–67.

110 Tosaka, *Nihon Ideorogiron*, 36.

111 *TJZ*, 5:66–67.

112 Tosaka, *Nihon Ideorogiron*, 226.

113 For more on the relationship of Tosaka's critique and the media, see
     Schafer, *Tosaka Jun*, 115–81; *TJZ*, 3:105–66 and 5:126–82.

114 Tosaka, *Nihon Ideorogiron*, 91.

115 Tosaka, *Nihon Ideorogiron*, 129.

116 Tosaka, *Nihon Ideorogiron*, 159.

117 Tosaka, *Nihon Ideorogiron*, 132 and 133.

118 Tosaka, *Nihon Ideorogiron*, 134.

119 Tosaka, *Nihon Ideorogiron*, 134. *Nippon* derived from Chinese pronuncia-
     tion used early (third century and after) and was associated with wartime
     nationalism; *Nihon* was less politically and emotionally charged, and the
     Japanese pronunciation of Chinese characters.

120 Tosaka, *Nihon Ideorogiron*, 136–37.

121 Tosaka, *Nihon Ideorogiron*, 197. See also *TJZ*, 2:322.

122 *TJZ*, 4:271.

123 Quoted in Person, *Arbiters of Patriotism*, 1. See also Tosaka, *Nihon Ideoro-
     gion*, 147. For more on Minoda's thought, see Person, *Arbiters of Patriotism*,
     chap. 3.

124 Tosaka, *Nihon Ideorogiron*, 198.

125 Tosaka, *Nihon Ideorogiron*, 199–200.

126   Tosaka, *Nihon Ideorogiron*, 202.

127   Tosaka, *Nihon Ideorogiron*, 36.

128   Tosaka, *Nihon Ideorogiron*, 231.

129   Tosaka, *Nihon Ideorogiron*, 203. For a translation by John Person, see "The Fate of Japanism," in Kawashima, Schäfer, and Stolz, *Tosaka Jun*, 65. I followed Person's translation of *bokuzen* as "ambivalent."

130   See Person, "The Fate of Japanism," 67, for a translation of Tosaka's text.

131   Tosaka, *Nihon Ideorogiron*, 206.

132   Tosaka, *Nihon Ideorogiron*, 179.

133   Tosaka, *Nihon Ideorogiron*, 175.

134   Tosaka, *Nihon Ideorogiron*, 175.

135   Tosaka, *Nihon Ideorogiron*, 176.

136   Tosaka, *Nihon Ideorogiron*, 177.

137   Tosaka, *Nihon Ideorogiron*, 178.

138   Tosaka, *Nihon Ideorogiron*, 179.

139   Tosaka, *Nihon Ideorogiron*, 180.

140   Tosaka, *Nihon Ideorogiron*, 178.

141   Tosaka, *Nihon Ideorogiron*, 179.

142   Tosaka, *Nihon Ideorogiron*, 182.

143   Tosaka, *Nihon Ideorogiron*, 181.

144   Tosaka, *Nihon Ideorogiron*, 183.

145   There is evidence throughout Tosaka's writings that he was frequently censored. But the censorship was uneven, and there is no sign that it occurred in this passage.

146   Tosaka, *Nihon Ideorogiron*, 184.

147   Tosaka, *Nihon Ideorogiron*, 149–50.

Epilogue: Déjà Vu

1   Virino, *Déjà Vu and the End of Theory*, 52–53.

2   Purposely using *Nippon*, as in prewar Japanism, rather than *Nihon*.

3   Takeuchi Yoshimi, *Shinpen Nihon Ideorogi*, 2:393 and 382.

4   Takeuchi Yoshimi, *Shinpen Nihon Ideorogi*, 2:393 and 382.

5   Quoted in Kan, *Tennōsei ronshū*, 1:159–51.

6   Kan, *Tennōsei ronshū*, 1:134–35.

7   Ollman, "Why Does the Emperor Need the Yakuza?"

8   Some people are convinced that this emphasis on the emperor in daily life appears to be receding into a forgettable past, especially in the reign of the current emperor, Reiwa. Only time will tell if this is only wishful thinking.

9   There is an English translation of Book I of Motoori, *Kojikiden*.

10   For a discussion between Kan Takyuki and Yasumaru Yoshio on Maruyama's *Kosō* and the "hopelessness seen" in that work and the author's

postwar attempt to show that the Japanese emperor was only a pale reflection of the figuration of Asia, although before the war Marxists had criticized the emperor system as an example of "Oriental despotism," see Kan, *Tennōsei ronshū*, 1:51, 54.

11 Maruyama, *Maruyama Masao shu*, 12:3–4.

12 Maruyama, *Maruyama Masao shu*, 12:112–14.

13 Maruyama, *Maruyama Masao shu*, 12:124.

14 Maruyama, *Kosō*, 10:4.

15 Maruyama, *Kosō*, 10:6.

16 Maruyama, *Kosō*, 10:10.

17 Maruyama, *Kosō*, 10:54.

18 Maruyama, *Kosō*, 10:54–55.

19 Maruyama, *Kosō*, 10:56.

20 Kobayashi's rejection of history and historical practice dates from the prewar days and was especially clear in his discussions at the 1942 symposium on "Overcoming the Modern." In his text on Motoori, he revealed familiar beliefs and returned to his older conviction that to "know history is to know the self," which historians are unable to do because "they have not captured history, only chronology which is the frame that limits it. The chronological framework, patterning the movement of affairs continues according to this inertia" (Kobayashi, *Motoori Norinaga*, 1:380).

21 Kobayashi, *Zenshū* (hereafter KHZ), 14:398.

22 *KHZ*, 14:398.

23 *KHZ*, 14:374.

24 *KHZ*, 14:299.

25 *KHZ*, 14:301.

26 *KHZ*, 14:324–25.

27 *KHZ*, 14:300–301.

28 *KHZ*, 14:300–301. See also Harootunian, *Things Seen and Unseen*, 59–60.

29 Kobayashi, *Motoori Norinaga*, 1:373.

30 Kobayashi, *Motoori Norinaga*, 1:362.

31 Kobayashi, *Motoori Norinaga*, 1:362–63.

32 *KHZ*, 14:324.

33 *KHZ*, 14:374.

34 *KHZ*, 14:378.

35 *KHZ*, 14:377–78.

BIBLIOGRAPHY

Adorno, Theodor W. *Critical Models*. Translated by Henry W. Pickford. New York: Columbia University Press, 1998.

Adorno, Theodor W. *History and Freedom: Lectures, 1964–1965*. Edited by Rolf Tiedemann. Translated by Rodney Livingstone. Cambridge: Polity Press, 2006.

Adorno, Theodor W. *Minima Moralia: Reflections from Damaged Life*. Translated by E. F. N. Jephcott. London: Verso, 1974.

Allinson, James C., and Alexander Anievas. "The Uneven and Combined Development of the Meiji Restoration: A Passive Revolutionary Road to Capitalist Modernity." *Capital and Class* 34, no. 3 (2010): 469–90.

Althusser, Louis. *On the Reproduction of Capitalism*. Translated by G. M. Goshgarian. London: Verso, 2014.

Arakawa Ikuo. *Miki Kiyoshi*. Tokyo: Kinokuniya, 1974.

Bakhtin, M. M. *The Dialogic Imagination: Four Essays*. Edited by Michael Holquist. Translated by Caryl Emerson and Michael Holquist. Austin: University of Texas Press, 1981.

Balibar, Étienne, and Immanuel Wallerstein. *Race, Nation, Class: Ambiguous Identities*. New York: Verso, 1980.

Barshay, Andrew. *State and Intellectual in Imperial Japan: The Public Man in Crisis*. Berkeley: University of California Press, 1988.

Benjamin, Walter. *The Arcades Project*. Translated by Howard Eiland and Kevin McLaughlin. Cambridge, MA: Belknap Press of Harvard University Press, 1999.

Benjamin, Walter. "Concept of History." In *Walter Benjamin: Selected Writings*, vol. 4, *1938–1940*, edited by Howard Eiland and Michael W. Jennings, 395. Cambridge, MA: Belknap Press of Harvard University Press, 2003.

Benjamin, Walter. *Origin of German Trauerspiel*. Translated by Howard Eiland. Cambridge, MA: Harvard University Press, 2019.

Bloch, Ernst. *Heritage of Our Times*. Translated by Neville Plaice and Steven Plaice. Berkeley: University of California Press, 1990.

Bloch, Ernst. *A Philosophy of the Future*. Translated by John Cumming. New York: Herder and Herder, 1970.

Bolz, Norbert, and Willem Van Reijen. *Walter Benjamin*. Translated by Laimdota Mazzarins. Atlantic Highlands, NJ: Humanities Press, 1996.

Clinton, Maggie. *Revolutionary Nativism: Fascism and Culture in China, 1927–1937*. Durham, NC: Duke University Press, 2017.

Davidson, Neil. *How Revolutionary Were the Bourgeois Revolutions?* Chicago: Haymarket Books, 2012.

DeBord, Guy. *Society of the Spectacle*. Detroit, MI: Red and Black, 1983.

Du Bois, W. E. B. *The Souls of Black Folk*. New York: Dover, 1994.

Edwards, Steve. "Time's Carcase, Art History, Capitalism and Temporality." Unpublished manuscript, last modified 2021.

Eliade, Mircea. *The Myth of the Eternal Return*. Translated by Willard R. Trask. Princeton, NJ: Princeton University Press, 1971.

Engels, Frederick. *The Peasant War in Germany*. Translated by Moissaye J. Olgin. Introduction by D. Riazanov. New York: International Publishers, 1926.

Fanon, Frantz. *The Wretched of the Earth*. Translated by Constance Farrington. New York: Grove Press, 1994.

Finchelstein, Federico. *A Brief History of Fascist Lies*. Oakland: University of California Press, 2020.

Foucault, Michel. *The Order of Things: An Archaeology of the Human Sciences*. New York: Pantheon, 1970.

Fujita Yukoku. "Seimeiron" [On correct names]. In *Mitogaku taikei*, vol. 3, edited by Takasu Yoshijirō. Tokyo: Mitogaku taikei kankōkai, 1941.

Fujitani, Takashi. *Splendid Monarchy: Power and Pageantry in Imperial Japan*. Berkeley: University of California Press, 1996.

Fukuda Yukie. *Sanrizuku andosoiru* [Sanrizuka underground]. Tokyo: Heigensha, 2001.

Gentile, Emilio. *Politics as Religion*. Translated by George Staunton. Princeton, NJ: Princeton University Press, 2006.

Gentile, Emilio. *The Struggle for Modernity, Nationalism, Futurism, and Fascism*. Translated by Stanley O. Payne. Westport, CT: Praeger, 2003.

Geoghegan, Vincent. *Ernst Bloch*. London: Routledge, 1995.

Gramsci, Antonio. *Further Selections from the Prison Notebooks*. Edited and translated by Derek Boothman. Minneapolis: University of Minnesota Press, 1995.

Gramsci, Antonio. *Prison Notebooks*. Edited and translated by Joseph Buttigieg. 3 vols. New York: Columbia University Press, 1996.

Gramsci, Antonio. *Selections from the Prison Notebooks*. Edited and translated by Quinton Hoare and Geoffrey Newell-Smith. New York: International Publishers, 1971.

Gramsci, Antonio. *The Southern Question*. New York: Bordighera Press, 2015.

Guterman, Norbert, and Henri Lefebvre. *La conscience mystifiee: Suivi de Henri Lefebvre, La Conscience priveé*. New ed. Paris: Syllepse, 1999.

Hani Gorō. *Hani Gorō rekishi ronshiron chosakushū* [Selection of Hani Gorō's histori-cal essays]. Vol. 1. Tokyo: Aoki Shōten, 1969.

Harootunian, Harry. *Things Seen and Unseen: Discourse and Ideology in Tokugawa Nativism*. Chicago: University of Chicago Press, 1988.

Harootunian, Harry. *Toward Restoration: The Growth of Political Consciousness in Tokugawa Japan*. Berkeley: University of California Press, 1970.

Harootunian, Harry. *Uneven Moments: Reflections on Japan's Modern History*. New York: Columbia University Press, 2019.

Hasegawa Nyozekan. *Hasegawa Nyozekan senshū* [Selected writings of Hasegawa Nyozekan]. Edited by Ōuchi Hyōhei. 2 vols. Tokyo: Kuita Shuppankai Kankō, 1969.

Hirano, Katsuya. "The Dialectic of Laughter and Tosaka's Critical Theory." In *Tosaka Jun: A Critical Reader*, edited by Ken C. Kawashima, Fabian Schäfer, and Robert Stolz, 176–93. Ithaca, NY: East Asia Program, Cornell University, 2013.

Hirano, Katsuya. *The Politics of Dialogical Imagination: Power and Popular Culture in Early Modern Japan*. Chicago: University of Chicago Press, 2014.

Hoffmann, Reto. *The Fascist Effect: Japan and Italy, 1915–1952*. Ithaca, NY: Cornell University Press, 2015.

Inoue, Isao. *Ōsei fukko* [Restoration of ancient imperial governance]. Tokyo: Chuko shinsho, 1991.

Inoue, Katsuo. *Bakumatsu Ishin* [Late Tokugawa renovation). Tokyo: Iwanami shinsho, 2016.

Irokawa, Daikichi. *The Culture of the Meiji Period*. Edited and translated by Marius B. Jansen. Princeton, NJ: Princeton University Press, 1985.

Iwasaki Chikatsugu. *Nihon Markusushgi tetsugakushi josetsu* [Introduction to the study of the philosophic history of Japanese Marxism]. Tokyo: Miraisha, 1976.

Jameson, Fredric. *Allegory and Ideology*. London: Verso, 2019.

Jameson, Fredric. *The Geopolitical Aesthetic: Cinema and Space in the World System*. Bloomington: Indiana University Press, 1992.

Jameson, Fredric. *Marxism and Form*. Princeton, NJ: Princeton University Press, 1971.

Kaishi suru fukei, sanrizuka nomin no sei kotoba [Landscape destroyed: Life and words of the Sanrizuka peasantry]. Edited by members of the Village Association. Tokyo: Sōdosha, 2005.

Kan Takayuki. *Tennōsei ronshū* [Symposium on the emperor system]. Vol. 1, *Tennōsei mondai to Nihonseishinshi* [The problem of the emperor system and the spiri-tual history of Japan]. Tokyo: Ochanomizu shobō, 2014.

Karatani, Kojin. *History and Repetition*. Translated by Seiji M. Lippit. New York: Columbia University Press, 2012.

Kawamura Nozomu. *Nihon Shakaigakushi Kenkyū* [Study of the history of Japanese sociology]. Vol. 2. Tokyo: Ningen no Kagakusha, 1975.

Kawashima, Ken C., Fabian Schäfer, and Robert Stolz, eds. *Tosaka Jun: A Critical Reader*. Ithaca, NY: East Asia Program, Cornell University, 2013.

Kita Ikki. *Nihon Kaizō hoantaikō* [An outline plan for the reorganization of Japan]. Tokyo: Nishida, 1925.

Kiyohara Sadao. *Kokutai ronshi* [Study of Japan's national body]. Edited by Naimusho Jinjakyoka. Tokyo: Seihon Goshi Kaisha, 1921.

Kobayashi Hideo. *Motoori Norinaga*. Vol. 1. Tokyo: Shinchōsha, 1992.

Kobayashi Hideo. *Zenshū* [Collected works]. Vol. 14. Tokyo: Shinchōsha, 2002.

Lenin, V. I. *Materialism and Empirico-Criticism: Critical Comments on a Reactionary Philosophy*. New York: International Publishers, 1927.

Lowy, Michael. *The Politics of Combined and Uneven Development: The Theory of Permanent Revolution*. London: Verso, 1981.

Lukács, Georg. *History and Class Consciousness*. Translated by Rodney Livingstone. London: Merlin Press, 1968.

Maruyama Masao. *Maruyama Masaoshū* [Collected works of Maruyama Masao]. *Kosō* [The archaic stratum]. 12 vols. Tokyo: Iwanami shōten, 1996.

Maruyama Masao. *Maruyama Masao shu* [Works of Maruyama Masao]. 12 vols. Tokyo: Iwanami shōten, 1996.

Maruyama Masao. *Thought and Behavior in Modern Japanese Politics*. Edited by Ivan Morris. London: Oxford University Press, 1969.

Marx, Karl. *Capital*. Vol. 1. Translated by Ben Fowkes. London: Penguin, 1990.

Marx, Karl. *The 18th Brumaire of Louis Bonaparte*. New York: International Publishers, 1963.

Marx, Karl. *Grundrisse: Foundations of the Critique of Political Economy*. Translated with a foreword by Martin Nicolaus. London: Penguin Books, 1993.

Marx, Karl, and V. I. Lenin. *Civil War in France: The Paris Commune*. New York: International Publishers, 1940.

Matsumura, Wendy. "Waiting for the Cool Moon: Subterranean Struggles in the Heart of the Japanese Empire." Forthcoming.

Miki Kiyoshi. *Essensu* [The essence of Miki Kiyoshi]. Edited by Uchida Hiroshi. Tokyo: Kobushi Bunko, 2000.

Miki Kiyoshi. *Zenshū* [Collected works]. 14 vols. Tokyo: Iwanami Shōten, 1966–1967.

Mitani Hiroshi. *Meiji Ishin o kangaeru* [Thinking the Meiji Restoration]. Tokyo: Yushisha, 2006.

Morfino, Vittorio, and Peter D. Thomas, eds. *The Government of Time*. Leiden: Brill, 2018.

Motoori Norinaga. *Kojikiden* [Reading the *Kojiki*]. Introduced, translated, and annotated by Anne Wehmeyer. Ithaca, NY: East Asia Program, Cornell University, 1997.

Murray, Patrick. *The Mismeasure of Wealth: Essays on Marx and Social Form*. Leiden, the Netherlands: Brill, 2016.

Najita, Tetsuo. *Ordinary Economies in Japan: A Historical Perspective, 1750–1950*. Berkeley: University of California Press, 2009.

Ollman, Bertell. "Why Does the Emperor Need the Yakuza? Toward a Marxist Theory of the Japanese State." *New Left Review*, Spring 2001. https://nyuscholars

.nyu.edu/en/publications/why-does-the-emperor-need-the-yakuza-toward
-a-marxist-theory-of-t.

Osborne, Peter. *The Politics of Time*. London: Verso, 1995.

Person, John. *Arbiters of Patriotism: Right Wing Scholars in Imperial Japan*. Honolulu: University of Hawai'i Press, 2020.

Pincus, Leslie. *Authenticating Culture in Imperial Japan: Shūzō Kuki and the Rise of National Aesthetics*. Berkeley: University of California Press, 1996.

Polanyi, Karl. "The Essence of Fascism." In *Christianity and the Social Revolution*, edited by J. Lewis, Karl Polanyi, and D. K. Kitchen, 359–94. London: Victor Gollanz, 1937.

Postone, Moishe. *Time, Labour and Social Domination: A Reinterpretation of Marx's Critical Theory*. Cambridge: Cambridge University Press, 1993.

Ramizi, Erag, ed. "Anachronism and Its Histories." Special issue, *Diacritics* 48, no. 2 (2020).

Rancière, Jacques. "The Concept of Anachronism and the Historian's Truth." Translated by Tim Stott and Noel Fitzpatrick. *InPrint* 3, no. 1 (2015): 13–52.

Riley, Dylan. *The Civic Foundations of Fascism in Europe*. London: Verso, 2019.

Roberts, John. *Philosophizing the Everyday*. London: Pluto Press, 2006.

Ross, Kristin. *L'imaginaire de la commune*. Translated by Etienne Dobensque. Paris: La Fabrique, 2015.

Sartre, Jean-Paul. *Search for a Method*. Translated by Hazel E. Barnes. New York: Vintage Books, 1968.

Satoshi, Yoshio. *Tosaka Jun Tetsugaku* [The philosophy of Tosaka Jun]. Tokyo: Kobushi, Shōbō 2001.

Schäfer, Fabian, *Tosaka Jun: Ideologie, Medien, Alltag*. Leipzig, Germany: Leipziger Universitatsverlag, 2011.

"Seikatsu bunka ni suite" [On cultural living]. *Fujin kōron* [Women's opinion] 22 (March 1937): 416–35.

Seki Eikichi. *Bunka shakaigaku gairon*. In Kawamura Nozomu, *Nihon Shakaigakushi Kenkyū*, vol. 2. Tokyo: Ningen no Kagaku,1975.

Shanin, Teodor, ed. *Late Marx and the Russian Road: Marx and the Peripheries of Capitalism*. New York: New York University Press, 1983.

Silverberg, Miriam. *Erotic Grotesque Nonsense: The Mass Culture of Japanese Modern Times*. Berkeley: University of California Press, 2009.

Skya, Walter. *Japan's Holy War: The Ideology of Radical Shintō Nationalism*. Durham, NC: Duke University Press, 2009.

Sohn-Rethel, Alfred. *Intellectual and Manual Labour: A Critique of Epistemology*. Translated by Martin Sohn-Rethel. Atlantic Highlands, NJ: Humanities Press, 1978.

Stolz, Robert. "Here, Now." In *Tosaka Jun: A Critical Reader*, edited by Ken C. Kawashima, Fabian Schäfer, and Robert Stolz, 125–49. Ithaca, NY: East Asia Program, Cornell University, 2013.

Suzuki Jun. *Ishin kōsō to tenkai* [Renovation's conception and its unfolding]. Tokyo: Kodansha bunko, 2010.

Takasu Yoshijirō, ed. *Mitogaku taikei* [Outline of Mito learning]. Vol. 3. Tokyo: Mitogaku Kankōkai, 1941.

Takeuchi Yoshimi. *Shinpen Nihon Ideorogi* [A new version of the Japan ideology]. Vol. 2. Tokyo: Chikuma Shōbō, 1962.

Tanaka, Stefan. *History without Chronology*. Mountain View, CA: Lever Press, 2019.

Tanaka, Stefan. *New Times in Modern Japan*. Princeton, NJ: Princeton University Press, 2004.

Tanka, Brij. *Kita Ikki and the Making of Modern Japan*. Leiden: Brill, 2006.

Tansman, Alan. *The Aesthetics of Japanese Fascism*. Berkeley: University of California Press, 2009.

Thomas, Peter D. *The Gramscian Moment: Philosophy, Hegemony and Marxism*. Chicago: Haymarket Books, 2010.

Thomas, Peter D. "Gramscian Plural Temporalities." In *The Government of Time*, edited by Vittorio Morfino and Peter D. Thomas, 174–209. Leiden: Brill, 2017.

Tierney, Robert Thomas. *Tropics of Savagery: The Culture of Japanese Empire in Comparative Frame*. Berkeley: University of California Press, 2010.

Tomba, Massimiliano. *Insurgent Universality, Historical Materialism: An Alternative Legacy of Modernity*. Oxford: Oxford University Press, 2019.

Tombazos, Stavros. *Time in Marx: The Categories of Time in Marx's Capital*. Chicago: Haymarket Books, 2014.

Tosaka Jun. *Nihon Ideorogion* [The Japan ideology]. Tokyo: Iwanami Shōten, 1978.

Tosaka Jun. *Zenshū* [Collected works]. 4 vols. Tokyo: Keisō Shōbō, 1966.

Toscano, Alberto. *Late Fascism*. London: Verso, 2023.

Tōyama Shigeki. *Meiji Ishin* [The Meiji Renovation]. Tokyo: Iwanami Bunko, 2018.

Traverso, Enzo. *The New Faces of Fascism: Populism and the Far Right*. Translated by David Broder. London: Verso, 2019.

Trotsky, Leon. *History of the Russian Revolution*. Translated by Max Eastman. Chicago: Haymarket Books, 2008.

Tsukui Tatsuo. *Nihonteki shakaishugi no Teishō* [Lectures on Japanese socialism]. Tokyo: Senshinsha, 1932.

Tsuneishi, Norihiko. "Rice and Coal: Worship of Inari Shrines in Japan's Commercial and Industrial Landscape, 1673–1833." PhD diss., Columbia University, 2019.

Tyner, James. *Dead Labor: Toward a Political Economy of Premature Death*. Minneapolis: University of Minnesota Press, 2020.

Virino, Paolo. *Déjà Vu and the End of Theory*. Translated by David Broder. London: Verso, 2015.

Volosinov, V. N. *Marxism and the Philosophy of Language*. Translated by Ladislav Matelka and I. R. Titunik. New York: Seminar Press, 1973.

Waite, Geoffrey. *Nietzsche's Corpse: Aesthetics, Politics, or the Spectacular Technoculture of Everyday Life*. Durham, NC: Duke University Press, 1996.

Walker, Gavin. *Marx et la politique du dehors*. Translated from English by Jonathan Martineau. Montreal: Lux Canada, 2022.

Ward, Max. *Thought Crime*. Durham, NC: Duke University Press, 2019.

Watsuji Tetsurō. *"Zoku Nippon Seishinshi kenkyū"* [Studies in Japanese spiritual history, continued]. In *Gendai Nihon shisō taikei* [Outline of contemporary thought], edited by Karaki Junzō, 28:377–78. Tokyo: Chikuma Shobou, 1963.

White, Hayden. *The Practical Past*. Evanston, IL: Northwestern University Press, 2014.

Yasumaru Yoshio. *Kindai tennōzō no keisei* [The formation of the image of the modern emperor system]. Tokyo: Iwanami Gendai Bunko, 2013.

Yoshida, Masatoshi. *Tosaka Jun no tetsugaku* [The philosophy of Tosaka Jun]. Tokyo: Kobushi Shōbō, 2001.

INDEX

absolutism: Hasegawa on, 118; Japanism
and, 135–36; Meiji restoration and,
65–66, 71–72
Achebe, Chinua, 13
actuality (*jissai*), 102, 174
Adorno, Theodor, 97, 101, 110, 246n.13
agrarianism: Japanese capitalism
and, 121–25; Japanists and, 207–12;
postwar return of, 230–31
Akamatsu Katsumaro, 129
allegorization, in Meiji Restoration,
102–9
allegorization of history, x–xi
Althusser, Louis, 105, 125
Amaterasu Ōmikami (sun goddess),
76, 133–34
anachrony: archaism and, 85–98; time
and, 33–35
Anderson, Benedict, 14
And Then (Natsume), 212
Anesaki Masaharu, 134
anticapitalism, Hasegawa on, 124–26
antiquity (*fukko*): Japan's postwar return
to, 228–29; Kobayashi's discussion of,
240–44
anti-Tokugawa movement, 59–61, 72–73
appropriation, passive revolution and, 9
archaism: capitalism and, 17–18, 136–37;
in China, 61; fascism and, 6–10,
83–84, 114; feudal remnants in Meiji
era and, 74–84; history and, 3, 8–10,

27–29, 84–98; ideology of, 99–101;
Japanese postwar intellectuals on,
233–44; Japanism and, 125–31,
139–44, 151–52, 204–7; Kobayashi
on, 238–44; Maruyama on archaic
stratum, 235–36; Marx and, 16; Meiji
Restoration and, 30–35, 44–45, 53–54,
64–66, 70–84; Miki on, 152–53,
158–60; postwar U.S. Occupation
and return to, 228–44; primitivization and, 208–12; in Russia, 29–30;
Tosaka's critique of, 71, 92, 134–35,
153, 192–99, 213–14, 217–22
Arrow of God, The (Achebe), 13
art, Hasegawa's view of, 140–44
Asianism, 204
Austria, U.S. postwar involvement
in, 226
authority hierarchy (*meibunron*): Meiji
Restoration and, 72–84, 249n.21; Mito
conception of, 65–70

Bakhtin, Mikhail, 193
Balibar, Étienne, 24, 28, 36
Barshay, Andrew, 139–40
Benjamin, Walter: fascism and, 16; on
history, xi–xvii, 11; on Marxism, 18–22;
on now of recognizability, 93–94; on
primitivization, 208; on time and
history, 13–22, 48–49, 93
Ben-Said, Daniel, xii

Bergson, Henri, 237
big lie phenomenon, ix–x
Bloch, Ernest, xii–xiii, 11, 14, 16–17; on capitalism, 26; on German fascism, 96; on history and time, 16–22; on ideology, 110; on Nazism, 130–31
Bolsonaro, Jair, x
Boshin War, 73
bourgeois culture: Hasegawa's view of, 141–44; Japanist hegemonization of, 127–31
British Union of Fascists, 112
Buddhism, Tosaka on, 198–99
bureaucracy, Japanese fascism and, 7, 175–76
Bushido ethos, 206–7
Buyō Inshi, 62

Cabral, Amilcar, 13
Calvinist Christianity, 87, 115–16
Capital (Marx), 24–25, 28–30, 193
capitalism: archaism and, 17, 89–90, 92–98; Balibar on history of, 24; Bloch's discussion of, 17–22; chronotope of, 247n.24; colonialism and, 13–14; in contemporary Asia, 26; culture and, 87–88, 95–98, 147–48; feudal remnants and, 73–74, 208–10; Hasegawa's critique of, 109–44; in Japan, 2–4, 51–54, 151–52, 209–10; Japanism (*Nipponshugi*) and, 221–22; Marx on, xiv–xv, 22; materialism and idealism and, 101–9; Meiji Restoration and, 31–35, 49–54, 74–84; Miki's analysis of, 157–58; in postwar Japan, 227–29; primitive accumulation and, 28–29, 54–55; Protestant Christianity and, 28–29; revolutionary consciousness and, xiii, 245n.2; sacralization of politics and, 92; Sartre on, 14–15; subsumption and, 8–9, 23–29; in Tokugawa shogunate, 55–66; Tosaka on, 110, 173, 187–90; unevenness of, 2–3, 14–16, 23–29, 46–54
catastrophe, Benjamin on progress and, 20–21

Chamberlain, Houston Stewart, 125–26, 253n.40
Charter Oath of 1868 (Meiji Restoration), 72, 94
China: archaism in, 61; capitalism in, 26; Communist takeover of, 226–27; ideology in, 106; Japanese war with, 120; nationalism in, 246n.7; political writing in, 150–51
Chinese ideographs, Japanese adaptation of, 67, 101–2, 135–36, 160, 236–39
chronology, Rancière on anachrony and, 86
chronotope, Trotsky's concept of, 247n.24
class structure: Hasegawa's analysis of, 121–22, 128–31, 143–44, 257n.77; history and, 184
clock time, Japanese introduction of, 31–35
cold fascism (*kurodo fuashizumu*), 111
Cold War politics, U.S. Occupation of Japan and, 226–29, 237
colonization: Fanon on, 12–13; Hasegawa's analysis of, 120–21; Japanese culture and, 165–66; noncontemporaneity and, 11–12; unevenness and, 13–14
Comintern, 130; Asian modernity and, 49–54; Japanese Marxists and, 56–58
communal organizations: formation of, 59–61; in Japan, 89–90, 231; Kobayashi on, 242–44; Marxist interpretation of, 34, 81–82, 92, 94–95
"Concept of History" (Benjamin), 18, 93
Confucianism, 99
constellation of dangers, Benjamin's concept of, 20–21
contemporization of noncontemporaneity: Bloch's concept of, 16–17; capitalism and, 26–27; colonization and, 11–12; of history, 12–35; Japanese culture and, 96–98; Japanism and, 128–31; memory and, 88–89
Contribution to the Critique of Political Economy, A (Marx), 29–30

cooperativism, Miki's discussion of, 167–69

coup d'état, Meiji initiation of, 70–72, 75–76

creationism, 135

"Critique of Fascism" (Hasegawa), 108, 139

Croce, Benedetto, 23

cultural living (*bunka seikatsu*), 165–69

culture: capitalism and, 87–88; climate and, 105–6; fascism and, 95–98, 104–9, 114–16; imperialism and, 231–32; Japanism and, 125–44; living culture ideology, 145–46, 156, 159–69; politics and, 59–61, 147–69, 175–76, 199–200, 232–33; postwar Japanese focus on, 229–30; Tosaka on, 106–7, 202–3, 257n.77

Cuoco, Vicenzo, 43

Da Charakter (Heidegger), 103

Davidson, Neil, 52–53

DeBord, Guy, 91

déjà vu, U.S. postwar occupation of Japan and, 228–29

Deleuze, Gilles, 230

de Martino, Ernesto, 91

Department of Divinities (*Jingikan*), Meiji creation of, 77

Destruction of Reason (Lukács), 172

dialectical theory, Benjamin and, 18–22

Du Bois, W. E. B., 12–13

Durkheim, Émile, 154

economic conditions: family system collapse and, 215–16; fascism in Japan and, 114–15; growthism in postwar Japan, 223–24; Japanism and, 8, 120–22; subsumption and, 24–29; temporality and, 17; in Tokugawa shogunate, 55–66

18th Brumaire of Louis Bonaparte, The (Marx), 18, 30, 35

Eliade, Mircea, 91

emperor: authority of, 133–34; as feudal remnant, 249n.21; Japanese designations for, 74–75; mythical origins of,

90; U.S. postwar protection and restoration of, 76–77, 227–44, 259n.8

enclosure, subsumption and, 27

Engels, Friedrich, 25–29, 53, 56–57, 119, 174

English culture, Japanese view of, 166

Enlightenment thought: Meiji Restoration and, 239; Tosaka and, 172

Erdoğan, Recep Tayyip, x, 10

everyday life: archaism and, 152–53; art and, 140, 148; capitalism and, 110, 142–44, 147, 174–76; history and, 102–3, 154, 162–64, 178–90; Japanism and, 166; Kobayashi on, 240–44; living culture and, 86, 164; Meiji Restoration and, 45, 55, 60–62; Miki's view of, 232–33; noncontemporaneity in, 127–28; postwar imperial saturation in, 231–33; social relations and, 73; Tosaka's view of, 232–33; Watsuji on, 31. *See also* folk community

failed model thesis, 44–45

familism, Tosaka's discussion of, 207–8, 213–22

Fanon, Frantz, xii, 12–14, 184

Farmer-Labor faction (Japan), 103

farmer-soldiers, 206–12

fascism: archaism and, 6–10, 83–84; capitalism and, 147–48, 246n.7; culture and, 95–98, 148–69; global context for, 246n.7; Hasegawa's discussion of, 110–14, 128–31, 143–44; historiography of, xii–xiv, 246n.8; Italian intellectuals and, 23–24; Japan's embrace of, ix–xvii, 3, 11, 99–101, 135–44, 204–7; microcosmic structures of, 230; Miki on, 100–101, 104, 113, 150–51, 154–55, 159–69; modernism and, 147–49; passive revolution and, 6–8; sacralization of politics and, 89–91; Tosaka on, 171–76, 201–2, 204–7

Febvre, Lucien, 41

feudal domains (remnants): capitalism and, 73–74, 207–10; Hasegawa's analysis of, 121–23, 142–44; history

feudal domains (continued)
and role of, 27, 73–84, 173, 181–82; Japanism and, 127–28; Marxist perspective on, 86–87, 147–48, 161–69; Meiji Restoration and, 70–84, 94–98, 104–5; postwar pervasiveness of, 230–31; in Tokugawa shogunate, 37–39, 54–55, 63–66, 68–70; Tosaka on, 122–23, 206–12, 217–22, 253n.32; U.S. postwar campaign against, 224–25

folk community: fascism and, 107–8, 137, 149; Hasegawa on, 108–9, 115, 130–31, 138–39; Japanism and, 106; Miki on, 158–60, 166, 168–69; Tosaka on, 129, 131, 203, 206–10. *See also* everyday life

foreign interaction with Japan: cultural impact of, 132, 159–69; in Meiji era, 78–79; Tokugawa shogunate and, 63–66, 69–70. *See also* isolationism

form, Tosaka's discussion of, 179–90

formless form, Miki's discussion of, 156–59

Formosa, colonization of, 122

Formosa culture, 48

Foucault, Michel, 83; on historiography, xi

Frankfurt school, 7–8

French Revolution: Meiji Restoration and, 43–46, 52, 71–72; Rome compared to, 93

Freud, Sigmund: dreamwork of, 105–6; psychoanalysis of, 19

Fujita Yūkoku, 69

Gemeinschaft, 218

Gentile, Emilio, 90

Gentile, Giovanni, 23, 130

geopolitics, U.S. Occupation in Japan and, 226–27

German Ideology, The (Marx and Engels), 25–26, 94, 119, 174

German intellectuals, on history and politics, 22–23

Germany: archaism in, 10; culture concepts in, 166; fascism in, 90–91,
130–31; historicism crisis in, 10–11, 218; history in, 153–55; Japan and, 108–9, 204; *Lebensphilosophie* of, 172; Nazi book burnings in, 149–50; U.S. postwar involvement in, 224–26

Gesellschaft, 218

Gramsci, Antonio, xiii–xiv, 1, 11; on historical time, 29; on ideology, 110; Italian philosophy and, 23; on liberalism and fascism, 169, 201; passive revolution concept of, 5–7, 36–37, 40–54, 128; on politics, 11, 18–19, 22, 148

Greater East Asia Co-Prosperity Sphere, 169

Great Japanism Party/Greater Japanism Party, 135–36

Gregorian calendar, Japanese use of, 31–35

"Growth of Japan's Fascism, The" (*Nihon fuashizumu no hatsuiku*), 174–76

Grundrisse (Marx), 50–51, 89, 122

Guattari, Félix, 230

Guterman, Norbert, 109–10

Hani Gorō, x, 186

Hasegawa Nyozekan, 53; critique of capitalism and, 109–44; on fascism, 149, 154–55; Japanism and, 99–101, 105, 108–16, 119–21, 145–46, 198; Marxism and, 151; postwar obscurity of, 223

Hashimoto Sanai, 61–66

Hattori Shisō, 146, 151, 255n.8

Hayashi Fusao, 150

Hegel, G. W. F., 151, 155–56, 182

Heidegger, Martin, 103, 146, 155, 167, 174, 184, 194–95

hermeneutics: Japanism and, 236; Tosaka's work on ideology and, 172–73, 194–95

Hiraizumi Kiyoshi, 176

Hirata Atsutane, 60–61, 87–88, 127, 137, 155–56

Hirata school, 250n.35

Hirohito (Emperor), funeral of, 227–28

historicism: crisis of, 10–11; Marx's conception of, 25–29, 221–22

history: allegorization of, x–xi; anach-
ronism and, 40–41; archaism and,
3, 8–10, 27–29, 84–98; contem-
porization of, 12–35; culture and,
154–55; Kobayashi's discussion of,
xi, 260n.20; Maruyama on, 235–36;
Meiji Restoration concept of, 38–54;
Miki's discussion of, 145–46, 150–51,
158–59, 163–69; politics of, 18–22;
Tosaka's critique of historical time
and, 173–90; of U.S. Occupation in
Japan, 226–27; value theory and, 110
Hitler, Adolf, 108
Hitotsubashi Keiki, 76
Holy Alliance, 120
Horkheimer, Max, 110

idealism: materialism and, 101–9;
Tosaka on, 170–76, 185–92
ideology: Althusser on, 105–6, 125;
archaism and, 99–101; myth and, 23,
27–29; primitivization and, 208–10;
Tosaka's study of, 170–222
ignorantization, Tosaka's concept
of, 203
Imperial Charter Oath of 1868, 48
imperialism: archaism and, 85–86; capitalism and, 123–24; Meiji Restoration
and, 71–84; in Tokugawa shogunate,
55–66, 231; U.S. Occupation and restoration of, 227–44
India, capitalism in, 26
"Inei raisan" (Praising shadows)
(Tanizaki), 165
Inoue Isao, 70–72
international relations, Japan and,
117–21
"Introduction to Japan's Cultural
History" (*Nihon bunkashi josetsu*)
(Nishida), 176
Iraq War, U.S. nation rebuilding in, 225
Island of Doctor Moreau, The (Wells), 226
isolationism: Japanism and, 132–33;
Meiji-era end to, 78–84; in Tokugawa
shogunate, 63–68, 248n.65. *See also*
foreign interaction with Japan

Italy: archaism in, 10, 90; history and,
153–55; Japan and, 204; Japanism and,
108–9, 111–13, 138; U.S. postwar involvement in, 224–25
Iwakura Tomomi, 68, 72–73, 76–77, 80,
82–83

Jameson, Fredric, 14, 104
Japan: archaism in, 10; capitalism in,
2–4, 26; culture and politics in,
147–69; diachronic history in, 154–55;
fascism in, 99–101, 111–44, 175–76;
historicism crisis in, 10–11; isolation
policy of, 248n.65; Maruyama on history of, 234–36; Mito discourse in,
60–61; modernity in, xv–xvii, 30–35;
passive revolution in, 3–4, 36–54;
postwar subjectivity in, 251n.69; restoration in, 5–6; sacralization of fascism in, 90–91; U.S. Occupation of,
35, 223–29; U.S.-sponsored postwar
constitution in, 82, 224–25, 229; war
with China, 120; Watsuji's cultural
history of, 31–35. *See also* Meiji Restoration; Tokugawa shogunate
Japan Communist Party, 50–51
Japan Conference (*Nippon kaigi*), 230
"Japanese Character and Fascism" (Miki
Kiyoshi), 145–46, 149–50
"Japanese spirit," 109–10, 125, 158,
170–72, 212
Japan Ideology (Tasaka). See *Nihon
Ideorogion* (The Japan ideology)
(Tosaka Jun)
Japanism (*Nipponshugi*), xii, xvi–xvii;
allegorization of, 105–6; anachrony
and, 33–35; archaism and, 125–31,
139–44, 151–53, 204–7; capitalism
and, 221–22; cultural and politics
and, 150–69; familism and, 215–16;
fascism and, 8, 90; Hasegawa's analysis of, 109–16, 119–21, 124–31; ideology of, 99–101, 132–34; international
relations and, 132–33; living culture
ideology and, 145–46, 156, 159–69;
materialism and idealism and, 102–9;

Japanism (continued)
Meiji Restoration and, 42–43; Miki's analysis of, 145–49, 151–53, 159–69; postwar return of, 227–29; primitivism and, 217–22; restorationism and, 207–12; sacralization of politics and, 92–93; Tosaka on, 99–101, 121, 139, 146, 203–8, 211–12
Jinmu (Emperor), 64, 71–72, 75–76, 78–81, 91, 107, 113, 218

Kakehi Katsuhiko, 134
Kant, Immanuel, 12
Kan Takayuki, 94–95, 231–32, 259n.10
Kautsky, Karl, 51
Kawai Eijirō, 200
Kita Ikki, 89, 108, 130, 150
Kiyohara Sadao, 99
Kobayashi Hideo, xi, 101, 126, 192–93, 196, 199, 233–34, 238–44
Kojiki (Chronicle of ancient history), 141, 220, 234, 237, 241
Kojikiden (Motoori), 234, 239–44
kokutai (mystic body politic), 84–85
Kokutai no hongi, 134–35, 160
Kokutai ronshi (Kiyohara), 99, 132–37
Komatsu, 72
Kōmei (Emperor), 67, 78–80
Kōmin shinbun newspaper, 107
Konoe Fumimaro, 140
Korean War, 226–27
Kōsaka, 186
Kosellek, Reinhart, xii, 11–12
Kosō (Maruyama), 233–37, 243–44, 259n.10
Kōyama, 186
Kuki Shūzō, 95
Kyoto school of philosophy, 145–46, 152, 186

Labor-Farmer faction (Japan), 50, 53–54
language: Japanese culture and, 192–93; Kobayashi on importance of, 239–44
La nuit proletaires (Rancière), 34–35
lateness, capitalism and, 2–3, 116–17

League of Nations, 120
lecture faction (Japan): failed model thesis, 44–45, 249n.32; fascism and, 114, 210; feudal remnants and, 225; Marxism and, 32–33, 50–51, 53–54; Meiji Restoration and, 104, 207–8; Tokugawa popular uprisings, 56–58
Lefebvre, Henri, xii, 109–10
legal fascism (*gōhōteki fuashizmu*), 111
Lenin, Vladimir, 15–16, 252n.8
Liberal Democratic Party (Japan), 230
liberalism: Miki's discussion of, 168–69; Tosaka on, 171–72, 200–202
literature: Kobayashi on, 239–44; Tosaka on, 199–200
literaturization of philosophy, 199–200, 203
living culture, philosophy of, 145–46, 156, 159–69; cultural living and, 166–67
Lowy, Michael, 53
Lukács, Georg, 19, 172, 186–87
Luxemburg, Rosa, 54, 172

MacArthur, Douglas, 224, 227
Malraux, André, 96
Manchuria, Japanese seizure of, 113
Mannheim, Karl, 57
Marcuse, Herbert, 7–8
Mariátegui, José Carlos, 13, 54
"Marrow of History" (*Rekishi no kotsuzui*) (Hiraizumi), 176
Maruyama Masao: on archaism, 53, 83–84, 158, 163, 233–38, 241, 243–44, 259n.10; on fascism, 83–84, 101; Marxism and, 81; on modernity, 35; on postwar modernization, 223–26; on sacralization of politics, 91–92
Marx, Karl: on capitalism, 122; on communal form, 34, 81–82, 92, 94; on history and time, xi–xii, 29, 178–82; on prehistory, 89; on primitive accumulation, 28–29, 54–55; on revolution, 4–6, 21; on subsumption, 8–9, 23–29; on unevenness and capitalism, 23–24; on world markets, 119

Marxism: Bloch and Benjamin on, 18–22; feudal remnants and, 86–87, 147–48, 161–69; on historicity of capitalism, 221–22; history and, xi–xv, 186–90, 245n.2; in Japan, 7, 51–54, 94–98; Japanism and, 100, 107–9; lecture faction and, 32–33; mass political action and, 56–58; Meiji Restoration in context of, 49–54; Miki's work with, 146–47; philologism and, 193; in postwar Japan, 223–29; stage theory and, 249n.32; temporality and, 14–15, 188–90; Tosaka on, 174, 199–200

mass belief, creation of, ix–x

mass political action, Tokugawa shogunate and, 55–58, 61–66

materialism: Hasegawa's rejection of, 139; idealism and, 101–9; Japanese fascism and, 100–101; Miki and, 146–47

Meiji (Emperor), 68; death of, 77

Meiji Restoration, xv–xvii, 1; capitalism and, 44–45; constitutional reforms during, 61–66, 82, 224–25, 229; criticism of, 107–8; fascism and, 113; French Revolution and, 43–46; Gramsci on, 47–54; history of, 37–54, 221–22; initiation of modernity and, 30–35; Japanism and, 125; loyalist activists in, 62–66; Maruyama on, 234–38; Marxist view of, 104, 207–8; materialist perspective on, 103; Mito discourse and, 39–41, 59–61; mythology and, 70–84, 102–3; as passive revolution, 42–44, 69–70; political character of, 69–70; principal actors in, 37–38; sacralization of politics in, 91–92; samurai-led reforms in, 52–54; theorists of, 250n.49; Tosaka on, 216–17

Mencius, 236

Michelangelo, 140

Miki Kiyoshi, 140; on archaism, 152–53, 158–60, 236–37; on capitalism, 86–87, 116, 210; on culture and politics, 148–69; on everyday life, 232–33; on

fascism, 100–101, 104, 113, 150–51, 154–55, 159–69; on history, 174–75, 182; on Japanism, 145–49, 151–53, 159–69; living culture philosophy of, 145–46, 156, 159–69, 223; on Marxism, 15, 23; Tosaka and, 146–70, 174–75

military forces: Hasegawa on, 118–19; Meiji Restoration and, 49, 52, 72–76; Miki on, 165–66; new sectionalism and, 63–66; rural alliances with, 206–12; Tosaka on, 206–12

mindfulness, Benjamin's concept of, 20–21

Minoda Muneki, 205

Mitani Hiroshi, 71, 250n.44, 251n.53

Mito discourse (Meiji Restoration), 39–41, 59–61, 65–70

modernization and modernism: culture and, 148–49; fascism and, 100–101, 147–49; Meiji Restoration and, 49–54; Miki's analysis of, 161–69; passive revolution and, 6–7; politics of time and, 11–12; in postwar Japan, 204–5, 225–29

Mosley, Oswald, 112

Motoori Norinaga, 101, 126–27, 192, 231, 233–44

Motoori Norinaga (Kobayashi), 233–34, 238–44, 260n.20

multiversum, Bloch's concept of, xiii

Muromachi period, 176

Murray, Patrick, 28

Mussolini, Benito, 90, 108, 111, 113, 138

mystery, Tosaka on, 178–80, 219–22

mysticism, Japanist ideology of, 99–101, 212, 219–22

mythology: Meiji Restoration and, 70–84, 91–98; right-wing politics and, 27–29

nariyuki (historical events), 236

naru (to become), 236

national anthem, postwar controversy over, 227

National Foundation Day (*Kenkoku Kinenbi*), 227

nationalism: agrarian anticapitalism and, 124; archaism and, 103–9; Miki's discussion of, 151–52
national regionalism in Japan, 114
national socialism, Japanism and, 8, 138–44
nation-state framework: Hasegawa's analysis of, 140–41; Japanese politics and, 117–21
nativism: capitalism and, 87–88; Japanism and, 99–101, 126–31; Kobayashi and, 243–44; Meiji Restoration and, 70, 74, 82–84, 250n.35; religion and, 60–61. See also *kokutai* (mystic body politic)
Natsume Sōseki, 212
neo-Kantian idealism, 170, 173
Neo-liberal capitalism, archaism and, 10
Neo-Ottomanism, in Turkey, 10
Neo-Slavism, 10
Nihon Ideorogion (The Japan ideology) (Tosaka Jun), 23, 146, 170, 172, 189, 196, 210, 212
Nihon shihonshugi bunseki (Essay on Japanese capitalism) (Yamada Moritarō), 44–45
Nihonshōki (Chronicles of early Japan), 133–34, 220
Nishida Kitarō, 176, 200, 205
Nishida Naojirō, 176
Nishitani Keiji, 186
noncontemporaneity. *See* contemporization of noncontemporaneity

Ōkawa Shūmei, 107–8
Ōkubo Toshimichi, 63–64, 72
Ōkuni Takamasa, 83
Ollman, Bertell, 231
"On Space" (Tosaka), 178
Orbán, Victor, 10
Orientalism, 204
Orikuchi Shinobu, 196, 234, 239, 242
Osborne, Peter, xii, 11–12
"Overcoming the Modern" symposium (1942), 129–30, 233, 260n.20

Paris Commune of 1871, 61
Parry, Benita, xiv, 42
Pascal, Blaise, 146
passive revolution: capitalism and, 123; formal subsumption and, 8–9; Gramsci's concept of, 1, 5–7, 36–37, 40–44; in Japan, 3–4, 36–54; Meiji Restoration as, 42–44, 69–70
peasant uprisings: in early Meiji era, 68–70; Japanese fascism and, 137–44; in Tokugawa shogunate, 55–59, 63–66
Peasant War in Germany, The (Engels), 57
Perry, Matthew (Commodore), 78, 248n.65
phenomenology, 2, 102, 146, 153–54
"philologism" (*bunkenshugi*), 191–92
philology, Tosaka on, 191–99, 258n.105
"Philosophical Explanation of the Consciousness of Crisis, A" (Miki), 147–69
philosophic history, 146
philosophy: Japanese culture and politics and, 150–69; Kyoto school of, 145–46, 152, 172, 186; literaturization of, 199–200, 203; Miki's focus on, 152–56, 167–69; Tosaka on, 172–74
Pincus, Leslie, 127–28
Polanyi, Karl, 90–91
politics: culture and, 59–61, 147–69, 175–76, 231–33; history and, 18–22; postwar restoration of archaism and, 230–44; sacralization of, 89–91; of time, 11–12
post-fascism, 246n.8
Postone, Moishe, 248n.60
present: figurability of, xvi; Miki's focus on, 153–54
primitive accumulation, Marx's concept of, 28–29, 54–55
primitivism, Tosaka's discussion of, 208–12, 217–22
Prison Notebooks (Gramsci), 7
production, Marx's subsumption and, 26–29, 90
progressivism, Benjamin on, 18

prostitution, Tosaka on legalization of, 213–14
Protestant Christianity, capitalism and, 28–29
pseudopast, archaism and, 88–89
public discussion (*kōron*), Mito concept of space for, 62
Putin, Vladimir, 10

Quinet, Edgar, 43

Rancière, Jacques, xii, 33–35, 86
reality (*genjitsu*), 19, 102–3, 162–69
religion: fascism and, 89–91; Japanism and, 125–31; postwar archaism as, 229; state and, 118
renovation (*ishin*), Japanese transformation and, 32–35
Research Center for the Study of the Japanese Spirit, 230
Research Institute of Japanese Spiritual Culture (*Nihon seishin bunka kenkyūjo*), 176
restorationism: fascism and, 35; Tokugawa shogunate and, 59–61; Tosaka on, 207–12, 216–22
revolution: fascism and, xii–xiv. *See also* passive revolution
revolution-restorations, Gramsci's concept of, 45–46
right-wing politics: in Meiji Restoration, 103–9; mythic ideology of, 27–29
Riley, Dylan, 130
Risorgimento, 6–7, 23, 36–37, 43, 46, 113
Robespierre, Maximilien, 93
Romanness (*Romanita*), Italian fascism and, 10, 90, 113
Ross, Kristin, xvi, 17–18
Rousseau, Jean-Jacques, 217–18
Russia: cultural nationalism in, 10; Marx's discussion of, 29–30; unevenness in, 15–16
Russian Revolution, capitalism and, xiii

Saigō Takamori, 65–66, 72, 76, 130, 150
Sakamoto Ryōma, 75

Sakuma Shōzan, 62, 166–67
samurai class: activism of, 3; Bushido ethos and, 206–7; Meiji Restoration and, 58–59, 63–66, 72; *sonnō-jōi* movement, 66–67
Sanrizuka protests, 250n.35
Sartre, Jean-Paul, xii, 11, 14–15, 188; on temporality, 23, 27, 30
Satō Haruo, 48
Satsuma-Chōshū conspiracy, 76
Scopes trial, 135
Second International, 14–15, 18, 130
sectionalism, in Tokukgawa shogunate, 63–66
Seji kemmonroku (Buyō Inshi), 62
Seki Eikichi, 106–7
Shinagawa, 72
Shintoism, 155–56, 205; archaism and, 10; revitalization of, 230
Shisō to fuzoku (Tosaka), 205
Shōwa Kenkyūkai (Shōwa Research Association), 105
Shōwa Restoration, 35, 42, 113, 150
Show Kenkyūkai, 140
Shrine Department of Compilation, 132–33
social organizations: formation of, 59–61; in Meiji Restoration, 73–84
Sohn-Rethel, Alfred, 170, 245n.2, 256n.53
sonnō-jōi movement, 66–67
Southern Question, The (Gramsci), 52
South Korea, U.S. postwar involvement in, 226
"Spirit of Japan." *See* "Japanese spirit"
spirit of language, Kobayashi on, 239–44
stadialization (*jūsōsei*), 159
status system (*mibunsei*), 73–84
Stirner, Max, 190
subsumption: Balibar's analysis of, 36; Japanese capitalism and, 86–87; Marx's concept of, 8–9, 23–30, 89–90; Meiji Restoration and, 47–54; passive revolution and, 40–41
synchronous nonsynchronicity, 16–17, 139
syncretic religions, 60–61, 65–66

Tachibana Kōsaburō, 208–9
Takabatake Motoyuki, 138
Takahashi Satomi, 176
Takasugi Shinsaku, 63–64
Takasu Yoshijirō, 250n.43
Takata Yasuma, 129–30
Takayoshi Kido, 71, 75–78
Takeuchi Yoshimi, 129, 158, 230
Tamamatsu Hisao, 83
Tanabe Hajime, 86–87, 184, 200
Tanaka, Stefan, 92
Tanigawa Tetsuzō, 165
Tanizaki Junichirō, 95, 165
temporality: archaism and, 85–86; Bloch
on, 16–17; Marxism and, 14–15
temporalization, Japanese history and,
1–3
tennō (heavenly emperor designation),
74–75, 79
Tenpō reforms, 65
terrorism, in Tokugawa shogunate, 61
Third International, 14–15, 18
Third Rome movement, 113
Three Dynasties (China), 61
Tiedemann, Rolf, 21–22
time: archaism and concepts of, 8–10;
Bloch's vision of, 16–17; capitalism
and, 96–98; colonialism and, 12–14;
historical time, xii–xiii, 1–2; imperial
time, 229, 232; Japanese concepts of,
40–41; Maruyama on, 237–38; politics
of, 11–12; Tosaka on historical time,
173–92; Tosaka on reality and, 19–20,
174–75
Tokugawa shogunate, 3; communal
order during, 321; feudal domains
in, 37–39, 54–55, 63–66; intellectuals
in, 61–62; isolationism and, 67–68,
248n.65; Japanese renovation and
transformation and, 32, 55–66; Meiji
overthrow of, 40–41, 43–44, 48–49;
nativism in, 243–44; political thinking in, 67–68; popular uprisings and,
55–58
Tolstoy, Leo, 140
Tomba, Massimiliano, xii–xiii, 8

Tönnies, Ferdinand, 155
Torii Ryūzō, 48
Tosaka Jun, xii, xvi, 2; on agrarianism, 207–12; on archaism, 71, 92,
134–35, 153, 192–99, 213–14, 217–22;
on capitalism, 110, 173, 187–90,
207–10; on culture, 106–7, 202–3;
on everyday life, 232–33; on fascism,
171–76, 201–2; on feudal domains
(remnants), 122–23, 206–10, 253n.32;
on history and time, 15, 19–20, 23,
164–65, 177–92; on idealism and materialism, 170; on ideology, 170–222;
on Japanism, 99–101, 121, 139, 146,
203–8; on liberalism, 200–202; on
literature, 199–200; Maruyama and,
238; Miki and, 146–70; on militarism
and Japanism, 206–7; on modernization, 7–8, 11, 232–33; on philology, 191–99; philosophy of, 154–55;
postwar obscurity of, 223; on primitivism, 128–31, 208–10; on reality
(*genjitsu*), 102–3; on young officers'
mutiny, 150
Toscano, Alberto, 110, 246n.7
Tōyama Shigeki: on Meiji Restoration,
71–72, 77; on Tokugawa feudal domains, 37–42, 55–57, 65–70
translation, Tosaka on, 197–98
Trotsky, Leon, 1, 15–16, 30, 113, 247n.24
Trump, Donald, x, 10
Tsukui Tatsuo, 8, 129–30, 138–39
tsukuru (to make), 236

umu (to give birth), 236
undercurrent (*kosō*), archaism and, 101
unevenness: Bloch on, 22; of capitalism,
2–3, 14–16, 23–29, 46–54; capitalism
and, 111–12; colonialism and, 13–14;
culture and politics and, 147–48; history and, ix–x, xv–xvii, 23–24; modern Japanese capitalism and, 86–87;
in Tokugawa shogunate, 55–66
United States: intervention in Japan by,
63–68, 235, 248n.65; postwar occupation of Japan by, 76–77, 96–97

Uno Kōzō, 53–54, 96
urban trashings (*uchikowashi*), 55–59, 65, 68–70
U.S. Occupation of Japan, 35, 223–29; Japanese intellectuals' criticism of, 243–44

value theory, 248n.60; elimination of history and, 110
Virino, Paolo, 88, 92, 228
Voloshinov, Valentin, 193–94

Watsuji Tetsurō: on capitalism, 13–14, 23; double life concept of, 127–28, 165–66; on Japanese culture, 31; Japanism and, 105–6; nativism and, 87, 127–28; stadialization concept of, 159; Tosaka's critique of, 176, 189–92, 198–99
Weber, Max, 28, 47–48, 87, 115, 175
Wells, H. G., 226
wholeness, philosophy of, 155
"why not?" (*ee ja nai ka*) protests, 55–56, 58–59, 65–66
Williams, Raymond, 148
women: financial independence for, 215–16; voting rights for, 227

Wretched of the Earth, The (Fanon), 12–13

Yamada Moritarō, 32–33, 44–45, 51, 53, 209–10
Yamagata, 72
Yamauchi of Tosa, 76–77
Yanagita Kunio, 23, 31, 125, 135–36, 242
Yano Gendō, 74, 80
Yasuda Yojūrō, 95, 148
Yasukuni (emperor's shrine), 74
Yasumaru Yoshio, 74–75, 259n.10
Yokoi Shōnan, 61–64
yonaoshi odori (dances of world renewal), 60–61, 65–66
Yoshida Shoin, 62–66, 236
Yoshimoto Takaaki, 230–31
young officers' mutiny (1936) (Japan), 150
Yuibutsu Kenkyūkai (Society for the Study of Materialism), 100–101, 110–11, 139

Zasulich, Vera, 16, 29–30, 34, 81–82
Zoku Nippon seishinshi kenkyū (Studies in the cultural history of Japan) (Watsuji), 31–35

www.ingramcontent.com/pod-product-compliance
Lightning Source LLC
Chambersburg PA
CBHW020840270326

41928CB00006B/493